THE BENEFIT OF STEEL

The Life and Times of Dr. Steve Foster

By Michael Hoskin

This is a work of biographical non-fiction. The events are described based on research, historical records, personal and public records, and interviews with many of the individuals referenced in the book whose versions of events were reported to the best of their memory and knowledge. While all the stories in this book are true, some names and identifying details have been changed to protect the privacy of the people involved. The views and opinions expressed in this book are the author's or those of the interviewees and do not necessarily represent those of SIM or any other missionary organization. The purpose of this book is to educate, inform and entertain, the information in this book does not constitute medical or other professional advice. The author disclaims any liability for direct or indirect losses or damages in association with this book, including errors or omissions.

Efforts have been made to identify and credit the photographers of all the photographs used throughout the book. However, in some cases due to the age of the photographs this was not always possible. If errors or omissions have been identified, please contact the author so they may be corrected in future editions.

ISBN-13: 978-1-9990990-0-8 (paperback)
ISBN-13: 978-1-9990990-1-5 (ebook)

Production Credits
Editing: Taija Morgan, T. Morgan Editing Services
Cover Design & Family Tree Graphic: Paul Warren, Immersion Design Inc.
Published by: Michael Hoskin | Calgary, Alberta, Canada

Dedication

To my Uncle Steve: a man as large as life, yet always focused on the One who is greatest.

And to Afonso Daniel, a man I never met, but whose story is permanently etched in my heart. - *Michael.*

TABLE OF CONTENTS

FOREWORD

For more than eleven decades, covering Africa's most turbulent century, several generations of the Foster family have played a front-line role in medical and general missionary work in the English-speaking and Portuguese-speaking nations of central and southern Africa. Told against the background of political upheaval during the years leading up to the demise of colonial rule, and the tribal conflicts that followed in its wake, this story is no dull narrative, it has everything in it! This is the biography of a family who integrated consistently with the hearts, minds, aspirations and fears of their adopted communities.

Their story is told with laughter and tears as they share their hopes and disappointments, successes and failures, risks and rewards, births and deaths, and most outstandingly, *courage*, in the face of heavy warfare, bandits, illnesses, martyrdom, a massacre and a thousand crises that would tempt many of us to quit. It is honest, not sensational. This family loves Africa and Jesus Christ. They bring diagnosis and remedy not just to the body but to the soul and spirit.

Countless people have benefited from the medical and material skills they have brought to them, and many have benefited more deeply, more richly and more satisfyingly by being introduced to a personal relationship with God, through Jesus Christ. This story doesn't avoid the issues they are forced to confront when straddling African and Western cultures, or which arise when members of a family well known for one thing opt for their own alternatives. God writes his story through ordinary people, and when he does, they become extraordinary. God is the 'extra' in the 'ordinary' who produces the 'extraordinary.' Such has been, and is, the extraordinary Foster family.

Charles Price
Minister at Large
The Peoples Church
Toronto

i

MICHAEL HOSKIN

PROLOGUE

I stood in the operating theatre, feeling useless.

On the operating table lay a small boy. A four-year-old, perhaps. He took up less than half of the table and neither of his shoulders reached the edges of the bed.

Only two people had scrubbed in for this procedure: my Uncle Steve and one of his nurses. I wanted to help them, but the boy was so tiny—there was simply no need or potential for need of anyone else. The most I did was to adjust the overhead lamp to aid my uncle as he stared down the boy's throat.

The boy had been to the Central Hospital in Lubango, but the physicians there were mystified by his condition. At times he would suddenly gasp for breath, but then normal breathing would resume. An X-ray revealed nothing. This was one of the ways my uncle's reputation proved helpful. After 40 years of medicine in Angola, he had a little bit of expertise in just about every kind of procedure. The name of Steve Foster had gained respect from his Angolan colleagues. Central Hospital referred the boy's family to Centro Evangélico Medicina do Lubango (CEML) and now my uncle was probing the boy's throat, looking for whatever was obstructing his breathing.

I had been at CEML long enough to learn a little about their practices. I knew I would be spending the entire day with my uncle, so at the end of the previous day I took a glance at the schedule in surgery. There were eleven procedures scheduled that day and my uncle was the only surgeon on duty; in the end, however, my uncle would see 17 patients in the theatre that day.

Most of my uncle's observations were delivered in curt Portuguese to his nurse, but he included a little English for my benefit. After all, the only reason I had joined him in the theatre was to collect material for the biography he asked me to write. By this time I had participated in more than two dozen procedures, despite my 100% lack of medical school. Although my uncle would usually entrust me with nothing more challenging than holding gauze or providing suction, his fellow surgeons would show me how to perform orthopaedic repair, suture, even assist in a caesarean-section!

My uncle's thin, delicate steel instruments examined the Angolan boy's throat. Although I could see nothing from where I stood, my uncle described with faint irritation what he was seeing. He had caught sight of the foreign object caught in the boy's throat, which was so far down that it was nearly impossible to see, especially since he had so little light to shine on the opening. Carefully, he attempted to grip the foreign object with his forceps.

He failed.

The object slipped from his forceps and fell across the windpipe. Although still sedated, the boy began to asphyxiate. In the amount of time it takes to draw breath, the child had lost his breath. Quickly, my uncle told the nurse he would prepare an emergency tracheotomy to open up the throat below the obstruction.

I stared, hands behind my back, thinking that being invisible might be the most helpful thing I could contribute. I began to notice the other hospital staff standing nearby: nurses, orderlies, custodians. Normally they would be busy getting the next table ready for a subsequent procedure. No one was working—all eyes were on the table as my uncle began cutting into the boy's throat.

People talk about "African Stoicism," the manner in which, when an African assumes a neutral expression, they seem much more emotionally reserved than any white person. If there is any truth to that idiom, it was found on the faces of the nursing staff. With surgical masks on, little could be seen of their faces—except for their eyes. I didn't recognize pain or concern in those pupils. All I could read was a sense of heightened interest. Much like my own.

I watched the little boy's stomach as he struggled to live. I didn't realize how flat the human stomach could become. I could well believe his navel was beating against his spine. With each glimpse of his intensely flattened abdomen, a hint of fear would crawl into my brain. I had seen many amazing and disgusting things inside the theatre. Was I about to witness death?

The emergency tracheotomy finished. I felt as tense as before, but my uncle seemed relieved. The boy could breathe again. Now that he had stabilized, my uncle could return to the forceps. It still took a solid minute for him to find the foreign object and grip it, but it felt like an hour. Finally, the object was loose and the nurse held out a pan to catch it as his forceps let it go. It was a thin white piece of plastic, like a chip from a venetian blind. It had been so well camouflaged that the X-ray had failed to catch it. It was so light the boy's windpipe had been able to keep functioning, but in those moments when it fell across his throat like a trap door, it had been cutting off his oxygen.

And then the nurses, orderlies and custodians did something I had never seen in any of my previous visits to the operating theatre: they burst into applause! With a smile hidden behind my surgical mask, I joined them. They weren't so stoic after all; neither was I.

The long steel instruments my uncle wielded that day brought to mind one of his favourite sayings: *the benefit of steel*. Steel, as he had told me, had traditionally been an alloy used to destroy the human body. For thousands of years, swords have been forged from steel, to the extent that *steel* had become a synonym for *sword*. Steel continues to be used in the construction of firearm, but, as my uncle says, "Come to my hospital and I will show you the benefit of steel! I will show you how steel can be used to *save* lives!"

My uncle's family have lived in Sub-Saharan Africa since 1917. What follows is my uncle's story, as told by his friends and family to me.

CHAPTER 1

"We Can Die for Christ, if it's Necessary." — Charles Foster

MUSONWEJI; MUKINGE (November 1917 – August 1929)

As Charles and June Foster sailed across the Atlantic Ocean in 1917, the United States had only recently begun to play its part in the so-called Great War which had spread across Europe and the Middle East. The Fosters were bound for Africa, a continent largely spared the carnage that had claimed so many millions of lives in Europe. Yet Africa's fate was intertwined with that of Europe, for this was the peak of the colonial era and the fissures exposed by the Great War would gradually sweep colonialism into the dustbin.

Considering the enormity of the impact colonialism had in Africa, it seems surprising that most of the colonies lasted less than a hundred years. It was only in 1884 that representatives of the European colonial empires met in Berlin, Germany, to discuss how they would partition the continent amongst themselves. Most of the continent was divided up by the European empires, forming maps based on expedience rather than any consideration of the peoples living within those borders. When one considers how the Europeans themselves had contested each other time and again over the borders of their own continent, it is surprising they gave so little thought to how history might repeat itself south of the Mediterranean, but so it transpired. At this time the first Pan-African Congress was still 2 years away, the philosophy of *Négritude* had not been coined and independence for the colonies lay even further afield.

As Charles and June waited in Cape Town, South Africa, to learn where the South African General Mission (SAGM) would assign them as missionaries, they were aware of their countrymen dying in Europe. Yet Charles philosophized, "If those young men can die for their country, then we can die for Christ, if it's necessary."

1

Although only 25 years old at the time, Charles Stephen Foster had already travelled far. Born in England at St. Leonards-on-Sea, Sussex, his family soon moved to a farm near Chatham in Southwestern Ontario, Canada. While still a boy, he moved to the United States for a job working on the assembly line at a Ford automobile factory in Detroit, Michigan. Later, he heard the Moody Bible Institute offered free tuition for students enrolled in its Evangelical training program. Moving to Chicago, Illinois, where Moody was headquartered, his training included a position as a student pastor at Roseland Baptist Church in Chicago. There, Charles first met June Violet Frost, an organist at the church. June likewise attended Moody and before long they had fallen in love and married in 1916. June hailed from a very mission-oriented family as both of her sisters became missionary wives.

Like many missionaries of the time, Charles and June were inspired by the example of Dr. David Livingstone, famed for his cross-Africa trek of 1854-1856. Livingstone christened Victoria Falls on what would become the borders of Zambia and Zimbabwe, spotlighting one of the continent's most famous landmarks. By venturing into lands few white men had seen, exposing the harsh slavery still being practised, and finding African hearts willing and eager for the Gospel message he stirred up the spirits of subsequent missionaries for generations. Livingstone's words: *"I am prepared to go anywhere, provided it be forward"* served as an electrifying rallying cry for the countless missionary societies that formed in his wake. SAGM was founded in 1889 at Cape Town as Cape General Mission, initially serving the needs of existent Christians in the area before expanding to perform outreach in southern Africa.

At Cape Town in November 1917, the Fosters were assigned to serve as missionaries in the landlocked nation of Northern Rhodesia, one of two countries named for the British businessman Cecil Rhodes. Northern Rhodesia lay in the lower centre of Africa, bordered by many neighbours, including the Belgian Congo to the north, German East Africa on the northeast, the British protectorate Nyasaland on the east, the Portuguese colony Mozambique to the southeast, Southern Rhodesia and the British protectorate Bechuanaland to the south, German South-West Africa on the southwest and the Portuguese colony of Angola on the western border. While Cecil Rhodes launched the massively successful company De Beers from extracting the wealth of diamonds found in the region, the Fosters entered Northern Rhodesia seeking precious hearts, not precious stones.

Before the lofty aspirations of the missionaries could be fulfilled, however, Charles first had to satisfy certain practical needs: SAGM's regional director required him to prove he could handle a rifle. Although the British had established an exemplary network of railroad lines across Africa, the Fosters' eventual destination, Musonweji, was a three-week walk from the nearest train station at Broken Hill. During that sojourn, the party of porters and guides accompanying the Fosters would depend upon Charles to supply meat to sustain them. Once Charles' marksmanship was proven, he and June travelled by train and on foot to Musonweji, rendezvousing with the husband and wife missionaries the Drummonds, who had hired 100 porters to carry the Fosters' possessions back to Musonweji.

All of Africa was new to the Fosters and they were seeing it in a time before electricity, pavement, mining, deforestation and excessive hunting would diminish the splendour. Amidst the natural beauty of subtropical Rhodesia, Charles' senses were as filled with wonder from the sights to the sounds. There were more than seventy languages spoken in Northern Rhodesia, and while previous missionaries provided some English classes, many of the Africans Charles met spoke only their tribal dialect. In the area of Musonweji, the Bakaonde people spoke Kikaonde, which had never been set down on paper. As the porters led Charles along the hills, he began to practise his Kikaonde. Charles had no particular training in linguistics, but his curiosity motivated him to learn more. As he came to learn about the Bakaonde, he realized that to effectively minister to them he would need to speak the people's native tongue.

While on the journey, the time finally came for Charles to prove his prowess as a hunter; when almost at Musonweji, his guides led him and Mr. Drummond to a field where an immense herd of wildebeest were grazing. Charles was excited by the opportunity to demonstrate his proficiency, but the rifle he had been outfitted with was a 9.3 mm, suitable for hunting large game but about the heaviest gun possible. Struggling with the weapon, his first five shots went wide, missing the creatures entirely. At last, his sixth shot struck an antelope and killed it; after two more shots, another wildebeest was dead. There was plenty of meat to bring back to camp to feed the massive contingent of porters and Charles, despite his initial misses, had earned his reputation as a hunter.

Charles and June arrived in Musonweji in mid-December. They were given a home and, obeying the custom, hired a number of Bakaonde boys to perform labour around the house. Charles threw himself wholeheartedly into teaching the Bakaonde lessons of the Gospel, while the Bakaonde taught Charles how to speak Kikaonde. Charles' overarching goal was to translate the entire Bible into Kikaonde—a difficult undertaking since there wasn't even a Kikaonde dictionary to draw from! In addition, the nature of languages can be very colloquial, as an expression common in one village may be conveyed entirely differently in another. It was a slow task, but Charles laboured over it while providing instruction to the villagers. As pastors such as Yoano Shikelenge, Yoba Shamambo and Ezekiel Musompa emerged from the ranks of Charles' pupils, Charles stepped back from his own preaching duties, knowing it would be best for the Bakaonde to be taught by people of their own tribe.

In 1918, June gave birth to Harold, their first son. More children followed as their daughter Mabel arrived in 1920 and their second son Edgar in 1921. By then, Charles was virtually fluent in Kikaonde and the family was well-accustomed to life in Musonweji. As the nearest store was in Bulawayo—a good thousand miles distant—June learned not to always rely upon cooking the foods she had been accustomed, instead growing what she could manage locally. Charles, of course, continued to supply wild-game meat.

Easily the most exciting game meat was that of the hippopotamus. Perhaps not so much because of its taste, but because the hippos were such massive creatures—larger than two cattle put together—and such destructive ones. The hippopotamuses we see in zoos may appear docile, even comical, but in the wild a hippopotamus is a danger to any human it encounters at close range. The hippopotamus is also a pest, bearing a ravenous appetite that, if given the opportunity, would gladly be sate by consuming gardens of vegetables grown by locals. The death of a hippopotamus, therefore, meant a celebration not only because of the generous supply of meat it provided, but because one fewer hippo would be frustrating the farmers. This was a state of affairs Charles was ignorant of—but not for long.

Charles' guide led him to a pool in which hippos were known to frequent. Sure enough, before long he spied the head of a hippopotamus rising from the water! Taking aim, he fired—then saw the hippo sink away from view. The guide shook his head. "Oh, *bwana*," (Swahili, meaning *boss*) he said, "you missed. That's terrible." The guide urged Charles to journey further upriver with him to a bend in the stream which was favourable for hippo sightings. The trip took an hour on foot, but the guide's instincts were correct: Charles spotted his second hippopotamus! This time, he resolved he would leave nothing to chance; he aimed his rifle most carefully, targeting the hippo's head. His powerful 9.3 mm rifle cracked out another shot—but this hippo, like the previous animal, disappeared from view.

"This is very bad luck!" the guide exclaimed. "Why, both of those hippos—you missed!" Charles was naive enough not to wonder why, if he had indeed missed both times, he hadn't heard his bullet splash into the water on either instance. Trusting in his guide's experience, he was led to yet another fine hunting spot. This time the hippopotamus they found was on the bank. Again Charles lined up his shot and fired; the hippo collapsed on the shore with a heavy thud. This time, there could be no mistake—Charles had killed his first hippo! The guide congratulated him exuberantly: "Oh, bwana, you finally got the hippo!"

Word was sent out to bring extra hands to help treat the hippo, for the process of tearing strips of hippo meat to be dried, smoked and cured is a lengthy operation because of the animals' massive size. Fortunately, this hippo had died on the shore, so they had been spared the extra effort of retrieving a hippopotamus from water. As the camp butchers began the process of carving up the carcass, Charles journeyed back down the river with his guide, pleased with himself. Yes, he had done well with his first hippo kill…

…Except it wasn't his *first* kill at all! As they returned to the bend in the river, Charles was alarmed to see four hippo legs sticking straight up out of the water! "Oh, bwana! You must have hit the hippo after all!" the guide innocently suggested. So the call went out to bring even more villagers to help butcher this hippo, and this time there would be the added labour of dragging its bulk to dry land.

Naive as he was, Charles began to wonder what had actually happened at the first pool. Returning there, he found his first target had also died, its carcass floating in the water. What Charles learned that day was that when a hippopotamus is killed in water, its body will sink to the bottom of the pool. It can take up to 4-5 hours for a hippo's post-mortem remains to bob back to the surface.

Sheepishly, Charles returned to the office of the game warden where he had obtained a licence to hunt 1 hippopotamus and informed the warden he had killed 3 hippopotamuses that day. It took three days for his hippos to be carved and carried home. There would be many more hippo hunts in Charles' future but from that point on he would be a little less credulous about his guides' motives.

The early years of Charles and June's time in Musonweji were overwhelmingly pleasant as many Bakaonde converted to the Christian faith and Charles made great progress in his translations, hoping to finish his Gospel of Mark before taking a furlough in 1922. However, those plans were marred by two tragedies that struck the family. One evening, Edgar, only three months old, began to thrash in his bed, his body hot with fever. June assumed Edgar had caught malaria and administered a dose of quinine to him, but the normally effective drug did nothing to halt his fever or his cries. Their missionary nurse friend Edith Shoosmith arrived to help June, but Edgar's sickness was outside even her ability to treat. The nearest doctor lived 300 miles away, so a messenger was sent to bring him, but it would take three weeks for him to arrive while June faced a malady she was ill-equipped to treat.

As they waited for the doctor, the situation worsened. Mabel had also become feverish, crying out "Hurt, hurt." Edgar was no longer crying, but his near-immobility had become a fresh source of concern. Charles and June gave every consideration they could to Mabel, from prayer to medicine, but after six days she died. Charles had adored Mabel and was shaken over her death, while

June consoled him, saying their daughter was "safe in the arms of Jesus."

At last the messenger returned—without the doctor. The doctor could not make the journey and had written a letter diagnosing Edgar's condition as cerebral meningitis, concluding that if he had made the trip it would have been to find either that Edgar had recovered or it would be too late to help him. Speeding up the date of their furlough, the family returned to the US to learn Edgar's brain had been "destroyed" by the fever; he would never develop beyond his infant state, never be able to care for himself or even speak. Charles and June had been willing to accept personal hardship when they first entered the mission field, but the grief of seeing their children as the ones suffering was a hardship for which they hadn't prepared.

Charles and June continued to care for Edgar as best as they could, returning with their two sons to Musonweji when the furlough ended. Charles resumed his work and finally published his Gospel of Mark in Kikaonde in 1923 (*Mambo-a-wama a nembele Mako*), a major achievement in Bible translation as well as for the identification of the Kikaonde language and a vital tool of evangelization amongst the Bakaonde. In 1924, June gave birth to their fourth child, another boy. Mindful of the tragedies Edgar and Mabel had fallen prey, and how the lack of physicians impacted so many lives, the couple named their third son Robert Livingstone Foster in honour of the inspirational missionary—and they prayed their son would become a missionary doctor.

MUKINGE

During this time, missionary couples sponsored by agencies such as SAGM at a ratio of 2:20,000. The Bakaonde numbered 40,000, therefore they never established more than two couples at a time. What this policy failed to consider was what a vast stretch of land the tribe lived upon, covering some 20,000 miles. With no vehicle more advanced than a bicycle to get around, the missionaries' ability to reach the Bakaonde was curtailed; they were simply too few and too slow.

Charles and another missionary, Herbert Pirouet, decided to move their station away from Musonweji and into a more central location. Scouting the lands in the heart of Bakaonde country, they realized Mukinge Hill was the perfect location. Mukinge rose from the Lufapa Valley and its higher altitude meant a somewhat more temperate climate than that of Musonweji. Further, the *boma* (chief of government) Chief Kasempa lived nearer to Mukinge, which would expedite the inevitable bureaucratic considerations every mission had to undertake. Fortunately, Chief Kasempa was eager to have the missionaries closer to his offices, knowing it would improve the education, economy and medical aid in his area. With the chief on their side, the mission won over the British officials governing Northern Rhodesia, establishing Mukinge as the new mission station for the Bakaonde.

It took some time to move the Fosters from Musonweji to Mukinge and slowly dismantle every valuable component of the Musonweji home to help construct their new one in Mukinge. Shortly after their move in 1926 June gave birth to their fourth son, whom they named after their missionary colleague: Herbert.

Mukinge would be Charles and June's home for most of their lives. There, Charles continued to busy himself with his translation work, completing the Gospel of Matthew in 1927 (*Mambo-a-wama a nembele Mateo*). The evangelization of the Bakaonde continued as well, with Chief Kasempa among those who converted.

Life in Mukinge came with challenges, however, including the factoring of wildlife into their daily routines. An outhouse lay beyond the Fosters' home in Mukinge, about 40 yards from their back door. In those days June didn't like keeping a chamber pot under her bed and so she would make the long walk to the outhouse when necessary, even at night. One evening she stepped out with her kerosene lantern to find the outhouse when the light revealed a frightening visitor on the path before her: a leopard! The leopard jumped back into the shadows while June sped a hasty retreat to her home and informed Charles of the predator. Immediately snatching his shotgun, Charles raced out on the stoop of the home to guard against the leopard, but having no flashlight it took time for him to prepare another lantern to make an investigation. When he arrived, there was no sign of the leopard, which had evidently been as startled by the sight of June as she had been of it. It's no surprise that from then on June kept a chamber pot for evening use!

As the years passed, Charles and June continued to care for Edgar, holding him when his limbs would thrash violently. Local boys were hired to help June care for him, principally to feed Edgar his meals. It would have been difficult for the Bakaonde to understand why Charles and June continued to care for their son as most families there would have abandoned a child so afflicted, rather than keep him alive year after year.

By 1928, Charles and June had to consider the long-term welfare of their other sons; Harold was 10 years old and June simply wasn't up to the challenge of teaching him—he required a formal education. Edgar and Mabel's maladies had also convinced the couple that their younger sons Robert and Herbert should grow up in a more secure environment. SAGM was insistent that they finally take a furlough (the previous one being in 1922), so it was decided the three healthy boys would return with them on furlough while Edith Shoosmith cared for Edgar.

After spending Christmas 1928 in Chicago with June's family, the Fosters began planning for their boys' futures. In the summer of 1929, before Charles and June returned to Mukinge, they brought Harold and Robert to Gowans' Home, a spacious 32-room manor situated on four acres in Collingwood, Ontario (near Toronto) which tended to dozens of children whose parents were international missionaries. The home was named after missionary Walter Gowans, one of the three founding members of SIM (at the time Soudan Interior Mission). Gowans had perished on the mission field but co-founder Rowland Bingham established the house in Gowans' name for mission families of all types. Run by SIM, the home promised a warm, Christian educational environment. They planned that Herbert would, when older, likewise come to Gowans' Home. Charles and June drew Harold and Robert close to them and prayed for them, reiterating their deep love for their sons. They trusted God had a plan for their sons; they didn't realize then it would be 8 years before they would meet again.

CHAPTER 2

"Your Dad Is a Wild Man." — Franklin Graham to Stirling Foster

COLLINGWOOD; TORONTO (September 1929 – July 1950)

Not only were Harold and Robert ("Bob") coming to grips with separation from their parents and immersion into a North American culture they had no experience with, they had also arrived just as the Great Depression disrupted the economy around the world. Gowans' Home weathered the storm, aided by the generosity of donors. It became difficult for Charles and June to afford their sons' fees as their own financial resources were diminished, but they kept the boys in school—and more importantly, wrote them letters weekly, so that even as years went by in Collingwood, Harold and Bob retained a relationship with their parents.

Bob also appreciated learning from the other MKs (Mission Kids) at Gowans' Home, hearing about the lands where their parents served in South America, Asia and Africa. Many of the children at Gowans' Home would grow up to become missionaries and Bob, who gave his life to Christ at age 10, aspired to do the same.

In 1937, Charles and June took another long-overdue furlough. This time SAGM insisted they not leave Edgar at Mukinge. Realizing they had to find a permanent home for Edgar, they relocated him to a care home in South Africa. Returning with the couple across the Atlantic were 11-year-old Herbert and 8-year-old Rhoda, who had been born shortly after the previous furlough ended. Reuniting with Harold and Bob at Gowans' Home could have been an especially awkward moment for the family, if not for the continued relationship established through their letters. As a result of that continuous connection, however, Harold and Bob quickly re-engaged with their parents.

Charles and June didn't wish to spend their furlough in Collingwood.

Instead they brought their boys to Chicago. Bob had already gone from Collingwood to another school in Lakefield—now he was transferred again, and out of the Canadian school system he'd been accustomed to. The change only lasted for the duration of the furlough as in 1938 Bob returned to Gowans' Home with Herbert and Rhoda in tow. 20-year-old Harold, having completed his schooling, returned to Africa with their parents, eventually settling permanently in Northern Rhodesia as a farmer. Rhoda was heartbroken to be separated from her parents and struggled to adjust to the strict teaching style at Gowans' Home. Fortunately, Bob remained to keep an eye on his little sister, reminding her of their parents' love for her and the importance of the family's mission in Africa.

With no children at their Mukinge home, Charles continued his labour on the Kikaonde translation, completing the New Testament in 1938 (*Lulayañano Lupya: lwa nkambo yetu ne mupulushi wetu Yesu Kilishitu*). This still left the entirety of the Old Testament to be translated, a project which would take Charles—and his committee of Bakaonde pastors and consultants—almost the remainder of his life to see complete. Charles was fortunate to have June as his secretary and redactor as she carefully carbon copied every page he wrote on thin onionskin paper, then sealed a copy of each page up in a vault so that nothing would be lost; an earlier fire in Charles' office had destroyed some of his papers years before, so they took steps to prevent against further loss. Additional duplicates of each page were crafted for each member of Charles' committee.

World War II broke out at this time, resulting in submarine warfare in the Atlantic, which would further restrict Charles and June from their children. By 1942, Edgar had died at his care home in South Africa. That same year, Bob was planning his post-secondary education, intending to become a missionary like his father, but specializing as a missionary surgeon—exactly what his parents had prayed for him. Bob had been an excellent student whose marks opened doors for him at the University of Toronto, but he was lacking in money and his father had none to lend.

To finance his education, Bob took a summer job at the shipyards in Collingwood where he operated a planer machine. On only his third day at the job, the tips of two fingers on Bob's left hand were caught in the machine's blade, mangling his hand! Bob was rushed to a hospital where the doctor, rather than amputate the injured digits, worked meticulously to repair the damage and save Bob's hand. Bob was relieved that his dream of being a surgeon would not be impeded by the injury, but it seemed doubtful he could afford his education as it had left him unable to perform physical labour.

However, something better was on the horizon, as Bob's friends at Gowans' Home directed him to a Christian youth camp in Keswick, Ontario.

While assisting the staff in teaching the children, Bob caught the eye of a teenage counsellor—a young lady named Belva Mark, who was born in Fort William in western Ontario. Belva became taken with Bob, but at age 18, he hadn't had a girlfriend before. The two agreed to remain in touch after the summer.

TORONTO

Bob came to the University of Toronto that fall still unable to pay for his schooling and facing fees of $450 per year—a considerable sum, especially as the medical program had been altered into a year-long format because of the war, meaning he could not work summer jobs between the spring and fall semesters. "Lord," he prayed, "You'll have to prove to me You are who You say You are, that if I give my life to You, You'll provide for my needs."

Bob approached the registrar trembling with nervous energy, prepared to explain why he could not afford his fees, when the officer brought him up short: "Your bill has been paid," she explained to him. "You won a scholarship from your final exams at high school and the money has already been credited to your account. All your fees have been taken care of for the year."

Bob was overjoyed at God's providence, all the more so when a Workman's Compensation payout for his injury wound up paying him more than he could have hoped to earn had he worked the full summer as planned. Additionally, he took on a weekend job selling Fuller Brushes door to door; his commanding, outgoing personality suited him well in sales.

By 1944, the submarine warfare in the Atlantic had all but abated, enabling Charles and June to once again visit North America. While Bob remained in Toronto with his studies, Herbert and Rhoda were uprooted once again to be in Chicago with their parents during the furlough.

With the end of World War II, there was a newfound sense of the bonds between the world's nations and an optimistic desire to improve international relations—expressed most obviously by the foundation of the United Nations in 1946. This outlook also affected Bob in University. Bob had joined IVCF (Inter-Varsity Christian Fellowship) and served as their chairman in 1946 when IVCF sponsored the first Urbana Conference in Toronto. The primary focus of Urbana (then and now) was to engage with university students on contemporary global issues and in particular the need for missionaries. Bob was himself still determined to become a missionary surgeon when his studies were complete.

While Bob was attending university in Toronto, Herbert was studying at LeTourneau University in Texas, and held similar hopes of becoming a missionary, inspired by the writings of missionary Roland Allen, author of *Missionary Methods: St. Paul's or Ours?* (1912) and *Spontaneous Expansion of the Church: and the Causes Which Hinder It* (1927). Allen had served as a missionary in China and both Herbert and Bob, despite their upbringing in Africa, were looking to serve in the mission field in China. However, when Bob approached representatives of the China Inland Mission (CIM) at Urbana he was rebuffed: "There's no use thinking of going under CIM to China," the representatives cautioned him. "The Marxists are taking over and missionaries are leaving. By the time you get ready to go, you won't be able to get in. You'd better ask God if He doesn't want you in some other place." Indeed, within a few years of Urbana, the People's Republic of China would officially close its doors to missionaries; CIM began withdrawing their missionaries from the country. China would not ease up on these restrictions until the 1970s.

Another person close to Bob was also feeling God calling her to the mission field—Belva Mark, who was now studying English at the University of Toronto, Belva had heard Rev. Tommy Titcombe speak of his work as a missionary in Nigeria and now discerned she was meant for mission ministry. She and Bob were dating, officially but not exclusively. Belva found herself drawn to Bob: "I had never experienced as much freedom in any relationship as I did with him. I thought, 'If I don't win him, I won't win anybody! I'm not embarrassed, self-conscious or uptight,'" she recalled. "That was the first time I'd ever felt that way."

However, Bob had become quite independent in his worldview, having grown up largely away from his parents. Although Bob had intentions of eventually marrying, he was in no rush to establish lasting commitments, not unless he found a partner who was prepared to meet the challenges he anticipated facing on the mission field. Trying to think through the matter rationally, Bob composed a list of pros and cons regarding a long-term future with Belva. Among the probable cons was the fact Belva had been operated on to remove an ovarian cyst and was left with only a 25% likelihood of ever getting pregnant. However, after hearing through the grapevine how Belva was becoming upset at his seeming aloofness, Bob brought the matter to a head, confronting Belva at her family home in Brantford in the summer of 1947 where he confessed he was in love with her. In April 1948, they were engaged.

While Bob was nearing the end of medical school, the globe continued to change in the aftermath of World War II. India had gained independence from the United Kingdom in 1947, heralding the gradual dissolution of the British Empire. At the same time the Cold War between communist and democratic nations had begun, causing both sides of the conflict to seek influence among the newly independent nations. And, particularly perniciously, in South Africa laws were put in place to officially codify Apartheid, a system that would enable the white minority to maintain rule over its black majority.

As Bob neared graduation he still had no conception of where he would serve as a missionary surgeon. The door to China truly seemed closed, as CIM had indicated, but where, then, did God want him to serve? In the spring of 1948, Bob attended a lecture by Ezra Shank, executive director of SAGM. Shank didn't know Bob was in the audience, but his lecture included an appeal on behalf of the mission station at Mukinge where Charles and June still lived. "We've been praying for a doctor for 27 years," Shank quoted Pastor Ezekiel Musompa, "but the mission has never sent us a doctor. We just get sick and die and nobody cares. If you really mean business about wanting to help us here, send us a doctor."

Convicted by this statement, Bob shared his sense of God's purpose with Belva, who encouraged him to speak with SAGM. Before Bob could make a decision, however, he received a letter from Charles which provided independent verification: "Robert, I know you're graduating soon," Charles wrote, "I don't know what you're going to do. I know you're interested in serving the Lord. Have you ever seriously considered serving the Lord in Northern Rhodesia? Your mother and I think that's something you ought to consider."

Bob went into his final exams for the Canadian Medical Council certain of his calling—but uncertain how to come up with the outstanding $50 he needed to pay for the exams. On the morning of the exams Bob received an envelope from an anonymous person in Winnipeg, Manitoba; inside was a $50-cheque. He would never learn whom his benefactor was, but once again he was reminded of God's constant support when all seemed hopeless.

With his residency in Toronto completed, Bob married Belva Mark on October 16, 1948, and honeymooned in Niagara Falls. Bob's next year of residency was in Nashville, Tennessee, where he served in a hospital treating primarily the poor black residents of the area. While Bob worked, Belva took classes at a Bible school to prepare for the mission field; both joined SAGM.

Thanks to his father and Ezra Shank, Bob had a specific target: to serve at Mukinge and bring quality medical care to the Bakaonde, whom his parents had lived with for 30 years. More than that, Bob was determined he would raise the funds to afford as highly advanced a hospital as he could hope for rather than settling for a modest clinic. As Bob began fundraising amongst friendly communities in Nashville, Toronto and Chicago, Belva became pregnant with their first child. On August 27, 1949 in Brantford, Ontario, Belva gave birth to Stephen James Foster, his given name taken from his grandfather Charles' middle name (Charles had himself inherited the name from his paternal grandfather).

During the fundraising efforts, the Bible Presbyterian Church of

Nashville aided Bob's mission by supplying an ambulance vehicle. Through his salesmanship skills Bob raised most of the money needed for the hospital, as well as the cost of transporting his equipment across the Atlantic Ocean to Durban, South Africa, then overland to Mukinge, Northern Rhodesia, which depleted virtually all of the money intended for his building funds.

In April 1950, Bob, Belva and their infant son Steve entered the mission field. As June greeted Bob at Mukinge she finally related to her son the reason she and Charles had given him the middle name Livingstone: "Because we prayed you would become the first medical missionary to serve among the Bakaonde." SAGM had very little experience overseeing medical missions and there was scepticism among their ranks about Bob's seemingly lofty goals but they would soon have reason to reconsider.

CHAPTER 3

"I Think You Need the Benefit of Steel." — Steve Foster

MUKINGE; SAKEJI; LUAMPA (August 1950 – September 1964)

Initially in Northern Rhodesia, Bob, Belva and Steve didn't have a roof of their own to live under but instead lived in Charles and June's Mukinge home. This quickly became all the more crowded on August 9, 1950 when Bob delivered his first daughter, Sharon June Foster (formalizing the pattern of the Foster children carrying the initials S. J.). Belva was so impressed with Bob's skill in the delivery that she insisted he be the attending physician at each of her future childbirths.

Sharing Charles and June's living space caused some friction within the family, however. Part of the difficulty was simply generational. Charles and June were trained as missionaries when the Great War was a current event; post-World War II, there was a growing sense of unease about the unequal relationship between missionaries and the local populations they served. Throughout Northern Rhodesia, Africans had been made to treat white people with deference. The new attitude was for whites to treat Africans as peers. African customs had previously been slighted or abolished by the colonizing Europeans. One interesting marker of how times were changing was in diet, for Charles and June had grown local vegetables but did not prepare local dishes such as *nshima* (a type of cornmeal porridge). Bob and Belva would make a stronger effort to eat local dishes. For Charles and June, who would employ Africans as servants but not invite them into their homes as guests, it was a difficult time of transition.

Although the elder Fosters' attitude may have seemed patronizing, Charles justified it to Bob by stating, "If you'd been here when we arrived and had seen what they've come from, you'd realize that they would have been embarrassed, and so would we, to invite them into our home for a meal."

15

But Bob gained enlightenment from Kyabasanga, a woman who had once been a servant in the Foster household. She had known Bob when he was a child and took offence one day when he passed her on his bicycle, calling out a Kikaonde greeting to her without stopping. "Young man, stop!" she commanded. "You've got to learn how to greet people right," she reproached him. "You don't say 'hello' and go riding along on your bike. You've got to stop and do it in a proper way—especially to people like me." It made a mark upon Bob that Kyabasanga felt familiar enough with him to admonish him and he strove to improve his interactions with Africans.

Belva looked to June for guidance in managing a household at Mukinge, learning how to prepare meals from the available foods and keeping the home clean were enormous tasks which June had long since mastered. One of the few roles Belva balked at was slaughtering animals. While June did this readily, Belva insisted Bob would have to butcher anything he wanted her to serve. The lessons Belva learned in hospitality would later be very important, as she would frequently be called on to help host visitors at the mission station.

While both Bob and Belva studied their Kikaonde, Bob toiled 300 miles away at the Luanshya hospital, established nearby the Copperbelt mines in Northern Rhodesia. Bob also ran a clinic down the hill from Charles and June's home where he treated emergency cases. The clinic's services were limited, but Bob's truck could transport complicated cases to Luanshya—cases such as that of his own daughter! Sharon had been born with an inguinal hernia which Bob intended to address later, but at three months her hernia had begun to strangulate her. Unless she received surgical attention, she would come down with gangrene and die. Bob transported Sharon as carefully as possible across the bumpy Copperbelt roads to Luanshya where the surgeons saved Sharon's life. Although the case had a happy outcome, it intensified Bob's determination to establish a hospital in Mukinge.

From the beginning of his return to Mukinge, Bob had been concerned with the case of Sarai, the 40-year-old wife of Chief Kasempa. Sarai had been unable to become pregnant, but there was little Bob could do for her initially with his limited resources. Later, after nurse Frances Woods arrived to assist Bob, they performed an examination on Sarai and discovered her infertility was due to cervical stenosis. Aware that the Bakaonde still preferred to visit their witchdoctors before seeing him, Bob devoted his utmost to the case, as he and Frances performed a surgical D&C (dilatation and curettage). Two months later, Sarai proudly informed Bob she was pregnant. Sarai's infertility was so well known that word of Bob's accomplishment spread quickly. Comparisons were drawn between Bob and a powerful witchdoctor named Kahaya who had lived at the turn of the century. Some people concluded Bob was the reincarnation of Kahaya; ergo, he was given the nickname 'Kahaya,' which many Bakaonde would continue to use for the rest of his life.

Meanwhile, Herbert had completed his studies at LeTourneau with a Master's of Theology. Now married to Elenore Thomas, he too had conceded China was not currently receptive to missions and he would do better to return to Northern Rhodesia. Because Herbert had spent more of his growing years at Mukinge, he had already learned and retained Kikaonde, rendering him a valuable mission asset. Herbert and Elenore settled at Chizera in 1952, located to the northwest of Mukinge and began raising a family just as large as Bob and Belva's.

In 1952, 3-year-old Steve accompanied his father and grandfather to a mission conference, during which the attendees indulged in the sport of hippo hunting. By now Charles was an old hand at killing hippos and took a photograph of one of his trophies, its immense mouth propped open while tiny Steve stood inside. Returning to Mukinge and joined by Dr. Alex Henderson, Bob delivered his third child, Sheila Joan Foster, on May 3, 1952. By then, the tensions between the two Foster families at Mukinge were becoming untenable. Along with the considerations of space and privacy, there were also concerns about the servants and from which Fosters they were to take orders. The time for Bob and Belva to live in their own home was past due.

Fortunately, Bob had chosen the location of the new hospital on the mission-owned grounds. He chose to situate the hospital in the northern part of the property, near the river, and his new home would be close by. This would place both the hospital and home downhill from Charles and June, an idea which was somewhat against the perceived wisdom of the times, when all mission property was built at as high an altitude as possible so as to minimize the amount of mosquitoes. It was also a minor scandal when Bob planned to install indoor plumbing in his home—a flagrant luxury by the standards of most bush missionaries! It was even more scandalous when Belva later installed a gas-powered Maytag washing machine, instead of cleaning her clothes by hand!

MUKINGE MISSION HOSPITAL

Mukinge Mission Hospital opened on July 25, 1953. Throughout the process, Bob had pushed ahead by faith to see the building's completion, choosing the site and designing the plans himself despite his lack of experience and the initial lack of funds. God provided for all the building's needs, from donations sent by overseas churches to the facilitation of the local government. In the first year of operation, Mukinge Mission Hospital treated 1,100 patients, with 200 surgeries among them. The hospital, church and mission home were built in a triangle, creating a large central courtyard. From their home, Bob and Belva's children would watch as buses pulled up at the hospital to deliver patients. So began young Steve's fascination with his father's vocation.

The children, quickly joined by their brother Stacey John Foster in 1953, grew up in awe of their grandparents upon the hill. They marvelled at the tangerine and grapefruit trees, gooseberry and youngberry bushes, sheep, chickens and goats on the property. Although Charles and June were not especially warm figures (remembered as "austere" and "stoic" by their grandchildren) they were still quite hospitable, especially if the grandchildren were canny enough to appear at tea time, when they might have a drink of Horlick's malted milk and cookies made with caraway seeds. Steve adored June's spinach soup and boiled peanuts, a specialty he called "beyond description." Charles was most often found in his study meeting with the committee overseeing translating the Bible into Kikaonde. Steve was particularly fond of the missionary translator Ernie Frost, a somewhat short man "almost as wide as he was tall" and possessing a spirit "as jovial as Santa Claus."

Bob bought a canning machine from South Africa to help preserve their meat for longer periods of time, as a single dead hartebeest provided more meat than their family could consume in one day. One afternoon, Bob had Steve help him send several cans of meat into storage in a shed behind their garage. As Steve went between the house and the shed for the cans, he came face-to-face with a cobra! The deadly snake spat its venom into Steve's eyes then slithered under the house. Bob heard Steve cry out in pain and arrived in time to see the cobra's exit. Working quickly, Bob brought Steve into the kitchen where Belva provided milk to splash over his eyes, which neutralized the effects of the venom, saving Steve's eyesight.

Cobras were all over Mukinge in those days. One morning Sharon went to play on the veranda with her toys and saw something moving inside the toy box. She ran back to her mother and told her "there's a froggy in my box." The 'froggy' was a very large cobra, which could have easily struck the toddler, but it was cool on the veranda and the cold had rendered the serpent sluggish. Bob quickly disposed of the intruder.

Bob had the most dramatic encounter with a cobra: one evening he heard a disturbance among the hens in his chicken house and, entering, felt something wet drip on the back of his neck. Turning around, he saw a cobra hiding in the rafters above! Calling upon Ken Askey, an electrician who was installing electric lights for the mission hospital, the two men clubbed the cobra and put its body in a box, planning to share the story with the locals the following day. Moving on from the incident, Bob went to work preserving fish in the garage. As Ken's electricity was not yet available, Bob toiled by the light of a hurricane lantern. Suddenly, a blue flame shot out of the lantern. Realizing he was in danger, Bob fled the garage as an explosion tore the building apart!

The blast quickly brought a crowd of startled Africans who wondered if *Kahaya* was all right. Bob quickly put together what had happened: the chemicals he had been using to preserve the fish had been so flammable that their proximity to the lantern had ignited the gases. He narrated his story to the astonished onlookers. "But that's just half the story," he began to explain, opening the box where he had deposited the cobra. However, upon opening the box, Bob and the Africans soon discovered that the clubbing the cobra had taken hadn't killed it and it readied to spring out of the box! Bob slammed the lid down just in time! Bob had come extremely close to death on at least two occasions that night.

One onlooker remarked, "If you'd been an African, Kahaya, you would have been dead twice." The Africans praised God for sparing Kahaya, then returned to their homes.

Two weeks later, a letter of support from a bedridden woman named Mrs. Hart revealed she had been praying intently for Bob on the evening of the cobra attack and explosion, having heard from God: "I really want you to pray for Bob Foster." Afterward, she had written Bob, wondering why he had needed prayers on that particular day.

In 1955 Bob and Belva brought the children with them on furlough to Toronto. Having grown up in the predictable climes of Africa, the more variable temperatures in Ontario were a new experience for the children. For Steve, it was fascinating to watch their neighbour's television, particularly seeing CFL football games. Of course, most football games were played on Sunday and, as Steve recalled, "in those days good Christians didn't turn on their TVs on Sundays." As Bob and Belva spoke to people in North America about their mission work, with Bob visiting Mrs. Hart to thank her for her prayers that evening he had escaped death twice, Belva found it difficult to justify her presence on the mission field. Belva spent so much time tending to the children, running her household and providing hospitality to mission people, visitors and patients. She thought she was "the biggest failure that ever existed" because "I had done no 'missionary work.' I discounted all the hospitality I had given which enabled other people to come for treatment and have their babies." Like many missionary wives, it took time for her to recognize the value of those contributions—that hospitality itself is part of mission work.

Soon after the end of the furlough in 1956, Bob and Belva decided it was time for 7-year-old Steve to begin his formal education. Rather than sending him to North America as Charles and June had with their children, a different option was selected: a boarding school for missionary kids called

Sakeji School.

SAKEJI SCHOOL

Operated by Christian Missions in Many Lands since its founding in 1925, Sakeji School lay far in the northern tip of Northern Rhodesia, close to the borders of both the Belgian Congo and Angola. The property gained its name from the Sakeji River, a nearby tributary of the Zambezi River. Several farms lay close by and would help supply food for the students and staff. Although today myriad students from various ages are taught at Sakeji, in the 1950s ages ranged from 7-14. Students came principally from nearby Angola, Belgian Congo, Southern Rhodesia (now Zimbabwe) and Northern Rhodesia and in addition to the Fosters, many other missionary families—such as the Biers, Bréchets, Coles, Hendersons and Stintons—availed themselves of the school.

At first, the sheer adventure of journeying to the north spoke to Steve's hardy spirit. It was only when Bob and Belva turned to leave that he began to cry. It was difficult for Bob and Belva to part ways with Steve; classes ran all year except for during June to September and a six-week Christmas vacation. Sakeji was a trying environment for many children as often MKs grow up in very relaxed home environments and are unable to adjust to the regimented behaviour expected at a boarding school. The style of teaching at Sakeji was modelled very closely on that of British boarding schools; the "stiff upper lip" format caused some children to feel they had been abandoned and were unloved by parents who considered them an obstacle to their mission. "It was a good school to discipline kids," former student Don Stinton recalled. "If you were independent-minded you could manage." Despite the rigid learning and living environment, Steve was the sort of person who could quickly adapt himself to the school.

The head of the school was Lyndon Hess, a very strict teacher who demanded obedience from his charges. Mr. Hess taught math, history and science, while Miss Mary Poole taught French, English, Latin, geography and social sciences. Mr. Hess' history classes would connect historical events to that of current events in international affairs, an approach Steve appreciated. Each Wednesday, Mr. Hess would give a one-hour synopsis of global events which occurred throughout that week, based on what was available to him over BBC Radio and in periodicals. Sakeji received the redoubtable London Illustrated News weekly paper and the children would assist in the binding of issues for storage in the library. Steve enjoyed leafing through the bound volumes, especially looking back into the archives on World War II from the paper's week-by-week perspective.

While these discussions appealed to Steve, he was happiest at Sakeji when he was on the sports field. Although Steve had short legs, which meant he couldn't run as fast as other students, he had good upper body strength for shot put, enjoyed baseball, soccer and field hockey. Steve especially enjoyed playing rugby, under the eye of their physical education teacher Mr. Wyatt. Mr. Wyatt was a farmer from nearby Hillwood Farms and volunteered his time once a week to teach the boys sports. Mr. Wyatt was a strong, 6'6" tall man whom Steve vividly recalled once picking up a pair of bags containing cornmeal, each one weighing 200 lbs., and loaded both into a pickup truck at the same time, doing the work of at least four men. Steve's exposure to CFL football in Canada helped him as many of his fellow students came from an American background and were accustomed to the forward pass of US football, whereas CFL football permits the backwards pass similar to rugby. Thus, Steve adapted more quickly than his American classmates and, owing to his size, played front row in games. He developed a reputation among the other boys for being "very sporty."

One year ahead of Steve was Jean-Pierre Bréchet, son of the Swiss missionary doctor Rodolphe Bréchet, who had been in Angola since 1943 and founded the Kalukembe Mission Hospital there. Jean-Pierre had to learn English as a second language to attend Sakeji, but he had learned enough by then to boast of his adopted homeland, especially remarking how much more topographical variety Angola had compared to Northern Rhodesia. Although Jean-Pierre spoke of Angola in glowing terms, Steve dismissed it as "typical mish kid talk," as many MKs would heap praise upon their parents' assigned countries, puffing up their adopted homes in a manner reminiscent of boasting "my dad can beat up your dad."

Another student Steve befriended was Danny Henk, a Methodist boy from the Belgian Congo who was obsessed with soldiering. As the library had many books on the subject of warfare, Danny became something of a specialist. While many MKs pondered if they would join the mission field as their parents had, Danny was certain he would become a soldier, once even building himself a wooden fort at Sakeji from a pile of leftover construction lumber. Little did Steve suspect that one day, Danny would realize that dream and would later become a colonel in the US Army, serving in the Africa Center for Strategic Studies!

Although Steve was a fine student in the classroom, outside of class was another matter. Steve's outgoing, exuberant personality made him a natural leader, so he would occasionally convince his friends to break curfew rules and sneak out at night to steal mangoes. Steve would also target some classmates for pranks, sending them on a "snipe hunt" into the woods to find a nonexistent animal.

At worship services, Steve had to adjust to Sakeji's style, which did not quite match his Baptist upbringing; instead of the Gospel choruses Steve had sung at home, Miss Poole and Mrs. Hess taught hymns such as "When Morning Gilds the Skies" and "Immortal, Invisible, God Only Wise." In the evenings at Sakeji, the staff would read a Bible story to the youngest children before sending them to bed. As he grew older, Steve would be allowed to stay up to hear the "big kids'" story, such as *Man-Eaters of Kumaon*, the 1944 account of Jim Corbett, famed British hunter of man-eating tigers in India. Steve adored those "hair-raising stories." "I don't know how any of us slept!" he recalled. There may not have been tigers in Africa, but Steve had an early love for hunting.

Perhaps the most valuable lesson Steve learned from Sakeji was the memorization of scripture. Bob and Belva trained their children at the dinner table to memorize certain passages just as Bob had at Gowans' Home, teaching them Psalms 23, 45 and 121. Sakeji further incentivized memorization by giving the students one piece of fudge each week if they could memorize all of the week's daily Bible verses (5 per week). Memorizing 100 verses (a full term of classes) would net a student their own New Testament; memorizing 200 verses (two terms) would reward the student with their own Bible. The discipline of memorizing long passages of the King James Bible eventually gave Steve most of Romans chapters 5-8.

It was good that the Sakeji school terms were not long because Steve's wardrobe was barely supporting itself. Most clothing was cleaned by hand and placed out in the African sun to dry, which "if it didn't dry your clothes in 15-20 minutes, something was wrong!" Steve noted. This was fine for most resilient garments but nylons and elastics couldn't manage such treatment indefinitely; Steve's underwear would begin to lose its elasticity, until by the end of the school term he would need replacements.

Speaking of replacements at Sakeji, Steve's younger siblings began joining in the subsequent years, along with their cousins, Herbert's children. Sharon started at Sakeji in 1957 while Sheila arrived in 1959. Sharon felt quite homesick, while Sheila adapted much like her brother and, being particularly studious, quickly became an excellent pupil. Herbert and Elenore's children were perhaps more in need of the discipline Sakeji provided. Bob's children were astonished that their cousins were permitted to go about barefoot and Sheila was particularly envious of how easily they spoke Kikaonde and interacted with Bakaonde children at Chizera. Although Bob was considered somewhat liberal in comparison to his parents, Herbert was himself less conventional than his older brother.

Although brothers Harold, Bob and Herbert all lived in Northern Rhodesia during those years, the three only got together on one occasion. Still,

Bob made frequent visits to Chizera to provide clinic duties. When not in school, Steve would accompany his father on these visits. On one trip, Steve went hunting with Herbert, marvelling at his uncle's superb marksmanship; Herbert brought down a roan antelope that day. "Uncle Herb used to carry one of those canvas water cooler sacks," Steve recalled, "the kind where you poured boiling water into it and let it evaporate on the front of the truck. Uncle Herb could swig one of those completely in one fell swoop."

Steve and Sharon had the opportunity to see their father in action as well. One day at Mukinge, a leopard was wounded by a trap a game warden had left to defend Charles' sheep and goats. The injured leopard had fled into the wild, now rendered extremely dangerous by its injury. Bob took up his rifle and permitted Steve and Sharon to join him in his jeep as he convened with fellow missionaries Dave Fields and Clarence Gifford, plus two African game wardens. The hunting party followed the leopard's trail into elephant grass so tall, even Bob's 6' frame was swallowed up by the blades. Dave Fields climbed a tree to see over the grass when he caught sight of movement. An exclamation of warning from Dave sent Bob scampering up the nearest tree, just in time to avoid the angry leopard. Fortunately, the wounded animal could not climb up the tree; unfortunately, Bob had dropped his rifle in his haste to escape.

The game wardens and other spectators made a hasty retreat. Dave sized up the animal with his own rifle: "I don't know if I should try to get him from here," he called.

"Don't shoot," Bob advised, "you might hit me." Just then, Bob's driver, Kibale, reappeared. As the leopard was focused on him, Bob hatched a plan to survive. "Kibale, crawl around behind the tree in the deep grass and pick up my gun. I'll keep teasing him so he won't notice you." Bob began hurtling sticks and make loud cries to keep the leopard distracted; the furious animal clawed and scraped at the base of the tree but still could not reach him. Kibale was uncertain of this plan, but as Bob continued to taunt the leopard and call upon Kibale for help, the driver gradually found his courage.

Dave kept his own rifle trained on the leopard, promising Kibale he would fire if the leopard caught sight of him. Ever so slowly, Kibale inched through the elephant grass, trying hard to avoid detection. Circling behind the tree, he found the fallen rifle. Carefully, shielded from sight of the leopard, he held the rifle up to Bob in the tree. Bob was so close to the animal that he couldn't miss; he stuck the barrel of his rifle into the snarling leopard's mouth and fired; the leopard fell over dead. Bob (and Kibale)'s courage facing the leopard made this encounter a favourite memory of the Fosters as Steve, Sharon and the other children would repeat the tale many times over the decades.

During a break from Sakeji, Steve, Sharon and Sheila accompanied their father on a camping trip to Kafue National Park, the largest game park in Northern Rhodesia. Because the children didn't often have time alone with their father, the special attention strengthened their bond with him. At home with Stacey, when the four children would play games or sports, they would always divide themselves into the same teams: Steve and Sheila against Sharon and Stacey. These relationships would remain much the same for decades. Although the two boys had many similar interests and likewise the two girls, "it was never boys against girls because Stephen and Stacey fought all the time as kids," Sheila remembered. Instead, Sharon looked out for Stacey while Sheila sided with Steve.

All around them, Africa was slowly changing. The gradual process of independence for colonies was speeding up. On March 6, 1957, the British colony 'The Gold Coast' up in northwestern Africa became the first African colony to gain independence, changing its name to Ghana. Although timetables for independence varied across the continent, most of the colonial powers were beginning to release their colonies. Independence movements were in full bloom around the Fosters, from the forces seeking to overthrow Apartheid in South Africa to the revolutionary armies forming in Angola and the Belgian Congo. Complicating matters was the Cold War, as communist powers (principally the USSR and China) offered sponsorship to communist-affiliated parties in African nations; this in turn compelled anti-communist powers such as the US to become involved in the independence movements.

Within Northern Rhodesia, matters were somewhat more peaceful than their neighbours, although not entirely so. While Northern and Southern Rhodesia were joining efforts to build the Kariba Dam which would result in Lake Kariba, the world's largest man-made lake, the black African population was seeking change. Although the Africans were not fully united in what course of action to pursue to achieve independence (strikes, boycotts and sit-ins were each attempted), they were unhappy at how they, the majority, were earning less money and obtaining fewer opportunities than the white population.

Among the political movements campaigning for independence was the Zambian African National Congress (*Zambia* derived from the Zambezi River), led by Kenneth Kaunda, a former schoolteacher. When Northern Rhodesia's Governor-General charged Kaunda with seditious acts and imprisoned him in 1959 on specious evidence, it served only to deepen the party's popularity, as well as making Kaunda's release from prison a *cause célèbre*. Time and again in these years, attempts to prevent African self-rule would only affirm the people's resolve to succeed; an independent Northern Rhodesia was not far off.

GRAPPLING WITH THE BLACK MAMBA!

Bob's most dramatic story came during a clinic visit in the village Mutanda where his former nurse Frances Woods lived with her husband Michael Warburton. Arriving around noon and taking lunch with the Warburtons, Bob went to visit patients Frances had indicated required his abilities. There were about 300 people outside of the clinic in the hot afternoon sun, 100 of them his patients. The first patient, a woman, entered the hut and lay down on the table for Bob to examine her with his stethoscope. Suddenly she sat upright, gathered her clothes and started to go.

"I have to leave," she insisted.

"But I'm not finished yet," Bob protested.

"No! I want to leave!" the woman insisted.

Through his stethoscope, Bob could hear her heart was pounding hard. With the exam complete, the woman immediately leaped off the table, went out of the hut and called to the hundreds of people present: "Don't anybody go into the clinic! There's a big snake in there!" Bob was startled and looked about, having seen no sign of a snake. He demanded to know where the creature was lurking. "Kahaya," she explained, "when I was lying down on your examining table, I looked up at the rafters and there was a big black mamba right above your head."

Returning inside, Bob gazed into the rafters. As the woman had said, a large black mamba was curled up near the gable of the thatch roof. It appeared to be almost as thick around as his arm and at least 8 feet long. The black mamba gained its name from its black-coloured mouth; if you see that black, poisonous mouth, you are flirting with death. Of all snakes, the black mamba is among the deadliest—not because they are the most venomous, but because they are not as easily frightened of humans. While most snakes will choose to hide when humans are around, black mambas are known to seek humans out. This was a dilemma; Bob knew that unless the snake was dealt with immediately, the clinic's reputation would be harmed and villagers would be less willing to use its services. There was no time to summon specialized aid—Bob needed to take charge of the situation. Turning to the crowd he asked, "Who will help me kill the snake?"

Although several hundred people were gathered there, the air was still. No one wanted to volunteer.

"We've got to kill it," Bob repeated. "We can't work as long as it's in there. Who will help me?" Again, Bob was met with silence. Finally a local pastor who had been meeting with patients stepped forward. "Kahaya, you go. We'll pray."

Although startled, Bob agreed. "All right. If you'll really pray, I'll go.

Does anyone have a gun?" The people shook their heads, but one enterprising fellow presented Bob with a six-foot-long spear; a wizened old man crippled by arthritis gave Bob his cane to use as a club. With a weapon in each hand, Bob re-entered the hut to take stock of the situation. The snake was alert, its eyes on Bob, waiting to see what his intentions were. Using a stepladder, Bob carefully raised himself to the snake's level, remaining a good four feet from its mouth. Bob knew if he came within range of the snake, it would easily bite and kill him. Finally, he settled on a plan of attack: "If I get him speared against the wall, I can hit him with the cane," he thought. He called aloud to the people outside: "Okay, now you pray!"

As the people outside prayed, Bob speared the black mamba in the middle of its body, burying the spearhead inside the wall. Furious, the snake lunged at Bob, its deadly fangs missing him by mere inches. While his left hand held the spear, Bob struck with his right hand, aiming the cane at the mamba's head. But the wily reptile dodged Bob's blow and readied another attack of its own. Again and again the snake would fling itself at Bob, unable to reach him; Bob, in turn, tried to club the snake, to no avail.

The people outside continued to pray; perhaps the struggle went on for an hour, scaly poisonous death lashing out at a man of God. However long it lasted, Bob's strength was not infinite. More and more, his left arm struggled to keep a tight grip on the spear; less and less power remained in Bob's right hand to swing the club. Finally, Bob knew he could not last any longer; he pulled the spear from the wall and let the snake fall to the ground; it slithered behind a cupboard. Shaken, but so far unharmed, Bob exited the hut. The people paused in their prayers, hoping to hear good news. "Look," he gasped, "I'm tired; the snake is tired. It's gone behind the cupboard. I need some help to finish him off."

Of all the able-bodied people in that crowd, the only one to answer Bob's plea proved to be the old man who had donated his cane. He was so short Bob could have tucked him under his armpit. "I'm old," the man explained. "If I die, no problem, I know where I'm going, I've lived my life." Bob guided his only aide inside the hut and explained the situation. Bob observed that if they pulled the cupboard away from the wall, the snake would try to escape. If the snake got loose, it would quickly kill them both. However, if they could press the cupboard tightly against the wall, their force would trap the snake. All Bob needed was for the snake to poke its head out from behind the cupboard so he could deliver a fatal clubbing. It was a dicey proposition.

With a shout, the two men slammed the cupboard against the wall. The snake's head popped out, but, as Bob had hoped, they pinned most of its body and it could not reach them. This time, the snake had less room to evade; with a shower of blows, Bob clubbed the snake to death.

Bob brought the snake's remains out to the waiting throng, which was impressed and grateful for his deeds. There was a quick service of thanksgiving for being delivered from the snake, but after this Bob called an end to his clinic visit; he was exhausted, but promised to return the next month.

The real importance of this story, as Bob would assert, was how it summed up so much of the missionary experience: "People say to me, 'Bob, you go; we'll pray.' And I go on to say that if they really pray, God will work." Further, he had seen time and again that when it comes to seeking volunteers for a difficulty ministry, it is often the old and decrepit who are willing while the young and seemingly strong hold themselves back.

As the family prepared for another furlough in 1960, many landmarks occurred: Bob was on the verge of bringing a hospital to Luampa along with airplane service; the fifth Foster child Stuart Jeremy was born; Charles published the Gospel of John (*Mambo awamá anembele Yoano*), and, tragically, Herbert Foster succumbed to cancer. He left behind six children: David, twins Carolyn and Stanley, Janet, Marguerite and Ken; Elenore was still pregnant with their seventh child, Roy. Most of Herbert's children were so young they could not remember their father—although they would come to know him and be inspired by him through their family's memories.

Bob worked hard during his furlough, taking refresher courses to improve his surgical skills and learn new techniques while spreading word of the need for air travel in Northern Rhodesia to safely transport critical cases. A great deal of fundraising had to be done to afford the airplane model Bob selected and he himself had to be trained as a pilot.

For the children, home was still not Toronto—home remained Mukinge—but soon, the family would move to Luampa. The family returned from furlough aboard a freighter, the only passengers being the Fosters, a dentist and the dentist's wife. The family was granted access to the behind-the-scenes operations of the freighter and Steve enjoyed touring the engine room and visiting the radio operator.

The children especially treasured that time because of how available Bob was to them. "We children had him to ourselves," Sharon enthused. "No one else could bother him or call him or summon him to a meeting."

STEVE'S FIRST ASSIST

Bob had been making visits out west to Luampa for several years, but the needs there were great and the 300-kilometre journey somewhat arduous. The people of Luampa had been calling out for a hospital of their own and, in 1961, the time had finally come. Luampa lay near the border of Angola. In those days, under the colonial rule of the Portuguese, the Angolans were subject to forced labour at the pleasure of the Portuguese. The indignity of forced labour was one of the earliest causes of the independence movement in Angola—but many Angolans simply wanted to live free. Because of this, Luampa had become home to a large refugee population of settlers who fled Angola. Some of the Angolan tribes who had immigrated to the Luampa area included the Luchazi, Mbundu, Chokwe, Luvale and Lozi. The Luchazi were so numerous that Bob and his family began learning their language. Fortunately, Luchazi had some similarities to Kikaonde and after six months, Bob was able to preach in Luchazi.

When he was home from Sakeji, Steve would accompany his father to work as often as possible. The hospital remained incomplete, but Bob strove to obtain the funding and loosen the bureaucracies slowing the progress. Steve noted his father had "a sense of the bigness of God and His generosity and willingness to bless those who live by faith. He believed God is as big as you are willing to let Him be in your life, in His ability to provide for your needs and provide for the task at hand." It was during one of Bob's absences that Steve had his first assist in the operating room. In 1962, while Bob was at a conference, a woman appeared at the Luampa hospital hemorrhaging blood. She was two months pregnant and required a D&C. A young South African doctor who was filling in for Bob took charge of the matter and recruited Steve's help as he drove the woman to Mankoya district hospital, the nearest properly equipped facility. Steve helped watch the road for obstacles and, even more importantly, when they came to Mankoya, vouched for the South African doctor, who was a stranger to the staff there—but everyone knew Bob's son.

Mankoya had no electricity so the operation had to be performed under a Tilley lantern—and here Steve found his first task in surgery: holding the lantern while the South African doctor operated. By now, the woman had lost a great deal of blood and there was a slight delay before they could operate as her hemoglobin type had to be confirmed. A D&C takes much longer to prepare than it does to perform; the operation itself inserts instruments into the patient's uterus to scrape out its contents. By the time the operation began, the doctor was "sweating bricks." Holding the hot lantern close so the doctor could perform the D&C, Steve's arms were so near to the lantern it felt as though they were cooking. D&Cs can be very bloody operations so between the blood and the heat, Steve was grateful he didn't faint.

The entire situation left a mark on Steve. Already he had been considering a career as a missionary doctor in Northern Rhodesia, but now there was certainty: he would become a surgeon. The D&C case had given him "the notion of how you can deal with an emergency in medicine, take a very ugly situation and turn it into something positive within a short period of time.

It was exciting to learn surgery was like that, to take a situation which was deteriorating and turn it around; to give people the benefit of steel." Acknowledging that surgeons are often typified as having more interest in cases than in people, Steve added: "People say there is a personality that goes with being a surgeon. The stereotype is a person who likes the hurly-burly and dynamic of telling someone, 'I think you need the benefit of steel' and sometimes the benefit of steel in the appropriate time and place can be the difference between life and death."

Out at Sakeji, repeated trips to drop off their sons had formed a bond between Bob Foster and Rodolphe Bréchet, all the more so now that Bob was treating people in Luampa who had fled Angola. Rodolphe and Bob became friends and it was Bob who performed Jean-Pierre's baptism in 1961. By the time Stacey Foster started attending Sakeji in 1962, the number of Fosters had grown to a multitude—the four eldest of Bob's and the three eldest of Elenore's being taught there.

January 1963 dawned with the birth of Bob and Belva's sixth child, Stirling Jeffrey. Steve and Stacey had suggested their brother's unique name, having heard of the famous British Formula One driver Stirling Moss. That same year, Charles Foster was awarded the title Officer of the Most Excellent Order of the British Empire by the Governor-General of Northern Rhodesia, "for services as a missionary in Northern Rhodesia"; the award included a certificate signed by Queen Elizabeth II. Steve was now nearing the end of his Sakeji education and had certainly benefited from the discipline for which the school excelled. He credited Sakeji for instilling respect for his elders and the view that "cultured people show respect." Nowhere at Sakeji were discipline and respect so vitally important as at the dinner table, where polite table manners were mandatory. Should a student reach across the table for a dish, they could expect to be ejected from the dining hall and ordered to run five laps around the playground while their food grew cold. Manners were especially paramount for those students fortunate (or, depending on one's view, unfortunate) enough to sit beside Mr. Hess himself. Heaven help you if you used your salad fork for anything other than salad!

Steve vividly recalled one Saturday morning in November of his last year when he sat beside Mr. Hess. Mr. Hess entered the hall with a sad look on his face, led grace for the meal, and then called the room to order: "I just wanted to let you all know that President John F. Kennedy was shot in an assassination yesterday afternoon and died last night. We had confirmation on the news this morning." Steve recalled the students were "aghast." It was surreal to receive such news at the breakfast hour. Even in a remote locale like Sakeji, tremors from the tumult in the US could still be felt.

Still, on the African continent, the news was concerned primarily with the growing number of independent nations; the French had divested themselves of virtually every one of their African colonies; the United Kingdom had released colonies ranging from far-off Sierra Leone to nearby Uganda; the Belgian Congo had become the Democratic Republic of the Congo; even in Kenya, where the British had attempted military force to maintain their hold over the colony, independence had won out. One of the few hold-outs to self-rule was South Africa, where Apartheid still held sway and had, in 1962, arrested rebel leader Nelson Mandela, whose continued imprisonment would only encourage resistance against white rule in the succeeding decades. Nearly all citizens of the continent were either independent or on the verge of obtaining independence—with the notable exceptions of all Portuguese-held colonies. The Portuguese claimed a long association with Africa, going back hundreds of years before the 'Scramble for Africa' had brought in the other colonial powers. In Africa, they controlled the southwestern nation of Angola and southeastern Mozambique, the island nations of Cape Verde and São Tomé and Príncipe and Portuguese Guinea (later Guinea-Bissau) in northwest Africa. Pedantically referring to their colonies as 'provinces' of Portugal (*províncias ultramarinas*), they were determined to remain in control—even as the struggle for independence heated up.

CHAPTER 4

"When Do We Operate?" — *Steve Foster*

LUSAKA; HAMILTON; TORONTO (October 1964 – August 1970)

On October 24, 1964, Northern Rhodesia officially became independent from the United Kingdom, changing its name to Zambia with Kenneth Kaunda as its first president. Luampa Mission Hospital hosted its own official opening only a few days after the transfer of power. Although many of the newly independent regimes in Africa proved weak and quickly toppled, or became dictatorial and oppressive, Zambia proved an exception as the country remained reasonably peaceful, even as its neighbours continued to wage war. That year, SAGM changed its name to the Africa Evangelical Fellowship (AEF). Their motto remained the same, words in the spirit of Dr. Livingstone: "God first—go forward."

Steve had moved from Sakeji to Lusaka, capital of Zambia, where he completed his secondary education in the all-boys' school Gilbert Rennie High School (soon to be renamed Kabulonga Boys' School). Bob and Belva asked a Baptist missionary couple in Lusaka—Darrell and Barb Hockersmith—to keep an eye on their son should he have any special requests. "Steve was ready for adventure," Barb recalled. "One day near the end of the school year, he came to us asking for permission to go with a number of school friends to Victoria Falls for the weekend. We prayed about the request and finally said no. The disappointment Steve accepted unhappily. The next day news was received that the vehicle he would have been in was involved in a serious accident and all occupants were killed or seriously injured. His disappointment turned to grateful praise."

The Hockersmiths had been serving in Angola in a remote village called Cavango. The pair had studied for 18 months to pass every entrance examination the Portuguese had demanded from missionaries—demands

31

which were all the more stringent when applied against Protestants. They had learned the Portuguese language as well as Portuguese geography, history and even poetry, then they defended themselves against a jury which would test their knowledge. Darrell had preached in villages while Barb tended to clinical needs as a nurse, but after the Hockersmiths took a furlough, the Portuguese refused to admit re-entry. Troubled and dejected, they went to serve in Zambia.

WHAT WAS GOING ON IN ANGOLA?

What had changed in Angola since the Hockersmiths' first arrival? From 1961 onward, Angola was in a state of war. By 1965 there were two major revolutionary parties: the ostensibly pro-democracy FNLA (*Frente Nacional de Libertação de Angola*) led by Holden Roberto and the ostensibly pro-communist MPLA (*Movimento Popular de Libertação de Angola*) led by poet/physician/politician Agostinho Neto. By 1966 a third party would emerge, splintering off from FNLA and amassing more and more importance as the years went by: UNITA (*União Nacional para a Independência Total de Angola*), led by Jonas Savimbi. Each of the three parties would receive notable international support, including the USSR and Cuba (MPLA), Zaire and Israel (FNLA), US and South Africa (UNITA) and China (FNLA and UNITA).

Portugal, which had been led by the authoritarian regime of António de Oliveira Salazar since 1932, was officially Catholic. They had long been uncomfortable by the numbers of Protestant missionaries entering Angola, believing they were undermining Catholic interests and 'radicalizing' the populace. Agostinho Neto himself was the son of a Methodist pastor, Holden Roberto was taught in a Baptist school and Jonas Savimbi had been taught by Congregationalists. Many regions of the country were still unreached by missionaries; indeed, many residents of Angola would not have even recognized the name of their homeland if it had been told to them. Angola is a vast territory—in fact, it is 14 times the size of mother Portugal! Portugal tried to keep Protestants out of its urban centres, sending them into the 'bush' instead—which was fine for the Protestants, for they could access many unreached peoples the Catholics had never encountered.

Protestant missionaries were also outspoken about what was going on in Angola. "I must stand with the Africans," Rev. E. Edwin LeMaster (a Methodist) told the *Saturday Evening Post* in 1962. "Protestant churches alone have educated more Africans than has the government," he observed. The Portuguese secret police force, PIDE (Polícia Internacional e de Defesa do Estado) accused Rev. LeMaster of running a "school for terrorists" and LeMaster told the press stories of church leaders being arrested, interrogated and beaten by PIDE. Finally, LeMaster was arrested and deported home to the US.

Of Angola, Salazar would say, *"Isto é nosso"* (This is ours). This nationalism went beyond religion or even pride; as any Catechist could have observed, "Money is the root of all evil" (1 Timothy 6:10) and Angola was in the midst of a startling economic transformation. Oil and gas had been found only in the most recent years, propping up Portugal and catching the eye of many international investors. The nation's greatest prize was yet to come: in 1966, vast quantities of oil would be discovered in the tiny patch of land they held within Congolese territory—Cabinda. "Africa is for us a moral justification and a *raison d'être* as a power," said Marcello Caetano (who would eventually succeed Salazar). "Without it we would be a small nation; with it, we are a great country."

In many parts of Africa, woodcarvers sell images of an African 'thinker.' Unlike the statue of Rodin's Thinker, this figure is an African person, hunched down on the ground, hands upon his head (this image is also a watermark on Angolan currency). Some Angolans say the most important part of the carving is its base—because it represents the African soil from which all the riches of the country originate. The thinker is in such a state of distress (so it is said) because he knows he has been denied access to that wealth.

Portugal had been late to realize the wealth to be exploited from Angola; although it had claimed it as a colony since 1575, Portugal had found it enormously difficult to settle willing Portuguese, much less people who could survive there before anti-malarial drugs were discovered. After hearing of the success the British had deporting criminals to Australia, there was an attempt in the nineteenth century to funnel Portugal's criminals to Angola. However, whereas many British convicts were petty thieves or debtors, the bulk of Portugal's jails were jammed with hardened criminals, leading to Angola's capital, Luanda, developing a reputation as one of the most violent, dangerous ports in Africa.

Since the 1910s Portugal had an official policy whereby any indigenous Angolan could obtain full citizenship rights—and become an *assimilado* ("assimilated"). "Now you've become a real person!" Steve would say in mockery of the European process; it was, after all, a procedure to determine if someone born in Angola were 'civilized' enough to be worthy of their homeland.

And yet, the percentage of assimilados was insignificant in Angola, never reaching a full 1% of the population. This was not due to lack of interest on the Angolans' side, but because the Portuguese made these tests as hard as possible. Assimilados needed a Portuguese name (rather than their village name), to read and write in Portuguese and be well-versed in Portuguese culture and geography—primarily the culture and geography of Portugal (down to "every single stream in Portugal," Steve noted). All of this was impeded by the simple fact that the Portuguese had established very few educational opportunities for Angolans; were it not for the many Protestant missionaries in Angola, the small percentage of assimilados would have been fewer still.

Portugal finally abolished the deeply unpopular forced labour program in 1961, but Angolans had little love for the colonial higher-ups. Even assimilados were barred from entering European-only buildings. Angolans could not travel from one town to another without reporting and justifying their presence to PIDE, and neither could the Protestant missionaries. Little wonder, then, that the Angolans and Protestants were increasingly drawn to each other as Angolans found it easy to accept the Protestant missionaries as their peers, as neither of them were beloved by Portugal.

SHELLEY: THE SEVENTH FOSTER

In 1965 Shelley Joy Foster was born, the seventh and last child of Bob and Belva. Belva—who was once considered unlikely to bear children—was by now wondering when the pregnancies would ever end! "I was resentful, I'm sure, for many years," she recalled. "Each pregnancy left me feeling dragged out and burdened, never really on top of it." Still, they had persisted in having children because as their elder children grew they realized they weren't ready to live in an 'empty nest.' Indeed, later in life Belva would reflect on the two youngest, Stirling and Shelley, as she and Bob's "greatest blessing" because tending to their needs provided much needed stability in times of upheaval. There was a 16-year age gap between Steve and Shelley, one so large they were almost in separate generations! Because of how Bob and Belva's ministry changed over the years, the younger Foster siblings would live rather different childhoods than their elder siblings.

One curious difference between the 7 Fosters and their parents is that Bob was ambidextrous, while all of his children were not; Belva and her two eldest (Steve and Sharon) and youngest (Shelley) were all right-handed, and the middle children (Sheila, Stacey, Stuart and Stirling) were left-handed.

One Sunday afternoon at Luampa in 1965, Bob had a pregnant woman who required a caesarean-section, but none of his staff were available. By this time, Sharon and Sheila had each been taught how to scrub in for surgery and accompanied their father into the OR on various cases. Now, Bob needed Sharon and Sheila because there was no one else to help him. With 15-year-old Sharon as his surgical assistant and 13-year-old Sheila on hand to catch the baby, the C-section was a success. Just as Steve was planning to become a surgeon, his eldest sisters were planning careers as nurses. On another occasion in the OR, Sharon helped her father remove a large goitre from a woman's thyroid; the operation was a difficult one which Bob was not entirely versed in. The surgical book containing instructions on the procedure was pressed up against the glass of a window looking into the OR and, as the case proceeded, Sharon would move from the table to the window, memorizing passages, relaying them to her father, assisting in the next step of the procedure, then returning to the window for the next paragraph.

Bob was content to remain in Luampa. "I was born in Zambia and I plan to die in Zambia," he would state. But times had changed; Ezra Shank, the man who helped direct Bob to Mukinge, had retired as head of AEF and now AEF was asking Bob to take his place. In the wake of the independence movement in Africa, AEF and other mission societies needed to reassert their purposes. There were those who questioned whether the practice of sending missionaries from the western nations into Africa should even continue. Bob had been gifted with the kind of forceful personality which made him a persuasive speaker and his decade and a half of service gave him practical experience and credibility. Finally, Bob confronted whether it was his own pride keeping him in medicine or God's will that he serve in a different capacity; concluding it was God's will, he prepared to return to the US.

Bob ultimately committed to three years in Glen Ridge, New Jersey, from 1966-69 as executive secretary of AEF. Stuart, who had only just begun learning at Sakeji, would be the last of the Fosters' kids to attend the boarding school. Bob and Belva auctioned off most of their household goods and returned to the US, with Bob placing his primary focus on recruiting new missionaries for the field. Sharon and Sheila both finished their high school education in Glen Ridge then began taking nursing courses via Rutgers University.

STEVE IN TORONTO

At the same time his family moved to the US, Steve had gone to Toronto to complete high school, taking Grade 13 there (schools in Ontario went up to Grade 13). Steve had it in his mind that he would like to attend his father's *alma mater*—the University of Toronto—but finishing his schooling in Ontario was very nearly a disaster. French was a mandatory class which was weighted very heavily on final marks and Steve hadn't taken any French since leaving Sakeji. Although he could manage the oral portion well enough, his written French was *très abominable*. The French alone brought Steve's average down to a miserable 33% in the first term. Mrs. Brewster, the woman he boarded with, kindly took him aside at one point and asked, "Are you sure you really want to go into medicine? Are you sure you don't want to become a carpenter or something?"

Chagrined, Steve answered wryly, "Well, ma'am, the girls with miniskirts sure are a great distraction!" Steve's English class went much more smoothly as he wrote an essay on William Shakespeare's Macbeth which his teacher graded 90%—then subtracted 20 points for spelling errors! It seems Steve had difficulty remembering how to apply apostrophes to Macbeth's wife, whom he repeatedly dubbed 'Macbeths' wife.'

During the summer, Steve went Brantford, where his grandparents (Belva's parents) lived. His Uncle Gil (Belva's brother) found Steve a job at Schultz Construction as a helper and coffee boy. Earning $1.75 an hour, he used his first paycheck to purchase a 10 speed bicycle to ride from his grandparents' house to work. "I was impressed by the speed and quality of the brick layer's work in comparison to what I had seen in Zambia." From his time in smaller Ontario towns Steve began to get a sense of the Canadian identity, an identity which up until then was largely confined to his passport. He was surprised at how 'provincial' small-town Canadians were. "There were people in Brantford who had never been to Toronto," he recalled. "They thought it was at the end of the world!"

Humbled by his poor marks, Steve was almost persuaded to turn away from his goal of attending the University of Toronto. From his family's new home in Glen Ridge, he came in touch with an athletics coach at nearby Bloomfield College who offered Steve a scholarship so he could play on the school's soccer team. Then as now, soccer was not an exceptionally popular sport in the US. The coach had heard Steve played in Zambia and remarked, "Nobody out here has heard of soccer, so you'll be a star!" But two days after the generous offer Steve received a letter of acceptance into the general sciences program at the University of Toronto and he had to scramble to find residence for the start of classes in September 1966.

On the first day of one of Steve's 101-level science classes, the professor asked the hundreds of students assembled, "Hands up, how many of you are going to become teachers?" A few hands rose. "Hands up, those who are going into dentistry?" A few more hands snaked up. "Hands up those of you who are going into medicine?" Upon which, two thirds of the room raised their hands. Most of Steve's classmates came from money, privilege or had excellent marks; Steve, who was ranked a B+ student, had none of those things and was well aware he was considered to be at the bottom of the barrel.

Initially Steve lived in Toronto with Bob and Ruth Stephens and their son Chuck Stephens became "like a brother" to him. If there were only one aspect of Canadian culture Steve loved it was the sports. He renewed his love of CFL football, especially during Grey Cup games, finding the quicker pace of CFL games much more to his liking than the NFL. It was also an excellent time for Canadian hockey as the local team—the Toronto Maple Leafs—were then playing their career-best games. Steve vividly recalls the days of players Frank Mahovlich, Davey Keon and Johnny Bower, and the voice of CBC-TV announcer Foster Hewitt covering the games. One of his fondest memories was in 1967 when the Maple Leafs won the much-coveted Stanley Cup, a feat that, at the time of this book's publication, has not been repeated.

During the summer of 1967 Steve returned to Brantford, boarding with the Loveday family instead of with his grandparents. Rev. Don Loveday was the man who married Bob and Belva almost two decades earlier. Steve's summer job was at Spauldings' Sporting Goods, a company which manufactured golf clubs. "I mastered making putter heads with sand blasting and sticking those on roughed up shafts. I discovered you can wreck a shaft in a few seconds if you hold it too long against the sander. You also get filthy with sand from the blaster. I soon discovered why no one else wanted that job." Although Steve had received a few lessons in operating manual vehicles from Bob's friend Don Amborski in Zambia, he didn't receive his certified lessons until 1967. "The instructor spoke as much Italian as English so it was an adventure!"

In the summer of 1968, Steve worked with Frontier College to help educate labourers on mining sites in northern Canada. Steve's assignment was at Tribag Mines, a copper mine 100 km from Sault Ste. Marie and 20 km from Batchewana Bay on Lake Superior. During the days, Steve participated in the labour, first by clearing brush from the roads but eventually journeying underground to help the long hole drill specialist. "I was his assistant taking the 150 lb drill up the ladder onto the platform from which he drilled 100 ft. deep holes into the rock. We did some 30 -40 holes in a radial fashion working suspended in space above a huge cavern where other guys dragged the broken ore into a shaft to be sent to the surface for crushing and grinding to make copper ore." In the evenings, Steve taught miners reading and math skills and helped organize movie nights with 16 mm films he rented from the National Film Board of Canada. "The total number of guys in the camp was about 60. The cook was our best friend as he made incredible pancakes and steaks." Steve's pay was a mere $2.25 an hour, "but as I did overtime I earned almost 3K that summer. I gained an appreciation for the hard work done to make Canada what it is."

Steve also got to experience the rise of drug culture in North America during his third year while staying in residence at Rochdale College. The building was run by a student co-op and "you could get high just by riding the elevator!" Steve typified the building's credo as "love your neighbour and smoke hash." There were financial advantages to living there because they offered spaces to prepare meals while the residents handled all the chores. However, the smell of hash in the building was so pungent Steve didn't enjoy eating in.

When the time came for Steve to fill out the medical college admissions test his form had spaces for six universities. At the time, Ontario had five renowned medical schools: University of Toronto, McGill University, University of Ottawa, University of Western Ontario, and Queen's University. To fill his sixth slot, Steve chose an Ontario school which, although it had been functioning since 1890, was only just then beginning to offer medical courses: McMaster University in Hamilton, less than 70 kilometres from Toronto.

In February 1969, Steve received a letter of acceptance from McMaster, the first post-secondary institution to respond as the other schools did not mail out letters until May, when students' final marks were available. Due to the fact that Steve had a 65.3% grade against a 65% minimum requirement he decided not to wait for a response from the other schools for fear McMaster might withdraw its offer. He believed in "going up against all these conventional schools, if this *crazy* school wants to accept me, I'm not going to reckon on a shot in the dark." Steve enrolled with McMaster, knowing little about the school, only that they were attempting 'problem-based learning' and it sounded "potentially exciting" to him.

Bob was surprised to learn Steve would not be attending the University of Toronto and reacted with befuddlement to hear he would be going to McMaster. "What? Isn't that a Baptist theological college?" Indeed, McMaster had been founded as a theological school. Steve was impatient to get into the mission field as a surgeon and part of the attraction McMaster held was that it was a 3-year program, as opposed to the 4-year programs at the other schools. "I must have qualified for the 'weird filter' effect," Steve mused of his acceptance. "They were looking for someone outside the box; I fit the category of students from different backgrounds."

The Faculty of Medicine were concerned that Steve's education had been heavily weighted in the sciences, so he took a summer course in sociology in June 1969. He spent the remainder of the summer working at Ontario Pioneer Camps, first in the ground maintenance crew, where he "fixed a lot of holes in fibreglass canoes." Later in the summer he served as a counselor "and saw what a positive influence camp life had on young men and women." On July 16, 1969, the camp set up a television set to watch the historic Apollo 11 moon landing. As Neil Armstrong made his "one small step for man," Steve's next step was medical school.

STEVE AT MCMASTER

There were no meaningful interviews at med schools in those days. McMaster asked only for Steve's references. In August 1969, Steve and the other first-year med students were invited to tea at the faculty club where they were seated in a circle while the 40 or so faculty members made introductions. The time came when the faculty asked if there were any questions; Steve raised his hand and asked, "When do we get to operate?" The whole room burst into laughter but Steve was, naturally, quite serious!

At McMaster, Steve began to understand what problem-based learning was all about. From his time at University of Toronto boarding among med students, Steve had seen the type of learning they were struggling with—the heavy loads of studying and homework. At other medical institutions, students were given 2-3 years of basic clinical sciences before being guided into gradual clinical exposure in their 3rd-4th years. He felt there was an obvious divorce between the times when the students studied anatomy in their first year to when they came back to it years later in clinical environments. This lag meant that for some students it was an ordeal to recall what they had previously learned. This divorce left many student unable to understand how the human body works, they were expected to simply regurgitate what had been taught to them earlier in their studies, but were fortunate to recall even 10% of what they had previously learned.

McMaster believed medical training was taking too long to turn out professionals and concluded students should have a more fulsome, clinical perspective directly from the beginning. Rather than studying about organs in isolation from each other, students would learn how each part of the anatomy related to the other. This created a way of thinking that allowed students to tie together their knowledge and improve their performance in clinical environments.

McMaster's philosophy was an unusual one in 1969 and other schools considered it an "unproven exercise" which would turn out students who wouldn't understand what they were doing. Conventional schools still swore by the tradition of thousands of hours spent studying anatomy, pathology, histology, and pathophysiology away from clinical environments. True, the professors at McMaster didn't realize quite where problem-based learning would lead the profession, but for Steve, it was a learning program sent from God.

Within three weeks, Steve understood fully what made McMaster's education different when they sent him to an operating room to observe a splenectomy. Steve had, by this time, spent many hours in the OR with Bob, primarily performing gynaecological surgeries such as hysterectomies and ovariectomies. He had never operated on a patient's stomach, much less taken the time to look around inside. The surgeon quizzed Steve throughout the operation and although Steve had studied (the night before), he felt quite foolish as the surgeon revealed the many different reasons why a patient would have their spleen removed. This line of questioning, of course, pointed to all the reasons why the human body had a spleen. What is the spleen there for? What does it do? *Where* is it? How big is it? What are the illnesses of the spleen? And, if your spleen is taken out, will you know it? (The answer, of course, is *yes!*) Through this line of thinking, Steve could see how microbiology, anatomy, and hematology were linked. He was taught to recognize vital signs and see the human body in an integrated manner. "I found that fascinating because you could see reasons you needed to know that, it wasn't an esoteric fact." Steve particularly perked his ears up when the surgeon mentioned malaria could cause a patient's spleen to swell up; intending to serve in tropical medicine, he could see direct applications for this knowledge in the field.

"Confronted with all of these new things to learn, instead of doing it in a pedantic way, why not learn it all together?" Steve mused. "I was always the kind of guy who wanted to know 'what's the relevance of that fact?' 'What am I learning about bacteria for?'" Learning in a more conventional school would have been a disjointed experience, he acknowledged. "It was like pulling teeth to get a professor to talk about clinical stuff. Whereas at Mac the guys were constantly bringing clinical into the day-to-day. So much more fun!" Steve was amazed at how problem-based learning delivered knowledge; it was precisely right for his personality.

Steve also found time to join McMaster's rugby team. He noted many of his teammates seemed to regard the sport as "an informal excuse to go get drunk at the end of the game." Steve limited himself to one beer. After all, he was "a liberated Evangelical!"

BOB AND ANGOLA

In Glen Ridge, Bob was meeting his obligations with AEF but his heart was still in medicine. He even made a return trip to serve temporarily at Mukinge when a replacement doctor was needed. During this time, Bob and Belva had changed their citizenship status from Canada to the US, which was done for pragmatic reasons, as they were paying into a US social security program through AEF and couldn't collect on it as Canadians. As a result, their three youngest (Stuart, Stirling and Shelley) were likewise made citizens of the US, but the first four Foster kids remained Canadians.

Bob was open to new opportunities and his long association with Dr.

Rodolphe Bréchet was finally about to bear fruit. In 1968, Portugal's Prime Minister Salazar suffered a cerebral hemorrhage. Although the new government was committed to maintaining the 'Estado Novo' Salazar spent his career promoting, some of the policies around their colonies had softened. Angola was still in a state of strife between the Portuguese, MPLA, FNLA and UNITA, but the anti-Protestantism was not as feverous. In the fall of 1969, at Rodolphe's prompting, Bob applied for visas to Angola, expecting to receive them in a few months (perhaps half a year). Much to his surprise, the typical bureaucracy of Portugal was strangely absent and the visas came within a single month! With only 90 days to enter the country, Bob had to scramble to get his family ready for the trip.

Upon arrival in Angola in January 1970, Bob was quickly questioned by the government. It seemed the officials in Portugal had granted his visa without consulting the Angolan governors or PIDE. PIDE was particularly paranoid and anti-Protestant—it did not want Bob in Angola, but could not reject him owing to his perfectly valid visa. Grudgingly, the police let Bob, Belva, Stacey, Stuart, Stirling and Shelley remain in the country. However, Bob had to make weekly visits to PIDE's offices to account for his activities and he could not travel between towns without obtaining papers from PIDE for a pass. PIDE's forlorn hope was that its bureaucracy might wear down Bob's determination to remain.

Bob and Belva lived in the town of Sá da Bandeira (today called Lubango) in Huíla province, southwestern Angola. The strong Catholic presence there could not be denied, for in 1957 they had raised the statue *Cristo Rei* upon the hillside overlooking the city; 30 metres tall and built from marble, this statue was carved in the form of Christ with His arms open wide, identical in shape to statues found in Lisbon and Rio de Janeiro. The statue was made so prominent that one could navigate the entire city by marking their position relative to *Cristo Rei*—Christ not only as a moral compass but a geographic one as well! Bob hoped that he might be allowed to practise on the mission station Catota almost 600 km away, but while the government had provisionally honoured his visa, he had not yet been granted a licence to practise medicine in Angola. While waiting faithfully to be awarded permission, Bob and Belva began learning Portuguese. Donald Lutes, the AEF director in Angola, helped the Fosters navigate the language barrier and found furniture for their temporary residence. As is often the case, the children picked up the new language much quicker than the grown-ups.

The crates containing the Fosters' household goods and Bob's medical supplies arrived in the country, but the government prohibited Bob from opening them. Finally the government rendered its final decision: they refused to permit Bob to practise medicine. Shattered by the news and frustrated by his own difficulty at mastering the Portuguese tongue, Bob nearly floundered. Looking into the Bible for words of consolation, he latched upon 2 Kings 19:6: "Be not afraid of the words which thou has heard." Indeed, Donald Lutes insisted Bob was being toyed with by the government, that they wanted him to leave of his own accord. Having come this far, there seemed to be little to do but, as AEF's motto read, "go forward." Despite any guarantee the government would change its minds, Bob remained in Sá da Bandeira. Here, his grasp of the language steadily improved until he could preach in the churches.

That October, Dr. Bréchet was holding an interview with the Governor-General in Luanda, the capital. After nearly 30 years of labour at Kalukembe Hospital, Rodolphe had many connections in the country, was respected for his years of service and, being Swiss, had his homeland's reputation for maintaining neutrality. Rodolphe was also in the process of composing a history of the Swiss mission in Angola which would be published as *J'ai Ouvert une Porte Devant Toi: Essai sur l'histoire de la Mission Philafricaine*. For these reasons, when the Portuguese government demanded the Protestant missionaries in Angola have a single representative to serve as their liaison, Rodolphe was acclaimed as a veritable ombudsman. The Governor-General unburdened himself to Dr. Bréchet: there were so many medical needs in Angola yet so few physicians. Rodolphe saw an opening: "We have a missionary doctor stuck in Sá da Bandeira and the secret police won't let him do anything." The Governor-General examined the issue, and admitted to Rodolphe there were certain matters troubling the government about Bob—chiefly that he had learned Luchazi while in Zambia and had taken up residence in Angola instead of returning to Zambia. The paranoid government saw Bob's foresight in acquiring Luchazi for future mission work with suspicion, especially since MPLA guerrillas warring with the government would travel across Angola's borders and were forming allies in neighbouring nations such as Zambia. After Rodolphe stifled these fears the Governor-General finally assented; although he could not authorize sending Bob to Catota, which was considered "unstable" by his government. Instead, he asked for another option. Dr. Bréchet had another opportunity in mind.

To the northeast of Sá da Bandeira in Huambo province was Cavango, the same village where the Hockersmiths had been stationed. The Cavango hospital had been run through a coordination of various mission agencies, including AEF, with church support from UIEA (*União De Igrejas Evangélicas De Angola*), an Evangelical denomination AEF had helped found. There had been no doctors stationed at Cavango since the government had removed them in the early 1960s; by the current timetable if no physician could be appointed there by 1971, the agencies would have to close the hospital. Huambo was considered to be a stable province, so the matter only needed Bob's consent.

"God has brought us here," he told Rodolphe. "Of course we'll go!" Bob was permitted to journey to Cavango and would arrive by Christmas 1970. The authorities told Bob to practise only "religious medicine"—an unclear term that seemed to indicate he could not run a for-profit hospital, a condition that in Bob's mind, was not a restriction at all.

A FATEFUL NEAR-ACCIDENT

Steve met Sheila Thomas during his time among the IVCF group at the University of Toronto and by his first year at McMaster they were dating casually. Steve was one of three men who were seeing Sheila at the time—quite a novel experience for Sheila, a quiet young woman who had never dated in high school and was somewhat overwhelmed by the sudden attention. Steve was slow to make friends at McMaster and so made many trips into Toronto to see his IVCF friends. Steve and classmate David Storey rented lodgings in Hamilton directly across the street from St. Joseph's Healthcare, enabling them to help out in the hospital's emergency room.

One weekend in the summer of 1970, a friend of David's invited him, Steve and their girlfriends to the harbour village Tobermory, where one of the girlfriends' family had a cottage. Steve and David took the bus to Toronto and collected Sheila and the others in a brand-new Ford Maverick which one of the girlfriends had bought only 3 weeks earlier. The party of six set out to Tobermory planning on a weekend of scuba diving at the lake, but as they were driving on Highway 401 and about to turn on to the 400, there was a suddenly a "terrible racket, screeching and burning rubber smell" all from the right rear wheel well. Blue smoke was coming from the car and they quickly pulled over to the shoulder. They soon discovered this supposedly top-of-the-line brand-new automobile was a textbook example of a 'lemon.' The C-clip in the semi-axle shaft in the drive member of the rear wheel had broken, causing the axle shaft and rear wheel to break free of their housing! By all rights, the wheel should have come off the car entirely, but the tire was held in place by the mudguard.

The new Ford Maverick was towed back to the Ford dealership where "we ignominiously left it," and there was little more for Steve and David to do; they didn't want to return to Hamilton, having come all that distance, but their weekend plans were ruined. They strolled back with Sheila to the hall at 429 Brunswick Avenue where she was living, an Inter-Varsity building comprised of students from both genders but housed on separate floors. Steve and David held court in the building's living room, telling the story of their near-accident to an amazed group of college students and Inter-Varsity staff.

As they spoke, Steve glimpsed someone coming down the stairs. "My goodness!" he recalled. "There're the longest, sexiest legs I've ever seen." Attached to those legs was a beautiful young woman who took a seat in the living room to hear the rest of their story. "This is Inter-Varsity?" Steve thought to himself. "Where'd this girl fall off the planet from? I've never seen a girl like that!" In fact, she was Sheila's roommate: Peggy Parkins.

CHAPTER 5

"This Is My Best for You." — Peggy Foster

TORONTO; CAVANGO (September 1970 – June 1975)

Margaret "Peggy" Ethel Parkins was born in 1948 at Fort William, Ontario, the same town where Belva had been born. In 1970, the year she met Steve Foster, Fort William and its neighbour Port Arthur merged together into the city of Thunder Bay. Peggy's father, Sidney 'Sid' Parkins, was a high school shop teacher originally born in the United Kingdom but raised in Canada, settling with his wife Frances ('Fran') in Fort William. Peggy had four siblings: her brothers Bob, Ted, and Richard and her younger sister Mary Lou.

Even as a child, Peggy had a very outgoing manner and found it very easy to make friends. She was "the apple of Mom's eye," opined her brother Richard. Mary Lou recalled how Peggy would rise early each morning, "hop" out of bed, go downstairs to greet their mother, iron her clean blouse, chat happily with her mother, then have breakfast. Mary Lou, on the other hand, wouldn't rise until breakfast was served, sleepily mumble a "good morning" to their mother, then go upstairs to don clothing she'd left on the floor. Mary Lou felt she was in her sister's shadow—not only as a younger sibling but because Peggy was more popular, more spiritual, prettier and thinner than she. This jealousy was something Mary Lou had to learn to overcome, as she truly adored her sister. Throughout high school and university Peggy had no difficulty attracting men who were interested in her—but ultimately, each one was interested in her for her looks, so the relationships didn't rise above a casual level.

Peggy also happened to be a very trusting soul, innocent to the point of naiveté. She often didn't understand jokes, which encouraged some people to play pranks on her at her expense—but for the very reason she didn't grasp the joke, she would spoil the punchlines. Once at age 12 while on a relaxing

Sunday car trip with her family, she noticed a field of cows grazing; some of the cattle had horns. Puzzled, because she had only previously seen dehorned cows, she asked her family: "Do cows have horns?" Her siblings erupted into laughter and never did explain to her why it was so funny to them.

Peggy's family consisted of staunch members of the Anglican Church of Canada and she had been brought up with a very intellectual understanding of faith. However, she lacked a deep, personal feeling *about* her faith; in those days it simply wasn't *de rigueur* for Anglicans to talk about their *feelings*. Peggy went to at least two church revival crusades where she had answered the church's altar call, but each time she had simply been caught up in the moment and none of the experiences made a difference in her walk with God.

Despite this lack of connection, Peggy's empathetic nature granted her a genuine interest in the welfare of others, leading her to eventually study sociology at Lakehead University, Thunder Bay. Her brother Ted was involved in Inter-Varsity and would "volunteer" Peggy's assistance at IVCF functions where she would play the piano. However, her naiveté would be the cause of much merriment, especially when the group once suggested going for dinner at a Harvey's franchise restaurant, to wit Peggy replied: "What's a Harvey?" Her IVCF friends would repeat that story frequently. After one IVCF party, the group was planning to visit a retreat in Duluth, Minnesota (just 300 km away). Someone asked, "Peggy, won't you come?" It felt to Peggy as though every eye in the room had fixed itself on her. Feeling unable to dissent, she agreed. The retreat's speaker was Paul E. Little, author of the book *How to Give Away Your Faith* (1966), a widely read book on personal evangelism. Through Paul's words Peggy realized "I had been holding God at arm's length in terms of a strong involvement in my life." At the past crusades, Peggy hadn't followed through in seeking God's ways and His will in her life; now she accepted real change. When Paul spoke about "facing God," she resolved she would seek that in her life. This was "strange" to her parents "because they were Anglican; you didn't talk about your faith!"

By her third year, Peggy had became the IVCF president and brought in an engaging speaker for one event: Rev. Harry Robinson. Robinson was then pastor of Little Trinity Anglican Church in Toronto, and would tour campuses across North America. As an Anglican, Peggy was very impressed with Rev. Robinson because he spoke intensely in defence of the Christian faith, demonstrating to her IVCF friends how Anglicans were as strong in their devotion as the Baptist and Alliance members among them.

During her time in the sociology program, preparing for a career as a social worker, Peggy discovered she had a particular passion for assisting the elderly and found great joy in visiting people who were otherwise left to themselves. During the summer of her third year Peggy volunteered at a chronic hospital. One patient there was a woman suffering from multiple sclerosis and couldn't perform any actions for herself. During her lunch break, Peggy would bring food to the bedridden woman and converse with her. One evening, when Peggy was chatting to her then-boyfriend about the seniors she had spoken with at the hospital earlier that day the boyfriend wondered, "Why don't you work with senior citizens?" Peggy had not considered that as her career until then.

After graduation, Peggy's Uncle Gil discovered the Toronto Home for the Aged was looking for a case worker. Taking the job, Peggy moved to Toronto and although she was not in college, her long association with IVCF netted her housing for the summer of 1970 at 429 Brunswick Avenue, sharing a room with Sheila Thomas. On her first Sunday in Toronto, Peggy asked the Inter-Varsity students if any of them were going to Little Trinity, as she wanted to visit Harry Robinson's parish. As it turned out, all of them were headed to Little Trinity and Peggy discovered the church was so popular with university students the seating was standing room only!

Although Sheila Thomas was dating Steve during this time, Steve lived in Hamilton and he was not in Toronto very often. Peggy once accompanied Sheila and Steve to a picnic in Hyde Park and Steve gave Peggy advice on an automobile purchase, and by the fall Peggy had moved into an apartment and Sheila soon moved on from Steve to one of her other three beaus, whom she later married.

BOB IN CAVANGO

When Bob, Belva, Stacey, Stuart, Stirling, and Shelley were led into Cavango by Dr. Bréchet around Christmas 1970, they were given a warm welcome. In spite of the continued political unrest and acts of violence in Angola, overall the country was in a very positive place due to the booming economy. That sense of optimism and positivity could also be felt in a locale as remote as Cavango. The staff at the Cavango Hospital saw Bob's arrival as the Lord's provision for them; in the previous nine years, their only physician had been Dr. George Burgess, who was based 150 km away in Dondi and only visited once per year!

The people of Cavango made a sign from banana leaves and hung it from the mission station reading: "Bem Vindo" (welcome). Stirling was impressed by the "euphoria" of the people around them. Throngs of people sang, danced and clapped, even those whose leprosy had left them with deformed hands and feet.

With no permanent missionaries established in Cavango for most of the decade, there was an unoccupied house already waiting for the Fosters to move into, still full of furniture and household items the previous missionary had left behind. It was a small house with only two bedrooms, but the family resolved to make it work. While Bob went to the hospital, the children continued their schooling at home as Belva taught the three youngest in history, literature, geography and other topics. When not teaching her children, Belva took on what seemed to her a more significant role in mission work as she led Bible studies and taught women of the village how to knit.

The whole expanse around Cavango was a paradise for the younger Fosters, who would call this period of their parents' ministry "the golden years." Cavango lay far from the big cities; there was no pavement and no electricity. By night, the stars would shine all the brighter from the lack of light pollution and the noises of the wilderness would carry all the further. As Bob and Belva began growing fruits and vegetables and raising geese and chicken, the children would assist in the harvesting chores.

Approximately 250 of the patients at Cavango Hospital were lepers. Bob had experience treating leprosy in Zambia and his heart went out to Cavango's lepers. Leprosy is an airborne disease transmitted by mycobacterium lepra. Acting as a parasite inside human nerve cells, it affects victims' skin by causing visible patches (red patches on people with white skin, pale patches on people with dark skin), eventually spreading across the victims' faces. In addition to the skin, it also affects the person's nerves and motor skills. The Cavango Hospital was a leprosarium and had been built in its particular location because it was remote and the traditional treatment for lepers was to isolate them from uninfected populations. However, by the 1970s the old ways of isolation were no longer necessary with new medications that could arrest the spread of leprosy. However, lepers still required constant medical care for the rest of their lives.

Bob intended to widen the hospital's scope, continuing to serve the lepers by supplying their medications, while providing health services for other ailments. The lepers populated three small villages around Cavango where Bob could visit them for treatment. The hospital had previously held about 30 beds for lepers; Bob now expanded its scope into general patient care with a full 60 beds. There were a few white Portuguese living in the area around Cavango in those days and many more who would drive up 150 kilometres for treatment in Cavango, but Thursdays were the only day in which they were invited to see Bob—the rest of the week belonged to the Angolans.

The people in Cavango fell in love with the Fosters and the affection was mutual. In Zambia, Bob had been considered important because of his profession, but the Zambians remained somewhat at arm's length. After all, for most of his time in Zambia the Zambians were trying to obtain independence and saw all white men, missionaries included, as tools of the state. Not so in

48

Cavango! Once again, the contempt the colonial Portuguese had for Protestant missionaries inched the Fosters even closer to the Angolans. "They knew we were there for only one reason," Belva observed, "because we loved them. They knew there would be no other reason for us to tolerate the kind of treatment we received."

The Portuguese themselves held doctors in very high regard and this attitude had filtered to the Angolans. Bob's commitment in Cavango was met by a tremendous outpouring of respect and appreciation from the Angolans. The Angolans in Cavango spoke primarily Ngangela, part of the same language family as Luchazi. This meant Bob's learning Luchazi in Luampa proved invaluable for reaching minds and winning hearts. The Fosters, being very outgoing people, were overjoyed at the easy friendships they forged with the Angolans and became engaged with their lives. Bob became especially close to Sr. Israel Canjila, the administrator of the hospital, who proved a loyal assistant and faithful friend.

Early in 1972, the Hockersmith family returned to Cavango, having likewise taken advantage of the ease on restrictions against Protestants. Darrell and Barb brought along their teenage son Paul. "Each of us were with growing families," Barb noted, "and enjoyed rich fellowship with one another." Paul joined the classroom being run by Belva while Darrell resumed his preaching duties. Darrell would hold a Bible study at the mission station every weekday morning and Sunday evening. He would also help lead Sunday morning church worship and on Sunday afternoons would venture out to other villages to evangelize nearby populations. Darrell lacked Bob's strong Luchazi so he employed interpreters while travelling. "For many people it was difficult for them to grasp salvation by grace through faith in Christ," Barb recalled, "but they were always eager to hear." At the time, the Portuguese government was relocating many villages out of their original locations to resettle closer to the highway where they could be more easily monitored. Many of these Angolans had never been visited by missionaries before, so it provided Bob and Darrell marvellous opportunities to witness.

Barb was herself a gift to the Cavango Hospital for her expertise as a surgical nurse. As a result, Steve would dub her "the matron of the hospital." Working alongside Bob she was impressed by his "unusual intuition in his medical and surgical abilities" which she attributed to his experience serving in Zambia. "It seemed God kept any emergency medical problems from happening on Sundays," Barb gratefully noted. Barb's strong organizational skills helped keep the hospital functioning and her own surgical skills were capable enough to handle some cases when Bob was elsewhere. Paul's own gift was his passion for sports, usually leading the other children in a game of volleyball each weekday and putting on soccer games with many of the local children on Saturdays.

One afternoon, three hippopotamuses were sighted down at the Okavango River and word was quickly sent to Bob and Darrell. Bob landed a successful rifle shot to the head of one of the hippos and it sank beneath the water. Some of the villagers had never seen a hippo hunt before and worried the meat had been lost, but Bob, having learned from his father's misadventure, knew better. In an hour, the hippo bobbed back to the surface. Tying a steel cable from one of the hippo's legs to a heavy truck, they dragged the two-ton beast to shore and began the long process of cutting and drying the meat. "It was as big as three cows," one villager recalled. Bob had so much hippo meat by the end of the process that for the next six months he would bring strips of hippo meat to his leprosy patients. The villagers found hippo meat so delicious that they kept hoping there would be another hippo sighting so that Bob could kill another for them!

NINE FOSTERS IN CAVANGO—AND ONE LION

As Bob found success establishing his work in Angola he invited his three eldest children to visit in the summer of 1971, providing an opportunity for Steve, Sharon, and Sheila to practise their medical skills in the Cavango Hospital. An invitation was also sent to Charles and June, who came from Mukinge to see how Bob's family was faring.

A friend of the Fosters had paid for Sheila and Sharon's airfare to Angola, but Steve was another matter. Steve had saved up as much money as he could from a summer job, but as the last week of June neared he was $350 short. He had already booked a plane reservation for July which needed to be paid! Steve's plans reached the ears of John Evans, the dean of McMaster, who invited Steve to his office and asked him to explain his trip to Angola. After hearing Steve was short of funds, Evans reached into his desk and pulled out an envelope. "We deans have a little slush fund. I don't want you to say too much about it, but I want to help you get to Angola." Within the envelope was the $350 Steve needed! Steve discerned the Lord's hand in this. He later realized he had been kept from getting the full amount until the last week so he could understand it had been orchestrated through God's efforts, not his own.

Before leaving to Angola, Steve had a free evening the night before his flight. Recalling Sheila Thomas was now in a serious relationship with another man (her eventual husband), he decided to phone Peggy. He had her number in his notebook and called her up, but there was no answer. He phoned again in another hour. Again, no response. While he still felt drawn to Peggy, he also felt those feelings couldn't be explored until after he returned from Angola.

Belva and Shelley were both present to greet Steve, Sharon and Sheila when they stepped off the plane at Luanda—and what a sight Steve made! He wore a loud Hawaiian shirt, had longish hair and a beard in the style of Franz Josef—muttonchops with a bare chin (this facial hair became one of Steve's defining traits). "My mom wasn't sure she wanted to claim him!" Shelley recollected, with a laugh. Although Shelley had spent time with Steve before, she had simply been so young that she had precious few memories of her eldest brother. In a certain sense, 6-year-old Shelley was having her 'first' meeting with Steve.

The massive Foster gathering was a thrill for all concerned. Steve was immensely impressed by his grandfather Charles, who preached via an interpreter on the subject of tithing. "Man!" Steve recalled, "The church elders came in at the end of the sermons and said, 'If that's what God says, then we want to get serious about this' and the offerings immediately increased five or six times over in one week. At the end of one month, they'd given more than they'd given in all the years before."

Sheila noticed how different the culture around Cavango was from what she had grown up in at Zambia and saw a change in how her parents responded. "Bob and Belva really liked Cavango. It was the first time they had true national colleagues to work with—a unity of purpose and sense of working together that hadn't been the case in Zambia." Steve noticed this as well: "Being oppressed together created common bedfellows."

Steve got to see how bad the colonial bureaucracy could be when he accompanied his mother on a shopping trip to Nova Lisboa (now called Huambo). The day before the trip, Belva had typed up a *guia* (government document) stating where they would be going, the purpose and duration of their trip, and a signature and stamp from the hospital. On the day of their departure they drove out early to Tchinhama to receive a stamp for their guia as soon as the office opened at 8:15 AM, then on to Bela Vista, where the municipal headquarters was located. A clerk examined their documents and verified all was in order; they merely required a signature from the *chefe de posto* (administrator).

From where he was standing, Steve could see into the chefe's office; the official did not appear to be busy, yet the clerk returned in minutes to claim, "O chefe está ocupada" (*he's busy*). Belva very gracefully asked when it would be convenient for them to return; the clerk suggested about 11:00. Belva had intended to meet friends in Nova Lisboa for lunch—it was now clear that would not happen, but she kept her cool. With no other course, mother and son performed a few tasks in Bela Vista and visited the local barber shop. Steve didn't have a haircut, but he knew his mother certainly wished he would have one. The Portuguese barber was quite friendly to the Fosters and invited them to his home for coffee to pass the time before returning to the office.

Belva and Steve returned the office at 11:00. By 11:30 there was still no action on their documents. Returning to the barber, they found their friend livid when he heard what had happened. "Oh, that man!" the barber fumed. "He has no interest in helping the missionaries because his sole purpose in life is to earn time off in purgatory! Our Catholic Father tells him for every missionary he holds up it takes time off his purgatory!" Steve realized that, unlike in Zambia, there was a cost to being a Protestant in Angola. Steve and Belva finally received their signature at 14:00 and arrived in Nova Lisboa an hour later—by which time most of the stores had closed. Their friend Peter Muir let them stay at his home overnight so they could finish their shopping in the morning. First, though, they had to report to the police in Nova Lisboa they would be staying overnight. Through all of it, Steve marvelled at his mother's serenity and in years to come would draw inspiration from her dignified response to being treated with such incivility.

One day in a village nearby Cavango, a woman and her child had the misfortune of encountering a pair of lion cubs. Fearfully protective, the mother lioness assaulted the woman, who was badly mauled while defending her child from harm. The woman's relatives carried her to Cavango where Bob treated the wounds.

The following day brought a visit from the soba (chief). He wanted to know what the missionaries intended to do about the dangerous lioness roaming about. As the missionaries were the only people nearby who owned guns, it was a fair question. Stacey, an enterprising hunter, was intrigued at the thought of hunting a lion. Steve too felt his adventurous spirit rise; after all, he was on vacation and this was an exploit his old hero Jim Corbett would have faced. It was settled: the two brothers would save the villagers from the dangerous lioness.

For all that Steve and Stacey had frequently clashed in their growing years, they put together a decent plan: journeying by Land Rover to the area where the lioness had attacked, they took a slaughtered animal to use as bait, leaving its bloody carcass out in the open. Situated in their Land Rover, the two brothers had their rifles loaded and ready for bear (or lion). They waited. Dusk fell. And then, far off in the jungle, they heard the lioness roar. Despite the creature lying far off, her roar carried through the quiet night, a terrifying noise unlike anything the brothers had heard. Steve shook "for more than 15 minutes." They climbed on the hood of the Land Rover to elevate themselves and spent a long night freezing the seats of their pants on the cool metal. By 3:00 AM the lioness had not appeared. Shaken and cold, the brothers gave up the hunt. Fortunately, there were no further attacks.

Just after the lioness hunt, Steve chanced to encounter his old Sakeji friend Jean-Pierre Bréchet (Steve liked to call him "John Peter") and went on an antelope hunt with him. Although Jean-Pierre had always been a year ahead of Steve at school, because of McMaster's three-year program they were now at the same point in their studies. Jean-Pierre's long-term mission prospects were not yet definite but he had come to Angola to observe his father's work in Kalukembe and to treat the lepers in Cavango, which was one of his passions. In their childhood, Steve had scoffed at Jean-Pierre's tales of Angola. Now, he was coming around to Jean-Pierre's point of view. On his way back to Luanda with Stacey, who was headed back to North America for college, Steve ascended Tundavala, a mountain just outside of Sá da Bandeira. Gaping in awe at the beautiful country around him, Steve mused on Jean-Pierre's words about Angola. As the Queen of Sheba once said to King Solomon, "I hadn't heard the half of it!"

Coming back to Canada from Angola, Steve felt he now knew where he wanted to serve as a missionary. Seeing the people of Cavango "was an eye-opener to me—just how much the day-to-day problems and ordinary people's lives revolved around the lack of access to surgical care." The entire experience reaffirmed Steve's passion for surgery. "I fell in love with surgery in 1971. I felt if I was ever going to go back to Africa that was what I needed to do."

Sharon had completed her nurse's training at Rutgers and while at Gordon-Conwell Theological Seminary, fell in love with fellow student Rob Arscott, a white man from Jamaica. They married in June 1972, then moved to Jamaica. Obviously, Gordon-Conwell had done well for Sharon. Sheila recalled her sister gushing, "Oh Sheila, you have to come to Gordon, it's a great place!" However, Sheila felt otherwise: "It was important to be somewhere where I was just me," she declared, having followed her sister's footprints throughout Sakeji and Rutger's. Seeking to move outside her family's usual haunts, she went all the way to the west coast of Canada—Regent College in Vancouver, British Columbia.

"I KNOW THIS GIRL!"

In the spring of 1972, Steve went to a concert by the Christian music duo Merv and Merla Watson. He briefly encountered Peggy Parkins there, but aside from recognizing her and saying "hi," the opportunity passed without incident. When Jean-Pierre came to visit Steve, his grandmother Helen Mark booked the duo into a speaking engagement where they could expound upon their experiences in Angola the previous year. En route to the gathering, Steve confused the directions he had been given and wound up getting lost. When he sped to make up time, Steve was pulled over by a traffic policeman.

Considering Steve's floppy hair, he could imagine the officer "was probably thinking he caught two hippies!" But the two young men patiently explained they were 20 minutes late to a speaking engagement at a church. Jean-Pierre's more refined bearing "added gravitas" to their account and the policeman let them go with a warning.

After finishing his studies at McMaster, Steve began an internship in Toronto, knowing it would please his father. For weeks he served at Toronto General Hospital in the emergency room, handling all manner of cases. He was on call for six weeks and would serve long 12-hour shifts which were staggered. It was difficult for him to maintain much of a social life. There was a young woman back in Hamilton he had been seeing casually, but he couldn't envision a long-term future in that relationship.

One Sunday in July Steve decided to visit Little Trinity so he could hear Harry Robinson speak. Although Steve's upbringing had not been in the Anglican Church, he had come to respect the Anglican traditions. "For all the talk of the freedom in Evangelical churches, after a while you see they're as set in a box as any group of people you care to meet," Steve opined. This caused some Evangelicals to flock into the mode of liturgical worship found in the Anglican Church: "People discovering the wonder of organ music, the wonder of prayers which are centuries old, the wonder of public confession." Front and centre, Little Trinity offered Harry's mode of evangelizing: "His teaching, his unconventional style, his simplicity and directness," Steve mused. "He was a big guy with wide arms but whose picture of the love of Jesus was exemplary." Although the Anglican liturgy caused Steve to fumble as he tried to follow the responses and the stand-up/sit-down reactions, he made an effort.

That Sunday, just after Steve took a seat he was stunned to see a familiar person walk by—Sheila Thomas' former roommate. Although she had been on his mind before, her name had slipped Steve's memory. She had also begun wearing her hair long instead of the shorter style he had first seen. "I recognize that girl!" he thought. "I must have her name written down!" Steve carried a Seven Star brand diary in those days to write down his patients' information, as well as to collect his friends' phone numbers. Instead of following Rev. Robinson's sermon Steve began leafing through the diary, starting in the letter As. Finally he got to P: "Peggy Parkins. That's it! I know this girl!" he realized. When the service ended he moved to the aisle so that she would have to walk past him. "Peggy Parkins?" he called out. She immediately greeted him as 'Stephen' and he thought, "She remembered my name! That's a good start!"

Little Trinity fed its parishioners sandwiches after services so Steve joined Peggy in the basement to quickly catch up with her, learning she was living in the Dufferin community. The meeting went well, but they parted without any particular plans; then God stepped in, through the person of Steve's old friend Nancy Wood. Nancy had met Steve at IVCF in 1966 and was on the verge of getting married. Buttonholing Steve before he could get away she told him her wedding was on the following Saturday. "Here's an invitation. You must bring a girl!" she insisted. Now Steve had a good reason to follow-up with Peggy.

At first, Steve's thoughts returned to the girl in Hamilton he had been dating—but he knew he wouldn't be returning to Hamilton in the long term and the relationship wasn't working out. By Wednesday of that week he finally gathered up his courage and phoned Peggy, unwittingly catching her while she was in the bath (a fact he remained ignorant of for years). With only so many evenings available due to the heavy workload at Toronto General, Steve opened by asking if she was free that Friday; no, she was not. "How about Saturday? I've got an invitation to a wedding, would you mind coming to a wedding with me?" Ever the good sport, Peggy agreed to this unusual first-date scenario.

Nancy's wedding went well that Saturday and the party adjourned to a reception at Inn on the Park. Steve was driving Peggy in his car when they came to a fateful intersection. From her experience travelling around Toronto working with Toronto Homes for the Aged, Peggy knew her directions and that they should head west. Steve turned east and drove a considerable distance before acknowledging his error and changing the course. It was ultimately good that they went off-course because the elongated car trip gave them a good opportunity to chat—for at the reception, they were seated at a table with another physician and Steve spent the entire time talking shop. Peggy accepted then that Steve was "an extra-extrovert" and didn't begrudge him anything (other than his wrong turn at the intersection) but she still wasn't entirely certain about him.

The next time Steve had a free day he planned a special outing with Peggy. Initially he explored visiting the 'African Lion Safari' at the Rockford zoo—but when he saw the cost was $5 he balked at the prices. They went for a hike, instead, although it was cut short by rainfall. Following their hike, they had supper at Steve's grandparents' home. Steve had an ulterior motive for introducing her to his grandparents; with his own parents an ocean away, the Marks were the nearest familial authority he could appeal to for either approval or disapproval of his new girlfriend. With her interest in the aged, Peggy got along famously with the Marks and Grandma Helen was surprised to learn Peggy had been born in Fort William like Belva, in the same hospital, no less! While Peggy chatted with his grandfather Fred after dinner, Steve helped his grandmother clear the dishes. She took her grandson aside and informed him: "Stephen! This is the one! Don't let her out of your sight!" Steve recalled with a laugh, "Only grandmas can hiss at you and say such things!"

On their third date, Steve brought Peggy along with him to say farewell to his former roommate Bruce Snyder and wife Helen Snyder, who were about to serve as missionaries in Nigeria. By now it was not lost on Peggy that Steve's intentions were to join the mission field. Cementing this notion, Steve showed Peggy a slideshow consisting of photographs he had taken in Africa. All of this was unusual to Peggy, whose home church in Thunder Bay had not been missionary-focused. But as she watched Steve's slides she thought, "I could love those people." She found herself being drawn in to Steve's mission.

After the first month of dating, Steve sat with his friend Stuart Archibald to hash out how he felt about Peggy. Although she hadn't been planning to join the mission field, he noted, "She really loved Jesus." Compared to other Canadians girls who "seemed to have talons out instead of hearts out" he "never got that sense with Peggy." By the end of the talk, he knew his grandmother had been right—Peggy was the one. After only three months of dating, Steve and Peggy were engaged on October 24, an easy date for Steve to remember because it was Zambian Independence Day!

Peggy's fascination with Steve was mutual: "He knew where he was going. I had dated so many guys who didn't know what they wanted to do in life." She especially loved listening to his stories about Africa and his broad sense of humour.

Steve wrote to Peggy's father Sid in Thunder Bay for his approval to marry Peggy; Sid wrote back to affirm their relationship. Steve also wrote to his own father, who delivered a somewhat sceptical approval, noting he thought three months was far too early for an engagement. Bob's only rule for his children in choosing a mate was to avoid marrying someone in medicine because of how it would impact their family life, so at least Peggy's career as a social worker suited him. Another uncertain voice was Harry Robinson, who was concerned Steve's Baptist upbringing was a poor fit for Peggy, but he agreed to officiate their wedding all the same.

When Peggy first told her mother about the engagement, her mother gave the guarded response "We'll wait and see." She warned Peggy "Not to analyze the relationship out of existence." In the past, Peggy had a habit of discussing her boyfriends with her sister Mary Lou and after weighing all the pros and cons of each beau, would inevitably decide to call off the relationship, which is why few of her boyfriends endured. In fact, after attending a conference led by Bob Gothard in Detroit, Michigan, Peggy heard a message of "knowing for sure" about God's call in her life and she expressed doubts to Steve about going through with a wedding, but ultimately she didn't sense God saying no, so continued the engagement.

Just before Christmas 1972, Peggy went to an IVCF party and her engagement ring was noticed. "Oh, Peggy, who are you engaged to?" one friend asked. "Steve Foster," Peggy answered proudly. "Steve Foster?!?" the friend retorted, then turned to other people in the room: "Do you know who Peggy's engaged to? Steve Foster!" A veritable chorus erupted: "*Steve Foster?!?!*" Peggy was a little taken aback, wondering, "What do I not know here?" Clearly some people couldn't see why they made a good match.

Steve and Peggy spent that Christmas in Thunder Bay with Peggy's parents and Mary Lou. Unfortunately, the airline was unable to fly them out because of mist so they took a long Greyhound bus ride instead. As was appropriate, Steve slept in the guest room and accompanied the Parkinses to their home church, St. Thomas, for the Christmas Eve service. Mary Lou couldn't help but notice Steve would whistle during the hymns and beat the pew in front of him like a drum; in that conservative crowd, he certainly stood apart! Peggy's mother was mostly distracted by how expressive Steve was, constantly hugging and kissing her beloved daughter. "Aren't you embarrassed?" she asked Peggy in confidence. But overall, Peggy's parents were quite in favour of Steve. They didn't know much about mission work, but they liked him.

Mary Lou could see Steve was entirely different from Peggy's earlier boyfriends. "It was clearly much more serious than she had been in the past," she recalled. Looking deeper, she observed, "He was affirming of her and she needed somebody who could give her that. She was very attractive and I think that's what her boyfriends had been looking for. Steve saw something deeper than that." Mary Lou concluded: "God had to have drawn them together."

WEDDING IN TORONTO, HONEYMOON IN ANGOLA

Having journeyed to North America for Sharon's wedding the year before, Bob and Belva couldn't afford another trip to be present for Steve and Peggy's wedding. However, Belva suggested they could spend their honeymoon in Angola and receive a special reception from the family there. Steve's internship was coming to an end and he just so happened to find himself with a six-week gap before the beginning of his residency—just enough time for the honeymoon! Steve still didn't know if Peggy could handle serving with him in the field as a mission wife, but he was encouraged by his mother's example. After all, Belva had adapted. Going on the honeymoon would be a fine means of testing Peggy. "Admittedly, the honeymoon's a little too late to be drawing lines in the sand," Steve realized in retrospect, but Peggy was willing: "I really, really trusted Steve. I had great faith in him that he knew what he was doing."

Steve had his friend Stuart Archibald as best man with Mary Lou as

Peggy's maid of honour. All of Steve's grandparents (Charles, June, and the Marks) attended the June 2, 1973, ceremony, along with Steve's siblings Sharon, Sheila and Stacey. Peggy's parents attended (in fact, they moved that year to live permanently in Toronto to be closer to their children), as did her siblings Bob, Ted, and Richard. Peggy's brothers hadn't seen much of Steve, but Bob quickly sized him up as a "salt-of-the-earth type" and liked him immediately. Richard was mainly surprised to find his sister marrying a man younger than her.

As Peggy stood in the back of Little Trinity with her father waiting to travel up the aisle where Rev. Harry Robinson and Steve awaited, she had an overwhelming sensation of joy. God's voice spoke to her: "This is my best for you." Those words carried her through the day and would continue to bolster her in the years to come. "I am so grateful to have a husband who is such a strong man of faith," she said. "He has a surgeon's mentality so when things aren't just where he wants them or where he thinks they should be it makes him very upset. But he is a very loving husband."

Journeying to Angola was an entirely new kind of experience for the new bride. "I had hardly been east of Montreal or south of Duluth!" she noted. They arrived at night in Luanda and were greeted by Bob, Belva, Stuart, Stirling and Shelley. It was overwhelming for Peggy and also a little overwhelming for young Shelley, who was so many years younger than her new sister-in-law and a bit bashful around her. The assembled family drove in a 1969 Chevy Suburban Carryall which had two bench seats. Belva insisted Steve and Peggy sit in the front of the vehicle with Bob so Peggy could take in more of the surroundings. "I saw Africa," Peggy confirmed. But she was also a new bride on her honeymoon with a desperately romantic husband who was constantly kissing her—Peggy couldn't quite keep from recalling her mother-in-law was seated practically at her shoulder. It was all a bit embarrassing.

Peggy also became a frequent source of amusement to the Fosters. Due to her lack of knowledge about Africa, as well as her naiveté, Steve would tease her by pointing out cattle and claiming they were buffalo while his siblings tittered with amusement. On their first morning, Peggy beheld a ghastly feathered creature in the yard where they were staying and asked what that grotesque bird could be; "a turkey," was the answer. Poor Peggy! "Peg's a good sport," Stirling reflected.

Peggy brought her wedding dress all the way from Toronto to Cavango so she could don it again for a special reception there. They spent two weeks in Cavango, during which time Peggy got to know her in-laws. Knowing she would have to prepare for this kind of life one day, she took note of how Belva ran the household and instructed their male servants. She hadn't realized Bob was a "statesman in the missionary world" and found him somewhat intimidating. "It was very difficult to disagree with him and hard to discuss things with him. It was a big challenge for me to feel at ease with him in some ways." But through all of the overwhelming sensations of this trip, however, "I had a strong man next to me and he was God's gift to me. A husband whose focus and whose *raison d'être* is to honour the Lord."

Steve spent most of his visit to Cavango with his wife rather than in the hospital. Fortunately, Bob was now very well-staffed with not only Barb Hockersmith but a second missionary nurse, Jane Williams, working at the hospital.

During the newlyweds stay, Bob was invited to a Christian Medical Fellowship conference being held in South Africa, amidst the majestic Drakensberg Mountains. The entire Foster assemblage drove down to the conference on the third week of the honeymoon, giving Peggy a larger view of what Africa was like. The conference was also a good opportunity for Steve to introduce his wife to friends of his youth. After four weeks in Africa they journeyed to Switzerland for a romantic mountain-climbing excursion. While there, they met Jean-Pierre Bréchet and his new bride Marie-Claude. The couple were about to head into the mission field in Nigeria. Steve had no idea then that he and Jean-Pierre's careers were headed to the same place. They returned to Canada in time for Steve to begin his residency in Toronto while Peggy went to Thunder Bay for Mary Lou's wedding to Rev. Andrew Hoskin.

AN INDEPENDENT ANGOLA

For all that the authoritarian regime in Portugal had vowed *"Isto é nosso,"* change had finally been enforced upon Portugal's colonies. Although the fractured independence parties in Angola had not met much success against Portugal in combat, at the same time Mozambique's independence army FRELIMO (*Frente de Libertação de Moçambique*) and Guinea-Bissau's army PAIGC (*Partido Africano da Independência da Guiné e Cabo Verde*) had obtained some victories and Portugal's military were tired of the unending wars. The military rose up against the government in Portugal and non-violently seized power in a *coup d'état* on April 25, 1974. The affair became known as the Carnation Revolution (*Revolução dos Cravos*) because of the carnations that decorated the soldiers who supported the coup. The new government promised democracy in Portugal—but more than that, opened negotiations with the colonies of Angola, Mozambique, Guinea-Bissau, Cape Verde and São Tomé and Príncipe with the intent of granting them independence. While the Portuguese wars were at an end, the fallout in the colonies still had to be reckoned with.

By this time Sheila had completed her year at Regent and had become a nursing practitioner in New Jersey. She asked the hospital if her father could be her supervisor, and they happily agreed. As part of her internship, Sheila went back to Cavango for a six-month assignment beginning December 1974. Although this was her second visit to Angola, it was at this time that Sheila fell in love with the country. Zambia had been home to her, but she appreciated the openness between missionaries and Angolans. "The nurses I was given to work with, they were just colleagues and teammates," she observed, rather than mere subordinates. She also saw in the Angolans a stronger sense of self-reliance, "because the Portuguese had held them at arm's length, it made them stand up for themselves." They had come to expect very little from their colonial government: "Angolans were not sitting around waiting for a handout," Sheila summed up.

There were other great changes in Cavango since Sheila's last visit. From the beginning, Bob had been hopeful to bring electricity to Cavango Hospital, just as he succeeded at Mukinge and Luampa. It had taken some time, but eventually he located an engineer from nearby Nova Lisboa who constructed a hydroelectric generator powered by a water wheel, using the current of the nearby Okavango River to supply power. At last, the hospital had electricity—although the strength of the electrical power was entirely dependant on the speed of the current. Bob wasted little time in seeking an X-ray machine for the hospital, planning the purchase in faith before the money had arrived, as he so often did. However, the bureaucracy around this purchase would prove tremendous in the years to follow.

On January 15, 1975, representatives of the MPLA, FNLA and UNITA met in Alvor, Portugal, to sign the Alvor Agreement, which assigned the following October as the date for their first democratic elections. Missing from the negotiations were FLEC (*Frente para a Libertação do Enclave de Cabinda*), an independence movement based in Cabinda that desired not simply freedom from Portugal but to be independent from Angola itself. However, one of the few items all three of the other parties agreed on was that Cabinda, with its vast quantities of oil and gas, would not be let go.

The uneasiness Angola's white Portuguese population felt during wartime was nothing compared to the tension leading up to the election. Many Portuguese began departing for Portugal. The MPLA turned to the communist government of Cuba for military support and UNITA and FNLA were in similar talks with other nations. At this stage, the FNLA was the most powerful party thanks to the military support it enjoyed from Zaire. Although the USSR was supplying the MPLA with weapons and training, Neto was suspicious of his allies. International observers wrongly thought the MPLA were being guided by the USSR—control which the Soviets certainly sought. The Soviets, on the other hand, urged the MPLA to be cautious, not wishing to become mired in Angola's conflict during those years while the USSR were in détente with the Western powers. Even Cuba and the USSR did not anticipate a civil war breaking out for at least two more years.

Although Portugal's army was ostensibly still present to keep the peace until the elections, violent clashes were breaking out between the parties, principally in the capital of Luanda; previously united in their distrust of the Portuguese, they now saw each other merely as rivals in their separate bids for total power. The MPLA slowly overtook the FNLA in military strength, aided politically by FNLA leader Holden Roberto's refusal to visit his homeland— Roberto had last been in Angola in 1956. UNITA, aware of its inferior firepower, simply sought politics as its means to power as its leader Savimbi toured across the nation to stoke up support for his party among both native Angolans and white Portuguese. Savimbi was perhaps the savviest player in the conflict, at various times shoring up alliances with most of the major players: FNLA, MPLA, Portugal, US and South Africa. But these ripples were slow to reach Cavango.

In addition to working at the Cavango Hospital on more than 100 cases per day, Sheila went to the surrounding villages to establish pediatric clinics for children under the age of five. The clinics helped provide mothers with basic advice on healthy child care, as well as provide medications. She was accompanied on these trips by Nurse Eliseu Herculano, who was also the local voter registration officer. At every village they visited, nurse Eliseu would take the time to perform a political speech, stressing the importance of voting. Prior to the Carnation Revolution, Stirling had noted "there wasn't really talk of independence" among the Angolans, but now that it had been granted people were developing an interest in politics. Sheila recalled most of the people around Cavango were "keen on UNITA." Although the Angolan political parties would present their perspectives through political philosophies to the rest of the world, within Angola they primarily appealed along lines of tribal divisions; UNITA was principally comprised of Ovimbundu, and so the Ovimbundu in Cavango were persuaded to vote for the party.

The time had come for Bob to start another furlough, but he was concerned about leaving Cavango Hospital unmanned for any great length of time. For the two years leading up to the furlough Bob asked other physicians to replace him, but was rebuffed. Knowing of his father's worries, Steve prayed for someone to answer. One night as he was praying, Steve heard the Lord's voice ask: "Stephen, why aren't you willing to go?" Not unlike Moses, Steve protested: "But Lord, you know that I don't have a Portuguese language certificate! You know that I don't have a tropical medicine certificate! I'm only halfway through my residency! How can I abandon all of this?"

Considering the matter soberly, Steve concluded, "If those were genuine issues then I had better put them on the table and test them." Steve wrote to his father and asked if he would be permitted to serve in Cavango despite his lack of certification on both scores. The very day Steve's letter arrived in Cavango, Bob was already beginning a trip to Luanda to see the Governor-General. Bob put the question to the Governor-General, who responded, "Things are changing. The regime is about ready to leave and we're trying to organize elections. If someone's willing to come and work in the country right now and knows the situation, we'll be prepared to grant him a visa." Bob felt he could have fallen off his chair in surprise! He wrote back to Steve to inform him the lack of certification would not be an issue; two out of three issues had been settled.

To address the third obstacle, Steve arranged an interview with the director of his program, Dr. Owen Gray, who was chair of general surgery. Steve explained the matter to Dr. Gray as it stood; he still didn't have the money he would need for a trip to Angola and he knew that by abandoning his residency midstream, he would have no job when he returned. Dr. Gray sank it all in for a moment, then answered: "Young man, this is the best idea anyone's come in here talking about for a long time. When do you need to leave?" Steve answered July 1. "Take a holiday at the end of June," Dr. Gray replied, "and you'll have a job waiting here when you come back, the first of January." Steve's time in Cavango would even be credited against his residency!

Even the money required was met by God; before Steve could begin formally requesting support, the Sunday after seeing Dr. Gray a man in church who had heard rumours about Steve and Peggy going to Angola handed him a $50 check, not unlike the ways in which supporters had always appeared to supply Bob with his support. In the end, more than $5000 would be received, enough to cover the airfare and expenses for the six months.

Steve had placed his issues on the table and each had been dismissed. There was no reason not to go—even knowing Peggy was pregnant with their first child, he was confident he could arrange the baby's delivery in Africa, just as his father had done for so many years.

This meant Steve and Peggy would be in Angola during the elections. Steve had witnessed the transition to independence in Zambia from afar and it had been a peaceful affair. He had no idea how different independence would be for Angola. He also "had no idea God was going to tie our hearts to the people of Cavango."

CHAPTER 6

"Running Away Has Never Been My Signature." — *Steve Foster*

CAVANGO (July – December 1975)

Everything seemed to be falling into place perfectly; Sheila's internship at Cavango ended in time for the start of furlough and, at the same time, the decision had been made for Charles and June to leave Mukinge and retire to the US with their daughter Rhoda. It was not an easy decision on any of the Fosters. Charles and June had lived for so many decades at Mukinge, but Charles was now 83 and June 82, and Bob worried for their well-being. Reluctantly, and with heavy hearts, his parents acquiesced.

Peggy's parents found it hard to accept their daughter would be going to Africa, but they tried to be supportive of her decision. Even in the midst of their doubts, they were "very proud of Steve and what he was doing and what he represented," Peggy recalled. Steve and Peggy journeyed to Angola in July by way of Jamaica so they could visit Sharon and Rob. During their week-long visit they celebrated the news that Sharon was also pregnant with her first child. From Jamaica they flew to Brazil, then South-West Africa and finally into Sá da Bandeira.

Steve spent the first three weeks of July working side by side with his father, seeing the state of affairs in Cavango. Although the news of fighting around the countryside continued, Bob and Belva fully expected to return. They left Steve and Peggy in custody of their home, knowing that capable men such as Sr. Israel and missionaries Darrell and Barb Hockersmith and Jane Williams would be there to assist them. Bob also hoped to sort out the confusion surrounding the receipt of his X-ray machine on his return. Peggy, meanwhile, had to take charge of running the household at Cavango, which was difficult for her without being able to speak the language. However, knowing the two servants would handle all the cooking and cleaning was a

63

relief.

Bob, Belva, Sheila, Stuart, Stirling and Shelley departed Cavango, not realizing how quickly the country would change. "Remember," Bob consoled Steve before boarding his flight, "if things get rough and you've got to leave, you send me an S.O.S. I'll come back and take over." Little did Bob know that the flight he was boarding would be among the last few commercial flights to depart from the country for quite some time.

The departing Fosters went to Mukinge to collect Charles and June. It was hard for the elder Fosters to leave Zambia behind, but Charles' legacy was the Kikaonde Bible he and the committee had worked hard to create. That same year, the full edition of the Kikaonde Bible (*Buk wa lesa: Lulayañano lwa Kala na Lulayañano Lupya*) was published and as they passed through England on their way to the US, Charles was presented with one of the first copies from the printers.

Returning from the airport where he saw off his family, Steve drove safely back to Cavango. "Not 10 days later," Steve mused, "there were 20 military checkpoints down all those roads." At each checkpoint, motorists had to present their guia, not unlike the old Portuguese rules. However, these checkpoints weren't run by the Portuguese. If they were run by the FNLA, then you had to present a guia stamped by the FNLA; if run by UNITA, then you needed to present a UNITA stamp; present the wrong guia to the soldier and you could be in for trouble. The soldiers, who were frequently teenagers without any uniform, were not easily identified by party affiliation. Before each checkpoint, savvy motorists would look ahead to see which flag was being flown, then collect the appropriate guia. "Sometimes you'd meet some friendly person whose family you had treated and he'd wave you through," Steve noted, "but you couldn't count on it."

Among the many projects Bob had been preparing at the time was an airfield at Cavango. To arrange for a bulldozer to clear the piece of land, Bob had to supply enough fuel for the vehicle. Darrell Hockersmith had gone into Nova Lisboa and collected 20 drums of diesel fuel which he kept at Cavango, waiting for the bulldozer. As Angola continued to fracture, that stockpile of diesel proved invaluable because Bob's Land Rover could run on it.

Steve was still a young surgeon with much to learn, but he was encouraged by Barb Hockersmith's easy command of the nurses at Cavango. One nurse in particular, a Sr. Silva, was responsible for preparing the operating room for surgeries and he would frequently advise Steve, saying, "This is what your father would do," when the solutions befuddled Steve. "He gave me courage as a young surgeon," Steve said in thankfulness.

Peggy adapted herself to the routine of the household and learned how to use some of the manual equipment such as the hand-operated washer/wringer and the wood-burning stove. She also took over a shop, which Belva had been running, where donated fabric and thread were sold to the local women. Not having any of the languages, Peggy was assisted by Julieta, a friendly leper who became her best friend—despite neither speaking the other's language! Julieta had only two fingers on each hand, having lost the others to leprosy, but she taught Peggy how to crochet. Julieta also knit baby clothes for Peggy's unborn child. In her spare time, Peggy began reading books. She had never been very interested in fiction as a young girl, much to the despair of her mother, but with little else to do for entertainment she discovered a fondness for C. S. Lewis' *Narnia* series and L. M. Montgomery's *Anne of Green Gables*.

One evening, Peggy and Steve visited the Hockersmiths and they sat around the fire talking about possible names for their baby. Although not knowing what gender to expect, Steve had already determined he wanted his son to be named Charles after his grandfather. Peggy had no love for the name and couldn't imagine a son who would be nicknamed Charlie. It was Barb who suggested the girl's name Rebecca after the wife of Isaac; Peggy latched on to the name. The people of Cavango were also excited for her pregnancy and one woman supplied a wicker cradle for the baby.

That July, the civil war had truly erupted. Holden Roberto declared "total war" and was now so committed to winning he had ended his exile in Zaire to be part of his army's march on Luanda, knowing whichever party held the capital could claim to be the national leaders. The US Secretary of State Henry Kissinger was interested in becoming involved in Angola, despite his nation's still-recent exit from the Vietnam War. He admitted "there was nothing needed or desired less than another crisis in a distant continent heretofore largely insulated from the Cold War and one likely to lead to another domestic controversy." Despite this sentiment, he convinced President Gerald Ford that the USSR was in direct control of the MPLA and that their communist threat had to be met. Kissinger arranged CIA support for the FNLA and UNITA. Consequently, as so often happened in the Cold War, the escalation by one side caused the other to increase the arms race as Cuba stepped up its own involvement, promising to land soldiers on the ground. Although the USSR thought increasing its involvement could damage relations with the US, the CIA involvement convinced it there was no shame in increasing its support for the MPLA. And Portugal? Portugal simply wanted out; the US National Security Council summed them up thusly: "The major Portuguese government objective in Angola is to get out, with honour if possible, but in any case to get out."

Only a few days after Bob's departure, there was fighting in Nova Lisboa and many Portuguese who had previously claimed they would remain in Angola "come hell or high water" began packing and leaving. Cavango remained cut off from much of the country, but over a high-frequency (HF) radio to the mission station in Catota, the missionaries would hear reports of the retreating Portuguese convoys; the people in Catota counted 3,000 vehicles pass through their town, heading for the border to South-West Africa in cars packed to the roof with household goods. Telephone lines were being taken down, but rumours seemed to travel just as quickly. In Luanda, Polish reporter Ryszard Kapuściński observed the departing Portuguese: "They said farewell to their African homes with mixed despair and rage, sorrow and impotence, with the feeling of leaving forever. All they wanted was to get out with their lives and to take their possessions with them." Angola had become the land of *confusão*.

In the second week of August, Steve and Darrell went into Nova Lisboa to purchase supplies and found much of the town abandoned, shops closed up and most of the remaining Portuguese packing up their possessions. At a hardware store they frequented, they discovered a heavy padlock on the door. An Angolan employee presented himself as "the new owner," explaining that his boss had left the previous week; unfortunately, his boss hadn't left behind the keys to the padlock.

One evening, a *mestiço* (half-Angolan, half-Portuguese) gentleman was out in his Land Rover when he spied a rabbit in his headlights. Having his shotgun nearby and loaded with birdshot, he fired a barrel at the creature. The rabbit spun around, dying but not yet dead. Leaping from the Land Rover, the man turned his shotgun around to club the rabbit to death with the butt of the gun. All at once, the shotgun fired its second barrel directly into his stomach. Wrapping his intestines into place with a blanket, the man climbed back into his Land Rover and drove to the nearest hospital—Cavango, a good four hours away across bumpy roads.

The night watchman at the hospital roused Steve from his bed to treat the wounded hunter. The birdshot had torn a 4-inch-diameter hole in his right upper quadrant, from which the intestines were spilling out. Steve and Barb opened him up and found an injury to the man's colon, so tacked the colon to two sides of the intestinal wall.

It wasn't until the next day that Steve realized there was an exit wound! The shot had gone through the transverse colon and into the abdominal wall of the back, next to the liver; the man was very, very fortunate the birdshot had missed his liver or he would have died before reaching Cavango. Steve opened him up a second time and cleaned out the exit wound, removing the dead skin, muscle and birdshot pellets, then patched him up again. Steve was still a young enough surgeon that he doubted his patient would survive, but the man rallied every day and left Cavango beaming with gratitude to Steve and Barb for saving his life.

"FAITHFUL IS HE WHO HAS CALLED YOU."

As the conflict escalated, the FNLA and UNITA formed a temporary alliance, hoping to drive the MPLA from Luanda. Fewer people came to Cavango hospital because the roads were either unsafe or covered by too many checkpoints. Those people who did brave their way to the hospital usually came because they had suffered an injury from one of the armed groups; no matter how the injury was received or what party they might support, Steve gave them the best care he could provide. One night at 2 AM Steve awoke to a tapping on his window. He arose to find a pair of South African diamond prospectors who were en route to the border. "We heard you guys are still here. Don't you know what's happening in this country?" Steve assented; he was treating plenty of wounded people in the hospital. "What are you doing here?" the prospectors wondered. "Don't you know all the white people are going to be killed?"

Steve disputed that; "Those are things which are being said, but I'm not so sure I've seen any evidence of that," he answered. "I'm the only doctor for 150 km, I can't leave these people now." Realizing Steve could not be budged, the prospectors moved on.

Two weeks later, the US State Department advised all non-essential personnel to evacuate the mission stations in Angola. Steve, the Hockersmiths and Jane all agreed they would remain at Cavango as long as possible, but they could not, by any means, call Peggy or 14-year-old Paul Hockersmith "essential." Paul's correspondence classes were complete so, simply, it was time for him to continue his education in the US with his elder siblings (being proud for his age, Paul wouldn't hear of being evacuated for any other reason). If there were a last-minute complication for Peggy, however, they would be putting Peggy and the baby's health at risk. It was agreed: Peggy and Paul would leave. Peggy was devastated; "I was sure I would never see my husband again." When the evacuation was delayed by one day, Peggy considered it a reprieve; "I had one more day with my husband."

Only one evacuation flight remained, heading to the US through Trans World Airlines (TWA). Steve, Peggy, Jane, Darrell, Barb, Paul and Sr. Israel journeyed together to Nova Lisboa to catch that flight, with Sr. Israel helping to safely guide their vehicle past the many military checkpoints. The terminal at Nova Lisboa was surrounded by mattresses as dozens of people sat, nervously hoping to be allowed aboard one of the evacuation flights. Because Peggy was Canadian and Paul an American, they were given priority ahead of those teeming throngs. While waiting for the flight, they stopped at a house where the TWA pilots were having their lunch. Peggy stepped into their washroom and cried.

Peggy said goodbye to Steve, boarded the plane, sat in her seat and in that moment heard the words of 1 Thessalonians 5:24: "Faithful is He who has called you." All at once, she felt fine and didn't shed another tear over the separation; "It just spoke to my life." Realizing she was fine, she wanted to reassure Steve and tried to get his attention from the window, but there was, of course, no way to relay her message. Peggy and Paul flew to Portugal and after finding their nearly lost luggage (which turned out to have been stowed with the crew's bags), they were greeted by another missionary who informed them the AEF missionaries William Brandle and Donald Lutes had both been arrested in Sá da Bandeira. They were flown to the US, where Peggy and Paul parted ways, Paul heading to his family in Zion, Illinois; Peggy reported on Brandle and Lutes' arrests to AEF headquarters, then continued home to Toronto.

As Peggy departed, the situation in Angola continued to deteriorate.

ACCUSED AS SPIES

Peggy's flight had left at about 2 PM, but Steve, Jane, Darrell, Barb and Sr. Israel had quite a time getting back to Cavango. The car broke down and with Nova Lisboa so bereft of supplies, there was no garage mechanic to examine the problem. As it became clear they wouldn't be roadworthy before dusk, Sr. Israel advised them to spend the night in Nova Lisboa and hopefully have the vehicle repaired by the morning. Fortunately, missionary Peter Muir was based in Nova Lisboa at Central Evangélicao de Literatura Bíblica, the local Christian bookstore. Peter's own family had been evacuated earlier and he was planning to depart, but for now they had a roof over their heads. By 7 PM, through trial and error, Steve and Darrell finally fixed the car. Sr. Israel had gone to visit friends, so they settled down for the night in Peter Muir's annex, giving the upper bedroom to Jane and Barb while Steve and Darrell tried to make beds from Peter's rather uncomfortable living room sofas.

Around 2 AM there was a loud banging at the front door. Steve and Darrell tried to ignore it, but after several minutes of knocks and yelling, Darrell finally opened the door, leaving the security cage shut. Before him stood a group of armed men who would ultimately prove to be from the FNLA. While Darrell tried to reason with the agitated soldiers, Steve, having so little Portuguese, barely had any idea how to help; he simply prayed. The soldiers began issuing a dizzying array of pronouncements and accusations: that they were going to requisition their car; that Darrell and Steve had to be brought to their commander; that they needed to *revistar* (inspect) the building;

and they were certain Steve and Darrell must be Soviet spies (there were known to be a tiny handful of Soviet agents in the country at the time).

Finally, they stopped asking and tried to grab Darrell by force. Darrell dug his hands into the doorframe, refusing to be budged even when they drew their pistols and struck him with the butt of a weapon. Giving up on that tactic, they barged into the room and began their *revistar*. They began overturning the room, continuing to yell accusations at the top of their lungs. One soldier noticed a radio/cassette player and yelled, "Comunicaçāo!" (communication), claiming it must surely be used for espionage; turning on the cassette player, they heard a recording which Peter had made the other day of UNITA's Jonas Savimbi speaking in Nova Lisboa, which seemed to prove their charge. They demanded to see Steve's and Darrell's passports, then declared both documents "had to be fakes."

Finally, Peter had arisen and flustered them by speaking in Mbundu. Peter's family had been missionaries in Angola since the 1930s "and he could speak Mbundu like a native," Steve noted. The tension finally dissolved when a man in a uniform with stripes on his shoulders arrived on the scene and addressed Darrell, Steve and Peter in English. He asked simple, direct questions, believed the explanations for their presence in Nova Lisboa and confirmed their passports as authentic. Ordering his subordinates to exit the room, he apologized that his "young fellows" had scared them. He didn't offer to clean up the rooms they had torn apart, but asked them to come visit his commanding officer in the morning. "I understand you might not want to after the way you've been treated, but it would be a great honour if you met my commander." What a difference in tone!

It was 6 AM by the time everything was cleared up. Peter and Steve read Psalm 121 together for comfort as the dawn broke. Sr. Israel returned to the group two hours later and they journeyed to the FNLA headquarters. The soldier from a few hours earlier greeted them and led them to his commanding officer. The commanding officer issued an abject apology for the manner in which they had been treated; "You have to realize in times of war things like this can happen," the officer stated, reiterating he had no ill will toward them. The reason for his apologetic stance? He wanted Steve to perform rounds in his sick ward.

Steve was willing; there were 50-60 wounded men in the military hospital, a building which had been a Portuguese centre, but was short on supplies and had no disinfectants to sterilize the surroundings. Even getting water to the building was a hardship under the present conditions and the sick men were suffering for it. Steve did what little he could for them considering the scarcity of supplies, but the army was very grateful for the gesture and in return, offered them gasoline—as much gasoline as they could carry. Taking out their jerrycans, they filled up, then finally got back on the road to Cavango.

While the four missionaries continued to serve in Cavango, the war heated up. The Cuban army landed thousands of troops in Angola; their Spanish tongue was mistaken by some of Steve's patients as "a strange Portuguese." Overwhelmed by the MPLA's renewed fighting strength, the FNLA retreated. The MPLA retained control over Luanda and would maintain control of Angola for the remainder of the civil war.

A HOLE IN THE HEART

Meanwhile in Toronto, Peggy lived with her parents, who had held some misgivings about the trip to Cavango to begin with; seeing Peggy return without her husband made them very unhappy. "I was absolutely fine," Peggy avowed. "Someone lent me a car, I was well taken care of; I wasn't upset."

One day she overheard her mother tell someone, "And she hasn't even cried!" It was true—she hadn't cried since her epiphany on the flight from Nova Lisboa. "That word from the Lord carried me through it all. There are times in your life when God speaks into your life in very clear ways."

On September 30, AEF chairman Rev. Phillip Gammon ordered all remaining AEF missionaries to evacuate Angola. Steve turned his "Nelsonian blind eye" to AEF, pretending he hadn't received the order. Even if he had wanted to comply with AEF, he refused to leave Cavango Hospital without a replacement physician. Without any additional flights in or out of Angola for the time being, it wasn't clear how he would get out. Frantically, the US State Department issued cables back and forth with AEF; were Steve Foster, Jane Williams and the Hockersmiths aware of the order to leave Angola? Confirmed, "Nevertheless, they have elected to remain at Cavango." More international players were becoming involved as South Africa formally invaded the country, lending its support to UNITA. The US Embassy had stripped down its staff to a skeleton crew; oil companies such as Chevron Corp. were evacuating their own employees.

In the rest of Angola, the other AEF missionaries were obeying orders. The Cavango team's friends in Catota contacted them by HF radio to inform them the station in Catota was being closed. The lines of combat had drawn near to the mission station and they feared for their lives. "We're leaving and we think you should too," they cautioned the Cavango team.

Steve dissented. "It's well and good for you to say God told you to go, but God hasn't told us that at all." Despite the wartime difficulties, Steve treated about 20 patients per day. They still had plenty of diesel in the drums Darrell had brought, plus the gasoline from the FNLA. "God had done all these things for us; why couldn't we trust him in these moments of uncertainty?" Steve wondered. He likened it to John 15:18-19:

"If the world hates you, keep in mind that it hated me first. If you belonged to the world, it would love you as its own. As it is, you do not belong to the world, but I have chosen you out of the world. That is why the world hates you."

Steve asked, "What kind of witness are we to be if we remain only when it's fine or if it suits us?" The morning devotionals Steve had with his hospital staff were a further reassurance to him. As he struggled each morning to follow along in his Portuguese-language Bible, Steve realized, "This life of faith was going on in the hearts and minds of the people I went to work with. I was used to this jaded university environment where you discussed the scripture but you didn't necessarily put it into practice. I think I'll always remember that excitement at Cavango."

The nurses vouched to Steve how much his ministry meant to them: "Your presence encourages us. Your willingness to be here in the midst of it all reminds us God has not taken his eye off us."

Steve was moved by their tribute and it steadied his resolve. "How could I say my skin was worth more than theirs?"

As he became more comfortable with the nurses, Steve would quiz them about their hopes and dreams for the future of Angola. "Now that Angola is independent, what do you hope will come?" he wondered. Sr. Silva was the most outspoken of the nurses; he was Ovimbundu, believed strongly in Savimbi's UNITA movement and that UNITA would come to power in Angola.

Although communications from Cavango to the outside world were tenuous, Darrell had made connections with the FNLA and UNITA leaders based around Nova Lisboa. Late in October, he asked for permission to use their radio so he could send a message to AEF alerting it of their status. UNITA refused, instead offering to fly him to Lusaka, Zambia. Although Zambia was not involved in the fighting of the Angolan Civil War, they were very free about permitting UNITA to violate its border. Boarding Savimbi's own plane in a highly illegal manoeuvre, Darrell crossed the border into Lusaka and spent three days there, informing AEF of the situation before returning to Angola. In turn, AEF alerted their families, including Peggy in Toronto.

On November 11, the departing Portuguese Governor-General transferred power to the MPLA. Despite a frantic push by UNITA and the FNLA to conquer Luanda, they had failed to oust the MPLA. Prior to independence, there had been some 340,000 Portuguese people in Angola; post-independence, there were around 40,000. Agostinho Neto ascended to the presidency of the country and Brazil became the first nation to formally recognize the new People's Republic of Angola.

In November, Bob Foster was determined to extricate his son, knowing how important it was for Steve to be at Peggy's side—and likewise aware Steve would refuse to be evacuated unless Bob returned himself. Using the connections Darrell had developed with UNITA, Bob arranged to ship medical relief supplies into Angola aboard an air freight vehicle headed to Nova Lisboa, with World Relief USA paying for the cost of the shipment. Landing with the supplies, Bob was recognized at the airport by a UNITA soldier. The soldier sought out the only missionary he could find: Dr. George Burgess. Burgess was stunned to hear out of the blue: "Dr. Foster needs a ride!"

That Sunday morning, November 30, Steve was having breakfast with Darrell and Barb when they heard the noise of an approaching car—an unusual sound in Cavango at any time. He was amazed to see Dr. Burgess pull up in his truck with Bob, carrying a massive amount of supplies. Bob waved and yelled "Hi!" in his booming voice, then helped Dr. Burgess unload the vehicle. They fed Dr. Burgess a quick meal so he could get back on the road to Nova Lisboa then back to his own mission station in Dondi.

Steve led Bob through the rounds at the hospital, then on Monday they made their plan: "Steve has to go back," Bob determined. "Peggy gives birth this week, he has to get back to Toronto." Jane Williams had also decided she should leave while opportunities remained available. Nova Lisboa was becoming more and more violent, but Jonas Savimbi was then based in the town of Silva Porto (today called Kuito), so they would attempt to board one of Savimbi's planes to Lusaka as Darrell had done.

The hospital staff understood why Steve had to depart, but first they gave him a proper send-off, singing hymns together and gathering around him in prayer. After Steve had said personal farewells to each nurse and climbed into Darrell's car, Sr. Silva climbed up through the open door to have one last conversation with Steve. "I want you to remember," Sr. Silva told him, "that I and the others are going to be praying that God will never let you forget the people here, that there will always be a place to work in Angola." Sr. Silva embraced him, and exited the car. Steve said farewell to his father, and Darrell drove Steve and Jane to Silva Porto.

AN INTRIGUE-FILLED EXIT

Heading to the UNITA headquarters they were told no one could confirm when they would be allowed to leave. The three missionaries wandered through Silva Porto to pass the time, ending up at a bookshop. Much to their amazement, they found a young American man in the shop, dressed in jeans, a

T-shirt and Ray-Ban sunglasses, his hair long and blond looking like he'd just stepped off a beach in California. "What is a Yankee boy like him doing here?" Steve wondered. They started up a conversation with the stranger, who identified himself as working in "communications." When he gave out a current address which matched that of Savimbi's headquarters, it confirmed everything in Steve's mind; he suspected he was speaking to a CIA operative. Steve and Jane explained they were waiting for a plane to Lusaka. The young man nodded, saying, "That makes sense." He advised them to be ready at a moment's notice. That night Steve, Darrell and Jane stayed at a local hotel, having no idea when their expected flight would occur.

During breakfast the next morning an airplane roared above the town. Soon, people from UNITA entered the hotel: "Get ready!" they called out. Darrell drove them to the UNITA airport, escorted by military vehicles. To their amazement, the Silva Porto airport was full of South African soldiers who had put up tents. With the UNITA men to vouch for them, there were minimal formal checks. Steve and Jane gave warm farewells to Darrell, and boarded an all-white Learjet; it had no markings or even a licence number and seated only eight passengers in total. A man and woman joined Steve and Jane, the man proving to be UNITA's vice-chair of Foreign Affairs. The plane took off and in 2.5 hours the Learjet landed in Lusaka; it taxied past the terminal, rolled far down the runway and finally entered a hangar whose doors closed behind them.

The UNITA official and his guest were taken away in a VIP car. An anonymous official greeted Steve and Jane, who wanted to know how immigration would be handled. "You are our guests, don't worry about anything," the official answered. He presented them with his business card and told them to call him before leaving Zambia. A driver escorted Steve and Jane to AEF's Lusaka headquarters. They drove from the hangar to a padlocked fence, where a guard unfastened the padlock, allowing them to merge with traffic.

In Lusaka, Steve and Jane greeted Keith Donald, the AEF director in Lusaka. "What are you guys doing here?" Keith wondered in astonishment. Jane decided to remain in Lusaka for a time before continuing on to the US, but Steve knew he had to keep moving to get back to Peggy. Keith phoned British Airways to see if they had compassion seats on an airplane for that evening that would arrive in Toronto by Thursday; it so happened they did. Keith brought Steve back to the airport and they obtained his ticket, then Steve phoned the official whose card he had been given.

It played out like a spy movie. "Ten minutes later, a man came to the British Airways counter and asked for Steve." Saying farewell to Keith, Steve surrendered his passport to the stranger, who guided Steve first to a VIP lounge in the terminal then into the airplane and took a seat next to him, chatting casually. At the moment before the cabin doors were ready to be closed, the mysterious man returned Steve's passport, then left the plane. Steve checked his passport: he had been given an immigration stamp out of the country.

At Heathrow, Steve was greeted by AEF's international director—the same man whose orders Steve had refused to obey months earlier. After a debriefing with AEF, Steve made an international phone call to Peggy to let her know he was coming home. In the end, Peggy's pregnancy was late by 8 days. Steve arrived for the due date, then had 8 days with Peggy before the December 12 birth of their first child, Rebecca Joy Foster, weighing 9 pounds, 14 ounces.

Steve saw God's hand in the friendships and relationships created in Cavango and in "the sense of belonging and being part of the team" as well as in their decision to remain when so many others fled.

Steve was out of Angola. But Sr. Silva's parting words were burning a hole in his heart.

CHAPTER 7

"I and the Others Are Going to Be Praying That God Will Never Let You Forget the People Here." — Sr. Silva

TORONTO; KALUKEMBE (January 1976 – March 1978)

Little did the average person in North America care about what was transpiring in Angola. As a whole, it seemed as though the continent of Africa only surfaced in the news to denote yet another regime toppled, another armed insurrection, more lives lost. A random person in North America could live a comfortable life without ever considering Africa, much less Angola. Even with so many major international players in the Cold War involved at some level in what was very much a hot war, the Angolan Civil War made few headlines in the years to come.

There were many great surgical positions in North America and Steve felt the temptation to accept such a posting after residency and simply tithe 10% of the salary back to Africa. His intention had been to journey to Lusaka, Zambia, and teach at the University of Zambia School of Medicine. He believed strongly in equipping African doctors with the skills they needed to become self-sufficient rather than an indefinite dependence on missionary doctors. Yet again and again, Steve would recall Sr. Silva's parting words. "Suppose I never went back to Angola and the next time I see Sr. Silva, we're in Heaven. If he asks me 'why didn't you return to us?' how could I say, 'I'm sorry, but my family was more important' or 'I have a really great job in Mississauga.'" Steve remained determined to serve as a missionary in Africa, but in his heart, Angola had displaced his homeland of Zambia.

First, Steve had a residency to complete; he had no means of returning to Angola for at least two more years. When he would try to express his compulsion to aid the people of Angola, North Americans would stare at him quizzically. "Angola? Aren't they a communist nation? Why would you want to help them?"

Steve conceded, "It wasn't easy to come up with answers! What kind of God allows us to get out scot-free and the rest to pay the price? Can we walk off the scene and let them stay? What are we saying about the Lord Jesus? What are we saying about the implications of the cross?" Steve pointed to the words of the prophet Isaiah: "Here I am; send me" (Isaiah 6:8).

There were also those critics who considered the work of a missionary doctor to be a compromise, believing that putting part of one's time into the work of the hospital was a distraction from the mission of spreading the Gospel. "I never accepted dichotomous thinking," Steve responded to such critics. "I have loved the symbolism of the Robe of Jesus at the foot of the cross. The soldiers could not find a seam to tear it up into pieces so they cast lots for it. …May our ministry be a seamless one where Christ crucified, resurrected and soon returning is what is preached in word and deed and the words [reportedly] of St. Francis of Assisi also ring clear: 'preach the Gospel at all times and if necessary use words.' My dad practised that seamlessness and his actions were always louder than his words."

THE FALL OF CAVANGO

Back in Cavango, Bob, Darrell and Barb continued to serve the locals' needs, but resources remained scarce and the perils were increasing. The time Darrell spent cultivating relations with UNITA offered them a few provisions; UNITA's leader Jonas Savimbi himself had asked them to remain at Cavango, promising them UNITA would defend the town and restock their supplies. Darrell continued to visit Silva Porto when possible, but the countryside was changing rapidly. The FNLA had mostly retreated to the north of the country, while the MPLA and Cuban armies were steadily pushing UNITA and its South African allies away.

On February 8, 1976, Huambo (the former Nova Lisboa) was captured by the MPLA. Soon after, a note written by Savimbi was delivered to Darrell. It informed the missionaries the Cuban army was on its way toward Cavango and UNITA was performing a strategic retreat. "I can no longer guarantee your safety," Savimbi cautioned them. The Cubans would arrive within days.

With a heavy heart, Bob went to the Cavango church and rang the bell. Many of the villagers gathered around to hear what he had to say. Bob let them know he, Darrell and Barb were being called "the enemy" by the MPLA, for accepting aid from UNITA, which made it appear that they were UNITA's allies. "If I stay here," Bob told the village, "they're either going to kill me or put me into prison." There was sorrow on both sides as the missionaries took their leave of Cavango, with no concept of what might become of the village without them. Bob gave an especially warm embrace to his friend Sr. Israel, who would now be left to manage the mission without the missionaries. Bob handed Sr. Israel the keys to the station; "Take care of everything 'til I get back," he said. Driving south via Menongue, the trio was escorted by the retreating South African Defence Force (SADF) across the border into South-West Africa. From there, they were transported back to the US.

Many of Cavango's population fled into the bush, abandoning their possessions in the hopes of finding a safer locale—but with the country collapsing into civil war and paranoia running riot, safety was not easily found. Some fled to Catota; others to Dondi. One villager, who had been a tractor operator and had often accompanied Bob on Sundays to hear him preach in the villages around Cavango, possessed a brilliant memory and stored up several of Bob's sermons and became a preacher to the villagers-in-exile. He recited Bob's sermons verbatim and even performed services of marriage and funerals.

Within a week, the Cuban army raided the defenceless village of Cavango. Cuban soldiers stole any medical equipment they had a use for from the hospital, then destroyed the remainder, rationalizing they were keeping it out of UNITA hands. Sr. Israel was forced to surrender the keys to the missionaries' homes, which were likewise pilfered. Disgusted by the leper villages, the Cubans turned on those lepers too slow or incapacitated to run and sealed them up in their grass huts, then lit the huts on fire. Thirty of the lepers were burned alive.

Around the country, the mission stations were in a state of collapse. Many missionaries fled the country to save their lives; others were thrown into prison. As the warring factions would destroy buildings they believed the other side could use for their encampments, many mission stations were utterly eradicated. Within a few months, every mission hospital in Angola had been either abandoned or demolished—with one exception.

RODOLPHE'S INTERVENTION

Kalukembe (depending who you ask, 'Caluquembe,' 'Caluguembe,' or 'Caluqueme') lies in the southwest quadrant of Angola, a little northeast of Lubango (formerly Sá da Bandeira). Much of the village of Kalukembe (called the 'sandula') lies close to the main highway which leads to Sá da Bandeira. Just a little off the highway lies Kalukembe Hospital, which Rodolphe Bréchet founded in 1944 through the support of the Swiss Alliance Missionaire

Evangelique. In 1952, a nursing school was added to the mission project. While the other mission hospitals fell during the civil war, Kalukembe Hospital remained open; because of its closer proximity to the highway than the other mission hospitals, and the government considered it more defensible than the Cavango Hospital. At the same time, Kalukembe Hospital remained neutral in the conflict, serving both MPLA and UNITA fighters—so UNITA had no reason to foment conflict either.

With 200 patient beds, Dr. Bréchet had sought to provide the best possible care at Kalukembe Hospital, just as his friend and colleague Bob Foster had in his own mission hospitals. However, by 1976 Dr. Bréchet was feeling his age, aggravated by a terrible case of kidney stones. While most of his missionary colleagues had fled Angola, Dr. Bréchet knew Bob wanted to return. Rodolphe extended a lifeline to Dr. Foster: come to Kalukembe Hospital to assist in the heavy caseload and perhaps, in time, there would be opportunities to reopen the other mission hospitals—even return to Cavango.

Bob needed only that very small amount of encouragement; "It was a wonderful answer to prayer," vouched Stirling. Bob had been unable to move on to other opportunities: "I don't want to go anywhere until I know I can't go back to Angola," he said. Emotionally, the Fosters wanted to return to Cavango, but there was no longer a safe means to return. Dr. Bréchet's offer came right when it was needed, for when Bob had officially exited Angola with his family on their 1975 furlough, his passport was stamped with a return visa. Consequently, there was already an official means for Bob to re-enter the country.

In April 1976, the Fosters convened a family reunion in Virginia at a vacation house owned by friends of Bob and Belva. With Bob, Belva, Stuart, Stirling and Shelley about to return to Angola it was an opportunity to send them off and welcome the Fosters' newest additions. Not only did Steve and Peggy bring little Rebecca with them, but Sharon came with her baby Tonya and Stacey brought his wife Ruth Walters, whom he had married the previous year. Stacey's passion was in video editing and Ruth worked in the same field.

The Angolan officials were amazed when the Fosters appeared at the border with re-entry visas in their passports, and permitted the family's return. Because so many missionaries had fled Kalukembe, furnished homes had been left behind—there was even a car! The Fosters settled in quickly. Stirling took note of the fleet of eight Land Rovers Rodolphe had in service—they were Rodolphe's favourite brand of vehicle for hospital uses and they soon became Stirling's car of choice. The durable and reliable English-made Land Rovers are a mechanic's delight—but one must be a mechanic if one is to keep them. One of the manufacturer's logos reads: "Turning Owners into Mechanics since 1948."

At the hospital, Bob lightened Rodolphe's workload by taking charge over the maternity ward and by overseeing surgery. At that time, the operating room ran two days per week. Bob attempted to bring in the X-ray machine he had bought years before, but it was still incomplete. He and Rodolphe used a radioscope instead to help treat cases of tuberculosis. Unfortunately, the radioscope exposed both physicians to large doses of radiation; this would cause troubles with lymphoma in later years.

Some refugees from Cavango made it all the way to Kalukembe. Bob was delighted to be reunited with them, but puzzled when they said, "Now we know that you really love us."

Bob replied, "What do you mean, *now* you know? I've lived here, I've worked here, I've done everything possible to show you that I really love you."

They answered, "Oh, no! For you to be willing to leave your home and come back and suffer with us shows us that you really do love us."

Bob began evangelizing among his patients, bringing his Bible with him as he visited with and witnessed to patients in the wards. Kalukembe Hospital was specifically an Evangelical hospital, so there was no tension between the sacred and the secular—or even the pagan, for "traditional medicine" was not permitted on the grounds. The hospital's nursing staff accompanied Bob as he ministered to the patients. "They didn't come to be authoritative, but to share what they knew," said Nurse Paulo Ismael. Just down the road from the main hospital was a small leper village with its own church, which Bob would also visit to preach to the lepers. Bob also gave talks to the villagers about family matters, delivering short lectures on the roles of family members, such as how to be a loving husband or wife.

Up in the sandula, Bob attended a church pastored by Paulo Mateus. Since his days in Zambia, Bob had been accustomed—whether at work or in church—to go about dressed in shorts. Pastor Mateus was the first church leader to push back, insisting Bob wear his best clothes during church services.

One day Stirling, Bob, Belva and pastor-in-training Moisés Miguel were out driving when they needed to stop for a bathroom break. Belva went to find some privacy further away from the men, and after she had finished she realized—with great astonishment—she had somehow lost her way from the road! Unable to locate the highway, Belva ventured deeper and deeper into the bush until she came upon a local cattleman. The helpful farmer guided Belva back to the highway where Bob and the others were still waiting; she had been missing for three hours. At the sight of his wife, Bob was overcome with joy and ran to meet her, embracing her warmly. This made a great impression on Moisés; he knew most Angolan men would have beaten a wife who had caused so much distress. Bob's behaviour to Belva was a great example to Moisés of what a Christian relationship should resemble. However, the Fosters had no idea what a stir they had caused and would retell the anecdote to others as an object lesson on why people shouldn't stray too far from the road when relieving themselves!

STEVE IN TORONTO

Steve finished his residency in 1977. He still had his general surgery exams to look forward to, but he wanted to obtain more medical experience to serve him in the mission field. He realized he might end up the only doctor within hundreds of kilometres, just as his father had so often found himself. The most relevant field of medicine for serving in Africa was tropical medicine, so he approached Dr. Jay Keystone and explained what he had been doing in Angola and his hopes for continued service. Dr. Keystone was fascinated by Steve's story and gave him a position as Clinical Fellow in his field, Tropical Disease and Parasitology at Toronto General Hospital. Many of the patients who came to Toronto General suffering from tropical diseases were themselves missionaries. This gave Steve an unusual series of opportunities to meet missionaries from around the world! Many of those he treated suffered from malaria, the most common of all tropical diseases, and Steve was enlightened to learn of the different ways malaria could present itself, such as the version living in the afflicted person's liver. One such woman he treated had been suffering from malaria since the 1940s!

In August 1977, Steve and Peggy's second child was born: another daughter, Heather Ann, weighing 10 pounds. That summer, the great excitement in North American culture was the release of the motion picture *Star Wars*, which Steve and Peggy saw with Mary Lou and her husband Andrew. Steve hadn't had many opportunities to watch films in theatres while growing up and *Star Wars* was a ground-breaking theatrical experience. Mary Lou was fascinated at Steve's reactions to the film. "I had never seen somebody watch a movie like that. I almost watched him as much as I watched the movie. He sat on the front edge of his seat with his hands on the seat in front of him." He was so giddy with enthusiasm over the picture that he was "almost bouncing and hitting the seat in front."

While Steve continued his final studies, he was formally contacted by Kalukembe Hospital, who asked him to come over as a surgeon and hopefully transfer to another Angolan hospital later on. Steve asked if he should first travel to Portugal and learn Portuguese. The response was quick: "No, no, no." At this time the MPLA was permitting missionaries to enter the country but there was no sense how long it might last—so the hospital encouraged Steve to learn the language once he was in the field, just as his parents had done. On

November 11, Steve and Peggy joined AEF as missionaries and one week later, Steve passed his general surgery exams in Montreal; he was now a certified surgeon. Over Christmas that year, Steve and Sheila met up with their brother Stuart, who had come back to the US to study history and literature at Harvard University. Sheila was still pondering whether she might return to Angola but both siblings were interested in hearing from their brother as to how the country had changed under MPLA rule.

At his exit from Kalukembe, Stuart had been deeply affected by one of his Angolan friends, who had been conscripted into service in FAPLA (*Forças Armadas Populares de Libertação de Angola*), the MPLA's army. The thought that he was allowed to go free and get an education while his friend was being marched off to die because of the difference of a passport hammered home one of the principles of the Gospel: "to whom much has been given, much shall be required from him" (Luke 12:48). Like his father and brother, Stuart hoped to become a missionary in Angola.

CHANGING FACES IN ANGOLA

Although the war was far from over, the MPLA maintained control over most of the country. However, the US continued to support UNITA and when Angola joined the United Nations on December 1, 1976, the US refused to recognize the MPLA government. South Africa had retreated from Angola, but remained watchful on the border. The Cuban army was now stationed in Angola indefinitely to ensure the MPLA remained in power.

One side effect of the civil war was the gradual depopulation of Angola's wildlife. The teeming forests where Stacey Foster had hunted were becoming less and less populous because of the Cuban armies. An army, as Napoleon Bonaparte said, travels on its stomach. To feed their thousands of soldiers in a nation whose formerly teeming agricultural industry had been disrupted or outright abandoned due to the war, the Cubans would go hunting for meat, even employing helicopter gunships to fire upon herds from the air. At the same time, Jonas Savimbi financed his UNITA forces in part by hunting elephants—not for their meat, but for their ivory tusks, which he fenced through his allies in the SADF to willing buyers in China. Between the Cubans' need for food and UNITA's need for money, the verdant land was being stripped bare.

Out in Kalukembe, a tremendous wave of refugees began pouring in. In all, some 36,000 refugees had fled to the southwest, having lost most of their homes to the war. These refugees had scarcely any clothing and food supplies were thin. As a result, the missionaries at Kalukembe began sending appeals to their supporters urging the need for food and clothes.

The surgical wing of Kalukembe Hospital was overwhelmed, with a waiting list of up to 150 people. At one point the MPLA toured the hospital and while impressed with what Bob and Rodolphe had accomplished, noted the strain on the duo and offered to send them Cuban doctors. Bob politely declined the offer; Cuban doctors in Angola operated on a triage basis, believing it more important to empty beds than offer patients the best outcomes—and would prefer to amputate broken legs rather than repair them. Cubans also weren't experienced with Angolan maladies; there were 100 beds set aside for tuberculosis but as Cuba had no cases of TB, virtually no Cuban doctors knew how to diagnose and treat the condition.

In summing up the state of mission hospitals in the late 70s, Bob said: "Having been involved in medical mission work and seeing the tremendous value both from the medical viewpoint and the spiritual, I believe there is a greater need today than there was in 1950 for medical missions. Governments that we hoped would be able to cope and take over mission hospitals are further from being able to do that today than they were twenty years ago." Unfortunately, the one-time explosion of mission-oriented doctors at the start of Charles Foster's mission had dimmed as more and more, doctors refused to leave their practice for the sake of mission work. Their reasons were many— family, unpaid medical school bills, career advancement. At the same time, efforts to raise generations of African doctors were stymied because so few African doctors were willing to serve in their own countries; Europe and the Americas had plenty of well-paying jobs for doctors compared to the cash-strapped African nations.

In December 1977, Rodolphe Bréchet's son Jean-Pierre came to Angola with his wife, Marie-Claude. At first they served at Cassua but the continued instability of the civil war finally brought them to Kalukembe. With Jean-Pierre on hand, Kalukembe Hospital now had three physicians to rely upon. Jean-Pierre took a particular interest in cases of tuberculosis and treating the lepers. About one kilometre from the main Kalukembe Hospital, there was a leprosarium and leper village at Kamunda. Jean-Pierre saw curing leprosy as being one of the most uniquely Christian causes a physician could perform. "Their lives have been transformed from a nobody to somebody loved by God," he explained. "It's not just treating people who have a disease, it's bringing them hope for a life transformed and to bring back to them this self-worth…for this identity that they are people who are loved by God and who have a contribution to make in present society."

THE NARROW GATE

On January 20, 1978, the government of Angola approved Steve and Peggy's visa application. Peggy was at her parents' home in Toronto when she heard the news. Excusing herself from her parents' sight, she hid and cried. While Peggy shared Steve's conviction that God had called them to Angola, she knew it would mean leaving her family and that it would hurt them. Peggy's siblings were very understanding. Her brother Bob was apprehensive, but concluded, "Steve is not stupid. If the risks were completely unacceptable, they wouldn't have gone."

Knowing Steve and Peggy would live primarily overseas from then on with only occasional furloughs in Canada, Peggy's mother Fran became upset because she wanted to see her grandchildren grow up. She had treasured the time she had spent with young Rebecca and Heather in Toronto. Peggy's father Sid took the news badly; a quiet, sensitive, pacifistic man who seldom raised his voice or showed his temper, he objected to their mission—not because he opposed Steve and Peggy's ministry, but because they were bringing Rebecca and Heather into the midst of a civil war. "It's not right," he would quietly repeat to his family. He felt Steve and Peggy were free to choose to serve in the midst of a war, but Rebecca and Heather had no choice. When Peggy solicited his opinion, he did not mince words: "I don't think it's right to take children to a war." He also objected to Peggy bringing family heirlooms overseas with her, fearing those items would be lost.

It was a good thing that Steve had come to love Canadian hockey, because it helped him bond with his father-in-law. The two men would watch the Toronto Maple Leafs play on the television set in the Parkins' basement; Bob Parkins would hear Steve's "exuberant laugh" echo up from the lower level. "You could hear it five blocks away!"

Still attending Little Trinity, Steve and Peggy befriended a new couple, Trevor and Peggy Smith, and informed them they would be heading overseas to Angola. Although the Smiths had only a short time with the Fosters at Little Trinity, the bond of their friendship would endure for decades, friends who could be entrusted with paperwork in Canada while they were overseas. The parish of Little Trinity would itself, through shifting congregations, continue to support Steve and Peggy across the decades.

In February 1978, Steve attended the Northside Baptist Church Missions Conference in St. Petersburg, Florida. Steve needed funds for a $5,000 diesel truck, aware he would need a strong, top-of-the-line vehicle overseas. The entirety of the money was given to him at the conference—as always, God provided for their mission's material needs.

Writing to his supporters, Steve explained why it was important for him to enter Angola:

"It is hard to convey the urgency of the task in view of the stated objectives of the Marxist government to unite all churches into a single 'state' church. In the confusion of civil war, the government is unwilling to antagonize the people more by closing churches. Thus, at this moment, the work of the Church visible is largely unrestricted. It is imperative that we grasp the opportunity to better prepare our brothers in Christ physically and spiritually for the increasing dangers ahead. The Angolan Christians have been praying for us personally and others to come over and help them."

Later that February, Steve and Peggy packed up their supplies and transported themselves and the two girls across the ocean to Luanda. Although in the past travel to Angola could be made through neighbouring countries such as South Africa, now that South Africa was at war with Angola having their country's stamp on one's passport could complicate entry at the border. As a result, many people who did have South African stamps would be denied entry, as the government feared spies were everywhere. For the duration of hostilities, missionaries had to take care to avoid provoking the government. In the past, it was the Portuguese government who accused the Protestants of being agitators; now the communist MPLA was in a position to exercise the same authoritarian measures.

In Charles and June's day, it had been acceptable to send MKs across the ocean to Collingwood, cut off from their parents for years at a time; for Bob and Belva, the tradition had been to send children away to a boarding school such as Sakeji; but Steve and Peggy belonged to a new generation of missionaries who saw their children as their most cherished possessions and an inseparable part of their ministry. Under God's grace, Rebecca and Heather would be raised on the mission field.

CHAPTER 8

*"An Island of Government Control in a Countryside That Was
Dominated by UNITA." — Ken Foster on Kalukembe*

KALUKEMBE (April 1978 – January 1983)

On April 3, 1978, Steve, Peggy, Rebecca and Heather arrived in Luanda. Much
to their joy, they found Bob Foster standing in the immigration line at the
airport, having just returned from a trip abroad. With Bob's guidance, all ten
of Steve and Peggy's suitcases were brought through customs. Steve had a
considerable amount of paperwork to finish in Luanda before he could begin
work in Kalukembe, but Peggy went ahead with the girls. Steve registered his
Angolan driver's licence and signed a government payment contract promising
$6,000 for working as a doctor in Angola. Steve doubted he would ever see the
money, but there was another advantage: it gave him the right to purchase plane
tickets to his country of origin (Canada) using the local currency, the kwanza.
Almost a decade later, the document would come in handy.

His time in Luanda gave Steve an opportunity to observe how Angolan
society was being reshaped under the MPLA. "This country is definitely in the
hands of the Marxist-Leninists and the Christians are gradually being forced to
decide whom they serve," he told his supporters. "You can imagine the anguish
for those Christians within the party who joined when its Marxism was not so
flagrant."

By the time Steve arrived in Kalukembe, a week behind Peggy, his
daughters were "already beginning to turn a lovely brown" under the African
sun. The family took up residence in Bicoque, a large manor on the mission
station located on a gentle slope below Kalukembe Hospital. There were four
apartments set up in Bicoque, one of which was occupied by Bob, Belva,
Stirling and Shelley. For the first few months, Steve and Peggy would take their

meals with Bob and Belva to help the new couple adjust. Outside the home stood a large tangerine tree; the smell of the tangerines being warmed by the sun became a strong scent-memory to Heather, and that smell is more vivid than any of her other early childhood memories.

It took a considerable amount of time for Steve and Peggy to unpack as the last of the crates containing their supplies would arrive four months later. There was also the matter of a shipping container holding 2 tons of clothing Little Trinity had arranged to ship over with the Fosters, but the government confiscated the container. Steve continued arguing for the container's release. As the young family began to adjust to Kalukembe, most of their time was spent learning Portuguese. Steve asked if they should also learn Mbundu, which was the primary tribal tongue. Other missionaries assured him there was "not much point," as they hoped and believed the civil war would be finished in another year, then they would be headed to Catota—where the local tongue was Ngangela. Steve's Portuguese studies were never quite complete as he developed many inaccuracies in his manner of speech, such as the always-tricky differences between the masculine and feminine. However, Steve's errors in Portuguese would always earn him a laugh from his nurses, so on some level he wasn't eager to improve.

Steve's arrival meant Kalukembe Hospital now had four physicians—although for the number of patient beds, they actually *needed* six to function properly. With Rodolphe and his son Jean-Pierre joined by Bob and his son Steve, there was a fine inter-generational staff (although Jean-Pierre spent most of 1978 in Kassua studying Mbundu). While he continued to learn his Portuguese, Steve began working in the operating room three afternoons a week. He brought with him a number of procedures the other physicians did not have, such as hip replacement surgery and draining fluid from the heads of hydrocephalic children by installing a shunt. Steve's expertise in emergency surgery also gifted him in treating bullet wounds, C-sections and hernia repairs.

Steve was only on his third week in the OR when Rodolphe made a fateful decision. Steve had observed that the practices in the OR were out-of-date; for example, they were using sulfa powder as an antibiotic. Sulfa powder had become a popular antibiotic in the 1930s, but by the 1970s it was clear that it was difficult to keep the powder sterile and if patients were allergic to the powder it could kill them. Realizing it was time to step aside, Rodolphe brought Steve to the operating room and summoned the head nurse Dona Julia and the other nursing staff. "I just want you to know," Rodolphe informed them, "this is my last moment in the operating room. This young man"—indicating Steve—"is going to be the director of the operating room. You're to listen to him." Then he turned and walked out.

One of the operations Steve gained notoriety for were

thyroidectomies. Every time Rodolphe had attempted a thyroidectomy, it had ended poorly—either the patient died on the table or would hemorrhage to death while in recovery. This was due partly to the kind of thyroid operations common in Angola—patients would develop goitres and wait so long to seek treatment that the surgery became life-threatening. When Steve announced his intention to perform his first thyroidectomy at Kalukembe, Dona Julia was sceptical; she had been serving at Kalukembe Hospital since it first opened and in 20,000 operations had never seen a successful thyroidectomy. "Wait and see, I think you'll be pleasantly surprised," he suggested. Sure enough, the operation was a success and the hospital saw an immediate benefit from Steve's skillset.

As Steve improved his ability to speak to the nurses in Portuguese, they were impressed by the differences between him and his father. One nurse noted Steve had "mais expertise" than Bob. Steve also gave instructions to his nurses: "when you see something not right, you tell me." A very simple concept, but it was an expression of trust the nurses had not been granted before. He also gave the nurses more room to make their own observations and recommendations. Steve's opinion of the Kalukembe nurses soared; he enjoyed working with them. As Steve began taking on consults (*consultas* in Portuguese), he would frequently meet patients in the corridor of the hospital and pause to examine some of them there, rather than insisting on formal consults in his office. The nurses noted how he "treated people equally no matter how unappreciated they were." By June 1978, Steve had begun Bible studies with the nurses, as he had done in Cavango. Just outside the hospital grounds lay the *sanzala*—the outpatient village—that was something of a shantytown occupied by the outpatients and their families. At times the population in the sanzala surged to 2-3,000 people and when Steve did not have medical duties he would preach and study with the outpatients.

Steve identified the goal of Kalukembe Hospital as to "live and testify to the love of Jesus Christ in our daily life; treat and relieve illness and suffering; develop primary health care and a preventive medicine program; train health-care workers to be capable of working in rural clinics independently; maintain an equilibrium between the medical work and that of the outreach of the Church."

Steve also kept an eye on the *oficina* (workshop) where the chief mechanic Claude Maeder would toil on the many Land Rovers, tractors and trucks the hospital utilized. Steve would begin each of his days at the oficina to help troubleshoot mechanical troubles, and then enter the hospital to begin his consultas.

Jean-Pierre appreciated Steve's "joie de vivre"—his ingenuity as a surgeon. As supplies were difficult to come by in Kalukembe, doctors could not always depend on having precisely what equipment they would prefer in any given situation. Steve would use old surgical gloves as drain stoppers for sinks; when he didn't have the prescribed suture, he would use whichever suture was available. To close up patients with abdominal cavities, Steve soaked 0.5 millimeter fishing line in alcohol to sterilize it so it would serve as a suture. When the hospital had no supplies to perform a proper osteosynthesis for patients with fractured femurs, Steve would simply place the patients into traction to repair the fractures. Blood was also difficult to come by, so Steve made it an accepted practice that before surgery, patients would donate a pint of their blood to be used in the operation. If the pint of blood was not needed, the hospital inherited another bag for its blood bank. This soon became the accepted practice at Kalukembe Hospital and in the other hospitals where Steve served. Steve was adaptable enough that he even put his surgical talents to use on Jean-Pierre's dog when it broke its leg!

Considering her upbringing was so different from Steve's, Peggy had done well up to this point, but early on at Kalukembe she found herself very lonely. Although Steve would return to Bicoque for lunch every day and she had many in-laws and the various Swiss missionaries nearby, she found it hard to relate to them. The Swiss were simply of a different culture and the only language they held in common was Portuguese. One of the Swiss missionaries was Betty Dauwalder, a midwife and nursing supervisor for the hospital. Betty had a wry sense of humour and, unfortunately, Peggy's trusting nature made her a prime target for Betty's jokes. One day Peggy asked Betty about a crop of bright red vegetables were growing in the courtyard at Bicoque. "Why don't you try one?" Betty suggested. Peggy took one of the vegetables into her mouth and bit it; it was a red-hot pepper and Betty burst into laughter at her great joke—however it was less funny for Peggy who took aspirin for the pain.

Of her husband's family, Peggy was slightly intimidated by her father-in-law. Although she felt "you always knew where you stood with him," she worried that she didn't meet his standards. She found it was difficult to relate to Bob on an emotional level. Eventually Peggy took on some office administration duties at the hospital so that she could provide helpful work.

Peggy frequently wrote letters to her mother, but it would take anywhere from 6 weeks to 3 months for their letters to reach one another; it was also somewhat unsettling to know their mail would constantly be opened and read by the government. Although it was hard for Peggy to maintain a connection to her friends in Canada, Marg Landry, a woman from her parish in Thunder Bay, took charge of the Fosters' prayer letter and for decades to come would copy and mail the letters Steve and Peggy sent to her.

On one occasion, Bob, Belva, Stirling and Shelley were driving out west to Benguela for a holiday when they passed a field where horses could be seen roaming. Shelley had been fascinated by horses since her father had taken her on a trail ride in Colorado a decade earlier and they were an uncommon sight in Angola. When Shelley evinced an interest in the horses, Bob turned off the highway and drove down the property road to find the owner. The property was a ranch, owned by a Portuguese couple. Bob told the rancher his children were interested in the horses and asked if any of them were for sale. The rancher replied "no," but Bob told him if he changed his mind, they would be interested.

Six months later, the Portuguese couple turned up at Kalukembe Hospital, where Bob treated the wife for a hysterectomy. Filled with gratitude toward Bob, the rancher gifted two of his horses to the Fosters. The horses were young—less than a year old. Unfortunately, one of them, named Roland, died from African horse sickness; the rancher generously supplied a replacement. At the time, Stirling and Shelley were both enjoying *The Lord of the Rings* by J. R. R. Tolkien, so they named the two horses after horses from the books: Hasufel (Aragorn's horse) and Windfola (Eowyn's horse).

Bob was so devoted to enabling Shelley's dream of owning horses that he had a stable built in the back of Bicoque, even outfitting it with running water so it could be more easily cleaned. Shelley found her horse Windfola was incredibly skittish around people and she had to ease the mare into accepting human contact. Stirling felt Windfola had been abused, as he once suffered a terrible kick from her. As Shelley won Windfola's trust the horse kicked people less frequently, but they would warn others to keep their distance. One day Stirling and Shelley were leading their horses when Rebecca toddled behind them. Distracted, they didn't see Rebecca walk up directly behind Windfola. "Instead of hauling off and walloping Rebecca," Stirling recalled, "she just picked up her one hoof, hardly even broke her stride as she was walking and gently just pushed Rebecca over so that Rebecca sat down on the ground." Stirling and Shelley sighed with relief. "The Lord was protecting Rebecca," said Stirling. "Maybe the horse realized Rebecca wasn't a danger. She wasn't happy about Rebecca walking behind her but wasn't nasty about it."

One day an MPLA commissar from the region came to Kalukembe for treatment. Bob had heard the commissar on the radio "calling us a hotbed of UNITA supporters and no one could be trusted. [Yet] here you are for a consulta?" The commissar grinned. "Oh, Doctor Foster, you just have to realize that we politicians have to say things but of course we don't mean them!" The wife of this commissar had been to Kalukembe the year before, when Bob delivered her child via C-section.

"It paved the way for relationships you didn't expect to get," Steve reflected. It planted "the seeds of trust, even with the most hostile attitudes on the part of political officials. The reality was day-to-day people knew they could count on us and trust us to care for them. …Whatever political banner was waving wouldn't affect the care they would get. We wouldn't play politics [and] we wouldn't take sides."

SAUDE PUBLICA

1979 brought a sea of changes to Angola and at Kalukembe. At Christmas, 1978, Sheila arrived at Kalukembe to begin serving as a missionary. First, of course, she needed to learn Portuguese and went to Kassua where a Swiss linguist began teaching her both Mbundu and Portuguese. Steve's car had been held up in Luanda since their arrival but in January it was finally released. Steve painted *Ambulancia – Hospital de Caluquembe* on the vehicle. He soon put the car to use as he made visits to other mission stations whose clinics had no residing physicians, such as Sussangue and Caia. "My visits there to the African staff who have stayed has helped their morale," he noted. That April most of the donated clothing was also released by the MPLA to Kalukembe and the missionaries began distributing the clothes to the many refugees who crowded the village. By the end of the year, the rest of the medical equipment shipping containers Steve had brought were also released.

Peggy began leading Bible study as well, with her first sessions being with teenage girls from the village. Keeping an eye on Rebecca and Heather continued to be a challenge. One day, Heather was attacked by red army ants which swarmed all over her body and into her thick curly hair; dousing the toddler in the bath removed most of the ants, but extricating them from her hair took much longer.

By the summer, Sheila began offering her public health clinics (*saude publica*) to villages around Kalukembe, offering under-5 care for children who required vaccinations. In her first two months she enrolled 1,000 children. Sheila was amazed to see how many cases of polio there were around Kalukembe, despite the polio vaccine being readily available. Checking in with the government medical officer, Sheila discovered the vaccines often sat in airports for days in the heat, destroying their effectiveness. Further, most of the vaccines were being supplied from the USSR and came in such a strong dosage they would have the opposite effect and actually infect children with polio! Sheila switched Kalukembe to UNICEF (United Nations Children's Fund, originally known as the United Nations International Children's Emergency Fund) as their supplier of vaccines.

Comparing this to her experiences as a nurse in the US she mused "it's not *boring*." Like her brother she enjoyed "the challenge to your creativity. To figure out ways to take care of people without the resources you have in North America." The saude publica also helped teach self-sufficiency to villagers, providing instructions on how to make soap, sugar, even a clay stove. She taught people how to spray their homes to remove parasites; dig clean water wells; construct latrines; perform first aid; utilize personal hygiene; grow vegetable gardens; dispose of garbage; tend to pregnancies; even identify tuberculosis and leprosy. "This is the way that God wants me to contribute to the kingdom," Sheila explained.

Sheila also toiled alongside Jean-Pierre at Kalukembe Hospital in its new pediatrics ward. Sheila "was a pioneer," said Nurse Paulo Ismael. "She was the first nurse dedicated to children." Children suffered in Kalukembe's measles epidemic, often being struck blind by the disease, but Sheila saved many of the children's eyesight by simply supplying them with vitamin A. Jean-Pierre noted how many villagers feared sending their children to the hospital because so frequently the hospital would be unable to help them and they would die; from their perspective, the hospital seemed to be a place where people went to die. As Sheila began saving children's lives it altered how they felt about hospital care. "They gained confidence," Jean-Pierre observed, while the hospital gained credibility.

On September 10, 1979, Angola's president Agostinho Neto died from cancer while visiting Moscow. Immediately, a faithful MPLA party member Eduardo dos Santos took charge of the country and would remain as the nation's leader for almost 40 years. Although initially the government sought to make Angola a truly atheistic communist nation like most Marxist-Leninist domains (as communist Ethiopia had attempted in that same time period), by 1979 the MPLA realized too many in the population were committed to their faith. As the MPLA was still at war with the FNLA and UNITA, it chose the better part of valour and halted its attempts to purge Christianity. Although the government had little love for religion, it was at least able to tolerate it. As one Angolan church leader stated, "Because of the ongoing war, the government cannot afford to persecute the church now as it could have done. The picture may be different once the war is over." However, it would not grant permits for new church buildings to be constructed and it did not want missionaries evangelizing among the unreached peoples.

In December 1979, Rodolphe Bréchet finally retired after more than 30 years at Kalukembe Hospital. As Rodolphe returned to Europe, Bob ascended to the position of medical director at the hospital, leaving them now with only three physicians. Fortunately, there were some medical students who would come through Kalukembe Hospital on short-term missions to help assist the staff. Among these were Paul and Susan Cole, Paul was an MK who was raised in Angola and could speak Mbundu, making him quite helpful.

Another bright spot came in the nearby town of Lubango, where the AEF mission headquarters had been seized by the government in 1975. In

March 1980, the government returned the keys of the building to AEF. Darrell and Barb Hockersmith were back in Angola and they took charge of the headquarters while continuing work on their next missionary venture—a seminary in Lubango in partnership with the Alliance of Evangelicals in Africa (AEA) and utilizing fellow missionaries from AEF, FELM (Finnish Evangelical Lutheran Mission) and SAM (Schweitz Alianz Mission). This seminary would finally open in 1981 as ISTEL (*Instituto Superior de Teologia Evangélica do Lubango*), with a vision to "prepare or train and equip servant leaders who live and teach sound doctrine, who promote unity in diversity, and who provide or stimulate holistic transformation in their communities."

However, other missionaries continued to leave Angola and soon Kassua lost its doctor. Kalukembe Hospital agreed to loan its physicians, each serving 3 days per month at Kassua. When Steve would take his turn serving in Kassua, Peggy found it quite to her liking; instead of running an entire household, she was treated as a guest, which calmed her nerves. All the same, Kassua lay much closer to the lines where UNITA guerrillas were operating than Kalukembe. Steve and Peggy knew danger lay nearby, but most of the time the only evidence of the ongoing civil war were those patients who came to Kalukembe suffering from combat wounds.

Peggy was now pregnant with their third child and Bob opted to deliver the baby just as he had done for his own offspring. It felt somewhat awkward to Peggy, especially as she hadn't had any prenatal visits with her father-in-law prior to the birth. Betty Dauwalder served as nurse for the delivery and as Peggy spent most of a day in labour, so the two spent quite a bit of time in each other's company. Peggy had thought of Betty as being very dour and the memory of being burned by hot peppers wasn't a pleasant one, but in the course of their time together they developed a better bond and finally became friends. Peggy learned how Betty had a particular place in her heart for babies from premature births; Betty eventually adopted a premature girl as her daughter. Ultimately on April 14, 1980, Bob performed a home delivery at Bicoque, delivering the 9-pound Rachel Frances Foster.

At four years old, Rebecca was old enough to appreciate her Rachel, but unfortunately she was also jealous of her newest sibling and would "blank" on Rachel, refusing at first to acknowledge her existence. Rebecca and Heather were both very keen on exploring the land around Kalukembe and required some looking after, more than Peggy could manage with Rachel to tend to, but virtually every adult in Kalukembe kept an eye on them. It was like having "a thousand babysitters," Peggy recalled, because her children "were so conspicuous."

Around June 1980, while Stuart was visiting Steve and Peggy, Steve attempted to visit Sierra de Neve ('Mountain of Snow'), an inactive volcano where the Ovakuando tribe lived—a people who had yet to hear the Gospel message. "This mountain and its people have had a long reputation as being the source of powerful sorceries. Soldiers over the years are known to have attempted the climb to procure so-called bulletproofing potions," Steve recounted. Steve hoped to ascend the volcano and meet the tribe, but the local administrator refused for the moment.

EZEKIEL FABIANO

One of the most notable families in Kalukembe was the Fabianos. Like the Fosters, the Fabianos consisted of seven siblings. Since the war began, the Fabiano siblings had been cut off from their parents, who were behind the lines of the conflict. However, the Bréchet family had been very welcoming to them, even sending some of them to Switzerland to further their education. Ambrosio Fabiano trained in theology while his sister Ermelinda Fabiano served as a secretary in the nursing school. Early in 1980, Ezekiel Fabiano returned from training in Switzerland to accept the post of assistant administrator at Kalukembe Hospital. Ezekiel was a very quiet man, but *simpatico* (pleasant) and loved by all. He had a gentle sense of humour and enjoyed a good game of checkers. Ezekiel lived in an annex behind Jean-Pierre and Marie-Claude's home.

Sheila began to befriend Ezekiel. Although he could not speak English, her Portuguese and Mbundu was sufficient and the two began spending more and more time together. They took long walks in the evening when people wouldn't notice them. They weren't ashamed to be known as friends, but wanted to avoid becoming the subject of gossip. As their friendship deepened, Sheila became impressed by the strength of Ezekiel's faith and devotion to Christ. "He had a gift of discernment," Sheila said. "He could be with you for 5 or 10 minutes and be able to figure out what your issues were." Finally one evening, Ezekiel became forward: would Sheila consent to marrying him? Ezekiel knew he would upset his relatives, especially his nearby uncle, by marrying outside of the Ovimbundu, but he loved her and was certain he could convince his family to accept her.

Sheila needed time to think. Immediately she thought of her older sister and wrote a letter to Sharon asking for advice. She gave the letter to her mother to be mailed and Belva innocently opened it; she was preparing her own letter to Sharon and wanted to avoid repeating anything Sheila might have written, as their supplies of paper were precious. Shocked, Belva discovered her daughter's relationship with Ezekiel in the pages of the letter.

Belva informed Bob, who grew incensed. In the heat of the moment, he assumed Ezekiel was simply seeking to obtain citizenship from Sheila. After a long conversation and prayers, Bob and Belva decided they wouldn't tell Sheila what they had learned, but asked one of the local pastors to speak with Ezekiel and tell him to "lay off the doctor's daughter." When the pastor spoke to Ezekiel, however, he was told the two were "just friends." Sheila had not made any firm decision about pursuing romance with Ezekiel and they each had concerns of how their own culture would accept the other. When Sharon's response to Sheila's letter arrived, Sharon advised Sheila to give the relationship more time and not to make a decision until after her upcoming furlough in 1981. Eventually, Sheila and Ezekiel decided to take a two-year break before revisiting the question, to see if the relationship would hold.

FATHERS' FAREWELLS

During this time, Bob Foster's name had been put forward for the post of International Director of AEF, which would require moving to the international offices in England. Bob was not interested in holding the position as he preferred his hands-on ministry as a missionary doctor. However, while performing his devotions one day he felt a nudge from God: "Bob, do you know why you're not willing to do this?" he heard. The voice continued: "Bob, you think more of medicine than you do of me." Convicted, to test the results he informed AEF he would not accept the position unless two-thirds of the voters voted for him. The results came in almost at two-thirds, so Bob took that as a fulfillment of the sign. Accepting the position, Bob left Kalukembe, leaving only Steve and Jean-Pierre as full-time staff physicians, with Jean-Pierre the new medical director. Bob, Belva, Stirling and Shelley resettled in Reading, a town in the south of England near Bristol.

In the fall of 1980, Steve and Peggy went on furlough for a few months, visiting supporters in Ontario, Illinois, North Carolina and Manitoba, as well as introducing Rachel to the Parkins family. Tragically, while in Ontario, Peggy's father Sid suffered a stroke on New Year's Eve. Steve assisted his father-in-law as they took him to a hospital, but Sid's stroke had weakened his right arm and robbed him of his ability to speak. Peggy knew it would be years until their next furlough and Steve did not mince words: he told her this would almost certainly be the last time she saw her father alive. Peggy's other siblings rallied around her parents at this time, but Peggy was on her way back to Angola. It was one of her most difficult farewells.

As Steve assumed more responsibilities at Kalukembe, some of his deficits began to emerge. Steve's tendency toward being an extra-extrovert worked against him in the hospital, due to his personality being so strong, he needed only to ponder an idea aloud to discover people thought he was delivering orders! Like his father, Steve was deeply empathetic toward his patients, but he struggled at the interpersonal dynamics of being part of a medical staff, especially when corrective discipline was involved.

In April 1981, the mission clinic sponsored by the UIEA church at Rio de Huíla reopened after an absence. The clinic had been previously run by William and Regina Brandle and Steve was now committed to visiting them every second month. At the reopening ceremony, Steve and the other staff were surprised when an elderly man rose to his feet and gave an unsolicited testimonial; he said that "Mr. Brandelley" had "told them of a God who loved them, but they had not been sure. Then came the Marxists who have told them since '75 that, after all, there was no God. But now he wants to let everyone know that indeed there is a God as He has sent another doctor and reopened the work."

Steve also ventured north with Darrell Hockersmith to again visit Cavango, this time escorted by the military because the roads remained dangerous. Some 500 people welcomed Steve at Cavango, among them 53 of the lepers he had met in 1975. Steve felt "greeted as the long-lost son come home." Seeing the great needs Cavango still had, "to leave behind needy patients without even a nurse to care for them tore at my heartstrings." Sadly, five days after Steve and Darrell's visit, guerrillas attacked Cavango and killed six people.

On May 26, 1981, Sidney Parkins died peacefully in Toronto. It took most of a week for the news to reach Kalukembe, where Steve had the sad duty of informing his wife. Peggy was pregnant yet again; to assist her in the household, she took on a helper named Conceição (nicknamed 'São'), an Angolan woman. São served principally as the family's cook and would become virtually part of the family, dubbed "Mana São" by the children. São cooked all of the family meals on a simple wood stove.

All around Kalukembe, the civil war raged on, coming within up to 12 kilometres of the mission grounds—but the guerillas still respected the work being done at Kalukembe and recognized the missionaries as impartial to the conflict. While some missionaries continued to exit amidst the many hardships in Angola, Steve wondered, "How can we who say we trust in God evacuate when the 'infidel' goes about his daily pursuits?" he admitted, "There are some who feel that it is too much to ask of new missionaries to come out now, and others who feel that our task is to [fulfill] the Great Commission and face the fact that the call of Christ to serve is always hard and fraught with danger—we should expect the privilege of suffering for His sake. As you can imagine I'm in the latter camp but we all need to be able to see together what God's purpose for this time is."

Still, as the number of injuries surged, Steve and Jean-Pierre struggled to maintain the hospital. Even with the expanded responsibilities granted to the nurses to ease the workload on the physicians, Steve's waiting list for consultas became backed up by two whole months!

STEVE'S SON

On September 16, 1981, Peggy gave birth to their fourth and final child, this time with Jean-Pierre and Betty Dauwalder at her side. The labour was shorter and easier than her three previous births, even without the benefit of epidurals. "Um rapaz, Peggy!" Betty exclaimed, meaning, "a boy!" Betty had admired both Bob and Steve Foster and was excited to know there would be a grandson with the Foster name. At first, Steve seemed very calm at the news, no more excited by the birth of his 8-pound son than any of the three girls; then he scooped up the newborn without a blanket or hat and went around the village, proudly introducing people to his son.

Steve had mellowed on the matter of his son's name. Peggy simply couldn't accept a son named "Charles," having little love for the nickname "Charlie." Instead, their son took three family names and was christened Robert Charles Sidney Foster after Bob and Charles Foster and Sidney Parkins. Although the people of Kalukembe were indeed happy "Doutor Estêvão" had a son, they were puzzled that, despite having had four children, Peggy was so thin—in fact, "too thin" was their opinion.

THE FIERY FREEZER

Among the materials Steve inherited from his parents when they left for England was a kerosene-powered freezer, which they kept in a room at Bicoque that served as Steve's office and Rebecca's schoolroom. Steve had worked with such equipment at various times growing up in Africa and although they were tricky to light correctly, he had enough experience to get the task done. To keep his supply of kerosene topped up, he ventured into Lubango to refill his jerrycan. He was quite proud of himself that when the gas station owner opened up his pump, he was the very first customer in line and filled the can. Just two weeks after Rob's birth, Steve was heading out to serve at a clinic in Benguela and Peggy asked him to refill the freezer before he left.

It was 10:30 PM when Steve poured his kerosene into the filter. The filter normally took some time to clear, but this time the liquid was flowing in very quickly, which seemed odd; the pungent odour from the jerrycan also struck Steve as strange. "Man, it smells like gasoline," Steve thought to himself. A little bit of the liquid spilled and ran down the back of the freezer. He filled the tank, lit the freezer, and then exited out of the office into the courtyard where his car was parked. He had just enough time to set down his jerrycan— when he heard the *whoosh* of a volatile ignition! Where the liquid had spilled down the back of the freezer, there was a trail of flame!

"Those first few moments were pandemonium." Steve had no fire extinguisher to combat the blaze. Fortunately, there was a space behind the freezer for ventilation and although the flame had travelled up the wall, it could not burn through the ceiling, thanks to the asbestos cement used in construction. Possessing the kind of adrenaline-fuelled strength people find in a crisis, Steve grabbed his metal filing cabinet and dragged it to the courtyard single-handed—giving himself terrible burns on his hands. He cried out for help, asking someone to bring a garden hose. But the perfect tool for putting out the fire was directly in front of him: the recently filled sandbox they had built for the children. Sand hurled from the sandbox smothered the flames. The formerly asleep children were brought to a neighbour's house while the blaze was fought. "When we went through the ruins the following morning," Steve noted, "I found my watch under a pile of sand and cinders completely intact and still working. We lost very little in it all apart from the actual freezer. My spare gastroscope was in one corner of the office and the fibreglass-plastic carrying case melted—but the actual scope survived unscathed, much to my relief."

As Steve continued his planned trip to Benguela, he prayed with his family before departure. Heather was flummoxed when she held her father's hand and discovered the bandages he was wearing over his burns. "In my mind, daddies weren't capable of being hurt." Steve's bandaged hands were not fit for surgery but he performed his consults. A month later Steve returned to Lubango and visited the gas station owner. As Steve informed the man what had happened, the serviceman's eyes sparkled with realization. "You were the first client," he recalled. It seems the pump which the man had used to deliver kerosene had previously been used to pump gasoline and there had been residual gasoline remaining in his hose, which had filled most of Steve's jerrycan!

During their last furlough, Steve and Peggy had put out a call for blanket donations which their supporters met. By October, the government finally released 75 of the crates. "Less than 5 crates were significantly pilfered from," Steve noted with gratitude. The initial cost of the freight for shipping the blankets had been quoted as $5,000; Steve and Peggy's supporters went above and beyond, raising $11,000—only for the actual amount to come out as $19,000! "I believe God is only testing us to believe that He alone is capable of meeting this need," Steve said with confidence. "I share this with you believing you will pray about it and not feel intimidated by my sharing this financial aspect of our adventure in proving God's faithfulness. For I can only see God's provident hand in sending the blankets so that they arrive in hand during this crisis time." To be sure, his supporters raised more than half of the outstanding balance within months and soon the full bill was paid. The blankets were distributed to leprosy and tuberculosis patients, refugees and displaced persons. "I cannot describe the impact of what this kind of tangible aid has upon folks," Steve thanked his supporters. "The joy and light that floods into faces when they've received a blanket makes all the hassles worthwhile."

Other great helps to Kalukembe Hospital were the donations of bandages, sutures and needles from North American institutions—most hospitals discarded the unused implements after opening a sterile package as, although perfectly good medical equipment, they were no longer sterile; Kalukembe Hospital gratefully accepted the surplus supplies, then resterilized them for use in its facility.

Among the friends the Fosters were making at Kalukembe were Avelino and Ludia Sayango. Avelino had served in Portugal's army prior to the civil war until a landmine injury in 1971 crippled him. The army supplied Avelino with a quality prosthetic leg and he became an administrator at Kalukembe Hospital, eventually an administrator within the IESA church as well. Avelino developed a reputation as a "missionary psychologist," for although he had no training in therapy, he was willing to listen and counsel the many missionaries serving at Kalukembe, particularly the single missionaries who had no spouses to whom to express their difficulties. In time, Avelino and Ludia's son Gil would become very precious to the Fosters.

In December 1981, Steve drove to Cavango in an 8-ton truck carrying 1.5 tons of blankets, 1,000 kilograms of salt and 2,500 kilograms of cornmeal flour. While he distributed the goods to the people of Cavango, Steve was shown an anti-truck mine which had emerged from concealment on the road only 2 kilometres from the mission entrance. It was the first time Steve had seen one of these deadly instruments. Some Cavango patients suffering from ulcers on their feet were brought back to Kalukembe with Steve for treatment, but he only had 12 hours of clinical work at Cavango, and that was a six-day trip! Steve began to see the need for an airplane in that area. On his way back to Kalukembe, Steve stopped in Chinhama where a new church had been opened, much to his joy.

After their 1981 Christmas service at Kalukembe, Steve and Peggy were amazed to find that hail had fallen, coating the ground like snow! Taking Rebecca and Heather into Bicoque's courtyard, they made snowballs from the hail and played outdoors with the children.

In January 1982, Steve's old friend Chuck Stephens came to Kalukembe to begin establishing himself as a building/project coordinator. By the end of the year Chuck and his wife Heather would formally begin their mission work, bringing their three children with them. At the same time, new physicians began to supplement Steve and Jean-Pierre's work, including Dr. Andreas Rohner and Dr. Cosima Chappuis. But across the Atlantic, tragedy was looming.

In Jamaica, Rob Arscott had developed cancer and the family rallied around him and Sharon, with Bob, Belva and Sheila journeying to Jamaica to support the family. "It meant so much to Rob that Dad would come to see us," Sharon stated. "Rob saw that tender side of Dad that he'd not seen before. I think he always thought of Dad as being very disciplined, able to cope in almost any situation." Rob finally succumbed to his illness on March 8; his daughter Tonya was only 6 and son Timothy aged 4. As Bob and Belva were still stationed in England, they urged Sharon, Tonya and Timothy to come back with them. "I knew I needed their love and support after he died," Sharon said, and agreed; she was amazed at her parents' willingness to let her family live with them after so many decades raising their children. Sharon wrote Steve a long letter describing all the details of Rob's final moments and sent it to Kalukembe. Rebecca and Heather barely knew their Uncle Rob but from the solemn way Steve and Peggy read the letter aloud at the dinner table, they sensed the weight of the moment.

In May, Steve and Peggy moved out of Bicoque and into a new home built for them in Kalukembe, a house which would remain theirs for the rest of their time at that mission station. Much like his father, Steve had drawn up plans showing what he wanted. This home boasted a large living room, four bedrooms, a large dining room, a pantry and a kitchen with a wood-burning stove. The floor was designed to be waterproof and ant-proof with plastic sheeting underneath the concrete. The family's home in Kalukembe would become the scene of many precious memories.

They hired another new housekeeper to join São: her name was Joaquina. Joaquina was hired primarily to help take care of young Rob and Rachel so Peggy could home school Rebecca and Heather. However, Joaquina was so efficient at tending to the children Peggy assigned her cleaning duties in the house to keep her feeling useful. Joaquina would finish her duties before dinner each day, her final act: bathing the children. The children much preferred Joaquina's hands to those of their father, who would bathe the children on Sunday nights—not knowing his own strength, he would scrub their hair so hard it hurt.

One night Rebecca awoke in the new room she shared with Heather and, "just knew" there was a large grasshopper on her leg. She asked Heather for help. Heather knew there was no grasshopper and that her sister had imagined it, but rather than argue she pretended she was capturing the grasshopper, first swatting at Rebecca's leg, then "catching it" and "releasing it." In retrospect, Rebecca marvelled at her little sister's gracious treatment. "She convinced me completely that the grasshopper was no longer on my leg and I was safe." It was an early sign of Heather's natural skill as a caregiver.

The mission hospitals gained a significant clinic thanks to the appointment of the nurses Afonso Daniel and his wife Carla to Caitovo. Although new mission stations had not been allowed by the national government, the local administrator had been aided by Kalukembe Hospital so often he consented to converting an abandoned tobacco farmhouse into a clinic. Afonso was one of the best and brightest amongst the nurses and had just returned from studying tropical medicine in London, during which he had learned English and studied in Addis Ababa, Ethiopia with ALERT (All African Leprosy Training and Rehabilitation Centre). The clinic at Caitovo was designed to cater specifically to lepers (20 beds) and tuberculosis patients (35 beds). Afonso was also deeply committed to sharing his faith among the unreached people of Angola and saw his work amongst lepers as a holy mission from God. "They have given of themselves unstintingly in this very difficult area where there had never existed a witness for Christ," said Steve of Afonso and Carla.

During the summer of 1982, Ken Foster, son of Bob's brother, the late Herbert Foster, came to Kalukembe Hospital. Like his cousin Steve, he had entered into medicine and at that point he was going into his final year at the University of Western Ontario. Ken spent 4 months at Kalukembe Hospital as his elective, gaining significant experience as he assisted on 500 operations! Ken got along well with his cousin's children, taking time to play with Rebecca and Heather.

A solar hot-water project also began that summer thanks to the Maranatha Foundation, Compassion of Canada, the Alberta Heritage Fund, the government of Canada and the Canadian International Development Agency (CIDA) through engineers Roy Barker and Garth Boak. The solar-energy collector the two engineers set up would help to heat water used in the operating room and in the recovery room's laundry room.

While they were in Angola, Roy and Garth got to sense some of the violence from the civil war. One evening around 10 PM there was a loud explosion from the village which shook the ground all the way down to the mission station! When Steve went to check on Roy and Garth, he found the two men hiding under their beds. They learned UNITA rebels had broken into a warehouse just a few yards from the mission station and blown the doors off the building using explosives. The unfortunate warehouse owner saw his entire food stocks cleaned out overnight.

One of Steve's all-time most unusual cases started out casually; a woman in her late 30s appeared at Steve's afternoon consult and claimed she had been pregnant for 9 years! She said her baby had stopped moving some time ago, but was vague about the details. Steve laughed and adopted a patronizing attitude. "We doctors know so much better," he assured her. "What's really happening inside your tummy is that you don't have a baby at all, this is all tumours that have grown in your uterus since your 20s."

One week later Steve had the woman in the operating theatre and opened up her belly; to his surprise, the uterus was completely normal. The location where he expected to find a tumour was, to his utter amazement, the site of a full-term calcified baby. The baby had died some nine years earlier and her body had slowly calcified it into a 3.5-kilogram statue. Steve likened it to "a Michelangelo statue in brown marble." The umbilical cord and placenta were likewise calcified and it was "amazing" that she had survived for nine years without any additional complications. Hers was a 1-in-100,000 case where a baby grows in the abdominal cavity instead of the uterus; the baby had only been protected by an amniotic sac rather than the uterine wall. Such unusual cases are all the more complicated in Angola, where access to quality medical resources is such a challenge. The woman made a full recovery after the operation and, with her family, buried the calcified remains of her baby.

In October, Steve and Darrell were preparing for another trip to Cavango, but in Katchiungo they met Adriano Gonçalves, who had been a nurse in Chinhama. Adriano informed them that guerrillas had attacked the town and massacred 297 people. The new church which had so impressed Steve had been burned down and the Bibles and hymn books destroyed—along with Adriano's home. Steve and Darrell were all the more eager to see Cavango, but now the military was skittish about entering that territory.

At the end of the year, Bob and Belva visited Kalukembe to hold a spiritual retreat for the missionary staff. Steve reflected on the challenges they had faced in 1982 and mused, "We accept that by human criteria, we should never have come here, but we didn't come here on human impulse. Thus, we have been encouraged in our faith and resolve to serve our Lord while we have strength and being."

While Bob and Belva were back in Kalukembe, Bob checked up on Ezekiel and Sheila, knowing nothing about the two-year break they had taken. Ezekiel had been back in Switzerland for training and corresponded with Sheila during that time. Through their letters, they both continued to feel drawn to each other, but little had changed. Sheila knew her father would have a difficult time accepting Ezekiel, and Ezekiel's uncle, as senior family member, tried to talk his nephew out of it. "We have another lady for you," he told Ezekiel.

Although Ezekiel's siblings worried their brother would be sacrificing their culture by marrying outside the tribe, they were not opposed to the relationship. Ezekiel had to admit he knew very little about the North American culture Sheila's family came from—the only parts of the western world he had seen were in Europe. "I know Portuguese, Swiss and French but not enough English to know her culture," he mused.

Steve and Peggy learned of Ezekiel and Sheila's relationship and Peggy lent her sister-in-law a sympathetic ear. Sheila, though, knew the one member of her family whom she most needed to convince was her father. While Bob and Belva were in Kalukembe, she took advantage of the situation and brought it up in conversation. She was unprepared for how close-minded her father was. He told her that her sense of isolation and growing older were responsible for her feelings and that if she transferred to a different mission field she would get over Ezekiel. For the first time in her life, Sheila became angry with her father. "What did you expect?" she wondered. "You raised us in Central Africa. We've grown up here and these are our roots—these are the people we've come to love; for whom we've worked all our lives. It would be natural to consider joining forces, wouldn't it?"

Steve summed up his father's perspective: "It was a sense of fatherly concern that his daughter might wake up and find out that confronting the realities of the stresses and strains of a black-white, Angolan-North American marriage was a more bitter pill than she thought. He was also concerned about who was going to carry the burden financially." Although Bob remained unmoved, Belva began to see Sheila's perspective.

On New Year's Eve 1982, a reveller in Lubango fired a gun into the air; unluckily, one of the bullets came down on the head of the provincial governor's chauffeur! Although Lubango had its own government-run hospital, the governor insisted on transporting his chauffeur down the 200 kilometre dangerous roads to Kalukembe because he had heard of Steve Foster's expertise. The newly arrived AEF missionary Rev. Paul Allen was stunned to hear Steve would be performing brain surgery to remove the bullet. He reminded Steve he wasn't a brain surgeon, but Steve sagely noted, "I'm the best they've got." When Paul followed up later, curious to hear if the chauffeur pulled through, Steve affirmed the operation was a success, but, "he won't be the first Angolan on the moon!"

Soon after, little Rob succumbed to a fever which lasted for four days. The reason for the fever was elusive—Steve first assumed it was malaria, as one normally expected from an African malady, but it was not so in this instance. The fever nearly killed Rob, but the Kalukembe community prayed fervently for his healing. Finally, the fever broke. Peggy placed Rob in his highchair for breakfast that morning. Going to the washroom, Peggy was arrested by a thought in her head, one that could only have come from God: "Rob has polio."

CHAPTER 9

"Thank You That You Are in All of This." — Peggy Foster

KALUKEMBE (January 1983 – December 1985)

Peggy returned to the highchair and took Rob out. He had been able to walk before and she needed to test what God had told her. As soon as she set him on the floor, his right leg crumpled beneath him. She carried Rob to Steve and asked him to examine their son—not sharing her insight. He quickly surmised, "It looks like he has polio." They summoned the pastors and elders of the church to lay their hands on Rob.

The polio vaccine which Rob had been receiving was delivered in a series of three doses. Sheila had retrieved the first two vaccines from Lubango, but when she went to collect the third, she learned they were out of stock— and remained out of stock for a year. "We had run out of vaccines before," Steve noted, "but we never realized how significant this one would be." Reeling from the diagnosis, Peggy went to see Miriam, a nurse friend of hers. When Miriam saw Peggy's face she knew she was distraught. In tears, Peggy told her what had happened to Rob.

Miriam prayed with her and Peggy was reminded of her most recent Bible study where she had been learning to give thanks to God in all things. And so she prayed: "Thank you that you are in all of this." At once, the burden she was carrying was taken away. "In the shock and fears I was able to affirm my love for Him and trust in His all-knowing."

After two weeks of forcing Rob to walk on his bad leg he regained strength and could move on his own again. "We can only say thank you to our Lord and to you all who have prayed," Steve offered up in gratitude. Still, the damage polio had wrought upon Rob would remain with him going forward. When news of Rob's diagnosis reached Canada, Fran Parkins grieved. To her it seemed "like Stephen was taking better care of Angolans than his own son,"

Richard Parkins recalled. Steve knew from his own family history of the death of his uncle Herbert in the field and of the tragedies of his Uncle Edgar and Aunt Mabel. "The lens you look through is what have others gone through?" he pondered. "What have others faced? It didn't seem too much and in the sense of [the] faithfulness of God, despite these issues I felt we might well have much more to gain than we had to lose." Decades later, Rob himself would affirm his father's hopes.

Despite the destruction at Chinhama, Steve, Darrell and Pastor José Abias tried to undertake a visit to Cavango in May 1983, but were informed that on that very week Cavango had been attacked by UNITA and destroyed. This time the guerrillas had been most methodical; not wanting to leave Cavango as a place the Cuban or MPLA armies could use for barracks, the guerrillas, acting on orders from Savimbi himself, forced the villagers to tear down their own buildings brick by brick. From the missionary houses to the church and hospital, not one structure was left standing.

Despite this destruction, at least one happy memory of Cavango was rekindled unexpectedly. While visiting Barb Hockersmith in Lubango, Steve and Barb were stopped in the street by a man who screeched his car to a halt and leaped out to greet them. "Do you remember me?" the mestiço driver asked. "I've been a prisoner of war since 1976!" Then he pulled up his shirt to expose an abdominal scar. Turning around, he showed off another scar on his back. It was the rabbit hunter Steve and Barb had saved in 1975! "I owe my life to you two people!" he said, grinning.

The outreach to the Ovakuando at Sierra de Neve finally went ahead thanks to the administrative efforts of the commissar of Mamue. On May 19, 1983, Steve ventured to the volcanic site alongside the commissar, Chuck Stephens, three nurses (including Afonso Daniel) and an old leper woman who had recently become a Christian. "This lady came as our guide as she was a native of the mountain and knew the trail. She was returning to gather up her idols and return with them to Catala, the leprosarium, for a public burning ceremony." After a nine-hour march and 6,000-foot climb over the rim of the volcano they meet the Ovakuando, who welcomed their guests with a great feast of kudu (antelope) steaks. Steve was especially fond of the liver, cooked over hot coals. They were amazed to discover the volcano's crater ran 20 kilometres across! 46 different villages of people dwelled upon the crater, some 500 people in total. Steve and Chuck observed the needs of the villagers and Chuck began making plans to drill a water well for them. "Lord willing, there will be Ovakuando at the return of the King of Kings," Steve prayed.

"Every day, there are services of public witness in the hospital and on the wards and in the outpatient compound or sanzala," Steve noted. "In these past years, hundreds have come to confess Christ as Saviour as direct result of evangelistic campaigns held amongst our outpatients and relatives." Steve was also impressed at how so many denominations could come together and put aside theological differences in the mission field. "It is hard to believe how difficult it is to get together until your buildings get knocked down, until your mission station is destroyed, until you go to the capital and the only accommodation is a Plymouth Brethren Guest House. Then, over a meal you discover that the love of Jesus is the same for all churches and the other theological differences are not so important after all. Maybe inter-church, inter-mission relationships are possible. Maybe it is even possible for a church to work with the government."

Nurse Ann Allen (Paul Allen's wife) would attend clinics alongside Steve and marvelled at his abilities. "This man is a wizard!" she would tell her husband. Without the benefit of "any diagnostic tools other than himself," she would see him accurately diagnose patients and perform surgeries under difficult situations, yet achieve many successes.

Paul laughed when he would see the gifts Angolans brought to the Fosters' doorstep, including rare commodities such as sugar. Paul wondered why he seldom saw gifts. "I'm here to tell them the eternal truth of God's word!" Paul noted, "But Steve Foster could save your child's life." Although Steve and Peggy received many generous gifts, they never hesitated to share them with the people of Kalukembe.

Johanna Kessler, a Swiss missionary who frequently drove between Kalukembe and Lubango in her grey Peugeot 404 pickup truck, brought many of the supplies which fed the people of Kalukembe and outfitted the hospital. "She reminded me of a sergeant major," Steve recalled, noting she had a remarkable ability for obtaining whatever was needed: soap, rice, flour, vegetable oil, beans and sugar.

One day in June, Johanna was attacked by UNITA guerrillas while driving her truck about 6 kilometres from Kalukembe. The burst of gunfire was brief and only 14 bullets struck the vehicle, but one of them went through the driver's door and hit Johanna in her calf. The bullets also hit a bottle of butane gas and a jerrycan of diesel fuel, but unlike a Hollywood movie, there was no explosion. Still in control of the vehicle, Johanna sped on to the hospital for treatment. As word of Johanna's injury spread through the village, word went back to UNITA. The recovering Johanna was subsequently contacted by a UNITA affiliate who told her it had all been a mistake; the ambush was meant for the local administrator, who also drove a grey Peugeot 404 pickup. As soon as she was able, Johanna returned to work.

"I personally feel privileged to work and share in an environment where colleagues of mine are prepared to lay down their lives for the opportunity to share Christ and make Him known," Steve said. "God alone knows our day and hour and He alone can protect us in our work of proclaiming the Good News in the face of the man-made horrors of Angola today."

It was only much later that Steve and the other missionaries would learn exactly why Kalukembe had received so much understanding from the UNITA guerrillas. The IESA church's Pastor Eliseu had gone to high school in Dondi with Jonas Savimbi and, at that time, was secretly a member of Savimbi's inner circle. From time to time, Pastor Eliseu would be picked up in a helicopter at night and flown to secret meetings with Savimbi. Pastor Eliseu was an imposing man, blunt in reminding the missionaries "the church is the dog and the hospital is the tail; the tail must not wag the dog." When he offered counsel to the missionaries at Kalukembe, informing them to adjust their calendar, the missionaries simply assumed it was "local wisdom," never suspecting their friend had Savimbi's ear. More than once, Pastor Eliseu would advise missionaries to cancel a trip down a certain road; on the day of the planned trip, there would be reports of guerrilla action on that road. In retrospect, it was a good thing the missionaries never knew of his connections—they had no secrets to conceal.

RECONCILIATION THROUGH WISDOM

As the Fosters planned for a large family reunion in Wales at the end of June, Bob went to the US to see his parents, whose health had begun to seriously decline. During his visit, June Foster passed away peacefully at age 90. At the end of June, Steve, Peggy and their four children began a lengthy furlough, targeting nine months away so Rebecca and Heather could enjoy a full semester of public school in Canada. Dr. Steve Duncan came to Kalukembe Hospital to cover during Steve's absence and Steve used his time away to take refresher courses in both medicine and Bible College. The furlough began with the Foster family reunion in Wales.

Ezekiel was still in Switzerland at the time and Sheila asked her parents if he could come to Wales. Bob refused. "I spent a lot of time crying and praying," Sheila recalled. "By this time, I was sure we should be married. Ezekiel had been in Switzerland for almost two years and our relationship had maintained itself." Bob remained firmly against inviting Ezekiel, but gradually, Belva convinced him he had not taken the time to get to know Ezekiel better. Only one day before Sheila's departure to Wales, Bob invited Ezekiel to join the family gathering.

All told, eighteen Fosters met at the family reunion: Bob, Belva, Steve, Peggy, as well as their children Rebecca, Heather, Rachel, and Rob; Sharon with her children Tonya and Timothy; Sheila, Stacey, Stuart and his wife Sindia, Stirling and Shelley. Stuart had met Sindia Patterson at Park Street Church, a congregational church in Boston while he studied history and literature of England at Harvard College and she studied journalism at Boston University. Although little more than the Charles River separates Harvard College from Boston University, students from the two schools did not often meet. Sindia had lived overseas as a child. Her overseas upbringing helped her relate to Stuart's African childhood. They fell in love and married two years later. They planned their wedding so that that when Bob and Belva came to Boston for Stuart's graduation on a Thursday, they could be there for the wedding on Saturday.

Scattered by their various commitments around the world, the Fosters enjoyed one another's company in what was a very warm and refreshing gathering. The one hiccup was the presence of Ezekiel; Bob's children were aware of the unhappy situation between Bob and Sheila. Even Rebecca was keen to the problem and knew it was centred about Ezekiel's race.

Lest his presence cast a pall over the happy time, Ezekiel decided he should speak with Bob sooner rather than later. Ezekiel and Sheila sat down with Bob and did their best to persuade him that their feelings for each other were genuine. However, Bob resisted their appeals; his mind was made up. Bob told them he did not approve of their relationship, would not support their union and that their cultural differences were, in his opinion, too great; he also believed Angola was too dangerous and doubted whether Ezekiel could provide for Sheila's future. The meeting did nothing to stir his heart.

Each evening of the reunion, the family would meet together for devotions, led by one of the men in the family. One evening, Bob read from 1 Kings 3:5-15. The passages recount the time in which God offered Solomon whatever he asked for; Solomon asked for wisdom and God replied: "Since you have asked for this and not for long life or wealth for yourself, nor have asked for the death of your enemies but for discernment in administering justice, I will do what you have asked. I will give you a wise and discerning heart…"

In teaching this passage, Bob felt God stirring him to communicate a message to his family about their common work in missions. Solomon had not asked for financial or personal security, nor protection from danger—he asked simply for wisdom, above all else. Bob believed his missions and those his children were performing or about to participate in, should do likewise—pray to God for wisdom. As he spoke, Sheila realized her father had been arguing against this idea when he opposed her and Ezekiel—all of his arguments boiled down to worries about finances and security.

She had anticipated where Bob was going with this teaching. He then turned to address Sheila and Ezekiel and told them God had spoken to him through this passage to show that he should give them his blessing on their marriage. Through tears and hugs, Sheila and Bob reconciled their differences and the Fosters welcomed Ezekiel into their family. Sheila was moved to tears not only by her father's blessing but because the division which had sprung up between them had been overcome. They had always been close and Sheila knew it was not pride or prejudice that motivated his earlier arguments, but his love for her which had made it so hard for him to come around. "Dad was willing to learn and grow," Sheila observed. "God gave him a vision of what he was supposed to do...a lot of people tried to dissuade him...but for the things he was really sure he was supposed to do he went ahead and did them. But he also had a capacity to listen to the Lord."

While in Wales, Stirling invited Steve and Peggy to visit an estate where he was serving in a summer job as groundskeeper for a Christian family. There was a swimming pool on the estate grounds and the Foster children were excited, never having seen a pool like it before. While Steve and Peggy were talking to the estate's owners, Rachel got too close to the edge and jumped into the water. She couldn't swim and started to go under. Seeing her in jeopardy, Stirling jumped in, fully clothed, and saved his niece; her head had barely gone underwater before Stirling caught her and brought her to shore. Little wonder he became Rachel's favourite uncle!

Arriving in Canada for furlough, Steve and Peggy settled in at Bramalea, a neighbourhood of Brampton in Toronto's greater metropolitan area. The Bramalea Baptist Church had a home for missionaries to rent but hadn't found anyone to claim the house. Although Steve and Peggy were not associated with their church, the Baptists happily accepted them as their tenants. The house held 4 bedrooms on a split-level and came fully furnished.

That September, Heather and Rebecca began going to school. Heather had been very socially withdrawn in Kalukembe, so Steve and Peggy assumed she would struggle at school. Much to their surprise, it was Rebecca who suffered the most. Rebecca returned from her first day "with misgivings and stomach pains from adjustment fears. She wasn't used to line-ups, classroom quizzes, and the routine." Heather had a poor start to her first day when her name wasn't called at assembly, leaving her unaware which classroom to go to. After that embarrassment, however, Heather rallied and soon began supporting her older sister "to have the courage to go to the bus on some of those tough mornings."

There were other cultural matters which flummoxed the Foster girls. Rebecca was shocked when children at school would ask her if she rode on elephants or lived in a hut; she realized children in Canada knew almost nothing about Africa. There was only one black girl in Rebecca's class and Rebecca made up her mind that the two of them should be friends as all of her friends in Kalukembe were black. "I was obsessed with her," she joked. "She probably thought I was weird and creepy." The girls had to dress themselves up in bulky winter clothing, which was "odd" to children who were accustomed to warmer climates. All the same, the young girls' personalities impressed their uncle Bob Parkins by how cosmopolitan they were: "Their sense of the world was way more profound than you would normally find, even as early as 7-8 years old."

Steve had doctors examine Rob, who confirmed the diagnosis of polio and did their best to strengthen him. When the children visited the Metro Toronto Zoo, the sight of the wildlife "provoked some nostalgic cries of 'when are we going home to Kalukembe?'"

While preparing for her marriage to Ezekiel, Sheila returned to Kalukembe to resume the public health program. "It was hard to believe that the situation could have changed so dramatically in the time I had been away," she exclaimed. She learned there were now at least 100,000 refugees within the radius of Kalukembe, among them Peggy's old friend Julieta from Cavango. "It's difficult to imagine the misery, suffering and apathy without seeing the reality—people homeless, literally living under a few cut branches in the worst rainy season anyone can remember; people without food, surviving on pitifully small government handouts of 2 kilograms of beans and 2 kilograms of cornmeal per family per month; many children dying of malnutrition, diarrhea and TB, not surprisingly." Sheila turned to the International Red Cross for aid and received 3 tons of food in response, but the Red Cross couldn't remain long term; Sheila began training village health workers who could help tend to the needs of their fellow villagers.

In the midst of the suffering, Sheila found the Gospel message was being well-received. "The hard-pressed Protestant church is not being snuffed out. On the contrary, over this timespan the number of adherents has nearly doubled to more than 400,000."

Steve used his time in North America to further his education and promote the mission in Kalukembe. Paul Allen saw Steve as a "prophetic voice", calling North American Christians and medical professionals to action. There was a steadily increasing famine in Angola due to overall reduced rainfall and government restrictions on access to land for cultivation. As the couple began informing their supporters of their needs in Kalukembe, among their requests was for a schoolteacher to help look after their children's education, as Peggy realized she could not handle teaching the four children all at once. Steve toured across Canada and the US, meeting with the College of Surgeons in Calgary and with the Christian Medical and Dental Society (CMDS) in Quebec City. He also began preparing a new vehicle for use in Angola—this one with a heavy armoured plate on its undercarriage to resist landmines.

The family also held reunions, visiting Peggy's sister Mary Lou in Brooks, Alberta, and seeing the rest of the Parkins family in Ontario, as well as seeing Bob, Belva, Stuart and Stirling in Greensboro. Christmas of 1983 was spent with Shelley, Stirling, Stacey, Belva's mother Helen Mark and Helen's sister Gertrude, plus the entire Parkins family except for Mary Lou.

In January 1984, Charles Stephen Foster died at the age of 91. He had been living in a nursing home in Greensboro with nearby family members tending to him. Steve attended his grandfather's memorial service alongside Bob, Stacey, Stuart, Stirling, Shelley and Charles' daughter Rhoda. Musing on his grandfather's life as a missionary Steve said on behalf of his brothers, "I personally feel a great mantle of responsibility has been handed down to us as grandsons to continue being found faithful men of God."

From February 17-25, Steve attended the World Congress on Leprosy in Delhi, India. Among the 1,350 delegates were his old friend from his tropical medicine fellowship Dr. Jay Keystone, Drs. Paul Brand and Margaret Brand, as well as two medical officers from Angola: Dr. Lidia Vaumard from the Ministry of Health in Luanda and Afonso Daniel from Caitovo. Steve and Afonso grew close as they journeyed together in India and became the best of friends.

At the World Congress on Leprosy and in visiting Indian facilities such as the Leprosy Research and Training Centre in Karigiri, Steve and Afonso witnessed what was cutting edge in leprosy treatment. They were particularly impressed to learn how India manufactures most of their own materials to meet their patients' needs; if only they could do the same in Angola! They also met Dr. Victor Smith of ALERT and as a follow-up to the congress, went with Dr. Smith to Addis Ababa, Ethiopia, where Steve received training in reconstructive surgery for lepers. Steve also took a course in treating vesico-vaginal fistulas while in Addis Ababa.

The very day Rebecca and Heather received their certificates from their schools, Steve and Peggy returned with the children to Angola, arriving back in Kalukembe at the start of June. They brought with them a shipping container full of supplies meant to address their needs for 4 years, which meant they had to predict just how tall their children would grow in the next four years and supply outfits accordingly. Peggy Smith helped them arrange many of the articles they needed and Fran Parkins had taken charge of preparing the correspondence lessons which would educate her grandchildren in Kalukembe. Their supporters had also arranged for the printing of a 450-page hymnbook with hymns in 3 languages (English, Portuguese and Mbundu).

On her return to Kalukembe, Rebecca was dismayed to find her Portuguese had suffered during their absence and she could not quite recall the language. Sheila and Ezekiel offered to help her and drove Rebecca to Caitovo, placing her in the care of Afonso Daniel's wife Carla for three days. Rebecca felt apprehensive as she didn't know Carla very well, but by the end of those three days her Portuguese had clicked back into place and Sheila and Ezekiel brought her back to Kalukembe.

Soon after the Fosters' return the hospital was aided by Ruth and Richard Brooks. Ruth was a medical student who worked in the hospital and Richard was an electrical technologist who used his gifts to install a new generator for the hospital. The generator had been donated by Jean-Pierre's younger brother Etienne, who had become a businessman working with Caterpillar, but remained devoted to the work their father had done in establishing Kalukembe Hospital. Richard also installed the X-ray machine Bob had bought more than a decade earlier and had languished all those years, only to find some of the parts had been misfiled, leaving the machine incomplete.

Steve had been painting red crosses on Kalukembe's Land Rovers to mark them as medical vehicles, but received a complaint from the International Red Cross, which claimed ownership of the decal. For his new Chevy Suburban, Steve instead painted a white cross on a red background and marked it with the logo of the IESA church and, of course: *Ambulancia – Hospital de Caluquembe*.

Other material acquisitions for the Foster household in Kalukembe included an electric freezer to replace the wrecked kerosene-powered model, a television set and a VCR. Peggy and Trevor Smith filled up several VHS tapes with good Canadian programming for the children to enjoy, sending the family additional tapes over the years such as the television shows *Today's Special*, *The Elephant Show* and the mini-series *Anne of Green Gables*. The television shows were a treat the family would turn on for Friday nights. On Sunday nights they would watch an educational video such as an episode of *Big Blue Marble*, and sing Baptist hymns such as "Blessed Assurance." With her Anglican upbringing, Peggy wasn't familiar with Steve's favourite tunes but she followed him as best as she could.

For a surgeon, Steve was immensely available to his family, more so than he would have been in any Canadian medical facility. Although he was extremely dedicated to his patients' welfare, he also knew that if he passed people waiting in the halls outside his office he would want to stop and check on almost every person. To avoid these impromptu assessments, when it was lunch time he would often climb out the window of his office (the office windows had a very low base). Almost every day he would return home for lunch with his wife and children and because of the enforced 6 PM curfew due to the war, he would return every evening for supper. On weekday nights Steve would relax in his easy chair and comb through the most recent medical journals (usually 6 months behind the rest of the world) while Peggy read stories to the children. Peggy read books such as C. S. Lewis' *Chronicles of*

Narnia, Laura Ingalls Wilder's *Little House on the Prairie* series, J. R. R. Tolkien's *The Hobbit*, Madeleine L'Engle's *Kairos* series, and Monica Hughes' *Isis* books. Although supposedly immersed in his journals, Peggy would hear Steve chuckle from his corner of the living room from time to time as she read a funny passage aloud to the children.

That summer, Shelley Foster returned to Angola to assist Sheila in her public health program. Shelley had switched from studying nursing to becoming a doctor but she was fascinated by the work her older sister was doing and began to hope she could become involved in the program. However, Sheila informed her that if she became a doctor she would manage the program from behind a desk—only nurses could be active in the field. Although she felt the nursing program in the US had been dumbed-down, Shelley swallowed her pride; she decided to finish her biology degree, then go back to nursing school.

That same summer on August 11, 1984, Sheila Foster married Ezekiel Fabiano in a ceremony at Kalukembe, joined by Steve and Peggy's family plus Bob and Belva. Prior to the ceremony, Bob sat down with the Fabiano family to make a formal arrangement—in the event something should happen to Ezekiel, Sheila would become a Foster again—she would not be treated like property of the Fabiano clan. The relatives agreed and threw a massive wedding for Sheila and Ezekiel, with more than one thousand guests in attendance and a great wedding feast. Bob and Belva let go of any lingering apprehension after seeing how welcoming the Fabianos were and the love they lavished upon Sheila, Ezekiel and their guests.

On September 30, 1984, the FNLA finally surrendered to the MPLA. The one-time "government in exile" of Angola had never recovered from their defeat in 1975. Although the party would endure and its leader Holden Roberto was permitted to pursue a political career in Angola, its former prestige had been lost. The civil war continued, but now UNITA was the MPLA's primary adversary.

During a visit to the US, Dr. Steve Duncan had met Franklin Graham, head of the charitable organization Samaritan's Purse and the son of evangelist Billy Graham. Dr. Duncan invited Franklin to come to Angola and see his medical practice. Franklin agreed and Dr. Duncan held him to his word; with some trepidation, Franklin visited Angola in November 1984. Franklin's time in Angola gave him an interest in using Samaritan's Purse to assist the medical missions in the country, raising money for seminary housing at ISTEL, Bibles, medicines for Rio de Huíla and Menongue, and a new ambulance. Although most of Franklin's visit was spent at Dr. Duncan's work in Lubango, he briefly encountered Steve Foster; Steve made an impression on him and he wrote about him in his 1998 book *Living Beyond the Limits*: "His thick, lamb-chop sideburns bristled up when he flashed his trademark grin the size of Africa."

Unfortunately, on his way out of the country, Franklin gave a copy of his father Billy Graham's book *Angels: God's Secret Agents* to Pastor Abias. As an American, Franklin's visit brought scrutiny from the secret police and they later arrested Pastor Abias, Paul Allen and Steve Duncan, claiming Graham's book as 'evidence' that Franklin had come as a spy. Fortunately, after a brief period of house arrest, the men were all released.

In Christmas 1984 at Kalukembe, the Fosters' presents to each other were "either items purchased while on furlough and shipped via container or local handicrafts such as cowhide-covered stools or woven baskets. Peg and our household help took tremendous pains in the kitchen to turn out delicious Christmas cakes and all manner of special things." Musing on how Angolans celebrated Christmas, Steve noted, "One of the positive aspects of all this is that it is easier to spend time on the real significance of Christmas. In the end, we witnessed the Christmas play enacted by 4 different church groups on various occasions on or before Christmas itself. It is always insightful to see this event interpreted through the eyes of others. The Angolan Christian is very sensitive and able to portray very vividly the sense of how the Jews were colonized and mistreated by the Romans—probably a reflection of 500 years of experience with the Portuguese."

The end of hostilities with the FNLA meant little to Kalukembe, where the threat of UNITA was never too distant. In the previous year there had been 1,866 major surgeries and 805 minor surgeries; 200 of the cases were war-related injuries. The typical cases in the hospital involved cataracts, hysterectomies, fistula repairs, sequestrectomies for osteomyelitis, bowel resections and amputations from landmine injuries.

Steve noted 460 landmine injuries at the hospital in 1984, many of which were treated with leg amputations; the numbers were due to rise as the pervasive weapons were utilized more and more by both sides. As anti-landmine activist Paul Jefferson, who was a landmine victim, remarked, "a landmine is the perfect soldier: Ever courageous, never sleeps, never misses." UNITA and the MPLA would use landmines to defend their positions, but because their battle lines were constantly changing—and almost no one was mapping the minefield locations—the danger of civilians walking across minefields continued to grow. Even then, that was an intended consequence: "Both sides laid mines defensively to protect military positions, and both practised what's euphemistically known as 'nuisance' or 'social' mining, setting out the weapons to terrorize civilians and control their movements," said Philip C. Winslow. "Land mines, or the perception of their presence, are an extraordinarily effective way of canalizing or confining human beings who might seek shelter or help somewhere else." The USSR, US, China, South Africa, Italy, Germany, France, Sweden, and Romania—manufactured landmines planted in Angola.

"If the victims were lucky," wrote journalist Marvin Ross, "they set off the mine with the anterior portion of their foot which would only blow off the toes. If they set off the mine with the mid-point or heel, then the device was designed to shatter and accelerate bone fragments up into the leg and torso. In the old type mines, most of the damage was done by metal fragments from the mine itself. With the new plastic devices, the shrapnel damage came from the victim's own body. These mines were made of plastic and could be purchased for less than $5 each." Comparing the cost of a landmine to that of an AK-47, Steve observed darkly, "you get a big bang for your buck."

"The absolute tragedy is the five- to eight-year-old kids," Steve said passionately. "They are being condemned to a lifetime of added handicaps like curvature of the spine or the thorax because we can't supply them with crutches or elementary prosthetic appliances. In a young person when the bones are still growing and pliable, they can be deformed permanently. If a child is wounded or loses part of a limb, he will compensate by twisting himself to balance so he can move around. If this is uncorrected, permanent damage results and he becomes a twisted cripple for the rest of his life."

Compounding this was the fact the landmines would insidiously lure children by being placed under a toy. At least Steve and Jean-Pierre's treatment of lepers who were missing limbs had given the doctors experience with prostheses. However, the number of leg and arm amputees continued to rise. "We started with crude materials—nails, wood, leather and glue. From glass fibre resin we can make a pylon, 'Captain Ahab' kind of artificial leg," Steve explained. "Man's inhumanity to man just beggars the imagination out here."

Then too, the effects of the famine in Angola were leading to increasingly large swathes of famished people. The International Red Cross sent Kalukembe 100 tons of cornmeal, vegetable oil and beans with a 10-ton truck and 10-ton trailer to carry them, while the Canadian Food Grains Bank in Winnipeg sent 60 tons of corn and beans. The war and the deadly landmines planted everywhere were starving the nation's people to death. Even if a farmer had good soil and arable conditions, he was apprehensive about venturing out into his field for fear he might step on a landmine.

Another problem facing Angolans were the *rusgas* (conscriptions) organized by the MPLA which would press young men into the ranks of the army. Steve had an agreement with the Ministry of Health that none of the nurses at Kalukembe could be conscripted; in return, Kalukembe's nursing school would provide nurses for the Ministry of Health. Although the agreement usually stood, a drunken commander who cared nothing for the order showed up one day, demanding several of the male nurses join his army. Steve placed himself in the doorframe of the school, barring the officer's path.

Enraged, the officer drew his gun and fired at the ground before Steve; still, Steve refused to move. Unwilling to shoot a foreigner, the officer departed, but the incident frightened many nurses away from Kalukembe.

There were also young men in Kalukembe who tried to hide in the village from the rusgas. Among them was Costa, who befriended the Fosters and would sleep in their schoolroom at night as the rusgas frequently rounded up men directly from their beds. Rachel worried about Costa, fearing that any morning he might be gone and that her parents could be in trouble for hiding him, but the Lord kept Costa safe. One night when the rusgas were known to be about, Rachel got up for a glass of water and saw an angel in their living room, holding a sword. Stunned, Rachel turned back to her room, startled by the vision, yet overwhelmed by a sense of security.

Another remarkable patient of Steve's was an unassuming man who appeared on the grassy rotunda at Kalukembe Hospital pushing a wheelbarrow. A member of the man's family drew Steve over to him. "Part of him is inside the wheelbarrow," the family member explained. Intrigued and confused, Steve raised the apron-like garment that hung over the man. Inside the wheelbarrow was the man's scrotum—it took up the entire wheelbarrow! Steve did a double-take. "You couldn't put your arms around it," he said; it weighed more than 20 kilograms. The afflicted man had been abandoned by his wife who thought him to be demon-possessed. He had travelled quite a distance on foot to arrive at Kalukembe, but one imagines that whether he had been stopped by the government or UNITA, neither would have mistaken him for a combatant!

Steve read up on the affliction and pinpointed it as Lymphatic filariasis (popularly called elephantiasis). The operation on the man took 6 hours because in those days, without an electrocautery device, after every cut was made the incisions had to be sutured together. Two hours into the operation, the local anaesthetic wore off and they began giving the patient ketamine; delirious from the drug but still awake, the man began singing hymns and telling rhymes about his girlfriends. After surgery, the man's scrotum weighed 17 kilograms; his skin grafts took and 6 months later he was in fine shape, appearing perfectly normal.

In August 1985, Steve caught a hepatitis A infection and spent six weeks recovering. The children were excited to have their father around the house and would read him stories and make him glasses of juice while he recuperated. During the last week of his recovery, Steve took the family with him to visit his friend Afonso in Caitovo. Afonso and his wife Carla Magna, an obstetrics nurse, became beloved by the rest of the family and the children took to calling him "Uncle Afonso."

Steve was impressed by the manner in which Afonso would reach out to others. "He was full of life," Steve recalled, "full of verve and keen to share his faith, but in a very wonderful way wasn't preachy in a negative sense. He just shared common-sense stuff and every day began with some opportunity to witness." As his health improved, Steve went hunting one day with a crossbow and successfully hit a guinea fowl in a thorn tree—but the bird remained on its perch and the thorns were too thick for Steve to climb up and claim his prize. A 12-year-old Angolan boy came to the rescue and speedily climbed the tree and shook the guinea fowl loose, amazing Steve when he wasn't pricked at all by the thorns.

Steve once journeyed out to the coastal town of Namibe and joined Paul Allen at a baptismal service. The church had an unusual architectural feature with a large spiral staircase looming above the baptismal tank. As Paul prepared the baptism, Steve traipsed upstairs to view from above. The man Paul baptized had an enormous afro and when Paul dunked the man underwater, part of his hair floated above the waterline, still dry. Amused, Steve called out in English (so the Angolans wouldn't understand): "I'm going to report you to the Baptists that you're not doing full immersion!"

The four growing Foster children loved their time in Kalukembe. Although the war was nearby, they were largely unaware of it. "It was like being in a cocoon," Rebecca said. The only definite restriction Steve and Peggy laid down was that the children must never mention dos Santos, Savimbi, the MPLA or UNITA. The children would climb every tree they could find and even play down near the river (which Peggy expressly ordered them to keep away from). They built mud castles and staged mock weddings between every conceivable pair of mission kids at the station. Under the tutelage of "Mana São," Heather learned to cook and would help make bread and the cinnamon rolls which São baked for the family every Sunday morning.

Every so often Kalukembe Hospital would hold a night of games and fun for the missionaries, nurses and their families. Those nights were "magical" to Heather because they were permitted to stay up past curfew. Jean-Pierre borrowed a film projector from the nearby Catholic mission and they would project old silent Charlie Chaplin films. The nurses would perform sketches, sing songs and play games, with Betty Dauwalder always keen to play her infamous jokes on hapless victims. In one game, men would remove their shoes and lie under a sheet with only their feet exposed while their wives tried to match the shoes to their husbands' feet! It was "such an oasis of laughter and fun," Heather recalled.

But not everything in Kalukembe was a delight for the children. Some Angolan children, curious about the Fosters' white skin, would poke and pinch them, pull the girls' long hair and press their nails into the children's skin so they could watch it change colour. Rebecca's green eyes were particularly fascinating as people would gaze at her, their faces mere inches away. "Cat's eyes!" they would remark. All of this attention "felt a little hostile," to Rebecca. There was one childish taunt that some Angolan children would sing at the Fosters: "Kachindele come banana; ele burro puxa carrosa," which essentially compared white people to donkeys. Rob in particular had a quick temper and would get upset when children sang it at him.

It was all the worse for Heather, who was very emotional and sensitive. Heather's name was difficult for Portuguese-speaking people to pronounce and to most it came out as "Ede." In retrospect, Peggy wished she had given Heather a more easily pronounceable name. Heather had her own trouble pronouncing r's and had to enrol in speech therapy, which she resisted. Attempting to overcome her speech impediment, Heather adopted an unusual accent in her voice which persists to this day. Heather's worst problems were with the Swiss missionaries; due to cultural differences, they assumed Heather's social awkwardness was simply rudeness and Heather, too young to understand, would simply avoid the Swiss out of timidity—thereby increasing the Swiss' criticisms about her.

In November, as an answer to Peggy's prayers and petitions, Muriel LeBreton came to Kalukembe. Muriel was a schoolteacher from Scarborough who worshipped at Little Trinity and had heard Peggy's call for a teacher at Kalukembe. Being highly valued by her district, she was granted a 2-year unpaid sabbatical. She spent the first 2 months in Portugal learning Portuguese then came to the mission station, bringing with her plans for the children's education. Peggy was somewhat ashamed of her children's behaviour, having been repeatedly told by the Swiss missionaries that her children were poorly behaved and "wild." Muriel was aghast at that criticism. "No, Peggy," she insisted, "they're good children."

Muriel set to work creating lesson plans for the four children. "She took our kids to the stars," Peggy said. Muriel made a strong effort to connect with the Angolans; she had brought with her plastic hockey sticks and balls to teach field hockey to the children and many of the Angolan kids quickly picked up the sport. Muriel once held a 25-kilometre cross-country run for all the mission kids to participate in. Most of all, Muriel "gave us structure," Rebecca said. "She worked around our quirks—made it fun." Rob agreed: "She gave such affirmation." Rachel most enjoyed the songs Muriel would teach them to sing. Steve said she "created a real atmosphere of delight for school (with the odd grumbling days)." As she won over the Fosters, Muriel expanded her mission to teach adult education classes in English at Kalukembe. She also brought a VHS tape of the 1939 *Wizard of Oz* film which became a Foster family favourite.

That November, Bob Foster was diagnosed with lymphoma—cancer in the marrow of his bones. It was a difficult reality to accept, but Bob's doctors encouraged him to keep at his normal activities. "Go home and live a normal life," they instructed him, "do whatever you have strength for as long as you are able." Steve observed a change in his father after this: "I think he has a sharpened sense of urgency; the sense that the sands of time are running through the timer," he observed. However, the sands of time in Bob's timer were considerably deeper than they might have supposed. Over the next several months, Bob's condition stabilized. Although he remained at risk of the cancer resurfacing, he completed his term as International Director of AEF.

Steve agreed with Rebecca's assessment of Kalukembe. "In many ways, we were cocooned to some degree, sheltered by the reality of being an oasis in the midst of a country at war. Both sides needed us in this mission hospital at Kalukembe, so we were in some sense protected from direct attack, even though guerrillas would raid villages within a mile or two of where we were." Amid the upheaval, plans were being made for Christmas 1985. Afonso Daniel and other missionaries intended to celebrate part of the holidays in Kalukembe. However, a great tragedy loomed ahead.

CHAPTER 10

"Your Husband Gave His Life for Us." — Quoted to Carla Magna

KALUKEMBE (December 1985 – November 1987)

In the summer, Steve had met Margarida and Mirian Horvath, two Brazilian sisters in their 20s who had come to Angola that year to serve as Sunday school teachers in Huambo. Thinking ahead, Steve asked them what their plans were that coming Christmas. They admitted they had no plans. Steve knew the road from Huambo to Kalukembe was long and in many places unsafe, so pointed out they could fly from Huambo to Lubango, then drive from Lubango to Kalukembe if they wanted to spend Christmas with Kalukembe's missionaries. The two women accepted the invitation and arrived at Kalukembe on December 23.

Meanwhile, Afonso Daniel went witnessing to the Mukubaish people in his area and on Christmas Day attempted to preach a sermon called "The Person of Jesus Christ" to an audience of 200 Mukubaish. However, the assembled villager elders found his sermon difficult to accept. "We don't get it," they admitted. "You're talking about a God who has a son who came to Earth? We just don't see that kind of love going on. It must be made-up. It can't possibly be true." Afonso had a heavy heart as he visited Kalukembe on December 27. Although he had come to deliver his year-end reports on Caitovo, he especially wanted Steve's counsel. He unburdened himself to his friend, expressing his concern. "What do I say, Steve?" he wondered, concerned that his outreach to the Mukubaish seemed unsuccessful.

Steve had no easy answers for him. "Afonso," he replied, "sometimes we just have to be faithful people who repeat and repeat and repeat the stories that God has given us to tell and at some point His spirit has to do the convicting and God's spirit has to be the agent by which things change in people's hearts."

Steve had intended to drive Margarida and Mirian to Lubango for his own planned trip on January 4, but the sisters decided they wanted to return sooner. When they asked Afonso if they could return with him on December 30, he happily agreed. His Land Rover and 2-ton trailer were full of supplies and with the two women he had 11 passengers total, but this was not unusual when preparing trips in Africa. Peggy waved Afonso and his passengers off at 11 AM; Steve was busy in the hospital.

Afonso was barely out of Kalukembe when he met a convoy of Cuban soldiers travelling the opposite direction. Knowing the army checked the roads on every trip for landmines, Afonso paused to check if the way ahead was clear of mines and, when confirmed, continued on his way. After about 85 kilometres of travel he had passed through Mauengue and was on his way to Cacula—about halfway to Lubango. In the stretch of road ahead of him, the grass and trees were so thick, the foliage came all the way down to the highway.

Suddenly, from the bushes, a rocket-propelled grenade (RPG) screamed through the air and exploded beneath Afonso's Land Rover! The blast from the RPG went through the driver's side and into the engine, wounding Afonso in the leg and blowing up the car's gearbox. As the vehicle skidded to a halt, flames burst through the dashboard and lit Margarida and Mirian's skirts on fire. Tumbling out of the stationary vehicle, they began smothering the flames.

Armed men emerged from the bushes—UNITA guerrillas. As they began firing on the occupants of the Land Rover, four of the passengers got out and ran for their lives; their fates remain unknown. Among those UNITA killed were Rebecca's Sunday school teacher and her two children. Another woman was shot in the thigh; she fell by the Land Rover and hid herself under the vehicle, doing her best to play dead.

Despite the burns they had received to their legs, Margarida and Mirian were about to follow the other fleeing people when they saw Afonso moving. Unwilling to abandon him, they went back. Shrapnel from the RPG had fractured Afonso's knee; upon opening the driver's door, he realized he couldn't stand on his fractured leg and he pulled himself up by gripping the door. The leader of the guerrillas came forward and Afonso remonstrated with him, furious they had attacked his vehicle which, of course, had been painted *Ambulancia – Hospital de Caluquembe*. Afonso noted he was constantly using this road—surely they must have known they were assaulting a hospital vehicle.

"No," the rebel replied. "You're taking advantage of the Cuban convoy." Afonso disputed this as well; the Cuban convoy was travelling in the opposite direction. He stated if he were working with the government, surely he would have remained in the safety of their convoy? Impatient, the rebel leader drew his pistol and shot Afonso in the head.

While Afonso lay dead, Margarida and Mirian were taken as prisoners by UNITA. The only surviving witness was the woman who had concealed herself under the vehicle. Although pained from the bullet in her thigh, she struggled her way back to Mauengue. The authorities returned to the scene of the crashed Land Rover and collected the bodies of Afonso and the four other victims (2 adults, 2 children). Steve had just finished scrubbing in for another surgery that afternoon when he heard a vehicle come "screeching to a halt" at the emergency department. Knowing emergency cases frequently required surgery, Steve sent his head nurse to investigate the commotion. The nurse returned "ashen-faced" to inform Steve of Afonso's death. "I was thunderstruck," Steve grieved.

Word spread around the mission compound. Rebecca heard about it from another MK who ran up saying, "Uncle Afonso is dead!" Rebecca thought it was a bad joke and laughed nervously. "It can't be real," she thought. "It must be impossible." As news got around, Steve heard the full account from the injured woman, who came to his operating table to have her injuries repaired. Steve wanted to travel to Caitovo and inform Carla what had happened to her husband, but owing to the UNITA attack, the authorities had ordered all traffic off the road.

On December 31, the funeral for Afonso was held in Kalukembe. Despite the travel ban, 3,000 people crowded the church, pressing up against the windows outside to witness the ceremony. Steve delivered the eulogy before Afonso was laid to rest. "His loss has left us all mourning and deeply moved as he was truly a brother to me in every sense," he announced passionately.

Rebecca had never seen her parents so deeply affected. "It was a very deep pain," she reflected. She saw her parents in a different light: "Parents can go through hard times," she learned.

On January 2, 1986, the roads reopened and word went to Caitovo. In an effort to soften the blow, the messengers told Carla that Afonso was sick. Then, the story changed and she heard he was in the ICU (intensive care unit). As a nurse, Carla knew many Angolans would use "ICU" to prepare loved ones for the news of their relative's death; even when she overheard people talking about a car being attacked and a nurse killed, the men who were transporting Carla and her three children to Kalukembe would deny that the story was about Afonso.

Of course, when Carla finally reached Kalukembe it was to learn not only that Afonso was dead but buried. Carla and her children visited the grave and Pastor Eliseu opened up his home, sharing it with them. He offered to let them remain in Kalukembe, but Carla felt resolved to return to Caitovo. The tradition among Ovimbundu is that wives do not inherit, only men can inherit property (and wives and children are often counted as property). Despite this,

Carla's deepest wish was to continue the work she and Afonso had began in Caitovo. She couldn't even drive a car at that point. Steve felt terrible sending a widow with three children home alone but mused, "Praise God with us for her courage."

Margarida and Mirian were marched across Angola into Jamba, deep in the southeast corner of the nation, where Savimbi's UNITA headquarters was based. They were not repatriated to Brazil until the middle of March (the sisters would later write a book about the experience: *Seqüestro em Angola*, 1987). In the aftermath of the attack, Steve cancelled some of his clinical visits to spend time with his children, who were all distraught by "Uncle Afonso's" death. The assembled missionaries began asking questions about how prepared they were in the event of an emergency. Steve likened their situation to 1 Peter 4:12: "We ought not to be surprised at these painful trials, but to rejoice that we participate in the sufferings of Christ."

"These events have brought into very sharp focus the precariousness of our lives and the fact that we are like flowers and grass that wither away. We want very much to be found faithful to the tasks entrusted to us and not to be found shying away from the tremendous responsibility, challenge and privilege it is to share the sufferings of Christ."

A few weeks later another mission vehicle was assaulted—this time, the car belonged to the Kassua clinic and the perpetrators were FAPLA. The Kassua clinic and other medical missions in Angola had accepted guidelines from the Red Cross on policies to adopt during the war. Among these, they agreed hospital vehicles would never be permitted to transport soldiers. The only way a soldier could be given a lift in a hospital car would be if he was dressed in civilian garb and not brandishing a rifle. In this way, the medical missions would remain neutral. Of course, this neutrality proved unacceptable to some soldiers, who decided to retaliate against Kassua. The vehicle they assaulted with machine guns had been carrying six people, including the administrator of the hospital; all six died. When Steve examined the remains of their vehicle, he counted up to 75 bullet holes—35 of which were in the driver's door.

As the missionaries waited for guidelines from their leaders, they attempted to carry on their lives as before. On February 4, Steve and Robbie watched "a reasonably aggressive" soccer match held in celebration of "Luta Armada"—which commemorated 25 years since the beginning of the struggle against the Portuguese. Even though the Portuguese had left 11 years earlier, for many Angolans the present civil war was simply a continuation of the colonial war. "If I hadn't married this guy, I wouldn't be in this mess!" Peggy would joke. "But I wouldn't trade it," she added. In spite of the war, the challenges to her children's education, and the ongoing famine, she echoed her husband's attitude. "What a chance to grow and see God's hand at work!"

A travel ban was enacted around Kalukembe; from then on, no one was permitted to be on the roads without a military escort. This meant Steve and Sheila's clinical work would be curtailed and they would be restricted to the medical and living supplies available in Kalukembe, without an easy means to shop in Lubango. Pastor Eliseu gathered all of the missionaries together and explained what these changes would mean for them. He said he understood if they wanted to leave. "In the end," Peggy gladly noted, "everybody stayed."

Preparations were made for a sudden evacuation. "I don't think we would have been killed," Peggy said in retrospect, but the usual practice for UNITA was to kidnap missionaries and march them to the border, similar to what had happened to the Horvath sisters. In case they were forced to march across the bush for weeks, each family prepared a backpack with clothing they could wear on the journey, leaving those bags where they could be easily reached in case of a sudden exit. One of the Swiss doctors supplied each bag with medications for treating dysentery and other diseases that might come up in the bush. Peggy also trained her children to hide in their house in case it came to that. "It was an anxious time for me," she confessed. "When it began to be clear that we were not exempt from anything. That was difficult."

Due to the travel ban, Steve had to take his holidays in Kalukembe—as it is almost impossible for a doctor to be on vacation when everyone knows where he lives. At times the family would relocate to a holiday house owned by the Bréchets so they could enjoy a little privacy. The closing of supply lines also made the provisions Johanna Kessler could provide all the sweeter—and nothing was sweeter to the Foster kids than the Cerelac (a Nestlé-brand baby food) she would occasionally supply as a treat. Overall, there were more positives than negatives to the travel ban. "We became so much closer to the Angolans," Peggy noted. "Difficulties?" Jean-Pierre queried. "There were many. But the strange thing is that you tend to forget some of the difficulties and you remember the good times. The rejoicing when food arrived, when medicines that were so long-awaited suddenly arrived."

THE PREGNANCY THAT SAVED THE MISSION

Sheila was pregnant with her and Ezekiel's first child, the due date set for March 7. Because of the travel ban and the increased awareness of UNITA's threat, Betty Dauwalder put together a special backpack for Sheila—an entire delivery pack in case they were abducted from Kalukembe and had to deliver the baby in the bush. Betty didn't share this with Sheila, for fear of upsetting her. But unknown to either woman, there was another person working in secret to defend Sheila's unborn child.

Samy Abel was a nurse at Kalukembe Hospital and, with his wife Maria, had served as padrinhos (godparents) at Sheila and Ezekiel's wedding. Unknown to the hospital staff, Samy was also a spy for UNITA. During the last week of February, UNITA guerrillas came within a few kilometres of Kalukembe Hospital and began holding meetings with the intent of raiding the mission grounds and kidnapping the missionaries. However, Samy opposed the idea and spoke passionately against it, informing the guerrillas of Sheila's pregnancy and what a terrible thing it would be for her to deliver her child in the bush. For an entire week, the UNITA guerrillas would plan to attack Kalukembe—and every night, Samy persuaded them against it. Finally, the guerrillas moved on.

On March 7, Sheila gave birth to her daughter Helena exactly on the due date after a long night's labour. Sheila would not learn how God had used Samy to protect the baby until Samy confessed his UNITA involvement 20 years later. Sheila and Ezekiel's home at Kalukembe lay next door to Steve and Peggy's. Rebecca, full of curiosity, sneaked to the new parents' home in the early hours of the morning so she could be the first among her siblings to see baby Helena. Sheila let her niece see the newborn, then Rebecca sped home—but Rebecca's absence had been noted at the breakfast table and caused Peggy to discipline her with a grounding. Despite the punishment, Rebecca decided, "it was worth it" because she had beaten her siblings to seeing Helena.

"They were young and vibrant," Rebecca said of her aunt and uncle. "They proved a cross-cultural relationship could work." Rebecca loved her uncle; "He was fun," she said. Rebecca called him "Tio 'Zekiel" (tio means uncle) he called her "Rebucca." Later that year, musician Paul Simon released his album *Graceland*, inspired by South African music; Ezekiel bought a copy and often played it; in an interesting connection, Steve's brother Stacey Foster would later toil on the sound recording for the concert video of Graceland.

In April, Jean-Pierre welcomed an International Red Cross delegation to Kalukembe to evaluate their location and provide recommendations on how they would transport supplies during the travel ban. Lubango remained Kalukembe's best hope for supplies, but the unsafe road remained an issue. For this reason, Steve and the IESA and UIEA churches implored MAF (Missionary Aviation Fellowship) to bring their planes to Kalukembe. Although it would be expensive to pay for MAF planes, the larger question was whether the Angolan government would permit MAF to fly to Kalukembe.

Following the Red Cross visit, the organization began to reconsider Kalukembe Hospital; they knew there was a strong pro-UNITA faction at Kalukembe and had assumed the entire hospital had a bias against the government. However, when the Red Cross met with UNITA in Jamba, they would hear vociferous complaints about how pro-MPLA the hospital was. Then, in Luanda, the MPLA would complain vociferously about how pro-UNITA the hospital was. After each side claimed lives in ambushes, the Red Cross began to realize the hospital was not partisan and trying to remain neutral in the midst of a very trying and dangerous situation.

Until MAF could be brought in, the Red Cross' airplanes were used in a variety of flights. In June, Steve and Pastor Eliseu visited Cubal-Ganda via the Red Cross so they could discuss redeploying staff there from Kassua, as the staff in Kassua was very tense after the recent assault on its members. Steve was justifiably unsettled by conditions in Cubal-Ganda. "I visited a Catholic clinic there and helped them cope with their large outpatient and TB patient load. Frankly, I haven't seen sicker people in a long time, reflecting the [dearth] of even the most simple anti-malarials in that region."

Steve went to the Minister of Health in Luanda to ask about opening an airfield at Kalukembe. "He told me that a certain body of opinion on the Central Committee of the Party is that we must all be evacuated to a 'safer place.' This, of course, was very serious news to us. The Minister went on to underline that he is prepared to defend our work for the present but on the following conditions: That we establish an airlink as rapidly as possible between Kalukembe – Lubango; we don't travel by road under any circumstance; that we cut all nonessential tasks and clinics; that we preserve people over places." The Minister promised to help get the airlink approved. After so many months of their father being stuck in Kalukembe, Rebecca and Robbie were particularly heartsick over his absence.

AFONSO'S LEGACY

After the attacks in Kassua, there was a long period of peace for the missionaries. This did not relieve the people of tension, however. The MPLA were allied with SWAPO from South-West Africa and at one time a squad of SWAPO soldiers put up camp on the road. After a patrol of SWAPO soldiers walked through the mission to the river, fully armed, it unnerved the mission families. The hospital administration spoke to the soldiers and, fortunately, they agreed to stay off the mission property. At night, explosions and gunshots could be heard in the once-peaceful darkness, but although they could tell the fighting was close, it didn't cross into Kalukembe.

All this time, Carla had continued to work in Caitovo to continue her and Afonso's mission. One day after a service to the Mukubaish, the village elders came to speak with her. "You know, we're starting to get it," the elders informed her. "You said God sent his son to give his life. Your husband gave his life too. He was only on that road because of us. He was bringing money, food, and medicine for us, and he had done that for 3 years. Now we're beginning to see." Afonso had been unable to reach these men at Christmas through his words, but his actions had spoken volumes.

"A human demonstration of love speaks far louder than any words that have ever been spoken," Steve reflected.

FOSTER KIDS IN THE OR

During the summer of 1986, Rebecca and Heather spent time working alongside their father in the operating theatre. As the children were not trained professionals this frustrated some of Steve's nurses. Regardless, the girls loved having an opportunity to share in their father's work. Rebecca was placed on "flyswatter duty" with the job of killing flies that entered the OR, provided she did not strike them while they were on an otherwise-sterile surface. Infestations with flies were such a common problem in the OR that there was usually a nurse on full-time fly-killing duty during operations. Rebecca also helped tie the strings on the surgical gowns and poured boiling water for cataract surgery. Being somewhat more passive, Heather usually observed the surgeries, but had a keener interest in the details than her sister. "Heather has a special liking for surgery and is very practical, often wanting me to explain what the various instruments do," Steve noted at the time. Heather began to fantasize about becoming a surgeon like her father and grandfather. When not working, Steve would tell familiar tales of family lore to the girls, such as their Great-Grandfather Charles' hippo hunt or Grandfather Bob's leopard hunt. Heather began to have a sense of the inter-generational work of her family and grasped "the significance of the pioneering work."

Some of the patients amused Rebecca; one woman had cooked a rabbit to appease her husband, then caught a rabbit bone in her throat. After Steve removed the bone, the woman fumed, "That's it, I don't care what my husband says! We are never having rabbit again!" Rebecca found it "weird," however, when the patients were people she knew. Most of all, it was strange for her when her own mother came in! Peggy had sliced her knuckles open on a tin can and required stitches.

There were 45 landmine injures in the month of August, people journeying to Kalukembe from as far as Chipindo. One truck came with about 11 people lined in the back of the vehicle "stacked almost like firewood," Steve recalled. They hadn't even had their wounds dressed. "The fact they hadn't died was amazing." Frequently, people injured by the landmines were the first ones to rise in the morning to draw water for their families—they would step across the new landmines which the soldiers had planted during the night. Consequently, about three-quarters of Steve's patients were women, many of them bearing small children on their backs.

Rebecca found it hard to watch her father perform amputations, especially when she heard the noise of the bonesaw cutting through their limbs. Rebecca's exposure to the horrors of landmine injuries would have a significant effect on her worldview and her passion to oppose injustice. She befriended a teenager named Mateus who had lost a leg to a landmine and remained at the hospital to be fitted for a prosthetic and undergo physiotherapy. Rebecca and Mateus found another boy who had received a tracheotomy to remove cancer from his voice box, leaving him unable to speak; the three of them invented their own sign language so he could communicate with them.

That winter, the Red Cross and FAPLA escorted Steve into Lubango where he visited the Rio de Huíla clinic. While at the clinic, Steve became friends with Pastor Eduardo Calenga of UIEA, who was impressed that Steve had "given himself entirely to his work." From Lubango, Steve journeyed to Luanda, then flew internationally on quick trips to Switzerland, Toronto (to see his mother-in-law Fran) and then attended the Mission Advance Conference in Hamilton, where he delivered a session on the "Call to Commitment."

As Steve's trips away from Kalukembe were beginning to resume, Heather mused, "I'm quite used to him going away so often, but it can be hard." Heather's siblings came down with a bout of chicken pox when Rob caught it then gave it to Rachel and Rebecca. "At first I thought it would be fun," Rebecca mused, but they had to be isolated from other children, which disappointed her. Still, the kids enjoyed days without school which they could spend watching TV and eating Jell-O. At this point, Kalukembe's 10-ton truck would travel to Lubango twice per month to bring supplies. "Sometimes a convoy will come and we all hope for mail," Heather said. "We have all been praying for mail."

At the year end, Heather shared some of her compositions with her family's supporters:

December in the Southern Hemisphere

Thick grass grows in unusual places.
Cool winds blow softly in the early morning and late afternoon.
Green trees sometimes fade, but they always stand straight and tall as if they are proud of Angola.
Leaves slowly fall making a thin carpet of leaves on the ground.
Rustling of trees can be heard on a calm day.
Christmas comes last.
Fun, enjoyable, thoughtful and happy Christmas.

Something we all share.
With gay flowers to make us happy, warm sunshine to make us glad, thick grass, big green
trees—they all join to make joy for a merry Christmas in Angola.

As Steve began his return journey to Angola in January 1987, he first stopped in Luanda to speak again to the Minister of Health about the progress in getting MAF permission to land at Kalukembe. The process had become repeatedly delayed by various bureaucracies and ultimately required President dos Santos to personally approve of the project. While speaking to the Minister, Steve brought up his great hope of training Angolan doctors. The Minister was very interested in Steve setting up the program, but informed him he would require additional training to become a faculty member in Angola's Department of Surgery. Steve told the IESA and UIEA churches about this and they began planning for Steve to acquire additional training at McMaster during his next furlough while the churches explored hospitals where Steve would teach surgery. Steve finally returned to Kalukembe in February thanks to a Red Cross airplane.

That August in Kalukembe, Ermelinda Fabiano, sister to Ezekiel, died of diphtheria. Rebecca was devastated by Ermelinda's death. "She was like extended family," she recalled. They sent word to Sheila and Ezekiel, who were studying in Vancouver. It was also this year that Jean-Pierre's father Rodolphe Bréchet passed away. While Ermelinda and Rodolphe's deaths were sorrowful, other cases gave the family cause for joy; Steve treated a 3-year-old girl who had mistakenly drunk from a pop bottle in her parents' home—a bottle filled with lye which burned her throat. "I took her short intestine and used it to replace her esophagus," Steve explained. "I'd never done it before. I'd only seen it done once in my life. That kind of case establishes your reputation."

LEAVING KALUKEMBE

Muriel LeBreton had finally reached the end of her 2-year visit and returned to Canada earlier in 1987. Although she remained a close friend of the family and would always answer to "Auntie Muriel" from the children, her time in Angola was over. Peggy once again had to take charge of the children's teaching, which was a trial because of the poor mail service, with the correspondence books falling behind by several months. Steve took a turn at teaching and taught science and math to the children to ease the burden on Peggy. When they ran out of official teaching materials, they would use National Geographic magazines as resources!

Before the end of the year it had been decided: Steve would return to

McMaster as a visiting fellow in order to obtain the additional training he required. This furlough would last about 18 months, giving the children a real chance to study in a formal classroom setting. In November, Paul and Susan Cole moved into the Fosters' house while most of the Fosters' possessions were placed into storage. As their vehicles were loaded, the family engaged in tearful farewells to the staff and citizens of Kalukembe, uncertain of the future, but aware that when they did return to Angola, Kalukembe might not be their home.

In order to return to Canada, they first had to transport themselves to Lubango to catch a plane to Luanda. "Going to Canada—that was the only reason I'd bring my children along that road," Steve remarked. A 40-person military convoy guided Steve's suburban down the road; it was the first time the children had seen the highway in the two years since Afonso's death.

"It was a scary feeling," Rebecca admitted.

When their car came close to where Afonso had been killed, Steve stopped his vehicle and unrolled the rear window of the suburban where his three daughters were sitting in the back. "If something happens," he told the girls, "you should jump out the window. Hide and wait for us."

Rachel was shocked by his words. "I couldn't believe he said that. It was one of the only times I felt scared about the war."

CHAPTER 11

"Each Time Leaving Africa Was Like Tearing a Piece Out of Me."
— Heather Foster

HAMILTON (December 1987 – August 1989)

The convoy arrived in Lubango without incident. The family prepared for a flight on the Angolan airline TAAG ('Transportes Aéreos de Angola'; many cheeky missionaries dubbed it 'Think Again About Going'). Before leaving Lubango, they met up with Janet Holden, one of Steve's cousins through his Uncle Herbert. Janet had married Jim Holden and both were missionaries with AEF, with Jim teaching at ISTEL. "Our trip by the Angolan airlines to Luanda was uneventful," Steve opined, "except that a pickpocket tried to get my wallet while going through the security check. I got the man arrested, but in the meantime, unbeknownst to me, he stole my sunglasses—something I was chagrined to discover the next day." While in Luanda Steve held meetings with Jean-Pierre and Steve Duncan about the future of the surgical program which would eventually be dubbed the Community Physician Training Project—or simply "The Project"—and of the MAF flights to Kalukembe.

Before continuing on, the family flew to Harare, Zimbabwe, to meet with Chuck and Heather Stephens and their children, where they spent a week's vacation. Even in Zimbabwe, the Fosters were struck by the differences from Angola. "We couldn't get over the quantity and quality of food for sale in the stores and local fruitstands, the organization and general vigour of the economy despite the hard times. It was all a great contrast to Luanda," Steve observed.

On Rebecca's birthday, the Fosters flew from Harare to England to see Bob and Belva. It was little Robbie's first time in a cool climate and after stepping off the plane he saw his breath hang in the air. "Dad, why am I smoking?" he wondered innocently. Bob hadn't yet recovered from lymphoma and, "wasn't quite himself," Steve noticed. They spent about two weeks in England, including Christmas with Bob and Belva, then flew on to Toronto and spent New Year's with the Parkins family.

To be close to McMaster, the Fosters settled down in Hamilton for the duration of their furlough. The home they rented in the Ontario city was located in Hamilton Mountain and was quite large, featuring four bedrooms one guest room, one living room and three family rooms. By this time, Rebecca was in Grade 7, Heather in Grade 5, Rachel in Grade 2 and Robbie in Grade 1. "They are adapting to the new social environment more slowly but have found their academic preparation in Angola by correspondence to have been very good with the exception of French," Steve noted. His children had the same issues with the mandatory French which had brought down his average some 20 years before, but they caught up quickly. Peggy packed school lunches for the children, but since Heather hadn't encountered luncheon meat or processed cheese before, she became disgusted by the food and throw them away, which landed her in trouble with the lunch-room monitor. Heather was quite a food critic, complaining, "Soups in Canada did *not* taste right." She had never eaten a soup with meat in it before. "Chicken noodle soup? *That's disgusting!*"

During Steve's years in Kalukembe, his brother Stacey had gone to work for Broadway Video, the company run by Lorne Michaels which produced television's *Saturday Night Live*. When Paul Allen asked Steve how much he thought his brother was making in television, Steve naively figured somewhere under $100,000. Paul shook his head, insisting Stacey must be earning several hundreds of thousands. This prompted them to do some math to determine how much Steve's services were worth. After figuring out how many surgeries he performed per year it came out to $3.75 CAD per surgery!

Paul admired Steve's boundless energy. He noticed Steve could drink mug after mug of coffee, yet still sleep at night. He once watched in fascination as Steve prepared a pot of espresso at 9 PM, drank it, and within the hour had fallen asleep, snoring!

In the spring, Steve, Peggy and the four children rented a large RV (recreational vehicle) and went on a lengthy tour of the United States and Canada, visiting all of the North America-based family. The only family members they had not seen the previous December were Mary Lou's family in Rocky Mountain House, Alberta. While in Rocky Mountain House that May, Steve took advantage of the opportunity to speak about his family's mission work at Holy Trinity Anglican Church, which was where Mary Lou's husband, Andrew Hoskin, served as rector.

Mary Lou and Andrew had four children, just like Steve and Peggy, although theirs were comprised of one girl (Janna) and three boys (Michael,

Jonathan, and Matthew). Before the Fosters came to visit, Andrew told his sons to tidy up all of their toy army soldiers and military-like vehicles as he was concerned they might bring up unpleasant memories for the Foster children. As Robbie went to play with Jonathan and Matthew, he began exploring their bedroom and took an interest in a certain closed drawer on Jonathan's bunkbed. Alarmed, Jonathan put his hand over the drawer. "Not in there!" Jonathan yelped.

"What's in there?" Rob wondered, his curiosity piqued.

"Toys," Jonathan admitted.

"What kind of toys?" Rob asked with rising interest.

"Army men," Jonathan confessed. He felt terrible for giving away the secret.

"Cool!" Rob exclaimed. "Let's get them out!" They went on to play with the toy soldiers without further incident.

Later, the male cousins went to play in the Hoskins' backyard, digging in the garden. Robbie and Matthew wondered if they could dig a hole to China. Struck by inspiration, Matthew suggested they could fly to China instead and simulated a helicopter by twirling a hoe around his head. The hoe struck Rob in the head, almost taking out one of his eyes. Peggy had to rush Robbie to the hospital, where stitches were put into his brow. His one mollification was the bubble-gum ice cream cone he was given as a treat. Later that year, Robbie would suffer a cut on the opposite side of his brow after falling on a pair of scissors, giving him a matching scar.

The Foster and Hoskin cousins got along well, although the Hoskin siblings did note some of the unusual things about their cousins, such as Heather's unique form of speech. The more startling revelation to them was that their family's favourite *Star Wars* character was Han Solo instead of Luke Skywalker. Despite these differences the cousins came together under Rebecca's leadership to perform the play *Beauty and the Beast* for their parents, and to gently tease Jonathan and Rachel for both being so good-looking. Later that summer, the Hoskins visited Hamilton themselves, one of the few times the Parkins family convened while Peggy was at hand.

The Fosters' RV trip took the family to Greensboro, St. Petersburg, Houston, Tempe, Los Angeles, Seattle, Vancouver, Calgary, Morden, Thunder Bay, Sault St. Marie, Chicago and Windsor. "We rather grew to like the RV except for its incredible thirst for gas," Steve remarked. In addition to seeing family members and speaking at churches, along the way they saw the Grand Canyon, went to Disney World and visited their friends Gordon and Melissa Wong.

Steve had many opportunities to speak to the press while in North America and did his best to impress on them the challenges facing Angola and how others could become involved. Oakland Ross, the African correspondent for the Globe & Mail newspaper, met Steve while reporting on Angola. Ross claimed Steve was "described as Angola's Norman Bethune," referencing the physician who became a noted twentieth-century humanitarian by serving in Spain and China, ultimately perishing in 1939 while helping the Chinese against Japanese invaders. However, Ross added, "While Bethune became known for communist sympathies, Foster is known for his Christian example and zeal." Indeed, as Bethune aided the Spanish and Chinese in part because he was devoted to the cause of communism, Ross recognized Steve was serving Communists and others from his Christian beliefs.

In July, the Fosters returned to Hamilton so Steve could begin his time as a visiting fellow at McMaster, which he served principally at St. Joseph's Health Care Hamilton. "It's hard to get used to the resources that are available," he gushed. "It's hard to comprehend that the hospital I'm working at spends in a year what the Angolan government has spent in health care for the nation since Independence 13 years ago."

The Fosters established themselves at Philpott Memorial Church in Hamilton because it had a strong youth group, which was important to Rebecca, although Heather shyly resisted involvement. Each Sunday after church the Fosters would drive to Toronto to spend the rest of the day with Peggy's mother Fran. Although Fran "was firm," as Rob recalls, the Foster children formed a bond with her and she enjoyed doting on them. Virtually every lunch she served them tomato soup and toasted cheese sandwiches, and her dinners were inevitably meatloaf and baked potatoes, knowing they were meals her daughter Peggy loved.

That fall, an accountant with the Angolan government, Faustino Sikila, came to Canada to receive cataract surgery. Although Sikila was only 38 years old, his cataracts had driven him completely blind. Sikila worked in Lubango where Dr. Steven Duncan arranged for his travel to Canada; although the procedure could have been performed in Lubango and despite Sikila being a government employee, he was not a member of the MPLA, so they would not approve of the operation. Bringing his wife and youngest child with him, Sikila was warmly welcomed by Steve, and his family lived with the Fosters in Hamilton during the operation. Peggy once took his wife to the grocery store and saw the woman gaze in awe; she had never seen so much food in one place! Steve made pleas on Sikila's behalf and Dr. Jim Martin at St. Joseph's hospital agreed to perform the operation without charge.

"It was a wonderful sight to see his personality change as he could see again," Steve said. Many people in Sikila's position would not have wished to return to Angola—but this was not an issue with him. Sikila had registered at ISTEL before leaving for Canada as a sign that he trusted God's future plans for him. Although his work as an accountant paid well, he no longer trusted the government because of their refusal to help him. Instead, "he had learned to trust in God's provision each step along the way." While still visiting, Sikila went to Redeemer Bible Church in Niagara Falls and delivered his testimony to the congregation, resulting in several parishioners pledging their financial support to his seminary training. Immediately upon his return he began his studies at ISTEL and would soon become a church pastor, then later served as financial manager of an orphanage.

Avelino Sayango also visited from Angola as he and Steve made plans for the future of "The Project." Steve had already begun drawing up the curriculum. "I am praying that God will raise up a group of committed Christian surgical specialists who will be able to come regularly to Angola to help in the teaching program." Major financial support came to The Project via Partnership Africa-Canada (PAC), a charitable organization which arose after the highly publicized 1983-1985 Ethiopian Famine resulted in an outpouring of charitable giving to relieve Ethiopia's population. With a $100 million surplus, PAC was created to find ways of spending the remainder for charitable works in Africa and they took an interest in The Project. The Canadian government was also interested in helping Angola in part because it was in opposition to South Africa; at that time, many western nations were placing political pressure on South Africa to abolish its Apartheid system and giving aid to Angola was intended to frustrate South Africa.

As Bob had reached the retirement age of 65, he finally stood down as AEF's international director, although he still intended to continue in God's service wherever it might be. In his time as international director, Bob had reopened doors for AEF into Madagascar, Gabon and Mozambique, as well as major initiatives in Namibia, South Africa, Botswana, Zaire, Guinea-Bissau and Tanzania. As a culmination of his service, on November 23, 1988, Bob was presented with World Vision's Robert Pierce Award. With their work in the international office completed and Rev. Ron Genheimer assuming directorship, Bob and Belva moved back to Greensboro, North Carolina, and bought a home near Shelley, Sharon and Sharon's new husband Martin Mills.

Back in Angola, great changes were well underway. In the summer of 1987, the battle of Cuito Cuanavale had been the largest engagement of MPLA, Cuban, South African and UNITA forces yet. Although that conflict ended as a veritable stalemate, it brought the opposing sides of the conflict to the negotiating table. In the New York Accord signed December 22, 1988 by Angola, Cuba, and South Africa, Cuba agreed to begin withdrawing its armies from Angola, under the guidance of the United Nations Verification Mission I (UNAVEM I). At the same time, South Africa agreed to withdraw its forces and to finally grant independence to South-West Africa, which formally reverted to its name Namibia. Although UNITA remained in opposition to the MPLA, its allies had been thinned—the MPLA had been aligned with Namibia's SWAPO, which soon rose to power in that nation, creating an ally and a buffer zone between Angola and South Africa. Despite all these changes, the US remained committed to UNITA and Savimbi even visited President Ronald Reagan at the White House during the summer of 1988. As the USSR was in a state of collapse, the MPLA was preparing for a post-Cold War world—whatever that might be.

FROM ANGOLA TO OZ

The Foster kids' school activities in 1989 included Rachel taking up gymnastics and performing in a school production of *The Music Man*, but much of the focus went to the middle school production of *The Wizard of Oz*, in which Rebecca and Heather performed. The production used the same songs as the motion picture which Muriel had brought to Kalukembe years earlier; Heather was a munchkin while Rebecca had the lead role: Dorothy Gale. Grandma Parkins was bursting with pride over her granddaughter and helped her obtain a pair of red running shoes which, by fastening on red sequins, became Rebecca's ruby slippers. "I want Rebecca to have voice lessons!" Grandma Parkins declared after seeing the school production. "It was fun and challenging," Rebecca mused. In retrospect she realized she "was used to standing out in Angola for looking different, sounding different, being different, being white, being a girl. I had already created a persona to deal with that in Angola but in Canada I didn't stand out in the same ways, I stood out in different ways. *The Wizard of Oz* gave me a chance to reinvent myself in other ways."

Rebecca's experiences at school in Canada made her realize what her schooling in Kalukembe had lacked: extracurricular activities. Outside of the sports Muriel had brought, there had been no sports at all. Becoming involved in extracurricular activities, forming teams and working with other students taught Rebecca valuable skills. At the same time, Robbie was struggling to keep up; his bad leg complicated his performance in sports, especially ice skating. Just walking 3-4 blocks from home to school was tiring on his body.

Steve had been working in the Head and Neck Cancer Division at St. Joseph's, reuniting him with his old schoolmate and best man Dr. Stuart Archibald. In February, Steve went to Angola with McMaster's Dr. Ev Sargeant and Canadian politician Iona Campagnolo (former president of the Liberal Party) to settle matters related to The Project. Over their meetings in Luanda with the Minister of Health, Dean of the Faculty of Medicine and Provincial

Government officials, it was decided The Project would be overseen jointly by the churches of IESA, UIEA, the Brethren Assemblies and AEF, with MAF providing aerial support for transporting patients. However, when they journeyed to Kalukembe to finalize the programming, Steve discovered Pastor Eliseu was giving him the cold shoulder.

Pastor Eliseu's refusal to admit The Project to operate at Kalukembe Hospital was, outwardly, presented as a matter of defending Christian culture. Pastor Eliseu claimed the doctors sent from Luanda for training would bring non-Christian values to the hospital, corrupt the people and impregnate local women. Steve saw working with the government as the "politically correct" action of the time, as the MPLA had been making good diplomatic overtures since the New York Accord. What Steve did not know then, of course, was Pastor Eliseu's involvement in UNITA; part of Pastor Eliseu's refusal stemmed from his wish to keep MPLA forces away from his UNITA allies.

When Steve reported these unhappy results to the Minister of Health, it was decided The Project would be based out of the Central Hospital in Lubango instead. This did not solve all of their problems, as among the reasons Steve wanted The Project to be set at Kalukembe were the already-standing residency housing. Holding the training program at Central Hospital meant developing housing for the missionaries and medical students. Plans began to develop Mitcha, a compound for AEF and MAF missionaries, but for the start, the staff would have to acquire regular housing in Lubango. Then too, the Central Hospital was not as well maintained as Kalukembe Hospital. When Steve visited its facility, he found there had been zero elective surgeries performed in the previous six months due to a lack of surgical material— despite eight Cuban surgeons being on staff. "Kalukembe Hospital last year did more surgery with 3 physicians than the provincial hospital did with 22," Steve observed.

With IESA distancing themselves from The Project, UIEA stepped in and asked Sheila and Ezekiel to join the staff, Sheila for her nursing abilities and Ezekiel with his skills as a hospital administrator; they agreed. They left Kalukembe without most of their possessions, which were packed into the 10-ton delivery truck that had been at Kalukembe since 1981. Until Steve returned to head up The Project, Sheila would assist two days a week at Rio de Huíla's clinic; by then, she was pregnant with her and Ezekiel's third child.

One week after Sheila and Ezekiel arrived in Lubango, another convoy was arranged to guide the 10-ton truck from Kalukembe. However, it was a smaller convoy than usual and some of the FAPLA soldiers protecting the trucks fell into an alliance with UNITA. When the truck came close to where Afonso Daniel died, an ambush hit the truck, killing the driver and a pastor who had been in the cab. The soldiers and rebels jointly sacked the truck and took everything of interest, then lit it on fire; the container on the back of the truck was made of fibreglass, so burned itself out quite easily.

When Ezekiel heard of the ambush and informed Sheila, she was despondent and horrified at the deaths of the driver and pastor. She was also disappointed; "That means we lost all of our stuff," she bemoaned. But Ezekiel was a born optimist: "Well, we don't know what was in the truck," he ventured. When staff from Kalukembe Hospital investigated the wreck, they found many of Sheila and Ezekiel's possessions scattered along the side of the road, abandoned by the same people who looted the truck. Jean-Pierre and Marie-Claude located most of a set of plastic dishes which had been a wedding gift to the couple, along with an embroidered picture Sheila had made, among other scavenged items. Store shelves were all but empty at this time, due to the war, so replacing the lost materials would be difficult, but when people heard of the attack they donated what they could to the couple—a towel here, a bedsheet there.

During the summer of 1989, Stirling went to work at Tchimbolelo, a farm outside of Lubango. Under the patronage of Sr. Fernando Borge, Stirling learned the ins and outs of practising agriculture and animal husbandry in that region of Angola, with the intent of opening a mission farm that would reach out to the Ovangambwe, a tribe of cattlemen. "Stirling came as an adventurer," opined Pastor Calenga, "but with a spirit to serve." Stirling's girlfriend Donna Gallant came out to Angola for six weeks to see Stirling. Stirling felt Donna had a "romanticized" view of Africa, but as she spent time with him in the bush she adapted herself to the reality. At the end of her visit, they were engaged. Sr. Borge arranged for the church mission to purchase farmland not too far from his own property with the understanding that when Stirling and Donna were married, they would come to operate the mission farm Tchincombe.

That June, Ezekiel journeyed to Luanda to help receive the Cessna Caravan airplane which supporters had purchased for MAF to inaugurate its Angolan fleet. Ezekiel stayed at a guest house in Luanda operated by the Brethren Assemblies, where he met Dr. Nicholas Comninellis, a missionary doctor who had only recently arrived with his family to begin their service in Angola. One evening, Ezekiel suddenly began thrashing and choking in his bed. Dr. Comninellis was summoned to his side and recognized Ezekiel was having a seizure. Ezekiel soon slipped into a coma as they rushed him to the nearest hospital—a military facility. The hospital received Ezekiel, but refused to let Dr. Comninellis or other mission people see him.

That very day in Lubango, Stirling and Donna were visiting the still-pregnant Sheila when the news arrived; leaving her daughters Helena and Sara under Stirling and Donna's care, Sheila and Ezekiel's brother Ambrosio flew to

Luanda as quickly they could. By the time they arrived, Ezekiel had come out of his coma and been released from the hospital with no tests or diagnosis of his condition. The attending physicians told Dr. Comninellis Ezekiel had diabetes. Prior to the seizure, Ezekiel had been having recurring dreams of a bus and of people getting on and off; soon, the dreams were of himself being forced aboard the bus. Ezekiel now believed the dreams were a portent of his death.

Sheila contacted Steve to request his advice. Steve told her the seizure should be investigated, but no one in Angola was qualified to diagnose the matter—they would have to return to North America. MAF transported Helena and Sara as their first-ever passengers in Angola, taking them from Lubango to Luanda so the whole family could hurry back to the US. Under the care of specialists, Ezekiel's medical condition was diagnosed: glioma, a form of brain cancer which transforms normal brain cells into malignant growths. There were no surgical options for Ezekiel, only the hope of radiation treatment. Sheila and Ezekiel relocated to High Point, North Carolina, relying on Sharon's hospitality.

As she saw Ezekiel's state and examined the prognosis, Sheila was overcome with grief. She questioned God: "Why did you let me get pregnant if this baby is never going to know his father?"

CHAPTER 12

*"The Way God Has Taken Care of You Now Is How He's Always
Going to Take Care of You." — Bob Foster*

KALUKEMBE; LUBANGO (September 1989 – May 1991)

In Greensboro, the Fosters rallied around Sheila and Ezekiel. Bob had been in South Africa to celebrate AEF's 100th anniversary when he heard about the seizure. Bob and Belva soon joined the other family members tending to the couple. Late in September, Sheila gave birth to her third child: a son, Daniel. Sharon and the local church community helped find a home in High Point for Sheila and Ezekiel to rent which was only a few blocks from Sharon's home and, as High Point was the "furniture capital" of the United States, church people donated furniture for the home.

As Steve and Peggy returned to Angola with their children they encountered only a few minor bureaucratic snafus on their return; Rebecca and Heather had been left off of Peggy's visa, but the matter was quickly settled and they were escorted back to Kalukembe to tidy up their home and prepare to move to Lubango. On their return, Heather was astonished to discover how differently Kalukembe seemed to her; while in Canada, she had pined for their home but upon their return was struck by "how small, dirty and dingy everything was. I hadn't remembered it that way at all. It had all been perfection. I felt very disloyal to see it as anything other than perfect." There had been another crop failure earlier that year and the need for famine relief was stronger than ever.

The continued famine had led to a daily food line at Kalukembe. Peggy and other missionaries would use the available donated foods to cook up pots of soup and serve 100 people per day, with even the Foster children taking a hand to pass out bowls to the people. Frequently it seemed as though they were about to run out of food, but God would always provide at the last moment as generous donations would come from local businessmen, such as a dealer in Luanda who couldn't find anyone to buy his grade 'B' beans and donated them all to Kalukembe.

During their time back in Kalukembe, the Fosters met the Comninellis family as Dr. Nicholas Comninellis prepared to take charge of the clinic in Huambo. Nicholas became a good friend of Steve and his family. Heather took an instant liking to Nicholas and his wife Teri's baby James and would help tend to him. In gratitude, Teri sewed a dress for Heather. During the Comninellis' seven-month tenure in Kalukembe, Nicholas worked at the hospital with Steve, giving him valuable experience in Angolan medicine.

When the time came for the Fosters to depart to Lubango, the staff at Kalukembe Hospital put on a grand farewell. As they had done at so many of their game nights, the nurses performed a skit in which Steve was portrayed by a nurse named Sr. Torres who donned a pair of shorts in imitation of the surgeon. The plot depicted the nurses in the operating theatre, anxiously wondering where Dr. Foster was, while Sr. Torres portrayed Steve as being out in the parking lot, stopping to greet every person who walked past him!

As the 1990s dawned, the collapse of the Soviet Union and end of the Cold War were at long last coming to bear, with the November destruction of the Berlin Wall.

Back in High Point, Sheila and Ezekiel decided to return to Lubango. Ezekiel responded well to his treatment, but the doctors could offer no guarantees—scans of Ezekiel's brain showed lines that might have been scar tissue—or cancer. Belva was certain that "even though we knew that without a miracle Ezekiel was going home to die, it was important that he go back to his family. As for Sheila—it was home for her." After the holidays, Sheila and Ezekiel began packing up their possessions. When their rented home was almost completely packed, they moved into Bob and Belva's house and where they lived in the basement in the last few days leading up to their departure.

Early on the morning after packing up their High Point home, Sheila was lying in bed with Ezekiel in her parents' home when she heard the phone ring upstairs. It was 6 AM. Knowing that there was a 6-hour time difference between Greensboro and Angola, Sheila became alert; perhaps her visa had been approved and there would be no further complications about their return. She heard her father holding a muffled conversation, then the sound of him descending the stairs. She arose to meet him.

The moment Sheila saw Bob's face, her heart jumped. Bob's expression was one of total shock. Still convinced the phone call must have come from Angola, Sheila blurted out: "Who died?"

Now Bob's expression shifted into one of confusion. "Nobody," he answered.

"Then why are you looking at me like that?" Sheila wondered.

"Your house burned down," he informed her.

"House?" Sheila wondered aloud. "What house?"

Her mind was still on Angola, so Bob had to spell it out. "Your house in High Point, it burned to the ground," he stated.

It seemed a short circuit in the wiring under the house had caused a fire which quickly engulfed the entire home in the early hours of the morning. By the time neighbours noticed and phoned the firefighters, it was too late to save the house. "It was the first time I really felt afraid," Sheila recalled. She had already lost most of her possessions in Kalukembe when the convoy had been attacked, now her possessions in High Point had been lost as well. Compounded with all the emotions around Daniel's birth and Ezekiel's health, Sheila cried out, "What have I done wrong? Doesn't the Lord love us?" In her mind, she thought, "I don't want to own another blessed thing, ever!"

Once again the church rallied around Sheila and Ezekiel, replacing all of the furniture which had been lost and even supplying toys for the children. Sheila had not been afraid during the years of the travel ban in Kalukembe— but now she was terrified. She believed a crisis such as this had been allowed by God to prepare her for another crisis later. "The only thing I could think of that would be worse would be if Ezekiel was going to die."

As Sheila, Ezekiel, Helena, Sara and Daniel set out for Angola once again, Bob told Sheila, "whatever happens, whatever the future holds, you can be sure that the way God has taken care of you now is how He's always going to take care of you." He also gave the couple this verse: *"Blessed is he, whosoever shall not be offended in me"* (Matthew 11:6).

LUBANGO

In the city of Lubango, the statue of Cristo Rei still sat upon the hill overlooking the landscape. Even in the most fiercely anti-Christian moments of the government regime, people could not bring themselves to take down the beautiful statue. Although only about 200 kilometres from Kalukembe, Lubango had a different feeling about it—more urban, certainly, as Lubango served as the administrative capital of Huíla Province; but it was also surrounded by hills, the very hills of Tundavala which had so impressed Steve in 1971. Lying upon the Huíla Plateau, Lubango rose higher than many sections of Angola, rising 1,760 metres above sea level.

An MAF plane brought Steve, Peggy, the children and their devoted housekeeper Joaquina in January 1990; the same airfield MAF and the national airline TAAG used in Lubango also housed the hangars for the Angolan air force and their fleet of MiGs (Russian fighter aircraft), a sign of how much more control the government enjoyed there relative to Kalukembe. The two trucks carrying their possessions made it safely down the same roads where both Afonso and Sheila's trucks had been ambushed. Unfortunately, Lubango was not quite ready to receive the Fosters—there was still no solution to the housing issue. AEF owned a guest house for visitors and so temporarily put the Fosters up there.

Steve finally found a home that seemed like it would be perfect for the family. As cars were very hard to come by, the purported owner agreed to sell the house to Steve in exchange for his six-year-old Chevy suburban. When Steve went to the notary office to settle the deal, the notary had unpleasant news: the woman selling the house was not the owner! The home had only ever had one owner and that man was chagrined to learn his tenant was trying to fence his property. For once, the bureaucrats had come to Steve's rescue!

Steve and the actual owner went ahead with the deal, but for a different home located in the neighbourhood of Benfica. The home had three bedrooms and a small adjacent annex. This house proved to be exceptionally dilapidated, but fortunately, though, they were being visited by Peter Damore, a registered nurse who was also an extremely good home renovator. Peter had met Steve during the previous furlough and had been inspired to help. Peter spruced up the home as best as he could and after five weeks in the guest house, Steve and his family finally had a home of their own! It was not an entirely pleasant house—there were cockroaches, no electricity and no running water. Still, the Fosters knew this home too was a temporary solution until the proposed complex at Mitcha could be built.

Meanwhile, Steve went to work at the Central Hospital in Lubango. Immediately, he found this would not be the laid-back environment he had grown accustomed to at Kalukembe—the staff insisted he could not wear shorts, but instead had to wear long trousers and buttoned-down shirts. This dress code extended to the patients as Central's security guards would turn away patients who did not dress in 'appropriate' attire—such as traditional African garb or ragged clothing. It was not so different from what the Portuguese officials had once demanded from Angolans.

The roster of physicians at Central comprised a veritable communist all-star team: Russians, Cubans, Vietnamese, North Korean and even Chinese doctors. The facility was, much like the Fosters' house, a fixer-upper. There were 500 beds with no sheets, blankets, pillows or towels. There was also no running water except on the first floor (for a few hours in the morning). The eight-storey building had an inoperable elevator—so patients had to be carried up flights of stairs to the wards. The operating room lay on the first floor, and during rain showers water would seep through the ceiling, enter the electrical lights and short them out.

Steve began establishing the space for The Project and conferred with his new colleagues. One day, he was invited by a Russian gynaecologist to operate with him on a lady with an intra-abdominal abscess; in return, the Russian asked Steve to teach him how to repair vesicovaginal fistulas. Steve observed "the Angolan doctors I've met are starved for clinical teaching."

As such, Steve quickly made an impression on the Angolan physicians. One Angolan doctor whom Steve invited into the operating theatre with him expressed his gratitude with tears in his eyes. "You have no idea what it is like to work 4 years with a Cuban doctor who pushes you out of the operating room every time you try to learn how to do a hernia," the Angolan told Steve. Either because of sensitivity over being observed or from fear of criticism, the other surgeons had not been welcoming the Angolans into the theatre.

What Steve also learned from interacting with the Cuban doctors was how ill-prepared they were to handle the caseloads of Angolan patients. Steve now had 12 years of experience treating Angolan medical issues and could prepare Angolan physicians to treat the type of cases most likely to emerge in their own nation. To Steve's surprise—and delight—many of the Angolan nurses at Kalukembe braved the dangerous roads and showed up in Lubango, eager to work alongside Steve at Central. In all, almost a third of Kalukembe's nurses would come to work at Central.

The Project was beginning to come together. Paul and Susan Cole joined; Paul as an internal-medicine specialist, Susan in pediatrics. Steve's ultimate hope in training physicians at Central was that "10-20% of our graduates will go back to serve the rural people." There were still many under-staffed or unstaffed clinics in Angola where such people could have a tremendous impact. Of course, Steve also saw The Project as an opportunity to evangelize: "We hope for Christian teachers for the most part to provide role models. What an excellent opportunity to demonstrate the love of Jesus."

"It will help train Angolan doctors to fill the 137 abandoned hospitals in the rural municipalities of Angola which at present do not even function. It will help rebuild an important segment of Angolan society with an international and interdenominational consortium of missionaries and non-government organizations in Angola and Canada. It will pioneer a new form of missionary medicine stressing the necessity of preparing indigenous physicians for their own hospitals and programs. It will further the credibility of the Church in a society that has on occasion mocked the efforts of God's people."

In those days, Lubango's streets were littered with Cuban vehicles—demobilizing tanks and Lorries on their way westward to the port and transport home to Cuba. One day it took Steve five hours to cross Lubango by car due to the constant traffic interruptions.

At Benfica, Steve's family was trying to settle into its new house. Most of their water had to be collected from a 250-gallon tank located 6 miles from home. When running water was available (1-2 nights every 2 weeks), it would only remain flowing for so long, so the children became used to turning on the bathtub to collect as much as they could while able. Although Peggy had Joaquina on hand for the household chores, she no longer had São and had to take up all the cooking, while also guiding the children's correspondence classes. Maintaining the household was difficult, for the war had caused a tremendous upheaval in prices; for instance, 30 eggs cost $80 USD! It became all the more difficult to attract new missionaries into the field with so much inflation.

The children reacted differently to their new locale. As Rebecca made friends, she discovered having grown up in Kalukembe she spoke her Portuguese with what, in comparison to the city dwellers, was a "hick accent." Her friends would ask Rebecca to read the newspaper to them for their enjoyment and laugh at how she pronounced words. For instance, instead of calling chewing gum *pastilha*, she called it *chuinga*. As a result, she soon realized the Angolans who used that term simply didn't have the word *pastilha* and had been trying to speak the English words *chewing gum*. She had also heard the expression meaning "to kick" (*ponta pê*) as *kunda pê*.

Rachel adapted very readily, proving to be the most outgoing of her siblings. Through the church choir, she made many new friends. Heather and Rob, however, struggled. Heather was instantly homesick for Kalukembe, while Rob was more comfortable in wide grassy spaces and hunting than in the urban environs.

On February 11, 1990, the South African government finally released Nelson Mandela from his long confinement in what would become a major step in ending Apartheid. Reconciliation was on Steve's mind as well, as he pondered the situation of Angolans who had been in combat against one another. "The only people I know with any solution to the Angolan dilemma are Christians who can love their brothers, who can pour coals of fire on his head, because the one who hated them, the one who killed them, the one who murdered their children, the one who raped their wives is the one today they receive back into the fellowship. That is the dilemma in Angola, it is brother against brother, cousin against cousin, it is just a terrible war that has divided the country. The only people who know how to love their enemies are those people with whom and in whom the spirit of God is resting. Christians are the only people who can say anything to a country that needs to be reconciled."

BEAUTY FOR ASHES

Back in Canada, Peggy's mother had been struggling with cancer and went through chemotherapy. Sanguine about her condition, when she parted from Peggy she made it clear she did not expect to live to see her daughter again. But instead of the cancer, it was a sudden aneurysm which hospitalized her. It became clear to her son Bob that she was nearing the end of her life—what was not clear to him was when he should inform Peggy. Bob struggled with sharing the news, not wanting to interrupt Peggy's life until he was absolutely certain their mother was about to die. Finally, he asked his secretary to put in a phone call to Peggy in Angola. In those days, an international phone call could take several hours to simply link up both parties because of the number of networks that had to be set up ("It was like moving mountains," Bob recalled). So the secretary faithfully kept at the task until she reached Peggy. When Peggy heard the news, she took a flight to Toronto as quickly as possible. Fortunately, Belva and Sharon had come to Lubango to help Sheila and had known about Fran Parkins' failing health. "The next five weeks were some of the most strenuous I've ever spent," Belva said, noting she had to prepare "meals for 8-10 people even with some household help, and supervising four children's schooling, in a house with no running water, but everything running hectically took everything I had."

While Sharon and Belva helped watch over Peggy's children, Peggy flew back to Toronto. When Peggy had seen her father for the last time in 1981, she didn't feel as though it was a proper farewell. She and her mother had always had a great bond and she wanted desperately to be present to say goodbye to Fran. Before departing she was informed of her mother's death, but still she *had* to know for certain. When her plane landed in Toronto, she came running from immigration to where her siblings were waiting. "Is she still here?" she asked frantically. Her siblings confirmed the difficult news: Frances Parkins had died one day before. Peggy burst into tears. "I just wanted to be here. I just wanted to say goodbye."

While Peggy saw to the funeral arrangements with her four siblings, Ezekiel's condition was becoming more and more obvious. Physically, Ezekiel had begun feeling weak in his right side. Mentally, he had trouble thinking clearly and concentrating. Sheila realized her husband was slowly dying. There were many matters which would have to be dealt with if he died, but Ezekiel refused to entertain those thoughts; always an optimist, Ezekiel hoped for his healing. Ezekiel's brother Ambrosio, who was teaching at ISTEL, was likewise confident that God would restore his body.

On Mother's Day, May 12, Peggy returned to Lubango, but it was not a happy return. She left the funeral of her mother only to return to see Ezekiel's diminishing condition; Peggy had also caught infectious hepatitis. She was put to bed, and Belva had to continue looking after the children—although Rebecca often vied with her for directing the household, causing some personality clashes. Fortunately, the family's faithful cook from Kalukembe, São, moved to Lubango that year and resumed service to the family, lightening the load of chores.

That June, *Sword & Scalpel: A Surgeon's Story of Faith and Courage* was published by author Lorry Lutz. The subject of this biography was Bob Foster (although the title was very similar to the 1952 biography of Dr. Norman Bethune: *The Scalpel, the Sword* by Ted Allan and Sydney Gordon). Lorry spent years coordinating efforts with Bob and his family to tell their story, from the journey of Charles Foster to Zambia up until Bob's retirement from AEF. Bob explained the title came from "The Sword of the Spirit, which is the Word of God (Ephesians 6:17) and the scalpel, representing the ministry of medicine; the two work together." The book became a significant tool for inspiring other people to become missionaries. MAF's Mark Faus was inspired by the book's stories of "people who are pioneers in missionary medicine that have a provoking story to tell of dedication and persistence."

Diminished in strength, Ezekiel would spend most of his time in bed. He spoke very little and what he did say came out garbled. The one mercy about his condition was that he felt very little pain. Belva finally had to depart; she gave her son-in-law a kiss goodbye, and hugged Sheila tightly. Fortunately, Ambrosio stepped up to aid the family and offered to take Ezekiel into his home so that Sheila would only have to tend to her three children. One morning, Sheila went to Ambrosio's to see how Ezekiel was faring, then went home to check on the children. When she returned, Ezekiel was dead.

Steve used an HF radio to contact Bob, who was with Samaritan's Purse at the time and when Franklin Graham heard about the situation he paid for Bob's ticket to Angola. Although Bob went to Angola as quickly as he could, the tradition in Angola was to hold the funeral as soon as possible. On June 21, Ezekiel's funeral service was held and he was buried in Lubango's city cemetery. Despite the ongoing war, a multitude of people from Kalukembe arrived for the service, including Ezekiel's family. UIEA, IESA and AEF were all represented at the service, in which the sermon preached was on Isaiah 61:3 *"And provide for those who grieve in Zion—to bestow on them a crown of beauty instead of ashes, the oil of joy instead of mourning, and a garment of praise instead of a spirit of despair. They will be called oaks of righteousness, a planting of the Lord for the display of His splendour."* Sheila took great meaning from that passage—it explained why Ezekiel had died and how she would respond. "The Lord has fulfilled those promises," Sheila confirmed.

Two days after the funeral, Bob arrived. He had known he would miss the ceremony but still had concerns about Ezekiel's family and wanted to be certain their agreement would be honoured. Ambrosio was heartbroken over his brother's death, but he was also faithful to the promise he had made years ago and insisted his other relations be true to their word. Bob satisfied the Fabiano family that Ezekiel's three children—Helena (4), Sara (2) and Daniel (9 months)—would be raised by the Fosters. In fact, Rebecca would spend time living with Sheila to help tend to her young cousins.

Sheila wasn't sure if she wanted to remain in Africa without Ezekiel, uncertain if she could manage as a single parent on the mission field. "I wasn't sure what the mission policy would be, or how useful I would be as a single parent, trying to keep the family together, as well as doing something that would justify my being in Angola."

Sheila continued to teach at ISTEL and would eventually become the institution's acting principal. "Sheila was courageous," said Pastor Calenga. "She never lost the vision of why she was in Angola."

Rachel was also impressed: "Auntie Sheila has such incredible grace."

THE GORILLA'S GRIP

Late that summer, Steve and Peggy were going to take a quick furlough back to Canada. Journeying back through Luanda, Steve took the opportunity to hold meetings with officials about The Project. Peggy left the children in the care of another missionary, a mother who brought her baby along as they visited the beach and went to a park where there was playground equipment.

Near the playground was a series of cages for zoo animals and Rachel grew curious about the animals. She spied a structure on the outside of the zoo wall which was like a ladder; although she was barefoot from visiting the beach she had plenty of experience climbing trees at Kalukembe and deftly climbed to stand on top of the wall surrounding the cage, looking down on the animal before her: a gorilla, who was being taunted by children inside the zoo. Throwing rocks and sticks, the children would tease the gorilla, riling it up until it would move to the back of the cage and charge at the bars, trying futilely to break free, angrily gripping the bars as it sought to attack its tormentors. Rachel stared at the scene in mute horror; it was terrifying to see how incensed the gorilla became, so much so that she was almost paralysed in fascination.

Rachel's babysitter finally noticed where she had gone and, gripping her baby, angrily remonstrated at Rachel, ordering her to get off the wall. If she had been wearing shoes, Rachel would have easily jumped down, but being barefoot she needed to find her courage. Just as she had summoned her strength, she leaped—but instead of landing feet-first, however, she found herself hanging upside-down. The gorilla had caught her by the right foot! More terrifying, he was biting down on her foot with his teeth! Unable to free herself, Rachel hung helplessly above the ground, looking down at the grass. She could feel the gorilla's teeth biting down on her foot, chewing at her toes. She reached out with her hands to grasp at the grass, trying ineffectively to pull herself free.

Startled, the babysitter dropped her baby and ran to Rachel's aid, trying to hoist her up for fear of what the gorilla might have done to her leg. People began grabbing sticks and beating at the gorilla, but he refused to let go of Rachel's foot. Finally, someone stuck fingers into the animal's eyes to force his release. The gorilla had disfigured Rachel's right foot, which was a bloody mess. The babysitter took a *pano* (piece of cloth) which Heather had been wearing and wrapped it around Rachel's foot. "She's going to be upset," complained Rachel, delirious. "You're going to get blood all over her pano!"

The babysitter had to abandon the other Foster children as she took Rachel in a car to the hospital. Every time the vehicle went over a bump, Rachel could feel the bone in her leg jiggle and screamed in pain. She was taken to the emergency ward while the babysitter went to find Steve and Peggy. Being alone in the hospital was a terrifying experience for Rachel; she wound up naked on a gurney, alone in a darkened corridor, screaming for a nurse to help her and without any clue what was going on. By the time Steve and Peggy arrived, Rachel was already in the operating theatre being treated by the Russian surgeons.

Rachel regained consciousness on a ward within the hospital, sharing a room with a woman suffering from malaria. Her right leg had been placed inside a cast. Peggy came to the hospital as often as she could, but the government-run facility was more restrictive about visiting hours than any of the church hospitals where Steve had worked. Rachel suffered from a seeming lack of caring in this hospital as she would be left in her bed without a bedpan and unable to rise, giving her no way to relieve herself without screaming for a nurse. Finally, Rachel was released and the family returned to Canada. They were going to stay with Trevor and Peggy Smith during this furlough and as soon as they were in the Smiths' house, Steve called in Dr. Muriel Henderson to bring the equipment they would need to remove the cast.

Steve was incensed to see the quality of care his youngest daughter had received; the cast had not been given a drain to prevent infection and the wound had been sutured closed, trapping bacteria inside her wound which resulted in gangrene on Rachel's foot. Rachel was taken to Sick Kids, the Toronto's children's hospital, where doctors confirmed her right lower leg was fractured. While they saved her leg, flesh lost on Rachel's foot had to be replaced with a graft from her thigh and her foot required some reconstruction. In the end, she was left without a baby toe on the right foot. Rachel's bed in the Sick Kids triage room had a picture of a baby monkey on the wall opposite; after seeing it, Rachel demanded the staff take it down.

While Rachel spent six weeks in the Toronto hospital, Steve took the opportunity to have an operation performed on Rob at the same time. Suffering from post-polio symptoms, Rob had a contracture in his Achilles tendon repaired. Both Rob and Heather suffered nightmares from the incident of the gorilla attack on Rachel. Rachel was given a plethora of gifts from well-wishers, making Rob jealous as his operation didn't yield anywhere near the amount of attention. For Rachel, constantly telling the story of the gorilla attack became tedious and she began suppressing it.

Rachel's physiotherapy took a long time as Peggy helped her regain her ability to walk. The nerves in her foot had been damaged and the pain of walking on her right leg was initially so intense that Rachel would scream in agony; Peggy would read stories to her to distract her from the pain. When Rachel's leg had regained mobility, she took to wearing closed shoes, hiding her amputation from sight.

Quickly returning to Lubango, Steve was much occupied in The Project, with Dr. Steve Duncan and Dr. Ken Foster having also joined; Carlos Velosa becoming the administrator and Dr. Filipe Matuba serving as college director. Dr. Stuart Archibald came out briefly as a visiting professor. Peter Damore was hard at work in teaching nurses to work in surgery and constructing homes for The Project's staff and students. Gerry Stanfield joined to set up the initiative's financial policy and accounting, while his wife Lois began teaching English to the med students as well as teaching the mission kids, including the Foster children. With Steve so busy at The Project and Central Hospital being further from home than Kalukembe Hospital had been from their mission station home, Steve's children missed having easy access to their father.

Helping Sheila tend to her children was at times a welcome distraction, and the Benfica home slowly improved as a water well with pump had been dug. The Foster kids also got to know Jim and Janet Holden's family. The Foster kids were surprised to learn the Holdens' kids were learning through the Canadian correspondence program as well as attending an Angolan school—twice as much schooling as what they were receiving!

At the start of 1991, The Project gained a significant new physician: Dr. Steve Collins. Although a Canadian citizen, Dr. Collins was a mission kid who had been born in Kamundongo, Angola, and spent many years with his family in Dondi. During the 1970s, Dr. Collins had met Steve at McMaster while undergoing his own training. In 1989, Bob Foster had come to speak at

Dr. Collins' church. Upon greeting him, Bob asked, "Steve, are you a doctor now?" After Dr. Collins confirmed it, Bob reacted, "Well, you've got to go to Angola, not stay out here!" Dr. Collins replied he had been trying to get into Angola but been unable to find a mission project that would accept him; Bob readily had him contact Steve and brought him into The Project. Dr. Collins' long association with Angola made him an easy fit into the mission staff at Central. Eventually, Central had three Steves working there: Steve Foster, Steve Duncan, and Steve Collins; their department was nicknamed "Bloco do Estêvão" ("Block of Steves"), a nickname which persisted long after all three men moved on.

One day, Darrell Hockersmith was transporting mail from the post office to Lubango's airport. En route, his pickup truck was rammed by a 20-ton truck. The other truck had failed to give Darrell the right-of-way at a roundabout and struck it on the left side, crashing the vehicle through an adobe wall. A young man from Darrell's church heard the crash, recognized Darrell's car and quickly informed Steve at Central. Steve tended to his old friend's injuries and saved Darrell's life. Darrell and Barb saw Steve's presence as a gift to them from God, but Darrell's injury unfortunately forced him and Barb out of the mission field.

While the homes at Mitcha began construction, the difficulties in Angola continued to escalate; inflation made the cost of living a great burden on the missionaries and it also made furloughs less practical as plane ticket costs in US dollars were so high as to be unaffordable. Dr. Steve Collins and Dr. Ken Foster were sent out to Kalukembe Hospital to help bolster their staff as Jean-Pierre Bréchet had left the previous year. Meanwhile, with the Cubans' retreat from Angola almost finished, in March 1991, UNITA moved into Kalukembe and officially occupied the town, driving out all MPLA elements and claiming control over Kalukembe Hospital. As noted, there were many in the mission station who supported UNITA, including Pastor Eliseu, which made the situation there all the more tense.

The United Nations' UNAVEM I had been a success as the last Cuban forces left during May 1991. At the same time, the MPLA were at last willing to negotiate with UNITA to end the war. Wanting to re-establish ties with the global marketplace and join the World Bank, the MPLA officially ceased being Marxist-Leninist. On May 31, 1991, the MPLA government and UNITA signed the Bicesse Accords in Lisbon which created a timetable for general elections in Angola for September 1992 with UNITA at last present on the ballot as an official political party. There were also provisions made for UNITA's guerrilla army to demobilize and unite its forces with those of the government into a single national army. As a result, UNAVEM II was established in order to observe Angola's changing political landscape. As the USSR continued to crumble, there was an increased sense of optimism about the future; it was the beginning of "the Year of Peace."

CHAPTER 13

"The Year of Peace."

LUBANGO (June 1991 – December 1992)

"Continue to pray for this process of reconciliation and reconstruction," Steve asked his supporters at the outset of The Year of Peace. There had been positive developments in The Project as well: the Ministry of Finance had delivered half of the budget which The Project requested (Steve hadn't expected the ministry to come through at all) and the European Economic Community Development Fund supplied the outstanding balance. Although the nation seemed to be on the verge of peace, heightened tensions in Huambo had forced Dr. Comninellis and his family back to the US.

John and Kathy Bloise, with their sons Mike and Joey, came to serve in Angola. John had been a lawyer with a practice in New York but gave it up after meeting Bob and hearing about the needs in Angola. Being skilled in construction, he joined the effort to build the Mitcha compound while Kathy pitched in to help Peggy run her household and occasionally provided her nursing skills at Central. Brazilian missionary Miriam Pereira took over most of the teaching duties for the MKs. Dr. Frank Timmerman came as a visiting surgeon, and anaesthetist Dr. Ken Thomas also joined the staff. The surgical staff was now so large they began holding weekly meetings with case presentations and discussions about difficulties in the operating room. When Steve began at Central, there were no surgical cases being performed; now they were up to 30 per week. As Steve prepared for a brief trip away, his old colleague Dr. George Burgess came to cover for him. Burgess had been gone from Angola for 14 years following the destruction of his own mission station.

In August, Steve and Peggy left Lubango for a brief visit to North America so they could place Rebecca in Canada. Rebecca was going into Grade 11 and simply needed to be within the school system rather than rely on the correspondence material, which she found dull. The Fosters' friends the McArthurs in Cambridge, Ontario, took Rebecca in as their guest for the year. Rebecca would record messages on tapes to send to her family so they could hear her voice in Lubango; phone calls were still immensely unreliable.

While the Fosters were away from Lubango, UNITA's leader Jonas Savimbi came to town to campaign for UNITA. The formerly spotty water supply suddenly became straightened out as city water became available just in time for Savimbi's arrival. UNITA had established itself as a party comprised primarily of the Ovimbundu, who were the most populous tribe in Angola (about 40% of the total population). Consequently, Savimbi was certain he would win the election as he expected every Ovimbundu to give him their vote. Steve's friend Quim Silva attended one of Savimbi's campaign speeches and marvelled at Savimbi's audacity; first he would address the crowd in Portuguese and assert 'equality for all'; then he would switch to Mbundu and inform the Ovimbundu that once he took power, they would take everything 'the white men' had.

On September 6, 1991, Stirling Foster and Donna Gallant were married. Their wedding had originally been scheduled for earlier that year, but Donna realized she had emotional issues stemming from sexual abuse she had suffered; having found healing through Christian counselling, she and Stirling finally tied the knot. Steve and Peggy attended the service with their family. After months of counselling, Donna felt God had redeemed her from her family's troubles. The Fosters became the supportive family unit Donna had lacked growing up; Peggy became like a sister and Bob and Belva like her parents. Now that Stirling and Donna were wed, they were ready to begin their mission in Angola.

Steve, Peggy and their three remaining children returned to Angola through France, stopping for a day to see such Parisian sights as the Eiffel Tower and the Seine River, as well as their friends William and Angela Brandle. On October 10, Angola's Minister of Health Dr. Flavio Fernandes came to Central Hospital for the ribbon-cutting ceremony on the teaching unit; the Community Physician Training Project had officially begun. Steve acknowledged there had been many barriers to overcome in reaching that point, "But, as long as I feel our presence here is helping alleviate the pain we share with the Angolans, and we are able to make some helpful contribution to improving the health care of the Angolan people through medicine, and that the message of Christ's love can be clearly communicated through us, then it's worth it."

On October 24, 1991, Angola's President José dos Santos visited Lubango for the first time, not to be outdone by Savimbi's earlier visit. Accompanying dos Santos was Sam Nujoma, the President of Namibia. The duo presidential visit caused the electricity in Lubango to switch back on. Noting how between Savimbi and dos Santos they had received both water and power, Steve mused the men "should work together." The MPLA were campaigning under the slogan 'O Futuro Certo' ('The Future Is Certain'), while in contrast, UNITA's campaign was the idiosyncratic 'Calças Novas em Setembro' ('New Trousers in September').

On one of his many flights around Angola with MAF, Steve journeyed to Catota with Pastor Calenga. Catota had suffered terribly in the war with its clinic destroyed by UNITA and it was one locale AEF remained interested in rebuilding. However, the church leaders in Catota hadn't expected Steve and Calenga's arrival and were out tending their gardens when the men arrived; the only people around town were the stationed UNAVEM. By the time the men returned from the fields it was late in the day and the quarters they had for Steve and Calenga had no electricity. The two men had a hand-cranked water filter to purify the local water, so in the dark, Steve picked up a pot left for them, which contained what he assumed to be water. It was actually a pot of *tchisangua*, a corn-based beverage. Not realizing this, Steve poured it into the filter and was amazed at how, despite his vigorous turning of the crank, precious little water was coming through. "Boy, this water is dirty!" he announced to Pastor Calenga, and he was quite embarrassed when he learned what he had poured into the filter.

On another trip, the two men travelled through Kuito and while passing through an open-air market, one of the vendors recognized Steve. "Doutor Estêvão!" the man exclaimed. "My doctor!" Steve's former patient was so overwhelmed by the reunion that he insisted Steve take a free sample of his wares: he was selling shorts. Fortunately, Steve had always been partial to shorts.

Many people gathered around the Fosters that Christmas, including missionary Rachel Newman, who helped Sheila manage her household. Steve, Peggy, Sheila, Jim and Janet Holden and all of their children celebrated Christmas with Ken Foster, as well as the newly arrived Dr. Karen Henriksen who was assisting at Rio de Huíla and Rob Cooper, a visiting med student who, although Jewish, happily joined in the festivities.

Another great present to the world came on December 26: the Soviet Union officially dissolved. Although Stirling and Donna had yet to arrive, the Fosters went out to the mission farm Tchincombe and celebrated New Year's Eve. The Year of Peace was half-over and although Bob's lymphoma had resurfaced, otherwise there seemed to be much to be hopeful for.

HARSH REALITIES

In January 1992, a small convoy of British tourists was travelling through the south of Angola when, about 90 miles from Quilengues, they drove by a UNITA camp at night. Although tourists are advised not to travel at night, they had been granted only a 3-day visa to get through the country and were trying to keep to schedule. Alarmed by the cars' presence, UNITA opened fire on the vehicles. In the chaos, four of the tourists were killed; the last vehicle in the convoy turned around and went for help, but only one passenger survived the onslaught upon the first two vehicles.

The survivor, David Sabin, was brought to Central Hospital in Lubango to be treated for gunshot injuries. The story brought a rare international focus on Angola and in particular on Steve as he filed reports with the British Embassy in Luanda while treating Sabin's injuries and delivering autopsy reports on the four dead tourists. Unprepared for the consequences of its actions, UNITA tried to claim rogue MPLA elements were responsible for the attacks. Although UNAVEM cast blame on UNITA, there was little hope of a thorough investigation; the ongoing effort to bring peace to Angola through the Bicesse Accords all but guaranteed the matter would be swept under the rug.

The UNAVEM forces monitoring events in Angola had done little to ensure the success of their mission; UNITA's armies were still armed and the government army had not been unified. Professor Assis Malaquias summed up UNAVEM II thusly: "The stated goal of the UN mission in Angola was neither peacebuilding, peacemaking, peacekeeping nor peace enforcement. It was vaguely defined as 'verification and monitoring.' Consequently, UNAVEM II was unable to act as a deterring factor within the framework of traditional peacekeeping."

In Lubango, the Fosters would see UN staffers carousing in the town; Lubango was the southern headquarters of UNAVEM II. "The UN in Lubango was a joke," Heather opined. "They would drive around in fancy cars, drive all the prices up and never did anything of use that I could see."

The Project had to make some hard decisions; 4 of the 5 residents who had been assigned by the Ministry of Health resigned from the initiative that January. "They have become disillusioned over the lack of political progress in recognizing the validity of their course by the Faculty of Medicine," Steve explained. "This despite advances in this area and signs of resolution to the crisis." Another sign of the unrest felt during The Year of Peace was an increase in theft. Within 2 weeks, 3 missionary homes were broken into. Worse still, Paul and Susan Cole were suffering marriage problems and finally left Angola. Fortunately, The Project soon received three new interns and the remaining resident was promising.

In May, Ken Foster and Steve Collins moved back to Lubango from Kalukembe, having grown uncomfortable with the situation there since UNITA occupied the town. Ken went to live with his sister Janet Holden and her family, who were helpfully situated close by Central Hospital. Dr. Ian Gilchrist also came to Lubango for a visit so he could assist Steve with the administrative details of running The Project, as administration remained one of Steve's weak spots.

THE KNIFE SWALLOWER

One of Dr. Collins' most memorable cases occurred while he was serving on call at Central. A patient who had been carried in by his family informed him: "I swallowed a knife." Being a very strange assertion, Dr. Collins wondered if the man was speaking in some sort of euphemism, so asked for an explanation. "Someone tried to stab me," the patient answered, "and I swallowed the knife."

Dr. Collins was confused. "Through your mouth?" he asked.

The patient gestured at his throat. "No, no, it's in here."

Dr. Collins examined the throat. A slight amount of swelling was apparent and there were two cuts beneath his jaw but he was extremely sceptical of this man's story. He wanted to take an X-ray, but the hospital was rationed and as it was evening, there were no plates available for the day.

Dr. Collins summoned Steve on the radio and Steve performed an examination with a gastroscope, but he couldn't see anything inside the man's throat. Steve cleaned up the man's wounds, but the following day they took an X-ray; Dr. Collins and Steve were amazed to see on the film an ordinary dinner knife lying in the man's right pleural cavity. "He's got a knife in there," Steve commented dryly. The knife had gone down his throat in precisely the right spot to save his life, landing between his esophagus and trachea without damaging either one, but his right lung had begun to collapse; if he had remained untreated, he would have slowly bled to death.

"He had no problems beyond the psychological," Dr. Collins explained. His story about being attacked was a lie: "He tried to kill himself."

Another welcome visitor from Kalukembe was Nurse Paulo Ismael, who was suffering from an abscess near his eye that was in danger of blinding him. He went to Central for treatment and, while waiting in a crowded hallway, he was spotted from afar by Steve. "What is it?" Steve asked with concern. When Paulo explained his condition, Steve gave him a warm hug, then brought him directly to the operating theatre for surgery. After recovering from his surgery, Paulo discovered he could not return to Kalukembe because of the strong UNITA presence. Instead, he went to work with Ambrosio Fabiano to establish a new clinic. When the clinic finally needed a name, Paulo was reminded of how Steve had saved his eyesight. Inspired by Jesus healing the blind man at Bethsaida (Mark 8:22-26), he named his clinic *Bethsaida*.

As a further sign of change in Angola, in June, Pope John Paul II visited Luanda to celebrate the end of Marxism in the country, observe the 500 year anniversary of the Catholic Church in Angola and encourage the new democratic process. President dos Santos and Jonas Savimbi were at hand to try and leverage the Pope's appearance to their advantage, knowing the majority of Angolans described themselves as Catholics. The Pope's message of reconciliation was simple: "I exhort each and every one of you, in particular those who are responsible for the destiny of the nation, to follow the path of solidarity toward a mutual acceptance of all Angolans."

Rachel and Heather took up sewing lessons with Janet Holden which they attended to every Saturday. One Saturday, Rachel began feeling numbness in her face and the side of her thigh. Steve was alerted and he quickly surmised she was suffering from malaria—cerebral malaria, to be exact. Steve quickly obtained IV fluid so he could treat her from home while Peggy brought Rachel there. Rachel lay on Heather's lap, suffering a horrible headache that made her cry in pain. Rachel was placed in their home's guest room as Steve tended to her. As he fed the IV line into her, she lashed out at her father in delirious anger. As she mended, she suffered through feverish moments, such as looking around the room "for Uncle Steve [Collins]' bag of jokes." Fortunately, Rachel eventually made a full recovery.

THE MISSION FARM

Stirling and Donna Foster had begun their mission work by journeying to Portugal in April so Donna could learn Portuguese, but the planned 3-month stay ended early as Donna, who already had Spanish, proved quite adept. In June, Stirling and Donna arrived in Angola and began establishing the mission farm at Tchincombe. Located about 250 kilometres from Lubango, it situated Stirling and Donna not too far from Steve's and Sheila's homes although it was quite remote—a bush ministry in the Foster tradition!

Excited, Bob planned to give Stirling a Luchazi Bible for his ministry at Tchincombe, but Stirling told him not to bother—as the people around Tchincombe were Ovangambwe. Stirling soon found the Ovangambwe were not very 'churched.' Although many had heard the Gospel message, they did not take it very seriously in their lives, so the need for spiritual discipline was clear. Many Ovangambwe could not read their own language in print—for precious little of it was in print—so Donna set up reading classes, teaching primarily the women of the nearby village.

The greatest change Stirling found between the farms he had been trained on in the US and those in Angola was the concept of managing personnel, as in the US it had become common for farms to be operated with a small handful of people, rather than the dozens whom Stirling would employ at Tchincombe. However, most farms in Angola were being run as a recreational activity instead of to support people's livelihoods; as a result, relatively few farms in Angola earn enough commercially to remain in business. However, Stirling knew from historical records that before 1975 Angola had been a major agricultural producer. In 1973, for example, the country had exported 218,660 tons of coffee, compared to the less than 5 tons in 1992. It would take time to reawaken forgotten agricultural practices.

Although Donna's medical training was primarily in veterinary fields, she found herself the most qualified medical professional in Tchincombe and would handle simple clinical work in the village; Steve and Sheila would offer her further advice over the radio. Donna provided some public health training to the villagers as well, teaching them how to clean wounds and improve their nutrition.

As Stirling and Donna settled in, Steve and Peggy finally moved out of Benfica and into the spacious new home built for them in Mitcha. Rob aided Ken Foster as he planted eucalyptus trees and elephant grass around the compound to beautify it.

Rebecca came to visit her family for the summer and they took a camper trailer on a cross-country vacation through Africa. While in Zambia, they went to Luampa and Mukinge, Steve's childhood homes. It made Steve "surprisingly nostalgic and homesick" to see those places and to "renew old friendships" with people he hadn't seen for 30 years. "I began to understand Kikaonde again but a week was too short." Visiting the University of Zambia, Steve was electrified to discover they were "beginning an analogous generalist specialty program." Comparing the Zambian program to The Project, Steve felt "vindicated that these two programs have been generated by people in similar situations for similar needs and yet without prior consultations. Our [curricula] are practically identical."

After journeying as far as Victoria Falls and through several game parks, Steve and Peggy wound up returning to Angola through Namibia, joining a convoy with Sheila, Stirling and Donna, who had also ventured out for holidays. Arriving at the border control, the Fosters had to wait overnight in their vehicles while the wheels of bureaucracy ground slowly. Donna hadn't prepared for this situation and had no food. She was impressed that Peggy had brought a rice casserole and Sheila cooked chickens as both women were experienced with such situations. Donna admired her sisters-in-law, viewing them as the sisters she had lacked growing up. "Peggy and Sheila were my heroes. They did so much to help me adjust to Angola."

In August 1992, Steve and Bob were both participants in a 2-week-long Pastors & Leaders Conference in Menongue, sponsored by the UIEA and led by Rev. Guy Davidson of Samaritan's Purse and the World Medical Mission. The event brought together 120 church leaders, many of whom had been separated by warfare for decades. The purpose of the conference was to reconcile the church leaders and inspire them to bring the Gospel to Angola's unreached tribes. Some of the pastors walked for 2 weeks to reach Menongue. "I was particularly touched by their humility, simplicity and great faith," Steve said. Bob was "glad to find despite diverse loyalties and tribal animosities, they were faithful to the Word of God."

Steve led a seminar on AIDS (acquired immunodeficiency syndrome) while Bob gave a series of 10 messages on Nehemiah and family life issues. Pastor Silva Kapamba, the leader of UIEA, saw how many of the pastors were dressed in tattered clothes and told the others, "If you have two shirts, or two pairs of trousers, share one of them with a brother who has nothing." Bob was very glad to see church leaders' desire to reach the unreached tribes of Angola. "God wonderfully answered prayer in reuniting the brethren and giving them a spirit of love and unity to press forward in the work of evangelization. Ten unreached tribes in the southern half of Angola were targeted by the church as their objective for missionary outreach during the next ten years in cooperation with the AEF." Steve was also fascinated to hear from one person who had seen Sr. Silva, his nurse from Cavango; he hoped they might yet be reunited.

Steve's shortcomings came to the forefront when his friend Rev. Paul Allen came to Lubango to help lead a mission conference, only to find Steve in conflict with other missionaries in the city. Paul joined Pastors Abias and Calenga in mediating the issue and it forced Paul to address some hard truths. Steve drove Paul to the meeting, then found himself on the end of a verbal tongue-lashing from his friend. "It's one thing to be a dictator in the operating room," Paul scolded him, "but you can't behave that way in the rest of the world." Paul understood why Steve reacted the way he did. "Steve is a surgeon, he's not looking for a consensus. He's looking for a life-saving answer every moment of the day." Steve repented his behaviour and promised to reconcile with the other missionaries. This left Paul in an uncomfortable position, needing Steve to drive him home afterwards. He began to wonder if he could find another ride back, when Steve came up to him, hugged him warmly, and thanked Paul for teaching him. Then he drove Paul home, still his good friend.

With Stirling and Donna in Tchincombe, the other Fosters would frequently visit them as a getaway from the urban life of Lubango. On one trip,

Stirling, Steve and Rob sat up most of the evening in Stirling's Land Rover overlooking a watering hole, hoping they might see elephants come to take a drink. Stirling and Steve chatted amongst themselves while Rob went to sleep. Around midnight they decided to call it off. Rob woke up and, needing to go pee, exited through the back of the Land Rover to find a bush. Moments later he jumped back into the Land Rover and slammed the door. "There are hyenas out there!" he informed his father and uncle. The adults scoffed at him because Rob had a great imagination, but as he breathlessly insisted they took out their flashlights to investigate. Stepping over to the bush where Rob had begun urinating, they found hyena tracks in the dirt on the other side of the bush. The hyena had evidently been waiting to pounce but, confused by Rob's behaviour, had lost its nerve and ran away. The grown-ups apologized to Rob for doubting him.

There was also an incident when Steve and Stirling went hunting for guinea fowl in a Land Rover. Their car didn't have a windscreen and when they sighted a flock of fowl Stirling decided to flush the birds with the Land Rover, while Steve would handle the shotgun. However, the fowl flushed a little sooner than they expected and, excited, Steve fired his shotgun while the Land Rover was still in motion! It was a dangerous manoeuvre, but no harm was done.

As a sign of how relaxed Angola had become during The Year of Peace, Peggy's brother Ted came to Lubango as a tourist. This marked the first time one of Peggy's birth family had been to the country. Ted stayed with the Fosters in Mitcha and was taken to see the sights, including Cristo Rei, Tundavala and the Tchincombe farm. The situation in Angola was beginning to feel 'normal.' The Angolans looked to the coming election and expected demobilizing of the guerrillas with a sense of hope.

THE WAR RESUMES

Between September 29-30, 1992, Angola held its first general election. Along with the MPLA and UNITA, there were 16 other smaller parties including the diminished FNLA. The MPLA won a majority of votes, but the title of president required a minimum 50% of the vote, necessitating a second round of voting. However, Jonas Savimbi rejected the results, claiming the election had been rigged. Due to Savimbi's intransigence, President dos Santos held on to power. "Never mind," one journalist noted, "the UN observers said the vote was reasonably free and fair—as fair as could be expected in a country that had never run democratic elections." In the aftermath, the nation tensed, certain fighting would soon resume. Savimbi had also been prepared for the resumption of warfare—not only by occupying locales such as Kalukembe, but by claiming many of Angola's diamond fields in the north to help finance his forces. He was soon making $60 million annually from trading in what the media would term "blood diamonds."

Near the end of October, Steve and Dr. Matuba left Angola to hold meetings on The Project in Canada. Although Mitcha's school for MKs had finally opened with Miriam Pereira as teacher, there was an increasing unrest in the nation and the city: "It is very tense with threats and rumours of war abounding," Peggy noted. MiGs had resumed daily patrols in the skies above the city and "There are gunshots heard at night but it's business as usual during daylight hours." The British Embassy suggested all non-essential foreign personnel should leave the country and most NGOs (Non-Governmental Organizations) had responded by leaving Angola. Mercifully, Sheila had gone to Greensboro on furlough with her three children and went to live with Bob and Belva.

"This is a real challenge to my faith and peaceful trust in the Lord," Peggy admitted. "These situations always cause us to draw closer to Him but there are moments that are difficult and I feel nervous (more than afraid) of what is going to happen." Peggy wanted to take her children to Namibia; Heather didn't want to leave, while Rob and Rachel thought the trip would be great until they were informed their school books would come with them! "Our leaving would be a big discouragement to the church," Peggy observed. "It's hard not having Steve here to share this with us." Reflecting on her past in Angola, Peggy concluded, "Both in 1975 and 1986 the Lord gave definite leading as to what we should do. He will do the same again."

Journalists and historians differ as to who was to blame for the resumption of hostilities—and as to which party was the first to officially resume the civil war. What was certain, though, was that during October 30 – November 1, 1992, the Halloween Massacre in Luanda saw the MPLA's FAPLA forces exterminating UNITA personnel in the city, subsequently claiming UNITA had attempted a coup. The civil war had once again gone hot and the massacre claimed more than 2,000 lives; "UNITA will never return here," the government vowed. Previously, the Angolan Civil War had been largely rural—fought in villages or in roadside ambushes. In this new stage, the fighting became urban—in spaces occupied with dense populations.

Alarmed, AEF ordered its missionaries to evacuate Angola using MAF planes. Peggy, Heather, Rachel and Rob were transported to Windhoek on October 31, only 3 hours before fighting broke out in Lubango. Stirling and Donna had come to town that day; unable to return to Tchincombe, they took up residence in the Benfica house and kept watch over 5 cars and 7 dogs, all of which belonged to evacuated missionaries. A few other missionaries remained to keep them company: Ken Foster, Steve Collins, Miriam Pereira and the entire

Holden family. Much like Steve and Peggy's children, the Holdens' children had difficulty comprehending what they were living through. Seeing the MiG jets fly over the city every day was "thrilling" to the kids and watching tracer bullets firing into the night sky was likewise fascinating to the children. The sound of gunshots and mortar fire could be heard throughout the evenings in Lubango, but AEF's fears of a bloodbath seemed to be groundless.

From Canada, Steve heard what had occurred in Angola. "I confess all of us were so delighted that things went so smoothly that it was hard to believe that the situation would deteriorate to its present degree." Changing his tickets, he flew to Windhoek to be with his family. Over the next six weeks, Steve began working with Samaritan's Purse and World Relief to accompany MAF on flights into Angola to provide medical supplies around the country. Steve did his best to assess the state of the country during his supply runs and each time, the country appeared stable. Central Hospital's staff was eager for him to return. "Times were very tough and discouraging for them in mid-November as tensions mounted and confusion existed as to why I was still out of the country."

In December, Steve, Peggy and their children joined John and Kathy Bloise as they drove from Windhoek to Lubango. Although the resumption of hostilities was discouraging, Steve sensed an opportunity for the family's witness: "Our partner churches in Angola have all felt that the situation in Lubango is tenable and offers a wonderful opportunity to show that Christians care. Our opportunities to serve have increased with the withdrawal of the Russian medical staff who make up two-thirds of the forty doctors in Lubango. The provincial governor was very grateful for the help provided and has asked for more medical staff to be sent to Lubango."

As 1992 drew to an end, the fighting had resumed and the flash of optimism had faded. The war was not over—and now it was headed to the missionaries' doorsteps.

CHAPTER 14

"A Certain Hope Left." — Heather Foster

LUBANGO (January 1993)

JANUARY 2

Margaret Anstee, a British official serving as head of the United Nations peacekeeping effort, visited Jonas Savimbi at his current headquarters, Huambo. Savimbi agreed to resume peace talks with the MPLA government. Anstee then flew to Luanda to meet with government officials. Although the MPLA had previously indicated they would not resume negotiations while UNITA remained armed, they stated they were willing to negotiate.

JANUARY 3 – 7:30 AM

It was Sunday morning; the first Sunday of the month and the first Sunday of the New Year. As was the custom, the churches in Lubango were scheduled to celebrate Holy Communion, with Mass being celebrated at the Catholic Church and a baptism at the UIEA church. At Central Hospital, Ken Foster and Steve Collins had arrived to perform early morning rounds as the nursing staff members provided updates on their current caseloads. Soon it would be time for the nurses' evening shift to go home while the next shift came to work.

At the airfield where the air force's MiGs were stationed, the planes were prepared—not for another routine patrol, but for combat. Outside the city, a battalion of T-55 and BMP-1 tanks commanded by FAPLA had assembled. With them was Angola's new Rapid Deployment Police, an elite unit trained in Spain to eliminate UNITA bases; this ruthless force was nicknamed 'ninjas' in the press. They were waiting for the signal to advance.

8:45 AM

At Mitcha, the Fosters and their friends the Bloises were preparing for church. John Bloise was feeling sick and remained at home in bed. With Sheila still out-of-country, Peggy was using her sister-in-law's car and took Kathy Bloise with her sons Joey and Mike in the borrowed vehicle. Steve was responsible for switching off Mitcha's generator, so he fell a few minutes behind Peggy. In his car, Steve was transporting 15-year old Heather, 12-year old Rachel, 11-year old Rob and Janet's daughter Esther Holden.

With the genset off, Steve started down the dirt road from Mitcha. At the time, Mitcha was still a rural location on the outside of Lubango, with most of the surrounding area taken up by grass and trees. As Steve went along he thought he saw a body lying across the road. "This is strange," he thought to himself, because although there were frequent hit-and-run accidents in Lubango, usually someone would drag the body away. The car windows were rolled up to keep out the dust from the road and music was playing, so Steve had no sense of what was going on.

As he reached the end of the dirt road and approached the asphalt of Lubango, Steve saw a number of people running and in a great state of excitement. Steve came to a halt, rolled down his window and hailed one of the people going by. "What's going on?" Steve asked. In answer, several of the passersby gestured upward: "Haven't you seen those explosions up in the sky?" they asked.

9:00 AM

In the sky over Lubango, almost level with the statue of Cristo Rei on the hillside, a signal rocket exploded in the air, leaving a white trail of smoke above the city. This was the alert to the forces waiting outside the city to begin to mobilize into Lubango. Their orders were to destroy the UNITA presence in the city, caring little that the UNITA members in Lubango were mostly office workers and had only a handful of weapons. However, the orders the forces received were so broad that it could be interpreted they were to kill anyone suspected of being in UNITA—or of being a UNITA supporter—for wearing one of the party's promotional T-shirts from the election or simply of being Ovimbundu, the largest ethnic group within UNITA.

"What's that?" Steve asked the passersby.

"That's the sign!" they answered. "Haven't you heard the gunfire down in the city?"

With both of the front windows in the car opened, Steve's ears finally detected "the popcorn sounds of small-arms fire."

The frightened people told him, "They're attacking in the city!"

Steve was startled. "Who's attacking?" he asked.

"We don't know," they answered, then continued their trek away from the city.

Steve's car was equipped with a CB radio, but Sheila's vehicle did not have one—he had no way to reach Peggy and warn her about what she was driving into. Pulling out the radio's microphone, Steve tried to reach Central Hospital, but no one answered him. He tried other frequencies, but none of the other missionaries answered his hails either. The missionaries kept their radios in either their houses or cars, so those who were barring the doors of their homes couldn't get to them, and those who had left early for church couldn't return home to the radios in their houses.

Whatever instincts might have compelled Steve to see to Peggy's safety or to check-in at Central, his immediate concern was the four children with him. He turned his car back to Mitcha and ushered Heather, Rachel, Rob and Esther back into the house. Steve ordered the children to keep away from the windows and remain as close to the centre of the house as they could. Entering the Bloises' home, Steve found John had rolled out of his bed to lie on the floor, afraid of bullets coming in through the window. After sharing what little he knew with John, Steve took out his binoculars and gazed at the city from the house windows, trying to see what was going on—and the severity of the fighting.

9:15 AM

As Peggy saw people running off the streets, she wondered what was going on. She began hearing scattered sounds of gunfire in the distance. As the noises of violence became more frequent, she turned to the home of Pastor Dinis, one of the church leaders, uncertain where else she could turn. Pastor Dinis was out but his wife ushered Peggy, Kathy, Mike and Joey into their house and they tried to comprehend what was happening.

"All of a sudden, all hell broke lose," said Dr. Collins. He and Ken were still at Central as the heavy fighting began. The sound of rockets and grenades exploding filled the air. Ken and Dr. Collins climbed to Central's upper storeys to look out into the city and try and grasp what was happening.

"Next thing you know there're MiGs flying across the town at treetop level!" Steve exclaimed. Through his binoculars he saw a formation of seven low-flying MiGs begin dropping bombs on the city! One of the bombs landed very close to the home of Steve's friend Pastor Abias.

The primary targets of the armed forces were the UNITA office which the United Nations had given the party for the election, and the downtown

Hotel Império where most of the UNITA employees were living. The UNITA office was within eyesight of Central where Ken and Dr. Collins watched as the army opened fire on the building; although FAPLA peppered the building, there was no exchange of fire—no one inside was shooting back. Anyone attempting to flee the scene was shot in the back. Finally, two young men emerged with their hands raised; they were thrown to the ground and sprayed with machine gun bullets. The army fired RPG rockets at the building, decimating it until it was an immense smoking wreck.

As the early church services were ending, across the city parishioners found themselves exiting into a war zone. At the Catholic Church, soldiers were stationed diagonally across from the entrance and began firing into congregants as they exited. People at the UIEA began running back inside their church, seeking safety from the soldiers outside. It was certainly no better for people who, like Peggy, had been on their way to church; some members of Peggy's choir were shot as they walked to church. A handful ran to the Holdens' house, where Jim and Janet granted them sanctuary. Jim sent his children into the central room of the house, locking them in and supplying them with their television set and VCR along with the longest movies they owned (1977's *Jesus of Nazareth* and 1970's *Patton*) to keep them occupied. The children were, indeed, little aware of what was going on; "I didn't ever question the war," Daniel Holden recalled.

Being out in public was not the only way to end up being targeted. One family who were friends of the Fosters had invited UNITA representatives into their house during the election campaign the previous August. The secret police took note of it at the time and on that morning, FAPLA soldiers invaded their home and executed the family for showing partiality to UNITA.

10:00 AM

The previous day's nursing staff remained at Central, too afraid of the violence to risk going home, which proved just as well—the new day shift failed to materialize. Likewise, none of the Angolan or expatriate physicians materialized. Ken and Dr. Collins realized they were the only physicians available—and the wounded were flooding Central. Not all of the injured were specifically targeted by FAPLA; the exuberant soldiers would fire their guns in the air, heedless that the bullets would eventually land and injure civilians. Ricocheted bullets injured many others.

At Mitcha, Steve continued to monitor the situation while the children, although concerned about Peggy, tried to tune out the sounds of violence from the city. Rachel and Esther took a bath together and sang "Old MacDonald" at top volume; it was how they coped with the situation. "We weren't stressed about it," Rachel recalled. "I don't know why. I think Dad has always been incredibly good under pressure and in those kinds of situations he is the most calm voice in the room and he does not get flustered. He may be a little bit more firm, he might tell you to relax. You felt everything was under control. I remember being worried for Mom, but not actually feeling anything could happen to her."

11:00 AM

One episode during the day became oft-repeated by missionaries for decades afterwards. Looking out of Central, Dr. Collins was incensed to see FAPLA soldiers on hospital property, setting up a rocket launcher and angling it down the slope from the hospital toward the UNITA office. "They were preparing to massacre more people there," Dr. Collins realized. His blood boiled. Fuelled by adrenaline and righteous indignation, Dr. Collins charged out of the hospital and walked in front of the rocket launcher. "That's fine!" he yelled at the soldiers. "That rocket goes right through me! I'm a physician at this hospital, this is neutral ground! There's nobody here that's UNITA, there's nobody here that's MPLA, these are patients and I will defend those patients. You want to put that rocket through me, you go right ahead and you'll answer to the Canadian government."

One of the nurses followed Dr. Collins outside and tried, nervously, to usher him back indoors, but Dr. Collins refused to budge. "Let them shoot me!" he yelled at the nurse. "I can observe from Heaven." An officer approached Dr. Collins and berated him for interfering with their operations, but didn't lay a finger on him. As a Canadian citizen, Dr. Collins knew he could afford to be bold. "Okay, have you finished?" he asked the officer at last. "Here I am. You can continue, nothing has changed." It was like a game of chicken and the officer simply could not risk creating an international incident by harming Dr. Collins. With no other choice, the army moved its rocket launcher to another location off the hospital grounds. "I was so mad," Dr. Collins admitted.

1:00 PM

From the vantage point of Pastor Dinis' house, Peggy had been seeing some of the horrors of the attack from close up. She witnessed an RPG fired at a residential home. The tanks were beginning to rumble through that part of town; one ran out of fuel and had to be refuelled in the street with a jerrycan. However, the sound of combat had lessened; the violence had reached a lull. Peggy felt God prompting her to get back in her car and return to Mitcha while the roads were still open, fearful of what the approaching tanks might do. Returning to the car, Peggy, Kathy, Mike and Joey returned to the road.

At the UN compound, its forces attempted to mobilize to help restore order in the city, only to be met by the Lubango police, which told the UN to return to its compound or its people would be shot. Three UNITA officials who had been working with the UN during the elections asked for sanctuary. But the UN had no authority to employ force; a squad of FAPLA soldiers surrounded the compound and executed one of the UNITA men on UN soil; the other two men were taken away, never to be seen again. Although the UN would express outrage at this incident and its Secretary Boutros Boutros-Ghali earned a personal apology from President dos Santos, apparently no one was punished. The UN had shown itself to be weak in the face of aggression, as would be demonstrated time and time again throughout human rights abuses in Africa during the 1990s.

1:45 PM

At Mitcha, Steve had assembled the other missionaries in his house and spent hours praying for Peggy, Kathy, Mike and Joey's safe return. Steve began reading from the Psalms, seeking comfort from Psalm 122. Then he began Psalm 121: "I lift up my eyes to the mountains; where does my help come from?" At that moment he heard the sound of Peggy's vehicle rumbling back into Mitcha! Steve and the children were overjoyed at their reunion, as was John Bloise to see his family safely returned. The Fosters sat down for a quick lunch.

2:00 PM

Steve's CB radio finally came back to life; Central was becoming overwhelmed with only Ken and Dr. Collins at hand so Dr. Collins had radioed to Steve— asking if he could come to work in surgery. Steve wasn't certain if it was possible. "At that point we weren't sure if fighting in the city was calming down or not," he recalled. "I've already come back home," Steve said to Dr. Collins, "there's no way to get into town. The road is littered with bodies and unless I get an escort I'm not coming down." Dr. Collins stepped out of Central; it was risky to be seen outdoors in the midst of this violence, but his inner outrage at the injuries he had seen gave him the adrenaline to propel himself forward. Finding a jeep full of drunken policemen he asked, "Does anybody know Doutor Estêvão?" One of them responded affirmatively. "Okay, somebody has to go up there and get Doutor Estêvão, we need him here."

In a few minutes, two police vehicles arrived at Mitcha. Steve said farewell to Peggy, and took his car into town, escorted by the police. The children were barely even aware their father had gone to work; Heather, assuming responsibility as the eldest, "kept us busy reading books, playing games, telling stories," Rachel recalled. "I don't think I knew how much danger we were in at any given time."

This time, Steve's drive down the Mitcha road was quite different; there were no longer any groups of people fleeing on foot. In fact, there wasn't a living soul to be seen—everyone was holed up in their homes. Along the roads, Steve could see the bodies of people who had been massacred. He arrived safely at Central, where Ken, Dr. Collins and the nursing staff were relieved to welcome him. "I was amazed at those people, the patience," Dr. Collins remarked of the nurses. The hospital's cooks had also remained in place and they provided food to the staff. It was going to be a very long day.

Steve and Ken took charge of surgery and began a marathon session of repairs, while Dr. Collins ran triage, ascertaining the most desperate cases. Many of the patients had suffered only superficial injuries and could be quickly discharged. However, one early outpatient, a woman in her 70s, walked only 30 yards from Central before being gunned down in the street. After that instance, the other patients refused to leave Central, so the hospital became their refuge.

"There was no clean up staff," Dr. Collins recalled. "Bloody bandages and amputated limbs simply lay around." The majority of the patients were women and children—with a few injured soldiers. "While Steve and Ken were operating there would be a **BOOM** and the whole hospital would shake," Dr. Collins remembered. "Steve would mutter in his way, 'What are they trying to do? Are they going to kill us all? We're saving lives and they're killing us?' Another explosion. 'Someone should talk to those guys.'"

Dr. Collins recalled one case in particular: while FAPLA were assaulting the Hotel Império, one woman came to the window of an upper storey holding her baby. "Please!" she screamed, and threw the baby to the soldiers below. One of the soldiers caught the infant, but the impact broke the baby's collarbone and dislocated its shoulder. The soldier brought the baby to Central and Steve saved its life, repairing the damage. Subsequently, the soldier adopted the orphan.

JANUARY 4, 3:00 AM

For 12 hours Steve and Ken laboured in surgery, operating on 26 patients. They slept at the hospital, but only "fitfully." In the morning, Steve, Ken and Dr. Collins performed rounds at Central. Ken noticed in the men's ward, the men would moan and cry; interestingly, in the women's ward he found the patients were much more stoic and reserved. The violence had quieted down and the steady flow of new patients had stopped. The three doctors and their nurses finally stepped aside and returned to their homes.

Life in Lubango slowly returned to normal; the people who hid with the Holdens were retrieved by family members who assured them it was safe to come home. However, many of slain or injured were abandoned by their families. "People were afraid to identify their relatives for fear of being seen as in cahoots with UNITA," Janet explained. Stories continued to circulate in the churches of people being dragged from their homes at night to be executed.

A mass grave was dug outside of Lubango near the base of Tundavala for all the unclaimed dead. Janet was visiting a Brazilian couple in their eighth-floor apartment. Looking out the window, she saw trucks going by carrying stacks of bodies to Tundavala. As Janet gazed at the bodies, saddened, another woman reprimanded her. "You'd better not look out the window looking sad or else you'll be incriminated as a sympathizer and they'll come for you as well," the woman cautioned Janet. "You had to mask all your pain and hate," Janet reflected.

However, Dr. Collins wore no such mask. Still incensed by what he had seen, he painted the symbol of the Red Cross on his car to help him get around Lubango. In the morgue at Central, he had taken a count of the bodies: 226. From there, he went to the city cemetery ("The graveyard caretaker was drunk; I don't blame him.") and out to the mass grave to collect more numbers. He took many photographs: "The mountains of bodies, pregnant women slashed open with bayonets, their babies at their side." All figures combined, Dr. Collins estimated at least 1,500 people had been killed.

DENIAL

The world outside knew little about what was going on in Lubango. There were no international journalists present during the massacre—the nearest were situated in Luanda and simply repeated the government's official statement on the incident. The MPLA claimed they had "taken back" Lubango from UNITA, referring to the Hotel Império as a "stronghold" of the rebels. The governor of Huíla, claimed only 30 people died in Lubango and referred to it as "an isolated incident." The governor stated, "What happened here in Lubango was a series of provocations by UNITA. It did so in the districts, against our armed forces and also here in the city. The climate of intimidation and insecurity is returning. An incident in which a hand grenade was hurled at a personnel carrier truck set off the clashes. That is what happened."

As missionaries began to spread the word of the actual numbers, they were quoted (anonymously) in newspapers with journalists identifying them as "pro-UNITA." Reports ranged wildly as to the number of people killed—

anywhere from 100 to 1500, which made doubting the accounts easier to accomplish. Although the Cold War was officially over, the outside world persisted in seeing the Angolan Civil War as something of the past; reports on the Lubango massacre consistently phrased the Angolan Civil War as having concluded two years earlier with the Bicesse Accord. During the Cold War, UNITA had been gladly embraced by other nations as fighters for democracy, but in the wake of the elections, the outside world was simply eager to open Angola up to business and saw UNITA as an impediment. Margaret Anstee summed up the newspaper coverage as "a conspiracy of silence by the international media."

UNITA had their own journalism correspondents reporting in Lubango, but their accounts of the massacre were full of invectives directed at the MPLA and its leaders. Jorge Alicerces Valentim, UNITA's information secretary, tried to involve Portugal in the massacre, claiming an international conspiracy against UNITA. Such missives did nothing to encourage international support for UNITA.

Savimbi again called for a mediated peace, but Prime Minister Marcolino Moco responded, "UNITA has this mania for proposing talks every time they lose territory. We are sick of this attitude. UNITA has to learn that neither side benefits from war. If UNITA wanted to comply with peace accords we wouldn't need a ceasefire."

As word reached North America, it made an impression on the other members of the Foster family. Rebecca was grateful her family had been spared: "It brought home how 'real' the civil war was." Sheila was relieved her own children were with her in Greensboro. "I was very glad not to be [there] because the kids were small and it would have been very traumatic for them."

When the Holdens' children returned to school, Daniel Holden began to understand something of how the massacre was viewed by the Angolans. He heard kids telling "stories of how their dads were heroes for looting. They had new fridges and TVs." One of the children asked Daniel if his father had looted anything; Daniel confessed no, they hadn't.

Dr. Collins and Ken once went to visit ISTEL's teachers Paul and Dorothy Kleiner and were told how on the day of the fighting, a UNITA soldier had shown up at their home and handed them his uniform and AK-47 to be hidden for safekeeping. Paul hid the items in his attic. When Dr. Collins heard this, his face lit up. Retrieving the AK-47, the incorrigible Collins took the rifle apart until he found the weapon's spring action mechanism, which he wrecked. Eventually the soldier returned for his weapon and was somewhat chagrined to find it rendered completely useless!

"These events and all the attendant wickedness were gruesome reminders of how close to the edge this society lives and the depths to which the roots of hatred have grown," Steve said. "The role for Christians in this land to show something of the opposite attitude has never been greater. The need to do it and show it in our lives and actions is all the more important. Most of the international community aid workers, etc., had left the country after the events of October 31, 1992, so that the few of us left as Christians stood out all the more."

"One can't survive emotionally, always thinking disaster is around the corner," Peggy philosophized. January 3 was the most catastrophic day of the civil war the Fosters had ever witnessed, but it garnered precious little interest internationally, even among human rights groups. The Angolans who lived through the massacre simply wanted to forget. "This nation is still in denial," Janet opined in retrospect. "This nation is reaping the denial of what our generation suffered or lived through."

AEF remained concerned for the lives of its missionaries; it had already evacuated the missionaries once, now it (and the Canadian government) began suggesting another evacuation was necessary. However, Steve and the other missionaries were quick to observe that while the violence on January 3 had been intense, "None of the expatriate Christian community were targets of either side in the fighting. We were able as physicians to bring help, care, and surgical attention when there are no other surgeons in this part of the world. To leave would abandon 2.5 million people who live in this region to **NO** surgical care. Our Angolan Christian brethren were encouraged by our presence and desired us to continue. Our families were secure at Mitcha and could go on with the tasks of daily living. As Christians, ultimately we decided that our priorities have to be what would honour God, not what would be safer for me."

"God has been gracious to us in not asking us to walk through too much fire," Steve added. "We have suffered almost nil personally. We have been encouraged by our ties in the community of Christians." Reminded of the ordeal in Cavango back in 1975, Steve wondered, "How can we leave and then come back and tell the people we're serving here that our God only takes care of us when we're in safe zones?"

"Afterward we saw the sadness and uncertainty," Heather recalled. "People had hope. After years of saying 'never take sides,' people began to feel they could be open about what they preferred, they could make political statements without being shot. All of that was torn away. Things were really sombre among the missionaries. Dad witnessed so much at Kalukembe but it all felt like the tide was turning. A certain hope left. Hope rekindled [then] squashed really hard."

THE LETTER

As Steve, Ken and Dr. Collins took stock of the international reaction, they felt their own stories needed to be set down in print. Each them independently wrote an account of what they had seen and done on January 3. Ken and Dr. Collins were both due to take a furlough via Namibia and Steve directed them to deliver copies of each letter to a friend of his in the Namibian government. "Unbeknownst to us," Dr. Collins revealed, "he was a traitor."

When Dr. Collins returned to Canada he received a summons to see the Department of Foreign Affairs. "What have I done?" he asked.

"You haven't done anything," the official answered. Dr. Collins set out to Parliament Hill, Ottawa, and the official showed him a copy of one of the three letters. "Did you write this?" the official asked. Dr. Collins was stunned; how had they obtained this copy? But more fantastically, why did the letter present Steve's account under Dr. Collins' signature?

The Foreign Affairs official explained the account had appeared translated into German in one of Namibia's newspapers. Dr. Collins explained to the official what had happened and shared his suspicion that Steve's "friend" in Namibia had leaked their papers.

At this, the official told Dr. Collins, "Don't go back. We don't know what they'll do to you if you go back." Dr. Collins notified Steve of what had occurred.

At the suggestion that his friend might suffer over this situation, Steve arranged a meeting with the provincial governor as quickly as he could. "Look here," Steve said to the governor, "this letter has appeared, you may have seen it. You may as well know what it says—and this letter was not by Dr. Collins, it was my letter. I wrote it, and I have no regrets having done so. And you need to know, sir, that we are here as missionaries. If we see an injustice that is intolerable, we will report it. If you want us to leave, tell us, we'll leave."

At this, the governor apologized. "Sometimes we make mistakes," the governor offered. Although Steve, Ken and Dr. Collins' actions ensured the secret police would continue to monitor their activities in Angola, there was no punishment handed down over the leak to the media. Paul Allen was impressed with Steve's actions. "He put his life on the line; it shows his character."

THE WORLD MOVES ON

One day a munitions dump in Lubango was set on fire, causing a great explosion. For a few hours, the people tensed up; was the war starting again? Thankfully, it was either an accident or a random instance of sabotage. The

MiGs resumed their usual (non-offensive) daily patrols. But the increase in combat had many ripple effects; the massive inflation which was already dwindling the missionaries' resources continued to widen as the war deceased the availability of goods.

In the midst of The Project's struggles, Steve saw cause for hope. The new interns the Ministry of Health had assigned to the initiative had all sequestered themselves in Luanda, refusing to come to Lubango because of the violence there. "At times," Steve observed, "Dr. Ken and I have been the only foreign doctors in the hospital. This has had the advantage in [focusing] as never before on the issue of how many doctors are needed to get the job done around here. Our thesis from the beginning has been that a few good generalists could do most of what needs to be done and this has been borne out by the realities of the present. Thus, our standing with government and colleagues has never been better. We believe that this 'pause' in normal events will lead us onto a new platform for the college." As ever, Steve's hope remained that a new generation of Angolan physicians would rise up. "It must become the Angolan College of Generalist Medicine, not Dr. Stephen Foster's personal hospital as so many view it."

Now that Lubango had been 'reclaimed' from UNITA, FAPLA's attention focused itself on other locales still under UNITA control—Kalukembe and Huambo, for example, where the Fosters still had many friends. More tragedies would follow...

CHAPTER 15

*"Never in the history of our partnership with God's people in
Angola has the situation looked so grim." — Steve Foster*

LUBANGO; HAMILTON (February 1993 – October 1996)

The civil war continued to be fought in the cities of Angola, and the outcomes
were never predictable. The United Nations delegation looked increasingly
powerless to affect the situation; "One could say," Margaret Anstee remarked,
"with the lessons of hindsight, that the UN should never have accepted the
mandate." As Mozambique's own peace process had begun, the United Nations
began moving staff out of Angola and into the more-promising stabilization
of Mozambique. Meanwhile, the US government officially recognized the
MPLA as the legitimate government of Angola, recognition it had pointedly
withheld ever since 1975. It became clear that UNITA's formerly staunch ally
in the US no longer supported it.

One day in Mitcha, it seemed as though the fighting was about to begin
again. Heather was standing in the doorway of the schoolhouse when mortar
came whistling through the air and struck the property! The shell landed in a
corner of the property, casting shrapnel at waist-height near one of the
missionary homes. The sound of the shell's impact was so intense, Heather lost
her hearing; for a moment, she was afraid she had gone permanently deaf. "It
was such a shock." Then, on the other side of the chain-link fence which
surrounded Mitcha, Heather saw a woman collapse on the road. Fearing she
was injured, Heather ran out of the compound and to the woman's side. Having
spent so much time learning from her father, Heather quickly saw the woman
had taken a piece of shrapnel through her arm. Creating a makeshift bandage,
Heather remained by the woman until she could be transported to Central. The
missionaries at Mitcha feared the mortar heralded the beginning of another

attack—but it never came. Some speculated that perhaps a drunken soldier had fired a shell by mistake—for the violence of January did not recur.

For years Heather had dealt with the difficulty Angolans had in pronouncing her name. She had spent time scouring dictionaries to find other versions of her name which would be easier for Portuguese-speaking people to adopt. Finally, she found one: *Erica*, a name shared within the family of heather plants. From then on, most Angolans would know her as Erica, causing minor confusion as her official name remained Heather.

In June 1993, World Relief Canada sent Ken Little to investigate The Project. The undertaking had not gone according to intent. "We've made many mistakes," Steve admitted, "but we can learn from these." Part of the problem the initiative was facing was that they had not originally seen the President of the University before speaking to the Dean of Medicine. As of August, The Project would be officially closed with the intent of reopening it as the College of Health Sciences in Lubango. However, this was effectively the end of The Project. Training Angolan physicians was still Steve's greatest desire, but the renewed intensity of the war coupled with government bureaucracy forced the worthy goal aside.

In the summer of 1993, Rebecca came over to visit for the holidays and Steve's family went to Namibia to celebrate. While there, they had another Foster family reunion with 19 members of the family gathering at Etosha Game Park to celebrate Bob and Belva's wedding anniversary. Stuart and his wife Sindia had been serving in Mozambique since 1985, where Stuart had helped aid the process of translating the Bible into the tribal language Lomwe; at this time they had two daughters, Cara and Belva (named for Stuart's mother) and Sindia was expecting their third child. The greatest surprise was the attendance of Shelley Foster, who claimed she couldn't afford the trip or obtain the time off, but at Sheila's insistence, she made the effort. Only Sheila and Stirling knew about Shelley's participation and while Bob and Belva were extremely pleased to see Shelley at the gathering, Steve was the family member most visibly emotional at seeing her. "It was not what I expected from him," Shelley mused, touched by his affection. At the end of the holidays Sheila and her children Helena, Sara and Daniel came back to Lubango, with Bob and Belva joining them for a while as Sheila taught at ISTEL.

On one visit to Tchincombe, Steve and Peggy's family was having breakfast with John and Kathy Bloise's family and a hot dish of oatmeal had been prepared. Suddenly, movement was noticed inside the oatmeal! Insect larvae had infested the supply of oatmeal at some point, and the insects had subsequently been cooked inside the pot. Almost everyone at the table was disgusted—except for Steve and his brother Stirling, who simply shrugged their shoulders and kept consuming the oatmeal. Donna shook her head. "I haven't been a missionary long enough to eat bugs," Donna stated. Kathy retorted, "Well I'm *not* a missionary and I'm *not* going to eat bugs!"

That fall, Steve's family returned to Canada so he could again sharpen his training at McMaster and provide the children with a chance at a full classroom education. "I left Angola on September 3 with a heavy heart," Steve confessed, noting both the heavy conflict and the lack of surgeons. "Never in the history of our partnership with God's people in Angola has the situation looked so grim." This time the family rented a house in Dundas, a town near Hamilton. The home was 110 years old and furnished full of antiques; it belonged to a professor at McMaster who had taken a sabbatical in Vancouver.

At one point the Fosters were pleased to be reunited with two of the Swiss nurses who had worked with them at Kalukembe: Betty Dauwalder and Johanna Kessler, who had retired by that point. The two women were looking for help in contacting an Amish colony in Ontario as they were curious to learn if the Amish there spoke the same dialect of German they did in Switzerland. The Fosters arranged a visit to the Amish community and found, indeed, they spoke the same German dialect.

Each of the Foster children had difficulties at school, but none more so than Rob. Rob entered Grade 7 in Hamilton and had great trouble trying to fit in. In Angola, Rob was a white boy in a place where white skin drew people's attention; he was the grandson of one famous missionary doctor and son of another; consequently, Rob had been used to being a big fish in a little pond and struggled to make sense of shifting to a much bigger pond. He had never learned how to make friends—children simply sought him out in Angola. As a result, other students bullied him that year, regularly pushing him into lockers. He blamed his mother for some of the bullying because all of his clothing had been donated—so he didn't have 'cool clothes' to wear.

Heather looked out for Rob when she could, but she also struggled at socializing. As third-culture kids, all of the Fosters had to deal with the struggle of fitting into a culture that was only nominally theirs. Instead of the idle chatter most kids their age indulged in, they enjoyed having deep, meaningful conversations with people. In addition, all of the Foster kids struggled with the mandatory French classes they had to take; despite their years learning from a Canadian correspondence program, they had still wound up academically behind their peers.

Rachel and Rebecca's relationship became stronger during this time, as the teenaged Rachel looked to her oldest sister for advice on boys, makeup and hair care. Rachel did better than Rob or Heather at adjusting to Canada, being the most social of the kids, but her year in Hamilton got off to a shaky start. When she received a check-up from the Missionary Health Institute, she tested positive for tuberculosis. The test proved she was carrying the antibodies of

TB, but she had no symptoms. Steve and Peggy decided to treat her in secret because if public health knew of her condition, they would insist she remain at home for the 9-month-long treatment.

Another kind of suffering had afflicted the Fosters, however. Peggy had developed problems which a doctor finally diagnosed as anxiety disorder. She had always been very sensitive, but exposure to the violence in Lubango had gradually preyed upon her mental health. As Peggy learned, under certain stresses or traumas, her brain had difficulty coping with troubles. Now that the problem had been diagnosed Peggy was at least better prepared for how to cope with new strains on her mental health as they arose.

THE FALL OF KALUKEMBE

Since UNITA had taken control of Kalukembe, the town became more and more cut off from the outside world. Preparing for an eventual siege, UNITA had destroyed all of the nearby bridges, so that the 'air bridge' of supplies brought by MAF pilots, including Mark Faus and Brad Fretz, who were instrumental in keeping the hospital stocked in supplies. UNITA claimed that regardless of what occurred, they would remain in Kalukembe until the last man.

Slowly and steadily, FAPLA advanced through UNITA-held territory, employing engineers to build new bridges. Huambo remained the seat of Savimbi's power and as FAPLA prepared to retake that city, Kalukembe became a lower priority. So it was that when FAPLA's army was one day away from Kalukembe, UNITA held a meeting. UNITA informed the nursing staff and missionaries they were abandoning the hospital and retreating toward Huambo. "If you stay," they stated, "you had better be ready to explain to the MPLA what's been going on for the last two years. If you come with us, maybe you'll be all right."

Having heard of the massacre in Lubango, many of the nurses and missionaries feared a similar fate; consequently, some of the missionaries—as well as two-thirds of the nurses—fled with UNITA. Others, including Avelino Sayango and his family, fled because they had hosted Savimbi himself at their house during the election and were certain there would be reprisals against them; although Avelino was a very diplomatic man, he was not very political and only hosted Savimbi from a sense of hospitality. The remaining missionaries were evacuated by MAF. FAPLA's forces stealthily moved into Kalukembe through the surrounding forest and laid a brief siege to the town before realizing UNITA had moved on. As the soldiers had not received their pay in some time, the army told them in lieu of pay, they could have whatever they wanted from the town. The hospital suffered some structural damage from mortar fire on the pediatrics wing and in the operating theatre and Pastor Eliseu's home was razed to the ground.

In the midst of the looting, one of the few remaining nurses was Antonio Chinjenque. At great risk to his own life, Antonio went to the dispensary and began filling a wheelbarrow full of medicine. Enlisting his wife and son to assist him, he began the long trek from the pharmacy warehouse to the leprosarium, where he deposited the wheelbarrow amongst the lepers. When people asked what he was doing, he claimed he was looting the hospital. In fact, he gambled that none of the actual looters would search the leper village because of the disdain people had for lepers; he gambled correctly. It took an entire week to empty the medical supplies.

Although MAF was forced to temporarily withdraw from Kalukembe, it kept in contact with the remaining staff through the radio and that continued connection encouraged the people of Kalukembe. Finally, 25 days after UNITA's departure, the staff decided it was safe to continue its work. The hidden medicines were restored to the dispensary—a prudent measure, for MAF could not resupply them for another six months—and the damages to the buildings were repaired as best as they could manage. With the hospital's leadership scattered, the quick-witted Antonio Chinjenque was made director of the hospital. In time, Avelino Sayango and his family were caught in the bush and brought to the MPLA in Luanda; much to their surprise, they were treated honourably and left alone. Pastor Eliseu, on the other hand, would eventually be caught in the bush and burned alive as punishment for being in Savimbi's inner circle.

Antonio Salomão, another senior nurse from Kalukembe fell into despair after retreating with UNITA. "We thought we would be out there only one day but one day turned into nearly 10 years," he reflected. "I lost almost everything." Antonio was treated as a privileged prisoner—but a prisoner all the same. Now that he was in UNITA's clutches, they would not allow him to depart, finding him useful for his medical skills and as a driver for collecting supplies. Knowing that Kalukembe Hospital had suffered from UNITA's departure, Antonio became angry with God: "Why did you let Kalukembe fall?" he prayed. "Why did you let me become a prisoner?"

In time, UNITA brought Antonio to a remote village and commanded him and his wife Marta to develop a clinic there. UNITA would perform such acts to help win allies from villages around the countryside. Operating the new clinic was more to Antonio's liking as he could finally return to the work he loved. As he treated people's ailments, he also resumed his ministry, sharing the Gospel message with them, as no one in the village had heard of Christ before.

After a few months of operating the clinic, Antonio was given an audience with a delegation of elders from the village. The elders first thanked him for the health care he had been providing, and said they had heard the stories about Jesus which he had been sharing and asked him to explain the message to them. Antonio repeated the Gospel message to the elders who then asked: "We really like what we're hearing about God and what He's done for us and who He is. But how come no one has ever come to tell us this story before?" That moment was a turning point for Antonio as, all of sudden, he knew exactly how to answer: "Because I had to lose everything so I could be brought here to care for you and share the Word."

Years later, Antonio smuggled a message to his old friend Sheila, telling her what had become of him. Antonio told her of the amazing encounter he had with the elders. "Whatever the circumstances," Sheila reflected, "God does and can use them for His purposes and we have to be open to being instruments." Antonio would remain 'protected' by UNITA until the end of the civil war.

Out at Tchincombe, Stirling was working on his and Donna's new house while Donna was pregnant with their first child. One day in April 1994, only eight months into the pregnancy, Donna's water broke but she didn't go into labour. It took six hours to get from Tchincombe to Lubango, so Stirling decided to be safe and transport her to his father. Bob examined Donna and determined since she wasn't in labour there was no need to rush anything. He took Donna for a walk around Mitcha but still she didn't go into labour.

Turning to MAF, Stirling and Donna were granted a medivac into Windhoek to see a physician there. The doctor in Windhoek examined Donna and agreed with Bob—she was not in labour so there was no need to hurry the baby along. After a week in the hospital, Donna was ready to be discharged—but all of a sudden, she went into labour. She gave birth to her and Stirling's son Jeffrey Williams Foster, his name taken from Stirling's middle name. Jeffrey was a thin baby because he hadn't reached full term, but he was healthy.

While the peace process in Angola was caught in a constant quagmire, international interest in Africa was constantly shifting from event to event; in October 1993 the great topic had been the Battle of Mogadishu, which led to the infamous "Black Hawk Down" incident; in April 1994, the Rwandan genocide shocked the globe; then the world celebrated the election of Nelson Mandela as President of South Africa the following month. The Angolan Civil War was now almost 20 years old and showed no sign of ceasing.

HEARTBREAK

Nine months after the birth of their son Luke, in June 1994, Stuart's family in

Alto Molocué, Mozambique lost their middle child. Belva, who was turning 7, had a mild fever for 5 days. They began malaria treatment, but on the fifth night, she seemed worse and so on the sixth day, Stuart and Sindia took her to a clinic for a blood test, which confirmed she had malaria. Within a few hours, she was dead. The church community organized a funeral for the next day (the normal custom) and as Stuart surveyed the mourners, he thought, "Every single parent here has a lost a child." Philosophically, Stuart realized "in some deep way their hearts were knit together with the people they had been serving."

Meanwhile back in Canada, Steve came into contact with a group called Physicians for Global Survival (formerly Canadian Physicians for Prevention of Nuclear War), an anti-war organization comprised of Canadian physicians. The group became very interested in hearing about landmines from Steve, who recounted, "If one could dream up a more dastardly weapon than a land mine I don't think you could do it. You can't do a more hideous thing to a young person in the Third World than to deny him his foot. These diabolical devices don't give up the ghost, they go on maiming and killing people for decades." Awareness of the global danger of landmines to civilian populations—especially in Angola—was beginning to rise and HALO Trust (Hazardous Area Life-support Organization), the world's largest humanitarian mine-clearing organization, began to remove landmines from Angola. Steve also encouraged fundraising for the ongoing famine relief needed in Angola, ultimately sending 10 tons of food.

As the year in Hamilton wound down, Rob had enjoyed playing sports in school such as basketball, swimming and skating, but he was also eager to return to Angola. His greatest prize that year was earning $200 shovelling snow and investing his money in a top-of-the-line mountain bike. Heather appreciated having a system with teachers who could assist her in her studies and to learn alongside classmates. "Not being used to working in groups and being involved in class presentations, they were somewhat of a trial for me, but I survived!"

Steve's family came to Namibia for a quick summer reunion with Stirling, Donna and Sheila. When Sharon's birthday came up in August, the three siblings phoned her to wish her a happy birthday. "It's not a happy birthday," Sharon informed them. "Martin's disappeared." Sharon had returned to the US to apply for citizenship and expected Martin to follow from Jamaica. However, he was missing from his flight—and on further investigation, his name wasn't on the flight manifesto. Sharon began to worry, fearing Martin was dead or had been mugged, but eventually her investigation uncovered that Martin had boarded a different plane with a woman he had known before marrying Sharon; he had been cheating on Sharon, and now he had abandoned her without even a word of warning. Bob and Belva went to comfort Sharon.

Sharon's daughter Tonya had just finished a span in New Jersey helping her Uncle Stacey and Aunt Ruth tend to their sons Wyatt and Tyler. Rebecca decided to take a year's break before starting university and spent the first three months on break in New Jersey, nannying for her cousins. She found her Uncle Stacey a quiet man who kept mostly to himself and his work on *Saturday Night Live*. For a time Rebecca kept up a friendship with her Aunt Ruth. Knowing Ruth collected eggcups from around the world, Rebecca sent several to her aunt as gifts.

As Steve returned to Lubango in the fall of 1994 he found Central Hospital was uncomfortable with the idea of continuing The Project. Remembering what he had seen in Zambia and elsewhere, Steve realized the program would have to change. He had tried to accommodate the government hospitals, but there were simply too many roadblocks; in the future, The Project would have to stand on its own as a private institution. Steve continued to perform a few surgeries each week at Central, but shifted most of his focus to serving patients at the Rio de Huíla clinic. At some expense he fitted out a truck to carry a mobile surgical unit, seeing it as a means to bring quality care to people in remote locations. The war had come to another ceasefire just after FAPLA won Huambo back from UNITA; the MPLA and UNITA signed the Lusaka Protocol in November, but the conflict was still unresolved.

ROADSIDE MEDICINE

Steve once went on a sightseeing excursion with a capable driver from Namibe into the area south of the Cunene River, some 20 kilometres into the desert of the Iona Game Park. At dusk, their vehicle was flagged down by a group of people at the roadside. They informed Steve and the driver they had a very sick old man in their village who was in great distress: he had been unable to urinate for 4 days. The old man (who later proved to be the village chief) lived in a hut shaped like an igloo built from sticks. Crawling into the hut, Steve found the old man lying on a cowhide. The man's bladder was distended so far out he looked pregnant!

Everywhere Steve went, he travelled with a full medical kit which included a catheter. A catheter was exactly what this old chief needed—but Steve had left his medical kit in Namibe that morning! Steve and the driver scoured the truck and toolbox trying to find something that could serve as a makeshift catheter. At last, popping the hood of the truck, the driver found the perfect substitute: a length of plastic tubing from the windshield washing fluid apparatus! They cut out the tube and bevelled the tip so that it could be inserted like a catheter. All they lacked was a lubricant for inserting the tube; spying a pot of souring, rancid milk that was separating into yogurt and buttermilk, Steve dipped the tube into the buttermilk. It worked! Lubricated with the buttermilk, the tube entered the man's urethra and in moments he could pee. Steve promised to return the next day to check on the old man.

When Steve came back the following day, the old man rose from his hut and greeted him. Steve removed the makeshift catheter (which the driver wanted back) and gave the old man a piece of paper directing him to the nearest hospital should there be any further complications. Steve wouldn't return to that part of Angola for six months, but when he did he met some of the old chief's grandchildren who happily informed him their grandfather was in good health.

Rebecca returned to Angola that December to work at an orphanage in Lubango. With the aid of UNICEF she had obtained yogurt and high-protein biscuits, which she mixed together to create a protein-rich food for the orphans. Rebecca spent time with the children, seeing to their basic hygiene needs, such as trimming their nails. She also arranged activities for children she found in the streets. Rebecca was still not entirely certain what her career goal was, but serving the needs of the orphans was very rewarding to her.

The United Nations finally ended UNAVEM II in February 1995; UNAVEM III took its place, although the peace process seemed as moribund as before. In May, Bob Foster and Dr. Don Mullen of the World Medical Mission took a tour of medical centres throughout Angola, including Huambo and Kuito, which had seen intense fighting. In Huambo they found entire city blocks had been levelled to the ground and the faces of high-rise apartments had been blown away. There were no electrical or water systems, or functional hospitals, and medical equipment had been pilfered with no means to restock medicines. The hospitals were in a terrible state. "On the other hand," Bob reported, "we were amazed at the resiliency of the Angolans, particularly of the Angolan Christians, who in every place we visited, were positive about the future. They not only had a vision for extending the work of God but also were involved in the ongoing ministry of the Word and in practical outreach to the community through the development of small church-based clinics."

For most of their ministry in Angola, the Fosters had curious people trying to understand why they were there; unable to accept the straightforward answer—they had come to serve others—whispers and conspiracies were bandied about, claims the Fosters had a fortune or were involved in criminal enterprises. Some security agents went to Fernando Borge and told him MAF was flying in guns to Tchincombe that Stirling would transport to Mitcha where Steve was storing them in shipping containers for UNITA. Fernando, who had mentored Stirling, took exception to those accusations. "I've known these people longer than you've been around! These people have a history of connectedness to Africa that dates to before you were born! These people are not running guns, they're here because they care about Angolans." Although Fernando had never professed any Christian beliefs to the Fosters, Steve sensed "a generous streak in him that was clearly the work of the Holy Spirit." Fernando put an end to the security agents' conspiracies by convening a meeting with Stirling and Steve, wherein the security agents apologized for their accusations.

In Hamilton, Rebecca began studying sociology at McMaster, in a sense following in the steps of her parents through her mother's vocation and her father's alma mater. She enjoyed meeting professors on campus who knew her father and began to see the positive side of the Fosters' legacy. She considered entering the medical program but realized her heart wasn't in it; she knew her father hoped to see another Foster continue in the same career as him and her grandfather, but there was never any pressure placed on her to become a doctor. Instead, she considered becoming a social worker before settling on teacher's college. In teaching, she found common ground with her father; like Steve, she loved that "every day is different." Instead of working behind a desk she worked best with other people.

In Lubango, Steve's other children were finding their paths. Heather decided to work with her father at his Rio de Huíla clinics and began aiding handicapped children and orphans. Rachel had become an excellent choral singer. Rob, like Rebecca, had begun feeling the sense of the Foster legacy weighing upon him, as he was Steve's only son. However, Rob had no aptitude for medicine so began looking for other mission opportunities he might enter; including piloting with MAF. Peggy took on new opportunities, assisting the production of a new hymnal for the UIEA church, leading Bible studies, teaching piano lessons and working as the radio liaison to the Menongue mission.

Among the many conferences Steve attended in 1995 was an AIDS seminar in Kenya. His host during the conference was the head of the national postal service maintenance department, who gave Steve room and board. As the host drove Steve from the airport to his home, Steve introduced himself and his life story, including his upbringing in Zambia. When they sat down that evening for dinner, Steve was very interested to note they had not set out knives, forks, or plates. Instead there were banana leaves, a big pot of nshima and relish. The host and his family said nothing about the meal presentation and neither did Steve comment on it; they said grace, then the hostess served the meal. The next morning Steve was given a traditional English breakfast with bacon, eggs, toast and cutlery; again, no one commented on the sudden appearance of utensils. From then on, all of Steve's meals were presented in a traditional western manner.

A few days into his visit, Steve brought up the first dinner to his host. "I'm amazed you had the courage to serve an unknown white man absolutely typical Kenyan food on the first night that you met [me]," he said.

His host answered, "When I learned you were an African and that you had been born to a father who had been born in Zambia, I just wanted to honour you as an African."

That moment spoke deeply to Steve because of what he had seen from his 20 years in Angola—in Angolan cities, the Angolans spoke Portuguese in the streets and served Portuguese meals in their homes. "Portuguese culture has separated Angolans from their roots," he said, sadly. In Kenya he heard people in the streets conversing in Swahili—but seldom do Angolans speak their tribal tongues in public. This, he laid at the feet of colonialism. "It is the shattering of African self-confidence," he said, that so many Africans believe the colonizer's culture is superior to their own.

Back in Lubango, Steve's medical work continued to fishtail. The mobile surgical unit he had built tore his truck apart, splitting both of the chassis rails. The truck had been rated to bear 2 tons but had been fitted with 2.5 tons of equipment and had often been made to bear up to 3 tons. Then, in February 1996, a new opportunity presented itself: AEF asked Steve to become its Canadian director. AEF Canada was concerned that the organization was standing still; their present director, John Pomeroy, was not comfortable with public speaking and preferred an administrative role, even though AEF Canada's Paul Russell was already its Administrative Director. Although Steve's heart was serving in the field in medical missions, he knew from his father's experiences that there was important work to be done. AEF asked Steve to accept a six-year term; he bartered them down to four years with the understanding that Paul Russell would be left to do the administrative functions while Steve toiled in the field.

When Rachel heard her father had accepted the post it caused her some consternation. Rachel had grown to love Angola so much that she didn't want to leave. She had an Angolan boyfriend at the time and wasn't eager to once again navigate an unfamiliar country. She actively prayed against her father's acceptance of the role.

In May 1996, Rebecca made another visit to Lubango, bringing with her two pre-med students from McMaster: Ari Ho and Raj. The young men had met Rebecca through McMaster's International Health Initiatives club and shared an interest in international medical issues, but neither was Christian. They came to perform a survey of Onjinua, 80 kilometres from Rio de Huíla, which had no health care available. Ari and Raj enjoyed working with Steve, and Ari in particular became a good friend of the family.

MADE WHOLE BY FAITH

Steve was scheduled to be installed as Canadian director of AEF in November 1996. The Fosters sold virtually everything they owned in Angola, packing only three extra suitcases to bring back to Canada. Peggy, Heather, Rachel and Rob left Angola ahead of him to write the kids' exams so his last three weeks in Angola were spent alone—a very difficult circumstance for Steve, who had always thrived on interaction with others and could not bear living alone. Steve also felt bad about leaving Angola. He had insisted to AEF that he would only serve as director for four years and then return to the field because he had seen so many missionaries leave the country in the 1990s. With The Project in disarray and Kalukembe Hospital in shambles, Steve worried his absence would only deepen the problems facing the country.

In his last weeks, Steve treated a woman at Rio de Huíla who was suffering from cancer and had already been to Namibia for treatment. Steve informed the woman he could do nothing for her with his resources and advised her to return to Namibia for more treatment. Sadly, she could not afford another trip to Namibia; Steve's words were like a death sentence to her and she left his consult room in tears.

The following Sunday Steve was preaching at the Congregational Church. After the service, the same woman approached him, tears still streaming from her eyes. "Can't you do something?" she persisted. "Please?" Steve suggested she return to Rio de Huíla on the next Wednesday so he could perform a biopsy. When the day came he found her at the clinic at 8 AM, waiting patiently with her entire family. To Steve's amazement, her leg was not as swollen as it had been the previous week. He palpated the area where he had found a tumour before; there was no tumour. Steve went ahead with the biopsy and, to his astonishment, found no evidence of cancer. "That was confusing," he admitted.

After sewing the woman up, he addressed her family to ask what had happened. The family answered they had done exactly what was written in James 5:14-15: "Is anyone among you sick? Let them call the elders of the church to pray over them and anoint them with oil in the name of the Lord. And the prayer offered in faith will make the sick person well; the Lord will raise them up." The woman's church had met together on the Tuesday night in a gathering of 400 people. They poured a full litre of oil over her head and prayed all night. When Steve heard this account, he realized how God was speaking to him. "I can handle this," is the message Steve sensed. "You can go, I'll take care of things." Reminded of God's faithfulness, Steve set his eyes to the challenge of leading AEF in Canada.

CHAPTER 16

"By Prayer. Go Forward." — *SIM Motto*

HAMILTON (September 1996 – October 2000)

In September 1996, Steve began his trip back to Canada to assume directorship of AEF Canada. On his way, he stopped in England to visit AEF's international office, before continuing onto Canada. By the time he joined his family at the home they were renting in Hamilton, the children were already getting settled. Heather was finishing her high school, then began a 4-year nursing program at McMaster, ultimately becoming the only one of Steve's children to take up a medical profession. "I loved the stories that Dad would tell about Great-Grandpa Charles and about his dad and his experiences. I really connected with the Foster legacy in Africa." Finding the midwifery program was too difficult to get into, Heather planned to work in public health. Rachel and Rob were enrolled in high school and once again had to navigate the unfamiliar aspects of Canadian culture. Although Rachel could adapt quickly, she didn't like becoming "the weirdo from Africa" again. In time, she grew to love Canada and Steve felt the change was ultimately good for his children. The next four years also served as a time for Steve to reflect upon his future in Angola and what the next phase of his ministry there would involve.

Peggy had struggles of her own as her anxiety disorder continued to trouble her, so she benefited from being back in a country where she could receive qualified treatment. As the family settled back into Philpott Memorial Church, Peggy befriended Beulah Sergeant, a 98-year-old woman who had been a missionary in Muie, Angola, but was now retired. Despite her age she was very independent and was very supportive of the younger generations of missionaries.

On November 4, 1996, Steve Foster was commissioned as director of AEF Canada at Ontario Bible College Chapel in Willowdale, a neighbourhood of Toronto. When Steve arrived at the office he had inherited with AEF in Cambridge, Ontario, he found his predecessor John Pomeroy had left him a three-foot-high stack of papers which he considered 'essential reading.' Steve called in Paul Russell and showed him the stack, then told Paul if there was anything in the pile he really needed to read, bring it to his attention, but otherwise it should all be put away.

Soon after taking his post, Steve was called to a lunch with Arnell Motz, who was the director of SIM Canada, the Canadian branch of the Sudan Interior Mission (although SIM was involved in many African locales other than the Sudan). Over lunch, Arnell told Steve their two organizations were on the cusp of a merger. This was a surprise to Steve, as the international office in England had not mentioned one word of it to him! Members of AEF had some concerns about merging with SIM as they enjoyed how small and intimate AEF was, and it was possible for every missionary in AEF to be acquainted with one another. Then too, there were financial considerations as SIM pooled the money of their missionaries together, while AEF kept the money separate. AEF's membership was also on a voluntary basis, so each member would have to choose to join SIM—it could not be mandated.

Steve's role as director drew upon one of his sharpest gifts as a missionary: his ability to speak in public. He travelled around to churches and Bible colleges to encourage support for AEF's missionaries and for new prospective missionaries to come join its ranks. Most frequently, Steve would speak passionately about the needs of Angola, which he knew all too well. It was because of Steve's advocacy for Angola that friends such as Pastor Calenga were glad he was in Canada. "We still felt connected and represented in Canada because we had someone there who could speak for Angola and knew what Angola was like."

Steve had been speaking most frequently on the issue of landmines, saying in one speech, "The knock-on effects of land mines can go on for years and years." The subject was becoming a major international topic. In January 1997, the world's most visible anti-landmine crusader, Princess Diana, journeyed to Angola to raise awareness of the landmine threat in that country. HALO Trust helped sponsor the Princess of Wales' visit and took her through a live minefield in Huambo. "In 1996, more than 65 varieties had been confirmed or reported in Angola," noted renowned Canadian journalist Philip C. Winslow. "Not one was made in Angola." Although the continuing civil war meant total landmine removal was impossible for the time being, the Princess' efforts would be long remembered; although she tragically died in Paris only 7 months after her visit to Huambo, her son Prince Harry would continue to raise support for landmine removal in Angola in later years.

Angola also made international waves when it supported the armies of

Rwanda, Uganda and Burundi as they invaded Zaire in 1997. The MPLA government had many reasons to seek the overthrow of Zaire's long-time dictator Mobutu, who had always opposed the MPLA and supported its rivals. By helping depose Mobutu, the MPLA eliminated a rival power and helped ensure the renamed country—the Democratic Republic of the Congo—would be an ally. Meanwhile, the fall of Mobutu removed one of UNITA's few remaining international supporters and exposed UNITA as Mobutu's allies, which hurt the rebels' image all the more. The US had long been Mobutu's allies since overseeing his installation during the Cold War, yet it did nothing to prevent his fall; this lack of involvement signalled that UNITA was similarly of little interest to the post-Cold War US. Soon after the foundation of the Democratic Republic of the Congo, UNAVEM III ended. Despite the fact the United Nations was still willing to help Angola achieve peace, it had been unable to forge any lasting agreements.

In the fall of 1997, Steve made his first trip to Mozambique on behalf of AEF. Having lived for so long in another ex-Portuguese colony he noted the comparisons: "Mozambique was always the poor cousin of Angola without the vast petroleum and mineral wealth. The war in Mozambique wasn't as intense and didn't have the superpower interests that have continued to create tensions in Angola." However, unlike in Angola, the peace accord of 1992 had been accomplished—the civil war was over. "Everywhere I went into small remote villages and bigger towns, I saw people rebuilding their homes, schools repaired, hospitals being refurbished, farms reopening, roads being repaired and a general sense of ebullience about their future. They are starting from a long way down."

While most of Steve's work was in Maputo with AEF's Dr. Mark Nelham and speaking to the Vice Minister of Health who was very interested in the curriculum The Project had developed, he also went to Alto Molocué to see Stuart, Sindia, Cara and Luke. Stuart booked his brother into a seminar for pastors and treasurers on how to encourage giving and tithing. "They have a very generous spirit toward visitors but don't think it necessary to support their full-time pastors," Steve observed. "Stuart as team leader is faced with the enormous difficulty of communicating to these fellow missionaries who are spread over 1800 km." While at Alto Molocué, Steve went to see the grave of his niece, little Belva. Her death caused him to reflect on what his family's calling to missions represented: "I was deeply moved to realize what it has cost to make possible the answer to the question: how shall they hear, except someone be sent?"

One day, four-year-old Luke was out with his Uncle Steve on the only road in Alto Molocué that had been paved with tar. Luke went running downhill and tripped, striking the pavement with his head. Luke blacked out and awoke being carried in his uncle's arms. Steve tended to the cut on Luke's head. For Luke, "It was comforting to have an actual doctor around."

That same fall, the Nobel committee gave the Nobel Peace Prize to the International Campaign to Ban Landmines. Amidst the growing international pressure against landmines, Canada had taken a leading role with the Ottawa Treaty to ban the production, sale and use of landmines, but the US and China—to this day—refused to sign the treaty. The resulting media blitz brought many journalists to Steve to learn from his experiences treating landmine victims. "This is one of the most visible human rights awards in the world," Steve told reporters. "An award like this can really mobilize people to do something."

Steve used these opportunities to relate the landmine issue directly to the Gospel message. "The old Biblical prophets used to talk to visiting the sins of the father on the third and fourth generation," Steve informed media outlets. "There's no better example I can think of than a landmine." The reporters were quite taken by Steve's breadth of knowledge on Angola, the issue of landmines and his sense of humour. "He seems somewhat restless," wrote one, "very energetic, and eager always for more challenges."

Steve also used these conversations with the media as opportunities to call on new missionaries. He emphasized his role in Angola had always been to better enable the Angolans to solve their own medical problems. "We are multipliers of effectiveness," he said. "With training, the Angolans won't be as dependent on outside help." Knowing that many North Americans' view of missionaries were of people sent to teach others from a position of superiority, he was quick to add, "You have to earn the right to preach. You have to live the message to earn credibility."

In January 1998, Bob returned to Angola to attend the Assembly of the AEA in Luanda, under whose authority fell the UIEA church. Bob was particularly impassioned on the matter of building a new medical centre in Angola and when rebuilding the clinic in Cavango was raised, he found the UIEA and AEA were very keen to the idea. Cavango's central location, with a large concentration of people and in an area with great polarization and political divisions due to the war, made it an ideal location for a mission hospital. In addition, Cavango also had an unlimited water supply from the Okavango River and good, arable soil. Bob turned a few heads at the assembly when he told the AEA leadership he wanted to sit down with someone from UNITA and "ask why Savimbi destroyed Cavango and Catota!" The men went pale; Savimbi's name was simply not thrown around so casually. However, Bob would never receive the explanations or apologies he would have appreciated. Dejected, Bob returned to the US to find support from his allies at Samaritan's Purse and the World Medical Mission.

Soon after, Mark Faus took Bob on an MAF flight over Cavango. There was no airstrip, but they made the flight principally to inform the people of Cavango they were coming. Bob dropped a bottle out of the plane containing a note which explained they would be driving into the village the following day. After all the Cavango residents had been through in the war and Bob didn't want them to be alarmed when they heard his car approaching.

Before entering her third year of McMaster's nursing program, Heather went back to Angola for a summer mission trip. "That trip was, in part, a searching for where the Lord wants me to serve Him down the road; it turned out to be a true confirmation of the burden that has been placed in my heart for the Angolan people. I went with my friend Julia, who, during her time in Angola, came to know God through the ministry of His people there. I had no expectation of this—my only hope had been that her heart might be softened toward Christianity! As always, God has shown Himself to have plans greater than anything we would dream. Julia continues with a heart that seeks the Lord, and she has the desire to one day help the process of peacebuilding in Angola."

In the fall of 1998, Steve oversaw the merger of AEF and SIM and his role was reduced to that of deputy director of SIM Canada, continuing work with Paul Russell and Pep Philpott. SIM had asked Steve to serve as their Canadian director, but he maintained he would stick to the agreement he made with AEF and serve four years only. SIM changed its acronym meaning to 'Serving in Mission' as a reflection on how generalized its international focus had become. From his increased presence in Canada, Steve had begun to comprehend what Canadian Christians believed. "Canadians struggle with pluralism in a way that our American friends rarely appreciate. We have become tuned to political correctness and the claims of Jesus of Nazareth are frankly embarrassing to some of us. I have been encouraged that frankness and simplicity from the pulpit have been appreciated."

At the same time, Rebecca's friend Ari Ho from McMaster had taken an interest in her and wanted to date her; Rebecca refused and insisted they should remain friends. However, Rebecca's family had come to love to Ari and would often invite him to their house for meals, even after Rebecca finished her sociology course in spring of 1998. When Rebecca would see Ari at the family dinner table she would "dramatically" run upstairs to her room rather than be around him. However, over time they began conversing via email and Rebecca wondered if they might be a good match after all. To determine if this was so, the two of them set aside a weekend and drove north to Gravenhurst, Ontario, to seclude themselves at a bed-and-breakfast establishment. In her very methodical way, Rebecca hashed out all of the problems she saw between herself and Ari. After everything had been aired and addressed they came to a logical conclusion: they should get married.

While in Gravenhurst, Rebecca and Ari visited the Bethune Memorial House, a National Historic Site that served as a museum to the life and career of Dr. Norman Bethune, the physician who had been compared to Rebecca's father. "We were pretty convinced that although both had carried out medical work overseas, recounts of Bethune's character and exploits suggested they are very, very different people!" Ari discerned.

In February 1999, Steve went back to Maputo, Mozambique, to participate in an Essential Surgical Skills Workshop CNIS (Canadian Network for International Surgery) had sponsored. This was an intensive, 40-hour course with an emphasis on the skills used in preventing unnecessary patient deaths. "The emphasis on such practical skills gave the participants a real sense of the do-ability of what the rural medical profession is all about," Steve said. "One of the students wrote on her evaluation that she had always avoided mothers giving birth because she felt so helpless but that after taking the course, she now knew what to do."

While in Africa, Steve went to White River, South Africa, to see his old friends Chuck and Heather Stephens, then flew to Namibia to greet his sister Sheila and help her transport medical supplies across the border into Angola. Back in Lubango, he was reunited with friends including Pastor Abias and Dr. Steve Collins. Dr. Collins had begun to specialize in eye surgery, using his God-blessed gifts to restore sight to the blind through procedures such as cataract surgery. While in Lubango, he was "particularly saddened by the death of the oldest member of the Lubango church, Dna. Henriqueta. She was 86. She developed cerebral malaria and despite what the 'best' private clinic could offer, she died on the Monday morning. Her death and the token efforts provided for her were a powerful indictment of the chaos and disorder that characterize the present state of affairs in the health system in Angola. Her funeral was one of the most moving I have ever been to. The choirs who sang continuously at the grave side were a testimony to God's love and graciousness. There was no bitterness. Many members of the extended family were there and for some it was the first time they had heard a clear presentation of why a Christian can face death with equanimity and hope."

From Lubango, Steve went to Luanda and met his old friends Jean-Pierre and Marie-Claude Bréchet. Jean-Pierre was now working with the American Leprosy Mission as a consultant to the Ministry of Health. Steve also met with the AEA to discuss what work Steve would be doing in Angola when his term with SIM Canada concluded. The AEA asked Steve to consider running a medical centre in Luanda, but when Steve brought the matter to his father and wife, Bob and Peggy observed their supporters wanted a medical centre in the southwest of the country, to better access the unreached peoples of Angola. Steve conceded the point: "I too feel that I want to work where we can contribute to the work begun years ago at Kalukembe with our friend Sr. Afonso who was killed in late '85 bringing the Good News to the Cuvale people at Caitovo."

As Steve witnessed the present state of Christians in Angola, he was impressed. "I am convinced that God's people have an important role to play in the country. Christians are fasting and praying for peace. They are building schools for their kids, developing outreach ministries to those who haven't heard, running the few health clinics that are accessible to common folk and generally standing firm in a time of great distress. This is not the time to leave but rather to prudently examine where and how we can be of help."

Back in Canada, Steve returned in March 1999 for Rebecca and Ari's engagement party, which was done in a traditional Chinese style according to the customs of Ari's family (Ari's family had come from Taiwan, but had been living in Canada since the 1960s). However, Rebecca was not in a hurry to be wed—she wanted time to appreciate living on her own before marriage. Fortunately, Ari's studies in epidemiology had him posted to Nova Scotia for a year's research, so they spent most of their year long engagement apart from each other while Rebecca graduated teacher's college.

DOING BUSINESS IN ANGOLA

Steve's old friend from Sakeji, Daniel Henk, had indeed become a soldier as he had dreamed of and by 1999 had served a distinguished 29 years in the US Army, retiring that year as a colonel. He then took up a post at the Air War College in the Department of Leadership and Ethics. One of Daniel's friends had become the head of security for Exxon Mobil (better known in Canada as Esso). As Exxon was putting together a security analysis of Angola to determine whether to continue pursuing oil and gas in that country, Daniel's friend wondered if there was someone who could speak to the on-ground situation in Angola. Daniel advised his friend to contact Steve Foster.

The head of security for Exxon Mobil asked Steve for a list of people he recommended as advisers to the corporation. Steve did so, but after a few minutes of conversing with Steve about Angola, the security chief changed his mind; he wanted Steve to be his adviser! When Exxon asked Steve what his 'professional' fee for this service was, Steve was stymied. He called up Daniel to find out how much money he should ask for. Daniel told him not to ask for less than $500 per day because the other consultants would be receiving $1000 per day. "Don't sell yourself short!" Daniel cautioned him. When Steve informed Exxon he wanted $1000 per day, they accepted it without further comment. "I probably should have asked for more!" Steve chuckled.

Having lived most of his life on the charity of monies raised by Christian fundraising, it was a very different experience for Steve to be flown around the world in the first-class compartment. Steve met with Exxon in Houston, Texas, then on to Angola for a 10-day visit. Steve was given the opportunity to see parts of the country which he had never visited as a missionary, including a tour of Exxon's offshore oil platforms. Nearly all of the consultants at the meetings were ex-military men and spoke as experts on international law and security issues; Steve's advice was valuable because he was an outsider. When they asked him about the political situation in Angola he spoke words of caution, noting if Jonas Savimbi could interfere with Exxon's operations, he absolutely would.

THE MILLION-DOLLAR STARTUP

While Steve was on this whirlwind trip, one of Bob Foster's cousins had invited him to speak one evening at a small church. Although the assembly was small, Bob went because of a rule he gave himself based on Zechariah 4:10: "Who dares despise the day of small things?" At the venue, Bob spoke passionately about the need for a new medical centre in Angola as the UIEA and AEA had impressed upon him. One of the few attendees asked Bob how much it would cost to establish a new medical facility. Bob responded, "$1 million would get us started."

Two days later, the man from church appeared at Bob's door in Greensboro to share a cup of tea. After a conversation with Bob about Angola and the medical centre, the man revealed he had just sold a piece of property for $10 million and intended to tithe 10%. He took out his chequebook and wrote a cheque for $1 million. Bob wasted little time in taking out his phone and calling his son Steve. "You're not going to believe this..." he began. After telling the story of the cheque he was then holding, Bob asked his son, "You wouldn't want to go back to Angola and get this started, would you?" Steve had a very pragmatic reply: "Dad, before we get started, we should find out if the cheque is any good!"

The cheque was good, but SIM Canada was a little out of its depth when it came to spending such sums. Bob turned again to his friend Franklin Graham, who brought in Samaritan's Purse and the World Medical Mission, who agreed to handle the money and become their partners in establishing the new medical centre. That same day, Pastor Abias contacted Steve to tell him there was a man in Lubango who wanted to give a gift of land to the church. So many elements were effortlessly falling into place. "I had been sharing how

God answers prayer with one of the members of the Esso team that week," Steve recalled. "You should have seen his face when I told him about the 2 phone calls. God is indeed doing things!"

With the million-dollar donation, Bob began exploring with the AEA and UIEA where in the country the new Evangelical Medical Centre would be situated. "One of the things I insisted on when we talked with UIEA," Steve said, "is to see that we are squarely interdenominational, no one denomination has hegemony, no one will sort of say that's our banner." Steve recalled all too well the problems that had come from Kalukembe Hospital being under the control of IESA. "Let's take pride in this as something as brothers in Christ, but not as saying it's our church. In that way try to honour our Lord, but at the same time recognize the human tendency to manipulate human power."

Back in Hamilton, Peggy was surprised when she learned from her brother Richard that their brother Ted was having a hernia repair performed and had not informed them. As Ted was a confirmed bachelor who lived on his own in Toronto, Peggy insisted he come to live with them in Hamilton while he regained strength. Ted's pet cat Rocky was also provided for, although he had to be sequestered from the Fosters' own territorial cats! Ted appreciated being cared for by the Fosters, especially as Steve tended to his health, just as he had for Peggy and Ted's father two decades before.

Rob had a procedure of his own that spring when he had reconstructive foot surgery performed to correct lingering issues caused by his childhood polio. The procedure granted him more mobility than he had enjoyed before. That summer, Rob worked as a counsellor at Pioneer Boys' Camp, working with children who had special needs. Still trying to seek his calling, Rob wondered if counselling was his strength.

THE OTHER FOSTER SON

Back in Angola, Steve and Peggy's friends Avelino and Ludia Sayango had been trying to stay out of trouble during the ongoing civil war, they were becoming concerned for their son Gil; the MPLA and UNITA liked to enforce rusgas to conscript able-bodied young men such as Gil. Brad Fretz, an MAF pilot from Canada, had befriended the Sayangos at Kalukembe and remained in touch with them. Aware of their fears for Gil, Brad told them that if need be, they could send Gil to Canada where the Fretz family would care for him.

Gil's status came to a head one night while travelling with his father, cousin and uncle. The car broke down outside of town and Gil went in with his cousin to obtain the spare parts they needed to effect repairs. About 5 kilometres from the town, they were apprehended by corrupt police officers.

The officers tied the hands of Gil and his cousin and set them aside with other people they had captured to search them for money. Gil heard the police arguing amongst themselves, with some of the police opining they should kill their prisoners immediately and throw them in the nearby river, but other policemen observed they were too close to town and the gunshots would be audible. Realizing the police wouldn't shoot them, Gil and his cousin sprang to their feet and ran into the woods. As the other captives had the same realization, they too fled. Gil and his cousin ultimately escaped their bonds, collected the spare parts in town and returned safely to the vehicle, but Avelino and Ludia were shaken to realize how close they had come to losing their son.

While Brad Fretz helped initiate the process of sending Gil to Canada as a refugee, Jean-Pierre and Marie-Claude Bréchet took Gil in at their home in Luanda, where he lived in their annex for six months lest he be found and conscripted by the army. Once Gil's refugee status was set, he travelled safely to Canada and began living with Brad and Maureen Fretz in Guelph, Ontario.

While picking up English at a camp, Gil suffered a fainting episode. Stumbling to the nurse's cabin, he collapsed before he could rouse the nurse, but fortunately her dog began barking to draw her attention. Gil was rushed to the nearest hospital, where the doctor on duty turned out to be a cardiologist. While the cardiologist worked on Gil—ultimately discovering he was suffering from Wolff-Parkinson-White Syndrome—Gil had a vision in which he saw a bottle being filled with blue liquid; somehow he knew if the bottle was filled, he would die and he heard a voice telling him, "Now you can go to be with God." But the cardiologist saved his life.

Brad and Maureen Fretz contacted the Fosters to let them know about Gil's condition. Peggy went to see Gil in the hospital and when she learned how the Fretz family didn't have quite enough space to accommodate Gil, Peggy welcomed Gil into the Fosters' house. Gil was aged 19, the same as Rachel, and fit into the Fosters' home-life well. While he took classes in easy English he put in a great amount of effort to be an ideal guest, taking the task of loading the dishwasher so seriously that he would instruct the Fosters on the 'best way' to do the job! Gil was a little taken aback at the generosity the Fosters showed him, as he recalled when they were children together in Kalukembe Rob "wouldn't even loan his bicycle!" In time, Gil took to calling Steve and Peggy 'Mom and Dad' and the Foster siblings referred to him as their brother—confusing those who knew Rob was Steve and Peggy's only son.

In September 1999, shortly after Steve's 50th birthday, almost the entire Foster clan convened at Outer Banks, North Carolina, for the wedding of Shelley Foster to Peter Duplantis, a nurse she had met through her church in Greensboro. Among the Fosters assembled was Meghan, Stirling and Donna's second child, who had been born the previous month. Peter's daughter Jasper

Duplantis from his prior marriage found herself welcomed by her father's new family; she took on Shelley as her stepmother.

In the fall, Rachel began studying business management at Sheridan College in Oakville, Ontario, not far from Hamilton. Rebecca had finished teacher's college and began working in substitute-teaching positions. Rebecca also began working with Christian Horizons, a charitable organization that assists adults with developmental disabilities. In the spring, Rob took a quick turn volunteering in the Dominican Republic, then in April he was given an adult baptism at Philpott Memorial Church, while Heather took a nursing elective in Angola as her training came to an end.

As Bob and Steve continued to plan the new Evangelical Medical Centre which the $1 million donation had helped spring into motion, Steve made a point of planning the facility slowly so as to avoid the problems The Project developed because of their earlier haste. He also "wanted to ensure there would be a sense of local ownership and participation in the decision making" and this meant allowing the Angolan churches the time they needed to be comfortable with the centre's planning. "I am beginning to see some of the problems Abraham must have faced when he set out for his uncertain place and future," Steve mused. "I would love to have a clearer picture but am certain that God is in this process and we simply need to learn to trust His character and capacity to do more than we can ask or even think of."

Steve returned to Maputo in February 2000 to teach another Essential Surgical Skills Workshop. Just ahead of his arrival, Mozambique had been hit by a series of cyclones, resulting in a dam collapse not far from the region where Stuart and Sindia lived. After the workshop, MAF took Steve on a flight to see the effects of the flooding. "The sight and smell of rotting vegetation, polluted water, dead animals hanging in trees, people still taking refuge in trees and the sheer extent of the event has left an indelible impact on my mind," he recalled. Soon after Steve's visit, Bob entered Mozambique with Samaritan's Purse to assist victims of the flood. While there, Bob preached an Easter sermon: "It was a great joy to be able to preach to hundreds of Mozambicans in Portuguese during the Easter season. So few know the liberating power of Christ in their lives."

On July 8, 2000, Rebecca Foster and Ari Ho were married in a service at the Ancaster Mill in Dundas. Rebecca was the first Foster of her generation to be married and the whole Foster and Parkins clan came to celebrate. By this time, Rob had become quite skilled with his guitar and one night he and his cousin Jonathan Hoskin began singing songs by the Christian band Jars of Clay, until the family complained about the noise; undaunted, the cousins went into the night air to sing and play on the porch of the house; neighbours looked on, but none complained.

The wedded Rebecca and Ari changed their surnames to 'Ho-Foster' and moved to Ottawa, where Rebecca continued to teach, work with Christian Horizons and give talks on landmines, which had become a personal cause of hers.

On September 30, 2000, Steve's 4-year directorship term, which had begun with AEF Canada and ended with SIM Canada, came to an end. He immediately began making plans to return to Angola to help oversee the continuation of the new Evangelical Medical Centre, with the intent of serving at Rio de Huíla's clinic during the interim. Much to his and Peggy's delight, Rob chose to return with them to Angola; in fact, Rob was once again seeking his long-term goals and had considered becoming a short-term associate missionary with SIM. Rob went back to Lubango two months before his parents so he could begin teaching at the Mitcha school—the same school which once taught him.

As Steve and Peggy returned to Lubango, Steve was as joyous as ever to be returning to the work he loved. However, Peggy suffered from misgivings; she felt the time in Canada had been good for her children and doubted Rob would have returned to Angola without them. As she gave farewell hugs to her three daughters (and son-in-law Ari) at the airport, she was especially concerned with Heather; although Heather was now 23 years old, Peggy felt she needed her mother. They parted with their children promising them "one hug every year" no matter where circumstances brought them.

CHAPTER 17

"The Bran Doctor."

LUBANGO (November 2000 – October 2006)

Angola had changed during the previous four years. Certainly, the civil war continued with no visible end, but since establishing good business relations with the US, Angola had welcomed many significant corporations. The Coca-Cola Company had fled Angola at independence, but in 2000 it opened its first new plant in Angola. Similarly, beer had begun rolling into the marketplace—and both beverages were bringing their own health problems as far too many Angolans would subsist on diets of Coke or beer, with those who consumed 6-9 beers in one day inflicting tremendous damage to their livers. Early in 2001, Angola's first cellphone company Unitel would launch.

Mitcha had undergone changes as well; the old chain-link fence had come down and a high stone wall had taken its place. This wall had been raised after concerns about MKs who had gone missing from their home. Although the children turned up in another house at Mitcha, it convinced the community to raise a proper wall.

Steve, Peggy and Rob took up residence in a flat within the city of Lubango. As Steve resumed his clinical work at Rio de Huíla with Dr. Collins and Dr. Karen Henriksen, he heard from many Angolans they had not expected to ever see him again; they assumed after four years of living in Canada he would become too accustomed to the lifestyle and remain there, so were pleased that Steve proved them wrong. Steve began to schedule a visit to Kalukembe Hospital for one week every three months. On his return there, he was alarmed to see that virtually all of the hospital's surgical equipment had been lost; he found only a pair of scissors in the operating theatre. Although the nursing staff remained depleted since UNITA had pulled out, as the hospital stabilized many of the nurses who had fled to Huambo began filtering back.

Steve was disturbed by what he saw in the hospitals and clinics. "It has been hard for me to believe the extent to which health services have degraded over these 4 years. Elective surgeries for many illnesses haven't been done and people have been neglected with seriously advanced states of diseases. People are left to fend for themselves in such a callous way that it makes me cringe sometimes to call oneself a member of what I hoped was an honourable profession. The variety and severity of the illnesses that I've been confronted with are some of the most advanced and seriously ill people I've ever seen. The impact of the withdrawal of all the Russian and Cuban specialists who were here until the last few years has now become apparent. In this town of 30-plus doctors, I am one of a few with a specialist training."

Peggy found more opportunities for service than ever before, teaching ESL (English as a Second Language) at ISTEL, leading two women's Bible studies, teaching piano and leading choir practice. Rob found himself to be the only teacher at Mitcha's school and while he had also planned to teach at ISTEL, the potential students did not materialize. By now, Rob had begun playing his guitar at any opportunity, not only at church events but even on the local radio in Lubango!

In the spring of 2001, Stuart, Sindia and their children Cara and Luke came from Mozambique to Angola for 6 weeks while Stuart taught a course module at ISTEL. One day, Luke threw out his knee while playing soccer. Squirming in pain, he begged his Uncle Steve to examine the injury. Steve looked, tested the knee and concluded, "You're fine, get up."

Luke protested, "But Uncle Steve, it hurts!"

His uncle assured him, "No, you're fine, get up."

Luke forced himself to walk on his knee and quickly found it was not as bad as it had seemed. Recalling how his uncle had tended to him at age four, Luke surmised, "I think that's pretty representative of his bedside manner: he will carry you if he has to, but most of the time he will tell you to pick yourself up and don't take yourself too seriously."

In the spring of 2001, Daniel "Danny" Estêvão was hired as project administrator for the Evangelical Medical Centre. Danny had previously served in the provincial government, making him an ideal man to facilitate the many bureaucracies involved in setting up a project in Angola. Beyond that, as Steve noted, "He is highly respected for his integrity and is a senior elder in the local church we are part of." By June, the property for the centre had been chosen: it lay in the hills above Lubango, near the town of Humpata and just down the road from Cristo Rei.

On Easter 2001, Steve visited a Pentecostal gathering of refugees near the border of Namibia in Caluque. "In a community of 5000, most of whom are dislocated peoples from the war in central Angola, are a number of Christians who are sharing their faith with people who have never heard the Gospel. The result has been about 8 new congregations totalling several hundred now." The displacement and suffering of the war had not prevented the spread of the Gospel but even aided its diffusion!

During the summer, Rebecca began a year-long internship with the Youth Mine Action Ambassador Programme (YMAAP), a Canadian initiative to educate young people about landmines and equip them with information to better facilitate teaching others about present landmine threats. As part of the internship, Rebecca went to observe the situation in Cambodia, one of the most heavily mined nations on Earth.

9/11

Peggy had been correct in her fears about Heather; months after her parents left Canada, Heather took a leave of absence from the nursing program. It had been difficult for Heather to live alone without family support especially as, much like her mother, she suffered from anxiety. Rachel was working in Oakville and found it hard to relate to her elder sister's issues, despite her wish to support her. Fortunately, Rob returned to Canada that fall to begin his university studies at McMaster and moved in with Heather. Steve and Peggy came out to Hamilton that September to help encourage their daughter—so were at home on September 11 when their television set began broadcasting a news report about a plane striking the World Trade Center.

When the World Trade Center was destroyed by terrorists working for al-Qaeda, Rob had not yet returned to Canada and, fortunately, his flight was not cancelled and he arrived a day later to begin his studies in political science and history at McMaster. Rob also returned to Philpott Memorial Church and became involved in IVCF, just as his parents and grandparents had been, joining a Christian worship band in the community. As the fallout from the 9/11 terrorism attack continued to be felt, it eventually led to the War in Afghanistan. Steve's cousin Ken Foster had been serving in Afghanistan with Interserve International, but was in Canada with his family on the day of the attack, and the resulting war prevented him from returning.

The events of 9/11 caused ripples around the world which were felt even in Angola. Many airports and airlines tightened their security policies and this was extended to Angola, where X-ray machines were brought in to scan luggage instead of performing physical searches. The 9/11 attack also had an indirect effect on the nation—one which could be said to have ended the 27-year civil war.

THE PATH TO PEACE

As the US began referring to its new 'War on Terror', many of the freedom fighters the nation had championed against communism in the 1980s (such as the Taliban) were now classified as 'terrorists.' This label now applied to Jonas Savimbi, much to the MPLA's delight. The MPLA had been referring to Savimbi as a terrorist in the media for years and in the wake of 9/11, the US were definitively his *former* allies. Over the years Savimbi had become paranoid, constantly purging UNITA's ranks of anyone he suspected of disloyalty. This only caused even further defections from UNITA.

On February 22, 2002, Savimbi's location in Moxico province had been given to the MPLA by his former allies in Israel. The army assaulted Savimbi's base and slew him. As Savimbi's death had been reported in the media at least 15 times over the year, the government released photographs of his dead body to silence any doubters. Janet Holden's daughter Esther was in Luanda when the news of Savimbi's death demise: In reaction, the city erupted into a massive celebration; parties were thrown in Lubango and cheering could be heard in the streets. Even in Ottawa, where Rebecca was spreading landmine awareness in schools the news of Savimbi's death reached her and she hoped the peace which had long been hoped for might finally arrive. To Steve, Savimbi's death heralded "the end of an era where the ambitions of one man have held the country hostage."

While the nation waited to see how UNITA would react to Savimbi's death, work went on for Steve in Lubango. One particular incident forcefully demonstrated why the Evangelical Medical Centre was deeply desired. As Steve was leaving one of the clinics, "I was asked to see a 27-year-old man who had awakened feeling nauseated and unwell and developed a major hemorrhage that very morning. He was vomiting bright-red blood. I got him settled down and he stopped bleeding, but I was unable to scope him as my endoscopy instruments are out of town at Rio de Huíla clinic 37 km away, so I was unable to confirm the actual source of the bleeding. As it happened, 8 years ago I had looked after the same fellow when he had had a similar bleed. Then I had scoped him and discovered a duodenal ulcer. I presumed he had the same problem. There was no chart to be found from 8 years ago so I couldn't be sure.

"At 6 PM, I went back to see him after my full clinic day at Rio de Huíla. He hadn't bled any more so I was thankful. At midnight, the phone rang to say that he was bleeding and in shock. I asked them to get the OR ready for an emergency operation, only to be told that the OR nurse had left for home and that there was no phone where she was and no one knew where she lived. To further heat things up, there was no blood in the blood bank and no phone numbers of next of kin to get hold of at that hour. Well, I was fit to be tied but after due consideration decided we could find a substitute for the missing OR nurse with a volunteer nurse who has scrubbed with me this last year. We press-ganged the X-ray tech and lab tech at the clinic to serve as circulating nurses and got on with the laparotomy. After 2 hours, we found the source of bleeding. It was a tear at the upper end of the stomach from his powerful vomiting. This responded to suturing and he stopped bleeding. We finally got home at 4 AM. The people whom we had asked to help didn't do a thing to help clean up but fell onto their mattresses, demonstrating an absolute disdain for a spirit of team.

"Five days later, the whole scene was repeated when the same lad bled again. It was 1:30 AM this time. He ruptured his suture line in the duodenum where I had looked first. He also bled from a second tear close to the first one in the stomach. This time, we had no anaesthetist as he had taken off for a trip to Namibia. We still had only one bottle of blood on hand but could find the family at least. It took another 2 hours to get him sorted out again after we borrowed an anaesthetist from the maternity hospital. Today I had the patient shipped out to Windhoek, Namibia, by air ambulance, as he is a high risk for further bleeding or complications. When the clinic opens, we will have the tools and staff under one roof to deal with this kind of trouble and save many unnecessary evacuations."

THE NEW GENERATION

Ari Ho-Foster spent some time in South Africa on a short contract assessing the prevalence of sexual violence in that country, but returned to Ottawa in time for the birth of his and Rebecca's first child, Lucas, mere weeks after Rebecca finished her internship with YMAAP. Lucas was the first Foster born in his generation. Although Rebecca had been hoping to adopt a child since she had been a teenager, she was happy to become pregnant. Heather served as Rebecca's *doula* and it was a great bonding experience for the two sisters because Rebecca needed Heather and Heather wanted to be needed. The day after Lucas' birth, Steve and Peggy came to Ottawa to meet their grandson.

In July, Rebecca, Ari and Lucas went out to Johannesburg, South Africa, so Ari could take another short-term posting, this time a 6-month project where he was analyzing the AIDS epidemic in the country. The Ho-Fosters were certain they would be back in Canada at the end of the term and left their pet cats with Ari's mother—but as it turned out, Africa would become their permanent home. Despite her upbringing in Angola, Rebecca found South African culture quite different. She was accustomed to being treated like a peer by Africans and found it difficult when Africans older than her would treat her with deference or refer to her as "madam."

Events moved quickly in Angola—quicker than the outside world assumed. On April 4, 2002, UNITA signed a ceasefire agreement with the government and began disarming its forces the following month. Around the world, politicians urged caution, believing the conflict could resume at a moment's notice and offering their assistance to help the Angolans negotiate the peace process. However, the civil war was declared over on August 2, 2002—pointedly, one day before UN Secretary Kofi Anan and US Secretary of State Colin Powell would arrive; the two politicians came to Angola to find their presence was not needed at all.

The Angolan Civil War had lasted 27 years! An estimated half a million people had perished in the conflict! Including the war with Portugal, Angola had been at war for 42 years!

The only true hotspot in Angola remained the situation in Cabinda, where FLEC continued to vie with the government for independence. For once, this proved helpful to the MPLA as they deployed UNITA soldiers into Cabinda as a means to bond those forces with FAPLA; having a conflict where the soldiers could fight side by side suited the government better than a 100% peaceful nation would have done. As UNITA's guerrillas transitioned into a political party, the people who had been trapped behind lines of fire were once more at their liberty. This resulted in many joyous reunions between family members and church congregations. Among them was Antonio Salomão, finally free of UNITA. "We cried for joy to be here again," Antonio said as he returned to Kalukembe Hospital, and eventually accepted the role of hospital administrator. In Greensboro, Bob received a letter from a church leader telling him of "the thousands of people who are coming out of the bush after the signing of the armistice several months ago. His word-pictures were heart-wrenching as he described the poverty and malnutrition of them all. Many had no clothes and only had a bark cloth to sleep under." Bob immediately put out word for a clothing drive and lined up more than 2 tons of used clothing. Cavango remained dear to Bob's heart and it was joyous to hear 169 former leprosy patients had returned to the village.

At the end of 2002, Steve and Peggy decided to sell their home in Hamilton. Heather had moved out and Rachel had become a logistics coordinator for Cambrian Chemicals in Oakville—they couldn't justify the continued expense of such a large house for Rob alone. As Rob moved into other accommodations, Steve and Peggy had to accept Angola now was their home. The Hamilton residence had been helpful during Steve's tenure leading

AEF Canada, but Canada would never be their permanent address.

Steve continued his surgical visits to Kalukembe Hospital and also performed surgery at the clinic in Xangalala. On the last day of one visit, he received a radio message that Pastor Calenga had malaria and was bleeding from his stomach. Steve sped back to Lubango and found Pastor Calenga on the brink of death. "Graciously, God saw fit to answer our prayers as the pastor responded to fresh whole blood transfusions requiring seven units to stabilize."

By this time Danny Estêvão and Steve had welcomed many more partners into the Evangelical Medical Centre project, including Eloa Jane, an architect from Curitiba, Brazil, and civil engineer Gordon Stephenson. Norm Henderson, a Canadian missionary who had been a student at Sakeji, donated his services to set up the hospital's computers and other information technologies. The $1 million donation which started the hospital could only cover a portion of the ultimate costs, but more donors continued to emerge and USAID pledged support as well. Samaritan's Purse deployed Minne Prins from Holland to serve as its country director in Angola. Minne's wife Joanna also served with Samaritan's Purse as a bookkeeper and spent some time observing Steve at his work. She once brought her son with her as they observed Steve perform an amputation of a gangrenous leg; Steve, in a moment of clinical detachment, handed the severed leg to Joanna's son to dispose of!

During this time, Gil Sayango had entered Mohawk College in Hamilton to study business administration. Tragically, one day his parents Avelino and Ludia were driving in Angola when they were struck by another car; they both died in the collision. Peggy was in Windhoek when she learned of their deaths and was charged with the task of informing Gil. Peggy quickly phoned Heather, Rachel and Rob to inform them of the tragedy, then asked them to be with Gil when she told him. With his 'siblings' at his side, Gil received the unfortunate word from Peggy in a calm fashion. Later, after the call, he broke down in tears, but Heather, Rachel and Rob helped to support him.

Gil continued to excel in Canada and eventually gained Canadian citizenship, but ultimately decided to return to Angola. With the war over, there were great business opportunities in the nation; the South African supermarket chain Shoprite, for example, had begun opening stores in Angola. As an educated businessman, Gil eventually opened a construction company in Benguela.

In May 2003, Rob came back to Lubango for a visit and brought two pre-med students with him to tour his father's work and assist alongside him at the clinics. Although Steve had welcomed med students in the past, the end of the war had made it somewhat easier to obtain a visa into Angola. These two guests were the first in a new era of visiting med students, most of who would come and live with Steve and Peggy at their flat. This provided many kinds of opportunities for Christian witnessing as it gave Christian med students a chance to practise medicine in the developing world and seek whether they had a calling to mission work—however, to non-Christian med students, it exposed them to the ministry Steve and the other missionaries in Lubango had taken on and thereby ministered to their spiritual growth.

Even in the Fosters' home there were opportunities for ministry to guests as Steve and Peggy held devotions every morning and said grace at every meal. At the same time, it required Peggy to assume new responsibilities as living quarters had to be arranged against the shifting schedules of student arrivals and departures and adjusting meal plans to accommodate dietary needs.

WANDERING SNAKE SYNDROME

Along with malaria, one of the most common health problems Steve treated was people suffering from IBS (irritable bowel syndrome). Because the patients would describe their ailment by referring to a snake in their stomach, it became known as Wandering Snake Syndrome or The Luanda Snake. Steve would have very similar conversations with his patients; here is a typical account of how many of those discussions would transpire:

Patient: "Oh, doctor, there is a snake in my stomach! First I feel him here—then I feel him here!"

Steve: "Mm-hm. The reason the snake keeps moving is because he is hungry. You have to feed the snake! Feed him bran!"

Patient: "Bran? Why, that's peasant food!"

Steve: "Let me ask you then, are you a son of Adam (or daughter of Eve) or are you a monkey?"

Patient (slightly offended): "I am son of Adam (or daughter of Eve), of course!"

Steve: "Mm-hm. Tell me, when Adam and Eve lived in the Garden of Eden, did Eve have a handmill? Did she have a Shoprite? No? So that means Eve had to pound the grain by hand, the same way your grandmother did. Eve and your grandmother didn't eat processed grain, they ate the bran! Tell me, how long ago did Shoprite open in your town?"

Patient: "Six months ago."

Steve: "When the village handmill closed?"

Patient: "Yes."

Steve: "And when did you begin feeling the snake in your belly?"

Patient: "In the last six months…oh! I understand!"

Steve would prescribe a diet of bran to these patients. He gave his 'bran' speech so often, other missionaries dubbed him "The Bran Doctor."

BACK TO CAVANGO

In June 2003, Steve journeyed with Stirling and Donna and their children Jeffrey and Meghan to Cavango. Still without airplane access, the Fosters had to drive the entire circuitous distance. Despite the length of the trip, Steve was fascinated to pass through towns and villages to see how they were faring post-war. In Huambo, which, as Bob had seen, had been blasted apart, Steve felt encouraged to see the city getting back on its feet. Passing through Dondi, where he saw ruins of the mission station where Dr. Collins grew up, Steve "was impressed by the zeal of the local congregation to begin a Christian school registering and catering for some 300 children through Grade 6. Their classes are mostly in the open air and the students who are boarders are sleeping in grass-roofed buildings built by the students and their families themselves." Seeing the determination of the Dondi Christians reminded Steve again of the passage from Zechariah: "Who dares despise the day of small things?" In Cavango, Steve treated people with active cases of leprosy, stabilizing their condition and "brought joy to their faces." The presence of lepers in Cavango had injured the village's reputation, so curing the lepers benefited the entire community.

While Heather continued her training in the nursing program, she made a return visit to Angola to assist Dr. Karen Henriksen in the public health program, principally by providing teaching to local women, much as her aunt Sheila had done around Kalukembe. Some of the problems women were facing were based on the assumed inferiority of females, so Heather would emphasize to husbands how they should take on some of the household work when their wives were pregnant. "It was great to see women's faces light up at the idea they had value," Heather said, beaming. After Heather treated a woman who had hypertension the patient remarked, "If I were always so well looked after, I'd want to be pregnant all the time!"

Heather also spent some time out by Tchincombe, living out of a camper trailer in the centre of the nearby town, close to the village water supply, which was built within a massive cement container. One night, Heather heard noises outside the trailer but didn't investigate; in the morning, she discovered elephant tracks all around the trailer! An elephant had strolled up to the water supply and drunk its fill, then lumbered away.

50 YEARS OF MUKINGE

In August, Mukinge Hospital celebrated their 50th anniversary and planned a special celebration, followed by its annual Bible conference. Bob and Belva Foster were invited back to Mukinge to commemorate the occasion and so that Bob could speak at the conference. Steve's sister Sharon met their parents at the airport in Lusaka then journeyed by road with them to the family's old hometown. At the hospital, they found many nurses who had graduated from the hospital's nursing program had come to join the festivities. Belva said, "For me the most thrilling part of our whole trip was to see and hear what God has done in and through the lives of these ladies. They gave tribute to the quality of their training, both professional and spiritual, and said they were the most respected and sought-after nurses in Zambia because of it."

By the time of the 50th anniversary ceremony, Steve, Peggy, Sheila and her children Helena, Sara and Daniel, Stirling, Donna and their children Jeffrey and Meghan, Rebecca and her son Lucas arrived to join the celebration; Zambia's Minister of Health also delivered a speech and the family toured the hospital, which was now home to 210 patient beds. Belva gasped "it wore me out just touring it."

While Bob went on to teach at the conference, Steve and Sheila attempted to visit their old school Sakeji, which was still open up in the north, but their Land Rover broke down on the road and they had to abandon the plan. The family had arranged to gather together in Katima Mulilo, Namibia, a lodge on the Zambezi River, once the conference had ended. However, the trip from Mukinge to Katima Mulilo was a long one. After nine hours of "a terrible jouncing journey through tsetse-fly-infested country," Bob and Belva arrived at the border to Namibia an hour after the gate had closed.

As the border town was quite small with no place for visitors to stay, Bob and Belva prayed about their plight. Not long afterward, they sighted a white man on top of a hill holding a cellphone, having come out there to improve his cell reception. "Whether he's ever been considered an angel before or since," Belva mused, "he was one for us that evening." The man with the phone was a contractor from South Africa and told them there was a campsite on an island in the Zambezi River about 5 kilometres back into Zambia. Bob and Belva sought the location out and, although the hosts were not taking guests at that time of the year, they didn't have the heart to turn away the couple and gave them lodging for the night.

Steve, Sheila and Stirling were quite worried about their parents' non-appearance and had pledged to set out first thing in the morning to find them, but at 9:15 AM Bob and Belva sped into the Zambezi Lodge. Bob and Belva's family were impressed that even after 50-plus years in Africa, they had not lost their adventurous spirit!

In May 2004, Angola passed laws protecting freedom of worship and religion, protections which the nation's Christians once lacked. As Angola's renewed economy boomed, the change could be felt particularly in the construction sector; Gil found himself with no end of building contracts as so many parts of the nation needed rebuilding. However, the scarcity of building supplies meant the price of concrete skyrocketed—further inflating the cost of building the Evangelical Medical Centre.

Angola adjusted itself to peacetime. There was much for all of the Fosters to rejoice in as Heather wrote and passed her nursing licence exams and began working for public health in Hamilton. But in the midst of these happy times, Peggy struggled internally. For the first time in her life, she found herself suffering from a crisis of faith, of uncertainty about what she believed. As a missionary's wife, she was afraid to express this to other people— missionaries are, unfortunately, expected to be immune to such struggles.

Peggy suffered mostly in silence, but then found a friend she could confide in: her sister-in-law Donna. Peggy unburdened herself to Donna and found someone who would listen. "I don't condemn you for feeling that," Donna would console her. "1 understand." Simply by being present for Peggy and willing to listen to her doubts without judging her, Donna helped usher Peggy through the year-long crisis. Donna used the struggles of her own life to provide a sympathetic ear to Peggy and the two became closer friends from then on. Over the years they would meet together to study texts including the novel *The Wounded Heart* by Adina Senft and the relationship aid *Married without Masks* by Nancy Bloom.

REBECCA'S SECOND CHILD

Rebecca had long hoped to adopt children; after Lucas' birth, Ari's parents assumed Rebecca had left that idea behind—but Rebecca and Ari continued to plan to adopt a child while living in Johannesburg. Finally, the adoption agency set up a meeting for Rebecca with Gabriel, a boy who lived in Durban. It so happened that Ari had a conference to attend in Durban so the entire Ho-Foster clan went to meet Gabe. Although Gabe had found a loving foster mother, Rebecca formed a true bond to the 16-month old; she and Ari adopted Gabe into their family, making him, at 10 months younger than Lucas, the 2nd of Steve and Peggy's grandchildren. The foster mother continued to remain in contact with Rebecca; she adored Gabe and lived for Rebecca's updates by telephone. Ari's parents and Steve and Peggy were ecstatic to bring him into their family.

Steve's work in Lubango received more support as his colleagues Dr. Nicholas Comninellis and Toronto cardiologist Dr. Michael Bentley-Taylor began making visits to work alongside him at the clinics. The work of SIM was also upheld thanks to Dagmar Henchoz, a German missionary who became the SIM field leader for Angola. The Evangelical Medical Center continued to move apace as it hoped to finally open its doors in 2005 and Samaritan's Purse's African Projects Director John Freyler visited to help the team press forward.

Minne Prins and Pastor Abias (who was now secretary of the AEA) determined they would employ a staff of Christian nurses at the hospital, for they would not be restricted from evangelizing to the patients because the hospital was a private institution. "Nurses will be trained to not only talk about the disease but also talk about Jesus," Minne stated. Pastor Abias added: "We do not say you have to be Christian or convert to Christianity to be treated, but we give you a chance or opportunity to listen to the Gospel."

In November 2004, Belva suffered a slight stroke that left her left leg and arm weakened; soon after, she suffered a transient ischemic attack. Since she had been the typist of her and Bob's newsletters for many years; Bob assumed that responsibility, but the gravity of Belva's condition pointed to her and Bob's advancing age. Despite that, Bob went out to Angola and journeyed to Kalukembe Hospital with Steve, where they performed 14 surgical cases together. "It felt like old times when we used to work together there in the '70s!" Bob beamed.

During 2005, Heather struck up a friendship in a Christian chatroom with a man named Georg Messner, who was dean of students at Tyndale Seminary, Amsterdam. Still a fairly shy young woman, Heather had never had a long-term boyfriend and, like many MKs, took the concept of dating very seriously. Communicating with Georg solely online proved to be a good match for Heather's personality as it kept the relationship at a casual level. "It helped mediate the intensity for us," Heather said.

Just ahead of the planned celebrations surrounding the opening of the Evangelical Medical Centre, Steve and Peggy went to visit Rebecca, Ari, Gabe and Lucas in Johannesburg and to see the regional SIM office. During their trip they passed through Kuruman in the Northern Cape province of South Africa. In 1841, it was the location where Dr. David Livingstone arrived to begin his first assignment as a missionary.

Seeing Kuruman put Steve in mind of that common missionary zeal which Livingstone had possessed and been passed down through the generations of Fosters beginning with his grandfather Charles. Still, the question of legacy remained ever present in his mind; would anyone in the next generation of Fosters chose to become a missionary? He needed only look to his eldest niece: Sharon's daughter Tonya Arscott-Mills, now a physician serving with Samaritan's Purse; and, as events would bear out, there would be more Fosters from Tonya's generation who would answer God's calling in missions.

THE FESTIVAL OF HOPE

On June 10, 2005, Huíla's provincial governor, José Ramos da Cruz, came to attend Franklin Graham's dedication of the Evangelical Medical Centre before a crowd of 400 people, including Shelley and her husband Peter Duplantis. "The one dark spot in the day," Bob Foster observed, "was the fact that the contractor hadn't finished what he had agreed to do. He tried to get out of his contract by doubling his fee, thus hoping he would be let go. However, eventually he agreed to stand by his commitment. He had just signed a contract for a huge building project and wanted out so he could be free to get on with this more lucrative one."

Despite the incomplete facility, the new hospital remained on track to be completed and Governor DaCruz stated, "This hospital is a great start in rebuilding our country. We are grateful for your generosity and what this will mean for our people. We are also thankful for the Festival, and I will work to protect the freedoms of our people to worship." Steve believed the centre would be "the best medical facility in Angola," and Franklin concurred: "The bar of quality for mission hospitals has just been raised," he beamed. Bob Foster and Pastor Chiquete (President of the AEA) unveiled the building's dedication plaque. "All of us were encouraged by how God has worked, multiplying the original gift of one million USD more than threefold," Steve celebrated.

Directly following the dedication, from June 10-12, 2005, Franklin Graham hosted his Festival of Hope in Lubango, a large rally intended to help celebrate the opening of the Evangelical Medical Centre and the nation's freedom to worship laws. "In a country that was once torn apart," Graham said, "we thank God for peace now that the war has ended. Now that there is peace in the land we have an opportunity to bring this Festival and spiritual peace to these people's hearts." Lubango had only recently opened a large soccer stadium in the city and the festival brought a crowd of 46,978 into the stands, with 13,496 of them coming forward to pledge their lives to Jesus. There was also a smaller festival for children (*festivalzinho*) which used drama and music to teach lessons about God's love and forgiveness. "The Lord really blessed the Festival of Hope evangelism campaign," a grateful Bob said.

"It was also the first time nearly all of the city's churches united for one purpose," reporters observed. Steve added, "More than 97 churches participated and one result has been an increased awareness of each other and a desire to continue to pray and work together. One church we know of has had to develop two additional worship services on Sunday just to handle the new attendees."

While Bob was still in Angola, he took the opportunity to visit Cavango, that place which still held a piece of his heart. After expressing his wish to rebuild at Cavango to Franklin Graham, Graham himself made the first donation to its renewal as a satellite of the Evangelical Medical Centre. Under this status, when Cavango's clinic was reopened they appealed to Lubango for staffing assistance and referrals. MAF pilot Brent Mudde brought Bob, Steve, Peggy and a pair of visiting med students as near to Cavango as he could—which still left them a long "12 hours of bouncing" down dirt roads to Cavango. It was Peggy's first trip to Cavango since 1975.

"The people have returned from refugee camps and hiding in the bush so that there are ten thousand or so in the immediate area," Bob noted. "We were received with great joy and they are asking for help to rebuild at least a clinic, school and church." Samaritan's Purse and the World Medical Mission again offered to help.

Steve's guests from North America included Dr. Collin Hong, a plastic surgeon from Scarborough who performed a free radial flap for one Kalukembe Hospital patient who "survived a gunshot wound to her face 4 years earlier, leaving her with a huge hole in her palate." That same week, Steve performed 91 operations at Kalukembe.

At the same time, Rob was again trying to find his place in the world and enrolled at Regent College, where his Aunt Sheila and Uncle Ezekiel had studied; Rob took up theology and wondered if he might have a calling as a pastor.

That Christmas, Rob went to Toronto to spend the holidays at his Uncle Richard and Aunt Sherri Parkins' home, along with Rachel and Heather. During the visit he met Heather's boyfriend Georg and on Christmas Eve, Georg proposed to Heather; she said yes.

ADVANCING THE GOSPEL IN ANGOLA

Bob Foster's determination to support the rebuilding of Cavango and the other mission projects the Fosters had become involved in over the years finally led to him developing an umbrella group called *Advancing the Gospel in Angola*. The organization described itself as its "sole purpose is to advance the Gospel in Angola through assistance to Evangelical churches in developing Christian schools, the seminary, hospitals and clinics, agricultural projects, etc." It had been born in part because of the aid agencies Bob had used in the past, which would each claim a certain percentage of donated monies in order to maintain their operations; Bob hoped this new organization would invest as much of the donated money as possible into the needs of Angola.

Steve joined the group on behalf of the Evangelical Medical Center, as did Sheila with her work at ISTEL and Stirling and Donna of the Tchincombe Ranch were also linked to their work. Among the many mission people who had supported efforts in Angola over the years and who joined this group were John Bloise (who would succeed Bob as President) and Paul Hockersmith, who particularly shared Bob's love for Cavango. A major goal of Advancing the Gospel in Angola was to build housing for missionaries, as the rising cost of building materials had driven up rental prices, making it hard for missionaries to afford living in Angola.

In June 2006, Bob was joined by Steve, Dr. Sean Reimer (an MK who had been born in Mukinge), Bob's grandson Daniel Fabiano, Shelley and Peter Duplantis on a visit to begin the rebuilding project. Shelley had resigned from her work as a midwife to assist at the Evangelical Medical Centre when it opened. A quick survey of the land uncovered the foundations of the houses, church, school and clinic all of which UNITA had torn down but the concrete floors remained quite usable. The group camped out on the cold ground ("It was hard but good," Daniel opined), and although Bob had the same spirit of adventure as in the past, his body did not take the rough living well; he would later develop pneumonia from the conditions, setting in motion a series of health complications that caused his slow decline.

The work in Cavango was successful as Peter worked diligently, laying 2.5 kilometres of pipe from a spring to the clinic grounds. The new clinic (initially 12x17 metres) was built on the base of its progenitor, with Sean, Shelley and Peter completing the roof. With the assistance of Charlie Rea, a civil engineer from Zambia and former Sakeji classmate of Sheila's, the villagers of Cavango were guided to help rebuild the lost structures, cleaning old bricks so they could be recycled. By the end of the trip, the clinic and village church were standing once again.

For Bob, it was as important to re-establish ties with the people of Cavango: "One of the great joys of the visit was to be able to speak and preach in Luchazi-Ngangela, a language I hadn't used for over 30 years. We met every morning at 7:30 AM to have devotions in their language and every evening at 7:30 PM around a campfire to memorize scripture, and share the Gospel." Sixteen-year-old Daniel took inspiration from his grandfather's seemingly endless energy. "Throughout our time at Cavango, Grandpa always took time to share with me and pass on his wisdom. His model as a husband, father, and grandfather are ones that I will aspire to."

THE ZEBRA HUNT

In the summer of 2006, Steve went on a hunting trip with John Bloise at the Schönfeld Game Park in Namibia, but by the time Steve arrived there he had only two days for hunting. Upon arrival, Steve met a Czechoslovakian woman who had come to hunt zebras; she told Steve she had been there for 10 days and had yet to land her targets. "I've seen a zebra every day," she said, "but they've never stopped." When she heard Steve had only two days to hunt and intended to land a zebra and a kudu, she was sceptical.

Steve, John and their guide set out into the hills. As they rounded a curve they sighted a herd of 5-6 zebras, but in an instant the animals thundered away "like life was too short." They stopped their vehicle and climbed to the top of a hill to watch the zebra run, wondering if they would stop; but the zebras kept going and going, moving about 900 yards. The guide informed Steve and John that this had happened to the Czech woman every day she went hunting.

As they rounded another hill, they spotted 6-8 zebras simply standing in the open; the wind was blowing from the zebras to the car and the vehicle was travelling slowly, not stirring up much dust. The guide examined the zebras with his field glasses. "There's a nice one," he directed, "the second one. Let the group disperse, they're going in single file." Perhaps the sun was in just the right position, because the zebras took no notice of the hunters. The guide told Steve to ready his rifle and wait until the second zebra separated from the first (as hitting two zebras when a hunter only has a licence for one is a costly problem). As if on cue, the first zebra stepped forward while the third stepped back, just as the guide predicted; Steve fired his shot and the zebra went down; they hadn't been out for even two hours and Steve already had his first trophy! They returned with the animal in time to greet the Czech woman, who was going home without landing a zebra; she was amazed at their good fortune. "It wasn't anything we did, just God's generosity," Steve admitted.

After lunch, Steve and John set out with the guide to hunt kudu. They followed a path down a dry riverbed because kudu like to come up underneath drooping plants along the riverbed to feed on overhanging bushes. After an hour and a half of driving they came up on a small ledge and saw a little valley where the water cut across. On the other side of the water, about 150 yards away, was a kudu walking parallel to the stream. The kudu must have left the riverbed about 15 minutes before the hunters' arrival and it did not see them. Once again, the wind was blowing from the animal to the hunters so that the hunters' scent was not detectable. The guide examined the kudu and determined it was an 8-year-old male and a good candidate for a trophy. They waited to see if he would come to a halt and drew their vehicle closer. They waited, with Steve's scope sighted on the animal until the kudu stopped; the guide ordered Steve to shoot and he did—the bullet struck the kudu head on and killed him. Steve had taken both of his trophies with only one shot each!

John had been less lucky, as he hadn't been able to hit an eland in all his time at the park prior to Steve's arrival. On their way back with the kudu, Steve, John and their guide came over a ridge when the guide spotted an eland a thousand yards away standing in an open area. Just as the final light of the day was descending, John fired on the eland at 85 yards as it strolled into the woods. It was a direct hit! Steve and John had both had a 100% successful day of hunting! The skins of the zebra and kudu became wall decorations at the Fosters' home in Lubango. They also brought home 70 kilograms of frozen eland meat, but gave the zebra and kudu meat to an orphanage.

On August 5, 2006, Steve and Peggy assembled their family in Amsterdam, Holland, for the wedding of Heather and Georg Messner. Guitar in hand, Rob played the processional as Steve led Heather up the aisle; Rebecca and Rachel sang a song to celebrate the wedding. The burgermeister (mayor) performed the civil ceremony and was amazed to learn Heather and Georg were not living together prior to their wedding, very much against the current western cultural trend. Heather learned Georg's parents had always wanted a daughter and would have named her 'Erica'; because 'Erica' was Heather's nickname, they had finally achieved that dream. "People are shocked when I tell them marriage is the hardest thing I've ever done," Heather said, adding, this is a reflection on herself, not on Georg. "It's also the best thing I've ever done." While Georg continued at Tyndale Seminary, Heather took a position there as caterer.

Nationally, the biggest headlines in Angola during 2006 was the country qualifying for the FIFA World Cup, as soccer is by far the most popular sport on the continent of Africa. But in the hills above Lubango, however, there was greater news: the Evangelical Medical Centre had finally opened on October 16 under the name *Centro Evangélico Medicina do Lubango* or CEML.

CHAPTER 18

"Health and Hope Through Christ." — *CEML Motto*

LUBANGO (October 2006 – December 2011)

CEML had been built in its location above Lubango in part to avoid the urban sprawl of the city and make it easier for the hospital to cater to the needs of rural people. Whereas Central Hospital still had dress code expectations for their patients, CEML would permit Africans to come dressed in rags or their traditional garb, unashamed. There was also the idea of competition—by placing themselves outside of the city, it could avoid being seen as a competitor of the city's clinics. The mission scriptures of the facility included Matthew 14:14: *"When Jesus landed and saw a large crowd, he had compassion on them and healed their sick."* and Luke 9:2: *"Jesus sent them out to preach the Kingdom of God and to heal the sick."* A painting by Nathan Greene entitled *Chief of the Medical Staff* was hung in the surgical ward; it depicts a surgeon in an operating theatre at work on a patient with Jesus Christ standing at the surgeon's side, encouraging him.

CEML rested upon a hefty 25 hectares but initially needed only five of those hectares. The large amount of surplus land would help it to slowly expand as funding became available. Unlike Kalukembe Hospital or Central Hospital, CEML was built entirely on one level—no upper storeys. The head building contained the consult rooms, administrative offices, dispensary, laboratories and emergency ward, while the buildings to the rear featured the men's and women's wards and surgical building. The facility featured 43 ward beds, 5 emergency beds and 2 operating beds.

The long delays in opening CEML had included a great deal of paperwork, including Steve's required licence in order to function as medical director of the facility. *Advancing the Gospel in Angola* stepped in at the last minute to cover the salaries of CEML's staff for the first two months, as initially the funding proved terribly tight. Samaritan's Purse celebrated the opening by issuing a new edition of Lorry Lutz's book *Sword and Scalpel* with new chapters added.

Out of nearly 150 staff members, initially there were only two physicians regularly available—Steve and Dr. Collins. "At times," Steve confessed, "if you write it all down on paper it looks rather silly. But at other times, you begin to say 'Well, somebody had to do something to start.' I've felt that was my responsibility and trusting this next generation of people will catch a vision." Fortunately, many of the capable nurses of Kalukembe who had previously followed him to the Central Hospital now continued in service beside him at CEML.

It was estimated that within a 250-kilometre radius of CEML, there were some 2.5 million Angolans. The tribes within that radius included Mumuila, Nganguela, Mucabal, Mundimba, Mungambwe, Kwangali, Himba and Nyaneka, all of whom were largely unreached people. However, the reputation of Steve Foster as a doctor with vast expertise would draw in patients from across the nation, even remote Cabinda, and they would find a steady flow of patients from the armed services, despite soldiers having their own army doctors.

Although it took time for patients to trust CEML, the many years Steve had spent treating people in Kalukembe, Lubango and elsewhere brought the facility some attention. "An institution is only as great as its people," Pastor Calenga mused. Steve's many contacts with physicians outside Angola brought helpers from time to time, including repeated visits from Dr. Collin Hong, North York General Hospital cardiologist Dr. Keith Kwok, Dr. Michael Bentley-Taylor, and physician couple Drs. Robert Riviello and Beth Riviello. The Riviellos hailed from Boston and had been friends with Stuart and Sindia for years. Shelley and Peter Duplantis assisted CEML; although Peter had his training as a nurse, being unable to speak Portuguese he instead assisted CEML with manual labour and maintenance. Shelley became CEML's midwifery and OBGYN specialist, managed the pharmacy and would even host consults!

As Cristo Rei stood as the most significant landmark along the hillside, many in Lubango would dub CEML 'Hospital Cristo Rei,' which was not entirely inaccurate. As Bob and Steve had intended, the hospital staff was encouraged to share its faith with patients. Pastor Moisés of IESA served as their chaplain, with many other pastors filling in when requested. "The churches saw it as an opportunity for evangelism," Pastor Calenga observed. The outdoor space included a simple chapel area—rows of wooden benches where church services could be held.

At the outset it was thought Dr. Collins would divide his time equally in ophthalmology and general medicine, but the sheer volume of patients with eye troubles quickly changed circumstances until Dr. Collins' typical workload comprised 90% ophthalmology, 10% general. Dr. Collins was also at work in Benguela at Boa Vista clinic where he was training nurses in ophthalmology.

In the first few months of CEML's work, Steve received a startling call: "Hello, Dr. Estêvão, this is Sr. Silva." Sr. Silva, the very man who had so strongly affected Steve when he left Cavango that he had felt compelled to return to Angola. It had been more than 30 years since he so much as heard the nurse's voice. Steve learned Sr. Silva had called on business—he was serving at a clinic in Menongue and needed to make a patient referral.

"When are you coming to see me?" Sr. Silva enquired.

"When are *you* coming to see *me?*" Steve laughed. Although his voice had changed with age, Sr. Silva's laughter sounded just as Steve remembered, and Silva rejoiced to hear Bob and Belva were still alive.

The efforts of Advancing the Gospel in Angola continued to progress in Cavango as Paul Hockersmith led the construction teams which completed the work on the new facilities. Having spent part of his childhood at Cavango, Paul felt the same determination as Bob to see the lost buildings restored. "We are thrilled and thankful for Paul's love of Angola and desire to see Cavango once again to have a full hospital," Darrell and Barb Hockersmith enthused. On May 1, 2007, the Cavango clinic was officially reopened. Steve, Peggy, Peter and Shelley brought Bob and Belva with them to the ceremony; it was Belva's first visit to Cavango since 1975. "The joy on the 1,000-plus who showed up to greet my folks was an awesome sight," Steve said.

More than 13 village sobas attended the festivities and a cow was slaughtered for the feast. Samaritan's Purse supplied Operation Christmas Child shoeboxes for several hundred village children. Although plans to open an airfield at Cavango continued to hit barriers with the local governor, CEML determined it would begin sending its physicians there on a regular basis, just as they were continuing to do at Kalukembe.

In June, Rachel Foster moved back to Angola to accept a position as regional manager for the Huíla and Namibe provinces at Jembas, the company owned by Jean-Pierre's younger brother Etienne Bréchet. Rachel had come to appreciate Canada and intended to return after one year in Angola, but instead she found a growing commitment to the work at Jembas. On some level she felt, "life was too easy in Canada, there was not enough of a challenge." Like her father, she wanted new inroads to make. In her work at Jembas, she could see how much the end of the war had begun to change the nation; there was a growing middle class in Angola, to say nothing of the wealthy upper classes. It was that same year that Angola joined the Organisation of the Petroleum Exporting Countries (OPEC) and, a further sign of the changing times, the FNLA's leader Holden Roberto died from heart failure, at age 84; with Neto, Savimbi and Roberto gone, the nation's three top political parties had each lost their initial leaders.

While Bob celebrated the 60th anniversary of his graduation from the University of Toronto, his first great-granddaughter was born: Olivia Ho-Foster was, like her brother Lucas, a happy surprise. Rebecca's intention to adopt children had been carried out through the adoption of Gabe. In due time, Rebecca would remind him of his special place in the family: "You are the only child your father and I planned; everyone else is a happy surprise."

Back at CEML, Shelley found herself quite busy guiding the nursing staff. Much like her sister Sheila, she had begun a community health program targeting the area around CEML, starting with a community called Campa, then moving into Mundindi. In addition to collecting statistics on the health and wellness of the people there, Shelley seized the opportunity as a Christian witness: "We also are ambassadors for Christ in these communities and want His love to shine to all these people more than anything else!"

Steve noted that while malaria remained the single greatest killer in Angola, "right after that, however, is a high-blood-pressure-related stroke, diabetes and cancer, so first-world diseases are marching in like a flood. All this is thanks to lots of salt, sugar in our Coca-Cola and refined bran-free foods." The Bran Doctor would time and again make his speech extolling the virtues of bran to all who would hear! Steve also had a new colleague at his side: Dr. Paulo Buaki, an Angolan surgical intern who had become CEML's first participant in the Pan-African Academy of Christian Surgeons (PAACS), an organization dedicated to training African surgeons to serve African health care needs. Steve had been waiting 30 years to prepare eager Christian surgeons such as Dr. Buaki.

Down the hill from CEML, Lubango had continued to change. In 2008, the Millennium Shopping Centre opened. Decorated with flourishes of elegant Portuguese architecture, the massive building boasted dozens of shops and the first movie theatre since independence—however, the mall acquired a terrible reputation due to its parking lot as the security force did little to defend space, which became the favourite place for robberies of unattended vehicles. If the mall was a sign of increased urbanity, then unfortunately the robberies also demonstrated the downsides of urban living!

ENTERING THE KINGDOM

Stirling and Steve's old friend Sr. Fernando Borge had developed prostate cancer and came to CEML for treatment. Sr. Fernando's large bowel was perforated and although Steve did his best to help the old gentleman in the operating theatre, he was nearing the end of his life. The evening before he passed away, Steve visited Sr. Fernando's bedside and heard him say: "I just want to say thank you for everything you've done for me. I am going to meet my maker." It amazed Steve to hear Sr. Fernando speak this way, for in all the years he had known him, Sr. Fernando had never spoken of his faith. At his funeral, friends shared reminiscences of Fernando's great generosity toward them in times of need. "Our lives were marked by people of this stature, this kind of generosity," Steve said. "You weren't even sure where they were in the Kingdom of God, which makes you glad God is the judge, not yourself. God alone sees the heart and reads the motives of others. I have great fears for those of us who are smug in our salvation and secure because of a baptismal certificate hanging on a wall someplace."

Meanwhile, Peggy suffered through a case of kidney stones. Ahead of a visit to Rebecca in May 2008, she had to detour to Johannesburg to receive lithotripsy and endoscopic surgery to remove a stuck kidney stone as her condition was more precarious than Steve had suspected because an infection had set in; Rebecca and Olivia came from Botswana to comfort Peggy and Rebecca summoned Steve to help her rally until she was well enough to travel to Gaborone.

By this time, Ari had been working with CIET (*Centro de Investigación de Enfermedades Tropicales*), formerly the Tropical Disease Research Centre, and took a new role as CIET opened a research office in Gaborone, Botswana, to perform HIV research. Eventually Ari moved there permanently with Rebecca, Lucas, Gabe and Olivia. While in Botswana, Rebecca resumed working as a teacher.

Heather and Georg had also taken on a new opportunity, moving to Mosbach, Germany, to serve with Operation Mobilization (OM), an international mission agency which was headquartered in Mosbach. Always sensitive to her environment, Heather couldn't help but note Mosbach lay within the Odenwald, forests supposedly dedicated to the Norse god Odin. Heather felt dark spiritual forces at work around Mosbach, but considered herself blessed to have been raised in Africa, where people take spiritual warfare seriously. Georg also found Mosbach spiritually troubling; once, he pointed to an unfamiliar couple walking on the street, asking Heather, "You see those people over there? They're not from around here." When Heather asked how he knew this, Georg answered, "They look healthy."

THE STRUGGLE OF LEGACY

Once again, Rob Foster found himself at a crisis point. Although neither Steve nor Bob had ever made demands on him to step into the Foster "legacy," as the son of Steve and the grandson of Bob, he decided he "had to live up to the Foster name and reputation or let everyone down." However, his classes at Regent College had not been going well; in fact, his faith had dimmed. Visiting his grandparents ahead of their 60th wedding anniversary, Rob noticed how their health had begun to fail when Belva didn't recognize him and he wondered if it might be the last time they would hold a lucid conversation.

Rob tried to express his doubts to his grandfather. "Grandpa," he sighed, "I've let you down."

Bob wouldn't hear of it: "You're going to be a pastor, so what's wrong with that?" he replied.

Rob was already ending his studies at Regent by this time. "Grandpa, I'm not. I don't want to be a pastor."

Bob thought for a moment. "You play the guitar very nicely," Bob observed and suggested Rob continue with a music ministry.

The celebration of Bob and Belva's 60th wedding anniversary occurred in the Drakensberg Mountains near Underburg, close to the border of Lesotho. Rob accompanied his grandparents out to the Drakensberg and, determined to "glean as much wisdom as I could from Grandpa," he asked, "Grandpa, if you could give me one piece of advice and only one, what would it be?"

Bob answered: "Believe God."

The joyous family reunion brought together Bob, Belva, Steve, Peggy, Rebecca, Ari, and their children Gabe, Lucas and Olivia; Heather and Georg; Rob; Sharon and her daughter Tonya; Sheila and her children Helena, Sara and Daniel; Stuart, Sindia and their children Cara and Luke; Stirling, Donna and their children Meghan and Jeffrey; Shelley and Peter Duplantis.

Just after Angola's 2008 general election—a peaceful affair, unlike that of 1992—the financial crisis in the US caused a global recession, provoking economic calamities which would grow to envelope Angola as well. Gil Sayango felt the pinch in Benguela as his construction firm suddenly found itself with clients who refused to pay their bills, for their finances had been wiped out.

In December 2008, Steve welcomed another visiting physician: Dr. Annelise Olson, daughter of an American missionary couple, but born in Denmark and raised in Portugal. Being fluent in Portuguese and passionate about serving in Africa, she had been looking for opportunities in a Portuguese-speaking country such as Guinea-Bissau, Mozambique or Angola when PAACS made her aware of CEML. Dr. Olson joined Steve in the operating theatre to enjoy his brand of "ridiculous surgery" and in her two weeks at Lubango she found the country "more Portuguese than Portugal! The same bureaucracy, the same architecture..." Steve had been hoping to find a missionary surgeon with a long-term interest in service and at last, she had appeared; however, it would take time for Dr. Olson to afford the transition into Angola full-time.

Steve once had the opportunity to aid his old friend Etienne Bréchet, who had been out one day to the farms run by Jembas near Lubango when a bit of fresh honey gave him an allergic reaction to pollen. Within minutes, Etienne was left struggling to breathe as his staff raced him to CEML. His blood pressure had dropped to 50 mm/hg when Steve intervened and revived him.

Etienne wasn't the only person at Jembas to benefit from Steve's expertise. One night, Jembas' security chief, Gordon van Slingeland had remained at the Lubango farm while his manager went to a formal dinner. Gordon had been feeling ill and taking antibiotics, but the antibiotics caused an allergic reaction and he fell into anaphylactic shock. Other staff members brought him to CEML, but the nurses could not treat him and called for Steve, who happened to be at the same formal dinner Gordon's manager had gone to, and Steve arrived at CEML in time to save Gordon's life. Gordon, a tough ex-soldier from South Africa, became overwhelmed by what Steve had done for him, much to the amusement of his co worker, Steve's daughter Rachel. "Rachel has stated that I have some sort of weird fascination or feelings for her father," Gordon mused. "Which is probably true, I find him to be inspirational on both a personal and professional level, and let's not forget that I owe him my life."

Just as Barack Obama became the US President, Steve joined Dr. Buaki on a trip to Nairobi, Kenya, organized by PAACS. "It was the first-ever meeting of surgical alumnae now totalling over 26 with program directors in five sites from 4 countries and all the residents we made up a group of over 50 doctors. It was the first time since PAACS' inception that such an event had occurred. It was intense but there was always something to learn. What an encouragement to me to see that surgical education is alive and well in mission hospitals. The clear lesson is that this is the way forward for medical missions. National docs given the training can be excellent. The trick is to find those with the right heart to serve."

Steve returned to CEML to be greeted by his old friend John Bloise, wagging his finger. On behalf of Advancing the Gospel in Angola, Bloise had been examining the books at CEML and found they were barely making payroll for the staff. Once again, Steve's shortcomings as an administrator were apparent; CEML began looking for a CEO who could better manage the hospital's administrative needs.

The development of the satellite clinic at Cavango took a major step forward as Shelley and Peter agreed be on-site missionaries, the first full-time missionaries to be stationed in Cavango since 1976! Paul Hockersmith again organized a construction team and, upon the foundation where his family's home had previously lain, began designing a new missionary residence. Until the home could be completed, Shelley and Peter simply lived out of a tent on the grounds for the first few months.

Much like Steve in Lubango, Shelley had to bear strange accusations brought by the villagers who simply couldn't understand why she had come there. At one point she heard a rumour that her father had buried diamonds in the 1970s and she had come there to dig them up! She understood why they came to these conclusions: "Why *would* a white person move to the bush if there weren't some hidden treasure? They don't realize *they* are the hidden treasure." Serving as a nurse in Cavango was "like a dream come true" for Shelley, who spent her childhood wishing she were a nurse like her older sisters so she could assist her father in the Cavango clinic. Now she had become the most knowledgeable medical professional in Cavango!

In the summer of 2009, SIM held its annual Spiritual Life Conference at Tchincombe with Pastor Abias as its speaker. Peggy's sister Mary Lou Hoskin and her husband Archdeacon Andrew Hoskin also attended as leaders of a mission team from their church in Peggy's hometown, Thunder Bay. It was the first time Mary Lou had seen the nation where her elder sister had grown up and it made a difficult impression on her. "I see a lot of poverty and hurting people. The need for the ministry that they have there. It was eye-opening. Up to that point I had no real understanding of what life was like for them. I think I had misconceptions—or rather, a lot of non-knowledge."

The reconstruction that had begun with CEML and Cavango continued despite the economic troubles as the Catota hospital in Bié province began to be rebuilt. At the same time, CEML had received a grant from the Fistula Foundation to help underwrite the provision of free care for all mothers who had an obstetric fistula. "This is a fancy word for inability to control urine after a complicated birth," Steve explained. Fistulas cause women to become incontinent, leaking urine and feces—which naturally gives them a terrible body odour that further ostracizes them. Fistulas are a common complication afflicting women who began having children during their teenage years. "Most of them never had a chance to go to school," Steve stated. "They didn't know they were too young to safely give birth, and sometimes only after 3-5 days in the travails of birth did someone go for help. These young women are soon abandoned by their erstwhile spouses and often don't have the means to afford the $1,100 USD it costs to put them back together. Providing safe caesareans to these women is one pillar of the prevention of injury and death strategy. Developing materials to educate every congregation in Angola about safe birthing is another challenge." Steve added that by performing this service he is saying to the afflicted women: "You are special, and in God's sight you are more than special, you are a special design."

Rob moved to Toronto and entered the Ontario Institute for Studies in Education (OISE) at the University of Toronto; at last, Rob felt certain he had found his calling—to become a teacher.

Steve visited Canada and the US in November of 2009, with Dr. Annelise Olson temporarily stepping in to cover his vacation—but she had only one day with him before he departed and trying to manage the surgical needs of CEML on her own proved a considerably overwhelming task for a physician only just out of residency. Steve had erred in assuming she would accept the workload as the sign of trust he intended, rather than the burden she found it to be. Back in Canada, Steve helped establish Angola Medical Outreach, a new non-profit organization that would provide charitable aid to CEML and other health initiatives in Angola.

In Greensboro, Steve found his parents in a diminished state; both had suffered strokes that greatly restricted their abilities. Belva could barely communicate, expressing herself in the phrases either "I think so" or "I don't think so." Bob had become partially paralysed in half of his body. "His problem defies adequate neurological diagnosis," Steve stated at the time, but after about two years it would finally be diagnosed as Progressive Supranuclear Palsy (PSP), a neurological disorder which typically runs 5 years; no cure exists, and Bob knew that. He now required an electric wheelchair to move around. Although Bob had a lot of spirit remaining, Steve felt uncomfortable seeing such independent people made wholly dependent on others. Sharon agreed, but acknowledged, "Dad never complained; he had such a sweet spirit to the very end. It amazed me he could accept such a terrible disability." Sheila and Helena assumed most of the responsibilities in caring for them.

From Greensboro, Steve and Peggy continued to Gaborone, then out to Victoria Falls, seeing Rebecca, Ari, Stirling, Shelley and their families. In Victoria Falls Steve found the old train station and hotel Charles and June Foster passed through on their way to Musonweji in 1917. Remembering how Dr. Livingstone—whose statue is on display at Victoria Falls—had been an inspiration to his grandfather, Steve mused on the mutual missionary calling that had inspired Livingstone and the Fosters: "I have been stirred by Livingstone's passion to see men and women understand that God, their maker, has a deep desire to receive his prodigal children and be reconciled to them." Soon after, Steve returned to CEML to respite a very grateful Dr. Olson.

By the end of 2009, Steve took a pragmatic view of CEML. For all that had been accomplished and for all his optimism, he and the other staff members were reaching their limits. "We have, however, recognized that we have reached the tipping point. We have to grow beyond where we are if we are truly to meet the challenges ahead of us. Without new staff to create a steady patient flow not dependent on my presence, the CEML will stagnate and run a serious risk of collapse." Fresh from seeing his father's condition, Steve commented on his own frailties: "The stiffness in my hands and back tells me I can't continue to operate at this pace too much longer."

RACHEL'S BEAU

In January 2010, Angola participated for the first time in soccer games for the African Cup of Nations, hosting them in Luanda, Benguela, Cabinda and Lubango. However, a different sort of excitement was stirring in Rachel's personal life. Through a friend, Rachel was introduced to Victor de Lemos and they quickly hit it off. Victor was 7 years younger than Rachel and she was a little sceptical about a long-term relationship with him because of the age difference, but she was pleasantly surprised to find he was far beyond his age in maturity. He was also incredibly kind, fun and down-to-earth.

Rachel wanted to be in a serious relationship and had no interest in someone who only wanted to date casually; Victor confirmed he too wanted a serious relationship. He was "unlike any other Angolan guy his age I had met." Victor de Lemos could be considered mestiço as both of his parents were classified as such; in fact, both of his grandmothers were black Angolans and both of his grandfathers were white Portuguese! Rachel found his family "very forgiving" as she committed a few social faux pas while getting to know them. She still resisted introducing Victor to her parents—not because Victor was black, but because she needed to be certain he was the right man. She knew her parents "are more interested in whether our partners are Christian and have faith in God than in race or culture." After six months of dating, Rachel finally introduced Victor to Steve and Peggy. Rachel appreciated what an intuitive thinker Victor was; he would take the time to learn things he didn't know. She also appreciated his deep capacity for patience, as she had inherited her father's impatience!

Steve continued to find aid for CEML as Steve Duncan covered for him during an ICMDA conference in Kenya and Dr. Michael Bentley-Taylor brought a team of seven doctors with him to serve in CEML. More significantly, CEML gained the services of Dr. Eduardo Ferreira, who had been trying for some eleven years to attain missionary status in Angola. Dr. Ferreira heralded a new era of participation from SIM Brazil and brought his family, including wife Norhina, with him to Lubango for the first of several lengthy periods at CEML. Steve even received a visit from Dr. Tonya Arscott-Mills, his eldest niece, who made her first-ever visit to Angola.

Tonya soon moved to work in Francistown, Botswana, and for the first time became very close to her cousin Rebecca, the two having spent much of their childhoods in Jamaica and Angola. As Botswana became Tonya's new home, Sharon would come to visit her from time to time, which also enabled Rebecca to develop a stronger bond with her aunt. Ari's work in Botswana moved into another HIV research project as both he and Tonya were serving as part of the Botswana-UPenn Partnership between the University of Botswana and University of Pennsylvania. Despite their different disciplines, Ari and Tonya would collaborate many times over the years, serving together on the partnership's senior management team in Botswana and would even co-author several papers. At the same time, Heather and Georg celebrated the birth of Kathryn Livingstone, their first child, in Germany and Rob graduated from OISE in Toronto.

RETIREMENT

Bob Foster had once stated he intended to "die in Zambia," but Angola had become the focus of his ministry and, as he reflected on where he would spend his final days, his hope became transfixed upon Angola. After expressing this to his children, it was Donna who proved to be the most excited; having long since accepted her in-laws as though they were her own, Donna felt it would be wonderful to have them live their remaining days at Tchincombe. Belva resisted, which puzzled her children who could not understand why Belva seemed so opposed to moving back to Angola, but Sharon surmised it was because her memories of the country were of it as being a very hard place.

The reality of Bob's and Belva's conditions proved difficult to accept; Donna still had a picture in her head of them as a capable, independent couple; accepting their limitations and the constant supervision they required proved a challenge to her. All the same, she, Stirling, Jeffrey and Meghan felt blessed to have them in their home and they received as much support from Steve, Sheila and Shelley's families as they could lend. "It was neat to see God's grace lived out the way Mom and Dad lived the last years of their lives," Sheila said. "There was no sense of bitterness or anger despite all the limitations and difficulties and dependencies (and Dad was always such an independent person)."

Helpers had to be hired to tend to Bob's and Belva's needs as they couldn't properly take care of themselves. Donna found the couple "so grateful to be cared for, so thankful for being helped and taken care of." Although the stroke made Bob's speech somewhat slurred, he remained quite intellectually adept and "still had such joy, could find humour in things." In the morning when the children would ask, "How are you, Dad?" he would respond each time: "I'm still here." It had become harder for Belva to communicate, but she could still follow familiar hymns. When the family would sing hymns together her mind would dig out the lyrics.

At times, caring for Bob could even be fun; when he needed help to use the toilet, Donna would carry him to the washroom and try to turn him around, but frequently he would slide to the floor—Donna would simply slide with him, both laughing. The worst times were when he would choke on food—the stress Donna felt in those moments, the fear that he could choke to death wore on her. As much as she tried to keep her spirits high, as the months wore on it became emotionally painful for Donna.

In October 2010, Steve and Peggy journeyed to Canada for a special occasion: Steve had been awarded the 2010 Teasdale-Corti Humanitarian Award, presented by the Royal College of Physicians and Surgeons of Canada, named for missionary Dr. Lucille Teasdale-Corti, who served for 35 years in Uganda. The award recognizes "a Canadian physician whose current practice reflects altruism and integrity, courage and perseverance in the alleviation of human suffering." During the ceremony held in Ottawa, Peggy and Rob were both summoned up to the platform with Steve by the president of the Royal College, who declared the award was "a family affair." Steve expressed pleasant surprise at the honour: "I thought I was rather forgotten out here in Angola. I hadn't really expected such a thing to happen."

Steve told the Royal College, "Despite the apparent dangers, I've had more fun here than I would have had anywhere else. The average general surgeon in Canada does five or six different types of operations. I do more than 100 procedures, 1,400 times in any given year." He also spoke on subjects near and dear to his practice: "One of the things I've fought for over these last 30-some years is to make sure that we don't divorce primary and secondary care, but that we keep them together and think about people's needs holistically and try to get at the root of the problem." The award brought Steve some notice and Angola Medical Outreach used the occasion to host a fund-raising dinner for CEML. The following year, Steve's cousin Ken Foster would win the same award for his services in Afghanistan. On their way back to Angola, Steve and Peggy visited Heather and Georg in Mosbach to meet their granddaughter Kathryn.

Big changes had come to CEML: Dr. Annelise Olson had finally obtained support through Samaritan's Purse and the World Medical Mission to serve at CEML and she took on 43 cases in the operating theatre within her first 2.5 days! Steve still needed to learn how to be a mentor to another surgeon but Annelise did her best to shape his mentorship. Dr. Olson also joined in the trips to Kalukembe and Cavango and quickly proved herself adept at the sort of surgery Steve had been practising. At the same time, SIM Canada sent Norm Henderson and his wife Audrey to serve at CEML. Norm took charge of the technology issues in the hospital as well as overseeing the custodial work, while Audrey, a nurse, continued the training Shelley had begun. They also took a mutual interest in outreach to the Nyaneka and founded a church for Nyaneka living in the Humpata area not far from CEML.

Amongst the other Fosters, Stuart's son Luke proved to be quite in the mold of his father as he began studying at Columbia University, the start of a brilliant post-secondary education. Luke's parents had taught him to see the mission field as wherever he happened to be; although he had no plans to become a 'capital M' missionary himself, Luke realized "academics are a lost tribe—unreached people, if you will."

By the end of the summer of 2011, the work of tending to Bob and Belva had worn too hard on Donna and she appealed to Steve and Peggy for help. Steve and Peggy left their downtown flat in Lubango and moved back into what had been their family home in the Mitcha compound (vacated for them by Eduardo Ferreira and his family). The Mitcha house had been chosen because "the only home that would truly allow them flexibility and capacity to move outside, with adequately sized bathrooms and ground floor access, was here at Mitcha," Steve explained.

At the same time they were caring for Bob and Belva, Steve and Peggy continued to host short-term medical missionaries. Household helpers Joaquina and São added to the three assistants helping Bob and Belva, which meant Peggy now had to manage a staff of five, in addition to the many med student guests! "It was a challenge," Peggy confessed, "but I was happy to do it." Sheila, Helena, Shelley, Peter, Stirling and Donna would each come as often as they could to assist. Belva would frequently watch videos of her favourite films and television programs such as *The Sound of Music, Seven Brides for Seven Brothers* and *As Time Goes By*.

Peggy was feeling a bit strained by all the activity in her home—and then a major crisis played even harder on her anxiety. Peggy received a letter summoning her to the local immigration office. She and Steve had entered the application process for residency cards seven years earlier and she hoped the card might finally be delivered. Much to her shock, the immigration official informed her he had an order from the national director in Luanda to expel her from Angola within eight days and delivered a $4,500 USD fine for being an illegal alien; the order went into effect on the very day Bob and Belva arrived at Mitcha. The official confiscated Peggy's passport, informing her it would be returned when she exited the country.

Fortunately, God had been at work among the Fosters. Only a few months earlier, Shelley had met a young woman in Cavango who had come as a translator for a visiting church team. The translator's father happened to be the Angolan consul in Namibia and the consul happened to be the brother of the Minister of External Affairs! When news of what had happened to Peggy reached the Minister, he immediately took action, as he had met Steve and Bob before—in fact, he had been born in Cavango. The Minister collected details on what had happened and, urging "esteja tranquilo" ("be calm"), he worked quickly to halt the order against Peggy. Peggy did not have to leave Angola or pay the fine, but her passport remained out of reach. As in James 1:2-3, Peggy and Steve had learned to "Consider it pure joy, my brothers and sisters, whenever you face trials of many kinds, because you know that the testing of your faith produces perseverance."

While Bob continued to weaken, his speech gradually became less intelligible, making it more difficult for him to communicate. Still, he found encouragement knowing how Lorry Lutz's book *Sword & Scalpel* continued to speak for him. He joyfully received letters from people who had discovered the book for the first time, and with the 2011 publication of the Portuguese version, *Espada e Bisturi*, the audience had expanded. Although he had been rendered incapable of almost any activity or even speech, Bob's eyes still sparkled with intelligence and he enjoyed sitting outdoors in Mitcha or watching the schoolroom where Helena taught the compound's MKs. In November he caught a case of pneumonia and came close to dying. Bob was so weakened nearly all of the Foster siblings—Steve, Sharon, Sheila, Stuart, Stirling and Shelley—convened in Mitcha to be at his side, but he rallied through.

For Christmas 2011, Steve and Peggy's children planned to gather their entire clan in Johannesburg for their first family reunion in several years. Unfortunately, Peggy's passport remained confiscated; Steve would not travel without Peggy, so the four Foster children and their families celebrated without them. Shelley and Peter had intended to live in Mitcha over Christmas so that Steve and Peggy could leave Bob and Belva's care to them. Instead, Shelley and Peter celebrated Christmas with Steve, Peggy and Sheila.

One day, Bob tried to say something to Peggy, but his speech came out so slurred she couldn't understand him. Summoning Shelley, they tried to puzzle out his words. Shelley wondered if he were asking for ice cream. "You mean you want ice cream?" Peggy asked him. Bob burst into fits of laughter. Finally, he managed to get across his message: he had been given a goat for Christmas and he wanted Stirling and Donna to have it. Peggy was amazed that even in the weakened state he was in, he could still laugh.

CHAPTER 19

"I Believed God." — Bob Foster

LUBANGO (January 2012 – 2018)

On the night of December 31, Bob Foster's health took a dramatic decline. By the morning of January 2, 2012, he could no longer get out of his bed. That evening, Shelley went to Bob's bedside and found his breathing had become rapid and laboured. Realizing how precarious her father's condition had become, Shelley woke up Steve for his judgment; concurring, they contacted their siblings to let them know—Bob did not have much longer to live.

From then on, Bob stopped taking food—eventually, he even refused ice chips. Bob had previously taken the time to make his wishes known to his children and he did not want any special measures taken when he neared the end—no oxygen, no IV fluids, and no resuscitation. Every hour he would be turned in his bed, given eye drops and massaged with lotion. Steve, Peggy, Stirling, Donna, Sheila, Shelley and Peter each took time with him over the week that followed, reading the Bible to him and praying with him. "Everyday we are 'sure' he can't physically make another day, but so far he is still here, giving me a more real understanding of the 'cords of death' and 'the anguish of the grave' from Psalm 116:3—Dad's favourite Psalm," Shelley recounted. "Later in the same Psalm the writer says, 'precious in the sight of the Lord is the death of his saints' and we know this to be true."

Bob's failing health was evident to Belva, even in the midst of her own struggles. "She can't express her grief per se, but seems to understand that things are not 'right' as she has been more frustrated and frustrating in the last couple of days," Shelley observed.

On Sunday, January 8, 2012, Dr. Robert Livingstone Foster passed from this life, at age 87. In his final moments, he was surrounded by loved ones: Steve, Peggy, Sheila, Helena, Stirling, Donna, Jeffrey, Meghan, Shelley and

Peter, who sang *Great Is Thy Faithfulness* and read Psalm 116 once again. "At 15:48 he took a long breath as if to say something and then he left us," Steve recounted. "It took a few moments for the reality to sink in." As Steve exited the room to begin funeral preparations, he "felt a great weight lift from my shoulders. I realized Dad is at rest and is in far more capable hands than mine."

As the Fosters consoled one another, many of their Angolan friends came forward to assist them, including CEML's nursing supervisor Alberto Sozinho Freitas and Danny Estêvão, the latter of whom took on the task of funeral coordinator for the family. Although neither Stacey nor Stuart could attend the funeral, Sharon made haste to return for the event, so Bob's body went to Central Hospital where it could be kept cool until the day of the funeral.

The seven children signed a letter exalting his life: "We are deeply grateful to God for Dad's life. Pray for us and with us as we praise his Lord."

STUART'S EULOGY

Stuart Foster had been present earlier when it seemed as though his father were about to die, but ultimately missed the moment of his passing. Reacting to the news, he declared: "A Christian's death is a moment of such power: thanking, praising God for his astonishing grace as lived out by this person; delight at their sharing with so many others now waiting for the final Resurrection day (Dad with his parents again, his two brothers, his sons-in-law Rob and Ezekiel, our daughter Belva); release from pain, relief; and hope, sheer overwhelming hope, as one person's wonderful story is caught up in God's big story of a people and a universe made new in Jesus.

"Dad's death makes me think afresh of our daughter Belva's death at seven, almost 18 years ago. His life was richly lived in service and blessing, hers so short yet full of joy and blessing for us. But in both cases death sharply breaks into the bustle of this-world activity, so demanding of our attention, with eternal reality. I am so glad we are not talking about feel-good platitudes, but about God's truth that lets us see beyond worn, breaking bodies.

"I was telling our son Luke this week that his grandfather was one of the most complete leaders I have known. He was not a mere manager, using people to get tasks done (though he got a lot of things done). He was not a mere carer, concerned for people's hurts and feelings (Dad was sensitive and discerning, but he tended to think that the solution to most troubles was to be tough, take risks and get on with it. Self-pity got little space.) He was not a mere visionary, seeing problems and dreaming up solutions without implementing anything. He was not a mere risk-taker, enjoying the thrill.

240

"He was a man who knew God, drenched in scripture, with a deep love for God's world. Serving God, he would do hard things, not because they were hard, but because God wanted them done and was going to do them. And he communicated that: his trusting, thrusting vision was infectious, drawing in hundreds of other people over the years. And he did it with a loud, bursting laugh—sheer joy."

A CELEBRATION OF BOB FOSTER'S LIFE

Other members of the family reacted to their patriarch's passing. "He was a pioneer and a true visionary," said Rob Foster, his grandfather's namesake. "He was an agent of change. With his hands and with his heart, he touched more lives than most of us can dream or even do dream of doing. Guided and strengthened by his faith, he wanted nothing more than to help and to serve and to love others. In this life, he walked with Jesus in his heart. In the midst of our sorrow, we can rejoice that he now walks with Him hand in hand."

Jasper Duplantis stated, "If there is testimony to one earthly man's humbly, happily and thoroughly lived service to the Lord Jesus Christ, it's Grandpa Robert Livingstone Foster's." Sara Fabiano called Bob "one of the greatest, most kind, and loving men of God that I know." Her brother Daniel stated, "I am filled with sadness as that booming laugh and Godly man will not be there any longer in person but only in memory. His memory and legacy will live on forever and his example of faith I will never forget."

Recalling the loss of his father Herbert at a young age, Ken Foster saw his Uncle Bob as "a medical role model. However, the thing that made me proud to be a nephew was his faith. As a man of action, he demonstrated dependence on God which is the *sine qua non* (essential ingredient) of faith. That is how I will remember him."

Tributes for "Dr. Bob" came from around the world, including the staff of Mukinge Hospital, the facility he helped found. "His book, *Sword and Scalpel* continues to be read by new missionaries. It always moves myself to tears when I read it," said Mukinge's Janet Matthews. Jean-Pierre and Marie-Claude Bréchet exclaimed, "[we] rejoice that he has completed his journey and rests in the presence of the Lord he faithfully served and loved all his life." His brother Etienne consoled the Fosters, saying, "We share your sorrow and pain for the departure to his Heavenly Father of a great man who has given a lifetime in saving Zambians and Angolans both physically and spiritually and brought his family in his footsteps."

"Dr. Robert Livingstone Foster answered the call to serve with his wife in many areas of ministry," said Gordon and Melissa Wong, "and only the Lord

knows how many lives and generations have been touched by his gifted hands."
Lorry Lutz, author of *Sword and Scalpel* stated, "Now he has his energy back
and I can imagine him letting out one of those great laughs as he meets so
many who are gathering up there for the final reunion at the throne." Bob
Stephens, who went to the University of Toronto with Bob, expressed his joy
that "his suffering is over and he is with his Lord." Dr. Michael Bentley-Taylor
rejoiced in "all he was able to do for the Kingdom of God during his time here
on earth."

Franklin Graham composed a personal letter to Belva Foster: "While
his family was close to his heart, he always found room for others because this
was God's call on his life, and you shared that call with him—to reach the
people of Angola, Zambia, and nations beyond its borders with the Gospel of
the Lord Jesus Christ through missionary medicine. He influenced your loving
family and his beloved Angola in monumental ways. But he also had an impact
on my life by demonstrating a selfless spirit of a true servant of the Lord.
Because Bob was a man of God, the Lord gifted him in various ways: as a
physician who served with the spirit of Jesus Christ; as a spiritual leader
throughout Africa, as an inspiration to others in mission work, as a mentor
encouraging many to be faithful in ministry; and as a man who challenged
others to live according to scripture and study God's Word.'"

At Bob's home church in Greensboro, Westover Church, Pastor Don
Miller said on behalf of the congregation, "Our lives have been enriched for
knowing Robert Livingstone Foster. We will miss him tremendously. But we do
not grieve his passing…because Dr. Bob exemplified the words of the Apostle
Paul: *'For me, to live is Christ, and to die is gain'* (Philippians 1:21)." Speaking on
behalf of Advancing the Gospel in Angola, John Bloise paid tribute saying,
"His life story is extraordinary and his family is a tremendous legacy."

UIEA President Rev. Eduardo Chiquete reflected on Bob choosing to
re-enter Angola during the civil war and that in this environment his
"characteristic pattern continued: proclaiming and demonstrating the Gospel
of Christ." AEA President Rev. Prince Mntambo likened Bob's dedication to
Africa by quoting from Dr. Livingstone: "It is the word of a gentleman of the
most strict and sacred honour, so there's an end of it! I will not cross furtively
tonight as I intended. Should such a man as I flee? Nay, verily, I shall take
observations for latitude and longitude to-night, though they may be the last. I
feel quite calm now, thank God." Rev. Mntambo prayed, "May his blood bring
more fruit of souls who will be touched by the testimony that will be repeated
to them for years."

Pastor Calenga felt "very impacted by both the fact that Bob dedicated
his life first and foremost to Christ and then in giving themselves to Christ,
gave themselves to the Angolan people. In terms of the medical profession,

which otherwise would provide a nice cushy life in North America instead they devoted themselves to Angolans and living for Christ in that way." Calenga cited the presence of four of Bob's children in Angola as "a testimony to Bob Foster's example."

THE FUNERAL

Danny Estêvão located a fine coffin for Bob—wooden, with a gilded cross on the lid. Sharon arrived on the Tuesday after her father's death and on Thursday the funeral service was held, first with a church service (broadcasted over the Internet for the benefit of distant friends and family), then a burial in the cemetery. The assembled mourners began by singing 'Tú És Fiel, Senhor' (the Portuguese version of 'Great Is Thy Faithfulness'). Steve, Sharon, Sheila, Stirling and Shelley brought Belva with them to both services. Each member of the family dropped a clod of dirt upon the grave, followed by members of the Angolan churches who did likewise and bouquets of flowers were placed on the mound at the end of the service. The assembly sang 'Castelo Forte' ('A Mighty Fortress Is Our God' by Martin Luther) before dispersal.

At the graveside, Bob's eldest child Steve was asked to speak a few words. Steve had always possessed a love of public speaking, but in that moment, "as I stood watching the many faces of dear friends, some of whom we have known for over 40 years now, I was temporarily overcome by the emotion of these events."

Subsequently, Steve said of his father, "What God has done amongst us because of a dad who was willing to follow his Lord to the tough places of this world is beyond our capacity to adequately recall or even give appropriate recognition to. There is no more fitting tribute to my dad than that he was simply a man who took God at face value. His going was God's command so he went. His protection was God's responsibility, the provisioning for building hospitals and sending personnel was God's job, his peace of mind faced with separation from parents for years as a child, death of brothers and sister and sons-in-law twice, a diagnosis of cancer twice at least, destruction of place he had worked to build—all brought him back to dependency on God. His simple confidence in God's faithfulness to us despite circumstances to the apparent contrary are what I believe will mark my dad out as a giant in his generation. We are now called to pick up the torch that has been passed to us. Do we believe God?"

Life went on. As Shelley and Peter left Angola for a furlough, Shelley stopped at Mitcha to say goodbye to her mother; she felt Belva squeeze her hand, and felt encouraged to know despite the circumstances, her mother retained some awareness. The drama surrounding Peggy's passport finally came to a head, thanks to the Minister of External Affairs and the assistance Etienne Bréchet offered in overcoming the obstacles. The director of immigration in Lubango finally summoned Peggy back to his office. As his final act as an official he returned her passport, and then cleaned out his desk.

On a trip to Luanda in March, Steve met several old friends from Cavango who expressed their condolences over his father's death. "As I was getting off the plane the young man beside asked me if I was indeed Dr. Foster. I replied in the affirmative and he went on to say that his mother had told him that when he was four months old, his mum had brought him to Kalukembe in April of 1978 with early hydrocephalus. I had operated on him, placing a bypass valve and shunt between his brain and abdominal cavity, one of the three I had been given by the head nurse in the OR at the Toronto General Hospital. In those days, those valves and tubes were close to a thousand dollars each. Anyway, this fellow had never returned for follow-up, left for Portugal as a teenager and has now become a lawyer and works for the National Commission on Human Rights. He has been back a year or so and had wanted to one day look me up to say thanks for his health but didn't know where to start. You can imagine what an encouragement that 34-year follow-up was to the two of us."

CEML obtained another able hand in surgery when it was sought out by Germans surgeon Dr. Birgit Lieske. Birgit was not a Christian but had learned Portuguese while working in Brazil and wanted to take the opportunity to perform surgery in the developing world. When Peggy came to Germany that March to meet Heather and Georg's newborn son David James, she developed pain in her left shoulder. Dr. Lieske took care of Peggy and guided her through Germany's medical system, even assisting in the orthopaedic surgery to repair the injury. Birgit went to work in CEML that May and enjoyed working alongside Steve. Although she acknowledged he struggled to be a mentor, she appreciated that "he takes people seriously." She admired Steve's visionary nature and called his surgical style "a unique way of being." From then on, she would make regular visits to CEML, usually to cover Steve's absences.

That summer, Dr. Annelise Olson completed her term with the World Medical Mission. She wanted to remain in Angola, but once again had to depart and arrange the support. Steve had grown to rely on Dr. Olson as his successor in surgery: "She is still seeking confirmation from the Lord as to her future. She knows we are convinced that it is right here at CEML. She is an incredibly gifted surgeon and teacher and has connected with people. I learned from her about needing to communicate and work with our team of doctors, something quite new for me." That same year, Dr. Sami Fabiano—son of Ambrosio and nephew of Sheila—began serving in PAACS as a surgical intern and assisted at CEML.

In September 2012, Steve went to Luanda to speak with the National Director of Immigration Services on various matters—Belva's visa had expired, his nephew Jeffrey's passport had gone missing and his and Peggy's residency cards remained in limbo. Etienne again used his networking skills to arrange a meeting with the director, Sr. Neto. When Sr. Neto summoned the National Director of Foreigners into the session, the other director proved to be an old patient of Steve's from 25 years before. Steve had told him to "go home and eat bran with food" and he testified he'd been healthy ever since. This story relaxed the mood of the meeting and by the end they had issued a new visa for Belva, initiated what would be a successful search for Jeffrey's missing passport, and Steve and Peggy were finally gifted with the residency cards they had sought for so many years, making their presence in Angola much less fraught with uncertainty.

The next month, Rob developed complications in his left leg from his childhood polio and once again required surgery. His family's old friends Trevor and Peggy Smith helped tend to him in Toronto, as well as Peggy, who came from Angola to mother her only son. On her way back to Angola she visited Germany and despite her absence the household staff "rose to the occasion and looked after Belva which increasingly now requires two people to help her to stand, transfer from bed to chair and commode."

Despite the downturn in the economy that began in 2008, Angola continued to be one of the fastest growing markets on Earth. In January 2013, Forbes magazine identified President dos Santos' daughter Isabel dos Santos as the first female African billionaire; much of her money came from being a board member on Sonangol, the national oil and gas company. Perhaps the most bizarre acknowledgement of Angola in the larger world came in the video game *Call of Duty: Black Ops II*, in which players were invited to re-enact the Angolan Civil War!

Over Easter 2013, Steve, Peggy, Sheila and Daniel joined Shelley and Peter for a vacation at Lake Kariba, Zimbabwe, which Steve had wanted to see since hearing of it in Sakeji as a boy. He even met a pastor in Zimbabwe whose cousin had gone to Sakeji and the pastor displayed a copy of *Sword and Scalpel* in his church library.

CEML continued its association with the Fistula Foundation and Dr. Steven Arrowsmith came in April 2013 to train Dr. Priscilla Cummings from the World Medical Mission to perform the procedure. Priscilla and her husband Dr. Daniel Cummings were assigned to Kalukembe Hospital, supplying long-term physician care. CEML finally received the CEO they had been seeking as Mark Faus from MAF stepped into the role. However, Mark made it clear he would only take the position as a means toward training an Angolan to succeed him. Mark had been in Angola through the most dangerous years of the war and felt convicted by the lack of assistance at CEML. "Where are all the other people to help?" he wondered. "The war is over, where are they?"

Also that April, Steve journeyed to Australia to learn how the training of physicians to serve in rural spaces had been developed in that nation. "We learned that there isn't a uniform approach to the rural doctor shortage nor to the definition of skill sets needed by said rural doctors, but there is a growing worldwide recognition of the problem and we are not alone in seeking solutions. There is a worldwide network of socially accountable medical schools, including ones in South Africa, Brazil and the Philippines, so I was encouraged that we are not alone. By being socially accountable, they intend to produce a physician with skill sets more closely matched to the needs of the communities that will be served and not just those of national capital regions or even of first-world countries where too many end up. One of my ongoing concerns remains the implications of weak-to-absent social fabric when one tries to measure honesty, integrity, human worth and such. Many of our senior church leaders are recognizing that the new generation of Angolans is weak in these areas with even seminary students widely plagiarizing [and] doctors not recognizing the implicit value of human life and all too frequently making decisions based primarily on financial gain."

Unfortunately, out in Cavango Peter had developed health problems. John Bloise intervened on behalf of Advancing the Gospel in Angola and guided Peter back to the US for treatment. Shelley briefly lingered in Lubango with Steve and Peggy before following Peter to the US. Dr. Tim Kubacki soon arrived in Cavango to assume responsibility for the clinic.

In October 2013, Tonya Arscott-Mills married Nyerere Otto Obita—nicknamed 'Jay', a man from Uganda whom she had met through a singles group in Botswana. Rebecca and Ari were privileged to help serve as Tonya's family during the ceremony, with Rebecca's daughter Olivia acting as flower girl. Rebecca found Jay to be "an outlier; kind of a radical guy," and appreciated the easy-going humour he brought to the family. In December 2013, Dr. Annelise Olson finally obtained the support she required to return to CEML, this time serving with Global Outreach International. "Annelise is so capable, energized and winsome," Steve enthused.

In the spring, Heather and Georg welcomed their third child, Emma Margaretha (her middle name honouring Georg's grandmother Margaretha but also Margaret 'Peggy' Foster). In July, Steve visited Catota to celebrate 100 years of SIM (and its predecessor agencies) and its involvement with the UIEA church. The occasion was attended by 17,000 people and Steve joined the other medical professionals present in administrating vaccinations and consults at

Catota's hospital. The UIEA presented Steve with its Certificado de Mérito in recognition of his work across the decades.

On August 9, 2014, 71 people stuffed themselves into the Fosters' Mitcha home for a civil marriage ceremony between Rachel Foster and Victor de Lemos. After the notary read the Angolan laws governing marriage, they awaited Rachel and Victor's declaration of vows, which they had not prepared, so had to invent their vows on the spot! Holding the ceremony in the Mitcha house allowed Belva to observe and Rob came from Canada for the ceremony. By marriage, Rachel's name became *Rachel Mota de Lemos*.

However, the church-blessed ceremony was held a few weeks later on August 21 in Sun Karros Daan Viljoen, Namibia, a game park and resort. Many of the Fosters attended, including Heather and Georg's family, Rebecca and Ari's family, Tonya and Jay, Stirling and Donna's family, Helena and Brent, Sheila, and Daniel Holden. Trevor and Peggy Smith came, as did Peggy's sister Mary Lou and her husband Archdeacon Andrew Hoskin and their son Michael. Archdeacon Hoskin performed the wedding ceremony for his niece, with Steve translating everything he said into Portuguese for the benefit of Victor's relations. During the sermon, it became clear to Andrew that Steve's translation was not 100% literal as Steve's version would receive laughter in places where Andrew had not intended it!

When it came time to recite the vows, Steve likewise translated each exchange. "Half way through Rachel's vows," Steve chuckled, "we realized we had been trapped by the classic mistake of translators where the two of us carried on in the repeat-after-me format without letting Rachel speak." Rachel finally interrupted them: "Hey, guys, can I say something here?" After a momentary pause for laughter the ceremony continued. Andrew preached on the concept of the church as the bride of Christ and that Christ's relationship to the church demonstrates the aspects of a loving Christian. "Several people at the ceremony were very appreciative," Steve noted, "saying they learned more from hearing the service in the two languages as the liturgical English tends to provoke automatic rote thinking."

After the marriage the Fosters crossed back to Angola by road, the Smiths joining their convoy. At the border, Steve noticed the immigration officials had upgraded their equipment to include a scanning device for passports. Despite this latest piece of technology, he found himself asked to step aside and visit the immigration officer's boss, who needed a consult, proving not much had changed!! Back in Lubango, Rachel and Victor had a new house built down the road from Mitcha, keeping them close to each of their families.

Rob went directly from the wedding in Namibia to Kuwait, where he had accepted a job teaching English at an international school. "In the front of my mind I meant to go back to Toronto," he recalled, "but I think I knew that my Toronto days were behind me." Rob seized on any opportunity to play his guitar and became involved with a Christian church in Kuwait, performing in its worship group.

Just as Dr. Sami Fabiano left CEML to continue his PAACS training in Gabon—promising to return to CEML when his was training completed— April Hall arrived at CEML. April Hall was an anaesthetist from Westover Church and assisted in the training of the anaesthetist nurses. Her husband, Danny, assisted in teaching at ISTEL and organizing youth activities at Tchincombe.

Angola's fast-growing economy had been the marvel of the world, but in 2015 oil prices tumbled; soon, inflation skyrocketed, with prices rising up to 400%! Luanda would be dubbed "the most expensive city in the world to live in for expatriates" by the Mercer consulting firm. The government's attempts to control the economic downturn resulted in a restriction on international trade, which made it even more challenging for businesses to function in Angola, as Angola's internal industries were still barely back on their feet. In addition, while its eastern neighbour Mozambique was declared landmine-free in 2015, Angola's landmines continued to be a problem in remote parts of the country where otherwise-productive land had been left untended.

Much worse, Angola responded to the crisis by cutting back on social programs, slashing the budget on health care at a time when it had already fallen well behind; for all the riches Angola enjoyed relative to other African nations, its child mortality rate ranked higher than locales such as Sierra Leone.

In the midst of these contrasts of wealth and poverty, Steve became the subject of an article written by journalist Nicholas Kristof for the New York Times. Writing for an assumed audience of non-believers presumed to have no great love for Christianity in general or Evangelicalism in particular, Kristof took pains to single Steve out as an Evangelical Christian even non-believers should admire. "The next time you hear someone at a cocktail party mock Evangelicals, think of Dr. Foster and those like him. These are folks who don't so much proclaim the Gospel as live it. They deserve better."

The article also proved notable because Kristof interviewed Rob, who seldom spoke about the polio that had crippled him as a child. In conversation with Kristof, however, he conversed candidly: "For a while, I blamed my dad and his high-risk dedication to others. Today, I no longer feel like that; I am no longer bitter or resentful. If me getting polio meant that thousands of lives were either saved or immeasurably improved by my father's work, then so be it."

In summer 2015, Steve went to the West African Health Consultation in Accra, Ghana, which was sponsored by SIM. It was the first time Steve had been to Accra and his "first opportunity to meet colleagues who have faced the Ebola crisis, radical Muslim dangers and many of the same issues emanating from government health systems where chronic under-investment has been the norm and our mission-related hospitals have been, and are being, stretched by increasing demands and shortage of personnel."

Although Steve had found it difficult to establish good relations with the communist surgeons at Central back in the 1990s, in the summer of 2015 he met Dr. Castilho, a Cuban physician who had made Luanda his home and worked at the Girasol Clinic. After encountering Steve, Dr. Castilho asked if he could donate time at Kalukembe and CEML; Steve happily accepted his offer. "He told me that although he wouldn't call himself religious, he knew he has been blessed by God and needed to give back to the ordinary people of Angola and not just the super rich patients of his oil company clients in Luanda. He and his wife, Marisa, have come and have shown interest in attending church for the first time in their lives, read Dad's book *Sword and Scalpel* (as *Espada e Bisturi*) and have expressed several times how they have been deeply impacted by the staff they have met both at Kalukembe and CEML."

Later that year, Dr. John Kraulis, who had served alongside Steve during his residency in Toronto, also visited CEML. Now retired, Dr. Kraulis came to aid in surgery at CEML and Kalukembe. "John was a great help when we had a 4-year-old child with a piece of electronics stuck in her trachea right at the division to right and left lungs. We tried for almost two hours to get the piece with an endoscope. The parents gave permission for a thoracotomy to get it out. I needed to explain all the options like going to South Africa or Luanda or simply leaving the object there with all its potential for complications. Fortunately, we had the piece in 15 minutes once we went in and the child recovered without a hitch."

As 2015 wound down, Belva Foster's health steadily declined. "She was failing and progressively frailer, requiring total bed care in the last few months of the year," Steve reported. On December 27, 2015, "We had a few hours of warning that allowed Stirling and Donna to be at her bedside as well as Rachel and Victor, Sheila and ourselves." Stirling and Donna arrived at Mitcha mere minutes before Belva breathed her last breath; Belva Mark Foster had died, age 89.

Sharon made haste to travel to Lubango while Shelley received a diplomatic visa, courtesy of the same minister who had helped Peggy retrieve her passport. The funeral was held at the UIEA church and the family were impressed to see the church full of people, friends who came from Kalukembe to celebrate Belva's life. As Belva had been Bob's wife, the family wondered if her passing would be overlooked, but the outpouring of affection toward her at the service impressed them; many Angolans rose to tell stories of small things Belva had done for them which were a great witness of Christ's love. The congregation sang "Tú És Fiel, Senhor," as they had at her husband's funeral.

"At the graveside," Steve recounted, "we had a short service blessed by a shower of rain that seemed fitting as it stopped when we lowered Mom into the ground." Etienne Bréchet delivered a eulogy at the grave and afterwards feted the Fosters at his home. "We were deeply blessed by the generosity and encouragement of God's people and will cherish those memories in our hearts," Steve said. "Life has slowly normalized with the first few days being rather strange as we kept expecting Mom's caregivers to show up and be part of our lives at mealtimes particularly."

"Belva was a beautiful woman," added Marie-Claude Bréchet. "She was very, very discrete but very efficient. She was never on the top—always in the background." Sharon opined, "Dad couldn't have done what he did without Mom's love and support." Pastor Calenga agreed: "Dona Belva was a warrior."

CEML continued with new staffing as Dr. Sarah Hudgins from Nova Scotia came for a year's term with the World Medical Mission working as an OB/GYN. Steve was nominated for the Gerson L'Chaim prize for outstanding Christian medical service, but ended as runner-up to another missionary surgeon, Dr. Jason Fader.

After Heather gave birth to her and Georg's fourth child, Nathan Ohenda (*Ohenda* is an Umbundu word meaning 'grace'), Peggy went to Mosbach to visit for six weeks. However, after only five weeks Steve begged her to return to Lubango; he was lonely. With his parents gone and the children long since moved out, he couldn't bear living in the house alone. Peggy complied and hastened her return. As Steve and Peggy adjusted to life without any family as permanent house guests, they decided to downsize into a smaller home. In fact, a brand-new house was constructed at Mitcha for them to reside in, while the newly arrived Swiss missionaries Drs. Ralph and Rebecca Zachariah moved their large family into the Fosters' old home.

Lubango continued to change as a new shopping mall opened in the city, one much less prone to theft than the Millennium Centre. The primary feature of this new mall was the Kero supermarket and so the entire complex became known as 'Kero' to residents (in something of a Portuguese culture in-joke, *quero* is the word which means *I want*).

Steve continued to attend conferences, including a speaking engagement in Portugal at the Maquina de Sonhos, where he challenged young people to serve the Lord in overseas missions. He also attended an ICMDA conference for Portuguese-speaking countries in Brazil. Among the attendees was Dr. Haniel Eller, a specialist in gerontology; Haniel and his wife Dr. Ana Peleja Eller, an OB/GYN, would eventually come to CEML through SIM

Brazil.

THE 'COOL' UNCLE

Once again, Rob's life had hit a rough patch. His work at the international school in Kuwait had been difficult and he finally resigned, taking a position at a different school in Kuwait. After visiting Rebecca and Ari in Gaborone and relishing his status as Lucas and Gabe's 'cool' uncle, they joined the other Fosters at Victoria Falls to celebrate 100 years since Charles and June had arrived in Northern Rhodesia. Steve and Peggy, Rebecca and Ari, Heather and Georg, Rachel and Victor, Rob, Sharon, Tonya and Jay, Sheila, Helena and her husband Brent, Sara, Daniel and his girlfriend (soon-to-be wife) Jenna, Stirling and Donna, Ken and his wife Winfer with their children Charis and Eran and all of the Foster grandchildren attended, prompting Steve to perform a mathematical trick: "Totalling the years of service to the Lord from those who followed in their train, I came to an incomplete tally of more than one thousand, one hundred and fifty life years. Praise God for those who didn't think burying children in Africa a price too great to serve our Precious Lord."

Steve, Peggy, Rachel, Victor and Rob returned to Angola where Dr. Nick Comninellis had been covering for Steve at CEML. Nevertheless, Steve found Annelise "about as close to being burned out as you could be while still functioning." Before Dr. Comninellis left he caught up with Rob and found him in a very lonely state; seeing so many family couples at the reunion had turned Rob melancholy, feeling he had been a failure to be the eldest unmarried Foster. During dinner with the Fosters, Rob mentioned the music he was writing to Nick. This prompted Peggy to ask, "Rob, have you heard any of Liz's music?" Nick's eldest child, Elizabeth Comninellis, happened to be a composer and she and Rob had met as children in Kalukembe some 30 years earlier. Nick showed Rob his daughter's website on his phone and when Rob saw an image of Liz he blurted out, "Whoa! She's pretty!"

Rob and Elizabeth Comninellis began communicating with each other over the Internet and despite the distance between them, their relationship quickly became serious; within two months, Liz had come to Kuwait to visit Rob and, being a pair of impatient missionary kids, they were engaged. Nick recalled how in college Liz had dated various musicians—an electric guitar player, a violist, a conductor, a double bassoon player—but in the end, "it was the acoustic guitar player who won her heart."

The Internet had facilitated many changes in Angola as well. At CEML, it became indispensable for Steve and his physicians as a means to assist them in diagnosing patients and to contact specialists for opinions. So too, the

Fosters in Angola were no longer cut off from North America as they had been from the 1970-1990s; Peggy now enjoyed a weekly video call with her brother Bob Parkins and sister Mary Lou Hoskin, for example. The Whatsapp app also became a means for the Fosters around the world to keep in touch with each other, whether on big changes in their families or to simply share a fun photo.

Great changes were happening around Africa as, following the 2017 election, President José Eduardo dos Santos retired and João Lourenço of the MPLA assumed the presidency. Around the same time, Robert Mugabe of Zimbabwe was driven from power in a coup, bringing two long-running African leaders to the end of their tenures.

In September 2017, Darrell Hockersmith came to see Angola. Now aged 87, his health had begun to fail, but he knew he could manage one last visit; he went to Cavango and saw the work his son Paul and others had done to refurbish the village, permitting him to return home to the US knowing the ministry he and Bob Foster had put their hearts into would continue.

Due to laws in Kuwait prohibiting unwed couples from sharing living spaces, Rob and Liz quickly had a civil ceremony and were married less than five months after being reintroduced, allowing Liz to move to Kuwait. In the summer of 2018, the newlyweds held their church-blessed ceremony in Mosbach, Germany with the cooperation of Georg's colleagues at OM. All of Liz's family attended, along with Rob's parents, all of his siblings, nieces and nephews (Rachel had recently given birth to her and Victor's first child, Selena), Trevor and Peggy Smith and two of Rob's cousins, one from each side of the family: Stuart's son Luke Foster and Mary Lou's son Michael Hoskin. Steve had the privilege of performing the blessing over his only son's wedding; Steve preached on the life and witness of his friend Afonso Daniel. Although Afonso's death may seem a strange topic for a wedding, Steve made his point: Afonso's actions demonstrated his deep love.

In June 2018, Mark Faus stepped aside from the role of CEO at CEML as Alberto Sozinho Freitas assumed the position of general director, passing the role to an Angolan as he had first hoped. Even after a lifetime spent primarily in Africa, Steve still found new areas to explore. At the end of 2018, he visited Rwanda for the first time when Dr. Robert Riviello invited him to Kigali. At a meeting of some 700 doctors from the College of Surgeons from East and Southern Africa, Steve felt disappointment to see Angola excluded from the proceedings. Although Sami Fabiano was still training in Gabon, Steve needed to know the generation of doctors following him would tend to Angola as he had, to let love and charity abound. Steve and Peggy both continue to learn and grow because God is not finished with them—nor is He finished with Angola. The mission continues…

CHAPTER 20

"Build God's Kingdom, No One Else's." — Sheila Foster Fabiano

LUBANGO (2019)

"Watch out," Steve frequently cautions listeners. "There is a love-of-Africa virus out there and it'll get under your skin and there's no immunization."

Angola has undergone great changes from the days of the colonial Portuguese to the civil war, from Marxism to capitalism. While the nation bears the scars of its past, great untapped potential remains in that country—unreached people who have never heard the Gospel message, an agricultural industry which could potentially challenge any country on Earth, and an increased awareness of the nutritional and health-care needs. Even in the worst days of the war, the missionaries who served in Angola had faith God would deliver the country through its crisis and better days would come.

The challenges in Angola today are somewhat different than those that greeted Bob Foster in 1970, but in many ways are more easily surmounted. Although landmines remain dotted across the country, Steve Foster has not treated a fresh landmine victim since 2002. The population of Angola is booming, yet there is a terrible "brain drain" pulling the best of the country's own surgeons into other nations rather than serving in Angola. Even then, most Angolan doctors graduate with only 'book knowledge', never having examined a patient or served in surgery during their education. The situation must change.

How does that change begin? Bob Foster put it simply: "Just go to Angola, stay with my family there, and you will be helpful to the suffering people and the mission work."

THE CHURCH IN ANGOLA

"What is needed are people who will stick it out and show people the love and compassion of Jesus Christ." – Bob Foster

It is attributed that Anglican priest John Stott said: "Numerical growth of Christianity in Africa is an inch deep and a mile wide." Pastor Abias sees some truth to that shallowness of faith when he looks at the practices of many of his fellow Angolans, who profess to be Christians, yet turn to the witchdoctor when facing health troubles. "You need to challenge the culture where the Gospel is preached," he says. "Do you submit your culture to the teaching of the Bible? Or when times are bad do you revert to the occult?" Pastor Abias feels this question needed to be asked of the first missionaries in Angola: "Did you transform my belief or my practice?"

Ken Foster believes, "Two things that scripture is all about are creation and covenant community, and Africans have a very strong sense of community. I'm not sure if it is that concept of covenant community, that kind of commitment that scripture is about. How do you tweak their concept?"

Fortunately, Pastor Abias has seen the rise of church leadership in Angola which stands on its own, rather than looking to the west for its answers. In doing so, it threatened to make a false idol of the western world. "Today's missionaries ask questions and allow themselves to be questioned," Pastor Abias says with approval.

"The church of God has no foreigners because all of us are here in the world as pilgrims," Pastor Abias continues. "I may be Angolan, you are not, but as Christians we belong to the same kingdom and we can work together."

MEDICINE IN ANGOLA

"The demonstration of the love and kindness of Christian nurses and doctors is a very practical evidence to the Africans that God really loves them." – Bob Foster

Malaria, acute diarrheal diseases, acute respiratory infections, measles and neonatal tetanus are directly responsible for 60% of child deaths in Angola, despite the fact that it is relatively easy to prevent or treat these problems at the level of primary health care services and through better practices and care at a household level.

Ken Foster believes increased vulnerability could transform medical missions. "Every clinical department should have a departmental discussion each week about a bad outcome. It would promote honesty and collegiality. It may cause problems initially and may take a while but if you made funding conditional on documenting discussion each week, it would transform the cultural practice of medicine."

Strangely, the recent investments China has made in Angola have led to CEML's second-most-common form of injury: bone fractures. "The love affair with speed and motorcycles has meant that the second-commonest cause of mortality and major morbidity between the ages of 15 to 40 is a traffic accident," Steve observes. "Long gone are the days of high velocity of AK-47 gun fire and their terrible injuries, thanks be to God. Many people on motorbikes have no experience on anything more than a bicycle but the velocity is much higher."

The cheap motorcycles which the Chinese have been selling in Angola cost about one month's wages—a worthy investment, most would think. But few riders wear helmets, the vehicles are frequently overburdened and the poorly maintained roads in Angola have all contributed to the endless wave of disastrous injuries.

Thanks to MAF flights, patients from remote locations can be ferried to CEML for life-saving surgery, and when CEML is itself unequipped to serve people's needs, now there are options for patients to journey into nearby Windhoek, Namibia—provided they can afford the expenses.

The internship program CEML has been operating under the oversight of Dr. Annelise Olson hopes to develop Angolan surgeons able to cope with a variety of surgical needs while witnessing to Christ, as well as producing successful interns who will set out to rural sections of Angola where medical needs are presently unfulfilled. The eventual goal is to develop an additive system where Angolan surgeons will be taught by fellow Angolans. It is hoped CEML will eventually qualify to join the PAACS program, through which they already have many connections, and that PAACS will help equip the next generation of Angolan surgeons. Surgery is the most important medical discipline to foster because it requires so many additional resources in order to function properly—therefore, by equipping even a single surgeon, a hospital gains a multitude of resources which serve non-surgical needs as well.

The support of North American health care professionals from locations such as McMaster University has been one way in which Angola has formed relationships outside its borders. Although the nation remains rather isolated, by opening the country's doors to physicians and nurses, the country's needs have been made known to countless numbers of people who would otherwise have never known about conditions in Angola.

CAVANGO

Dr. Tim Kubacki continues to serve at the Cavango clinic, utilizing MAF flights to send surgical cases to CEML. "One four-year-old arrived at our clinic one afternoon from a 'nearby' village. This little boy's father carried him for three hours on foot to another village where a man with a motorcycle transported him for an hour on his bike to our clinic. This beautiful, otherwise-healthy-appearing little boy was unresponsive. His eyes were rolled back and he was in severe respiratory distress, though moving very little air. None of the outpost clinic locations have a doctor within several days' walk or many hours by car. We resuscitated him with aggressive medication and within an hour, he was minimally improved and it looked as though he might survive. That evening, he was sitting up and sipping water, and he continued to slowly improve. He likely had a severe case of Pertussis (whooping cough), an illness we treat regularly and completely vaccine-preventable. We had the opportunity to be God's instruments in this boy's survival because of the many supporters who have placed us here for 'the least and forgotten' of rural Angola. The boy would not have survived another hour or two without intervention. He now has the opportunity to live and meet the One who made him and who so dearly loves him."

CEML

"We're excited to think that over these next several years God's going to multiply and give us opportunities to serve." – Steve Foster

With an ageing population, current health indicators and the influx of patient arrivals at CEML reflect the growing health care needs for the 60-plus age sector of Angolans. There are increasing needs to treat common geriatric conditions—surgeries to repair orthopaedic fractures from osteoporosis, arthroplasty procedures and angioplasty. Most of these advanced surgeries are currently only available in neighbouring countries.

CEML has virtually the same caseload today as it did when it opened in 2006: more than 1000 patients and approximately 225 surgeries per month. CEML rarely sees fresh trauma, however. Instead, people come days or even years later with misaligned bones, resulting in necrosis within the bone, meaning the bone has to be cleaned out. IV fluids are also hard to obtain in Angola.

Socially, women and children are only permitted to go to the doctor if the husband agrees. The cooperation of families is also key in prescribing treatment, as family members must encourage their relatives to follow prescriptions. Many people avoid treatment because they can't afford it, which

Ken Foster sees as an indication of the need for a stronger *fundo social* (social fund) to cover patient expenses. Other people are sceptical because CEML is a non-governmental facility.

There are many hopes of what can be done with CEML's land as the hospital continues to expand. Currently they hope to one day include staff, surgical training and visiting team/short-term housing; an ICU; expanded recovery room in ER; an eye clinic; a waiting area; professional education/ERC; a maternity centre; an imaging centre; a stand-alone warehouse for medications; an administration building; a new lab; an expanded morgue; expanded medical and surgical beds; a dialysis unit; physiotherapy; a patient villa expansion; a schoolhouse; an airstrip; improved roads; and a dental clinic.

"The challenges faced by CEML are typical for African Christian hospitals," opines Dr. Nicholas Comninellis. "**Funding:** how do we provide compassionate care to people in need and yet also stay in the black? **Personnel:** how do we attract individuals who have the skill and the spiritual perspective and are willing to work at a fraction of what they could earn in the private world? **Prevention vs. Cure:** CEML is focused on cure, but what are we doing to prevent malaria, typhoid or road trauma?"

Pastor Calenga adds, "Everyone needs to have a solid understanding of what the vision is—and the vision is 'health and hope through Christ,' to be an example of God's love and God's care. You can lose that in several ways, by only focusing on the health aspect or by the mission treating it as just a church project or conversely the church views it as just a mission project and then stops involving themselves as much. If that happens the hospital loses credibility with the people because eventually it will show there is a lack of purpose and direction. A secure future for CEML will involve a clear understanding and a strong pursuit of its core vision, which is making Christ's name known."

Steve Foster points out, "The best advertisement for CEML is the good word of mouth from patients who have been repaired telling others."

SHELLEY DUPLANTIS

Shelley Duplantis lives in Lansing, North Carolina, and works as a nurse. Her husband Peter remains by her side and she continues to have a healthy relationship with her stepdaughter Jasper. "She has a very positive personality," Sharon Arscott-Mills says. "She is my precious little sister." Rachel de Lemos calls her "the fun aunt." She keeps several horses in Lansing on her nephew

Tim's farm.

STIRLING FOSTER

Stirling Foster continues to serve at Tchincombe Ranch, Angola, with his wife Donna. Stirling hopes to eventually populate the property into a game farm where he can teach land and resource conservation. Stirling is looking for Angolans who want to work on a farm—not men who see the work as a stepping stone to a desk job, but to toil long term in the manual labour. Donna continues to teach the Mbongwe women to read and supplies a little clinical knowledge in the village.

Stirling loves the passage: "Take my yoke upon you, and learn of me; for I am meek and lowly in heart: and ye shall find rest unto your souls. For my yoke is easy, and my burden is light." (Matthew 11:29-30) He notes that a yoke is fitted into the right shape to fit the animal wearing it—and therefore, taking on the yoke should not be hard work. Stirling is "my best friend," says Shelley Duplantis.

Donna is proud of how her two children grew up at Tchincombe, away from any of the bad influences found in US public schools. "They grew up around nature, seeing how other people live...they have a great worldview."

Jeffrey Foster married fellow MK Breanna "Bree" Mueller in 2017. Having obtained Namibian citizenship, he planned to become a professional hunter/guide in Namibia. "Jeffrey enjoys helping people to find their dreams. It's always new and exciting," Donna says. "He is a wonderful, reliable, dependable, loving son." Rachel de Lemos giggles, "He is so much like his father! The same interests, the same clothing, the same laugh!" Luke Foster opines, "Jeff and I have exacerbated our father's tendencies!" Luke sees his cousin Jeffrey as being even more in love with hunting and Land Rover maintenance than his Uncle Stirling.

Meghan Foster is attending the University of North Carolina at Chapel Hill and entering pre-med. She wrestled with the decision, wishing to be certain it was something God wanted for her, and not out of expectations of following in the footsteps of her grandfather. "What has God given me skills and passion for? What does He want me to do versus what has my family been doing?" Whether she becomes a doctor or not, she knows from her family's experiences that "There is no skill set God can't use." When she decided on medicine as her goal, her grandfather was still alive. "Perhaps one day you'll be a doctor like me," Bob Foster mused.

STUART FOSTER

The Lomwe Bible which Stuart Foster helped translate was published in August 2017. Stuart continues to serve in Gurué, Mozambique with his wife Sindia. Their daughter Cara is married with two children and lives in Boston, where she is an oil painter. Visits with her and her family and with Luke are precious. Luke is a doctoral candidate at the University of Chicago in political philosophy. In 2016, Luke converted to Catholicism. "I can guess what Grandpa and Great-Grandpa would have said," he admitted. "I pray for the repose of their souls now…which they would not approve of."

"Stuart is incredibly smart, incredibly humble, incredibly Godly," says Shelley Duplantis. "Temperament-wise, he has the most in common with Uncle Stacey," says Luke, noting his father does not "dominate" the way Steve and Stirling do, but encourages others; "He leads by giving away." Luke also finds his father is "very much an African, culturally" and alters his accent, tone and body language to match whomever he is speaking to. "He is an intellectual and an adventurer," says Robert Riviello. Robert also commends Sindia as "warm, funny and hospitable." "Stuart is brilliant," says Sharon Arscott Mills. "He has an encyclopedic memory—and a tender heart. They have lived very sacrificially in a very lonely place with very little outside social life of any westerners on very meagre food sources and they never complain; they have a beautiful attitude." Pastor Calenga of UIEA was very impressed by the faithfulness Stuart exhibited during the long process of preparing the Lomwe Bible in collaboration with the Mozambique Bible Society.

STACEY FOSTER

Stacey Foster continues to work as a technical producer on *Saturday Night Live* and other television projects with Broadway Video including *Late Night with Jimmy Fallon*. His credits have also included the Canadian program *Kids in the Hall*; he received an Emmy Award nomination for sound design on Paul Simon's *Concert in the Park*. He and his wife Ruth have homes in New Jersey and Greensboro. "Stacey is very sweet, very soft-spoken," says Shelley Duplantis. Shelley recalls once attending an episode of *Saturday Night Live*. While she was backstage with Stacey, a man approached her brother asking for money; without a second thought, Stacey wrote a cheque for $500. Stacey's family has become distant to the other Fosters. "I am willing to reconnect when they are ready," Sharon says. Wyatt and Tyler remain in contact with many of their cousins. Rebecca Ho-Foster considers her Uncle Stacey "unknowable. He is very private, and that's okay."

SHEILA FOSTER FABIANO

Sheila Foster Fabiano continues to teach in Lubango at the ISTEL seminary. Sheila says one of the reasons she has remained in Lubango is for the privilege of seeing her former students become pastors, leaders and teachers. Pastor Calenga agrees: "Pastors and other leaders can look back at Sheila and say, she was my teacher and she was a great teacher and great example to me." Her little sister Shelley Duplantis says, "I wanted to be Sheila when I grew up!"

Sheila's daughter Helena is married to MAF pilot Brent Mudde in Lubango and they have three children. Sheila's daughter Sara has completed medical school and hopes to become a missionary doctor; in 2019 she married Nathanial Lynch. Sheila's son Daniel graduated from Regent College, the same school she and Ezekiel attended, and is married to Jenna Veenbaas—and he hopes to become a missionary and would like to find ways to reach young people using sports. Sheila is impressed at how Daniel and Sara are as at ease in North America as in Angola, unlike many third-culture kids. She believes Helena and Daniel have inherited Ezekiel's gift for discernment.

SHARON ARSCOTT-MILLS

Sharon Arscott-Mills is mostly retired but serves on the board of a non-profit organization which is developing a centre for cultural arts in Appalachia. Her daughter Tonya serves as a doctor in Botswana with her husband Jay and their two children. Her son Tim is married and they have two children; their family lives close by Sharon. Sharon's youngest sister Shelley Duplantis observes, "Sharon has had a hard life, a lot of hard knocks." But her sister-in-law Donna Foster calls her "a sincere woman of faith," and "a great example to me."

ROB FOSTER

Rob Foster works at an international school in Kuwait. His wife Liz is a music composer and the two frequently perform in public events, he with his guitar and she with her piano. Rob continues to make peace with his place as Steve Foster's son. "Grandpa and Dad were never biased toward medicine for us kids, but were adamant in their hope that whatever we did, we do it because God has called you to it. '*Seek ye first…*' I still have moments of doubt if I should have gone into medicine, but more wishing than wondering. I chased God with my head and hoped my heart would follow." His mother Peggy says, "Rob wears his heart on his sleeve." Rob is satisfied teaching in Kuwait but now believes Angola is his true home; he and Liz hope to move there in the future. "In many ways, our parents are teachers," Rachel de Lemos notes. "In that way, Rob and Rebecca are following their path."

RACHEL MOTA DE LEMOS

Rachel Mota de Lemos lives in Lubango, Angola, with her husband Victor and their daughter Selena. Rachel continues to work for Jembas as a regional manager. "Rachel is a very precious thing, and I don't mean fragile, but of great value," says her cousin Jonathan Hoskin. Sheila Foster Fabiano senses "Rachel has very personal faith." Rachel remains quite modest: "So many geniuses in the family! I always wonder what happened to me!" she laughs. It has been hard for her to be a third-culture kid but "I wouldn't change it for the world."

HEATHER MESSNER

Heather lives in Mosbach, Germany, with her husband Georg and their four children Kathryn, David, Emma, and Nathan. While Georg serves in Operation Mobilization, Heather has taken up using essential oils to cure ailments. She is very quick to note that she "hasn't abandoned evidence-based medicine" and avoids the New Age trappings some practitioners ascribe to the oils. "Heather is the caretaker," says her sister Rachel de Lemos. "She has a true healer's heart and soul." Her mother Peggy agrees: "Heather is very sensitive. She suffers with others because she feels their pain." Sheila recalls conversations she had with Heather in her teenage years: "Heather spent time questioning her faith in a way her siblings didn't. She opened up her concerns to 'Auntie Sheila' instead of her parents. She came through to a strong faith."

REBECCA HO-FOSTER

Rebecca Ho-Foster works as a schoolteacher in Gaborone, Botswana. Her husband Ari works as an epidemiologist. Their children Lucas and Olivia reside in Botswana while Gabe has gone to boarding school in South Africa, hoping he might one day play rugby nationally. Rebecca loves that her dad "always wonders, is always curious about the world and would wonder aloud about it; I inherited it." Her little sister Rachel de Lemos says, "I've always idolized her.

Rebecca has been my hero for as long as I can remember. She is an incredible mom, making sure her kids are well-rounded individuals who will get involved in their communities, get involved in social issues and give back to the community."

"Since childhood she seemed very self-determined," notes her aunt Mary Lou Hoskin. "'I am who I am, I am going to do what I want to do.'" Rebecca remains beloved by her family. "She is a very caring, dedicated person," says her aunt Shelley Duplantis.

PEGGY FOSTER

Peggy Foster lives in Lubango with her husband Steve. Much of her ministry is dedicated to the elderly, people who would otherwise be shut up in their homes, encouraging them visiting them for Bible studies. She also teaches piano, teaches music at the MK school run by her niece Helena, and hosts a literature club for young English students. Her sister-in-law Shelley Duplantis says, "Peggy and Donna are sisters to me, not sisters-in-law." Her eldest daughter Rebecca Ho-Foster states, "I feel they really modelled what Jesus intended. Everyone is welcome, no one should be excluded [and] no one is unacceptable. That's my parents' legacy."

Dr. Steve Collins dubs Peggy "the secret of Steve's success." Rachel de Lemos agrees. "Mom has had to deal with so much. She is the unsung hero." John Bloise calls Steve a workhorse but "Peggy was key. You can't be a workhorse if your home is unattended." So too from Sharon Arscott-Mills: "Peggy has accepted a lot married to Steve. She's such a sweetheart. She's very sensitive to people, she has a very sensitive heart and she sees what's beneath the surface, she understands what's going on with someone. She is a very kind and generous person." Melissa Wong believes, "in Peggy, Stephen has found a true companion and confidant who understands the calling and tremendous load for a missionary surgeon with a vision like CEML."

"Peggy is a rock," opines Paul Allen, "and she has rolled with Steve. She managed his surgeon's personality. When he was under pressure and not always a happy person, Peggy kept her dignity and kept the household running, kept her good humour." He notes that Steve is a man who appreciates routines in his life. "Peggy creates stability for him amidst chaos. She is a vital cog in the machine. Peggy is spiritually sharp and inquisitive, mature and winsome." Paul's wife Ann agrees: "Peggy is amazing to have hung in for so many years. She is a stabilizing force. She is able to manage because God has given her inner strength." She feels Peggy and Steve are now "more African than North American," but the Allens see it as one of their strengths as a multicultural couple. "They live in the moment, wherever they are."

Dr. Nicholas Comninellis called Peggy "a very classy woman. She's virtuous, she's artistic, she's expressive, she's graceful and I think that's given Steve a lot of resources that most married men don't have. She adores him." Peggy's sister Mary Lou Hoskin states, "I don't think people appreciate how much work Peggy does with seniors. Marrying into the Foster family has not given Peggy an easy life. But God is faithful. God is always faithful! God had a purpose for them."

STEVE FOSTER

Dr. Stephen Foster continues to be the medical director of CEML and lives with his wife Peggy in Angola. In the opinion of Gordon van Slingeland, Steve "has the qualities of a saint, which has yet to be fully recognized, but has been and continues to be appreciated by many." Dr. Collin Hong calls him "an incredible, jovial person with a lot of tenacity. He works against a lot of difficult situations amongst poor facilities, medical health and political unrest. He has chosen to serve with his family in this environment rather than indulge in a much more comfortable and stable Canadian lifestyle. This is all because he feels that he is being called by God and would like to serve."

Melissa Wong admires Steve's "strong work ethic balanced by a wonderful sense of humour." Melissa singles Steve out as "a dedicated servant of the Lord…who does not lose sight of what's really important." Dr. Steve Collins appreciates "his loyalty, his consistency and his friendship." He adds, "He is a rich, rich friend and a very powerful representative of Christ and a very conscientious and thorough surgeon." John Bloise admires "his zest for living while he was dealing with all of the heartache and problems that people had in Angola." Paul Hooper of Wycliffe Bible Translators believes "he revolutionized missionary medicine through his combination of spirituality and practical science."

Dr. Comninellis believes "the reason he has endured so long in this lifestyle and ministry is because he acknowledges tensions and imperfections but he can sleep at night. Whereas other people would say 'I can't tolerate this, I'm going to leave,' his ability to adjust his expectations for the sake of continuity or endurance has allowed him to keep at it for four decades. His focus on training others, informing others and casting a vision. I think it's been difficult because he has all of these urgent day-to-day matters of manning the hospital and caring for patients, but he still manages to take some time to do some teaching and vision-casting." Dr. Comninellis applauds Steve and Peggy's lengthy devotion to Angola. "In a time when short-term missions [are] becoming not just acceptable but mainstream, they are continuing to pursue this lifestyle and ministry year after year, and I think that gives them a lot of credibility that others don't have."

Shelley Duplantis calls her eldest brother "an ideas person and his creativity comes out in his ideas; he doesn't expect people to accept his ideas but because he's such a forceful person they think he wants them to agree. I like his optimism and willingness to believe in people. Dad was very much that way too." Danny Estêvão is at times overwhelmed by Steve's daily supply of new ideas: "Some days I say 'Steve, stop! These ideas are very good but let me work with *this* idea!'" Steve's steady flow of ideas help inspire others. "It's hard to talk to him without developing a passion for something he's passionate about," says Dr. Andrew Giles. Paul Allen jokes, "God loves you, and Steve has a wonderful plan for your life."

According to Sharon Arscott-Mills, "Stephen is a visionary, able to articulate well his vision and obviously his love over the Angolan people, that's been the driving force in his life. I don't think he's been a good administrator, he needs someone always with him or beside him to do the administrative side of life. Usually a visionary isn't a good administrator. I don't know if others in the mission realized it early enough to help him. You need a team approach [to] recognize people's gifts and abilities. Even when someone is not pulling their weight or failing, he gives people chance after chance."

When will Steve retire from full-time medicine? His son Rob Foster can only wonder, "What would Dad do without work?" Steve, on the other hand, has been dismissive of the idea: "When folk ask me about our future and the 'R' or retirement word comes up, my only response is to walk them around and ask them if the task is anywhere near done." As Steve so often repeats: "Retirement is *not* in the Bible!" However, he does concede that, "My aching hands remind me that several thousand OR cases a year isn't sustainable." His colleague Dr. Steve Collins notes how Dr. Annelise Olson is "becoming on par" with Steve.

People close to Steve have noticed changes in recent years. Danny Estêvão has observed Steve spends most of his time in consults rather than surgery. "Steve has become more accepting of a wide range of ideas," Peggy Smith suggests. Paul and Ann Allen credit Steve's children with changing Steve's personality. "In the OR he is not your friend, he is a dictator, he's under pressure; he knows the life of child is at stake, he's not looking for opinions or to keep people happy. He tended to roll over people." But over the decades the Allens saw him change: "Young men will head off to war," Ann philosophizes, "mature men think more of their family. Steve appreciates his family more now." Paul concurs: "He has continued to mature in grace and love. Steve is much easier-going today, quicker to laugh and he understands grace, he is growing into the path of grace."

"I used to find Steve larger than life," his sister-in-law Mary Lou Hoskin states. "He was hard to relate to, but he has mellowed a lot in the last decade, he is more approachable and willing to talk and share." Fellow sister-in-law, Donna Foster, has similar thoughts: "He still loves medicine and he loves helping people. I know he's getting a wee [bit] tired now, I mean his back and his hands," but Donna quickly adds what has not grown tired: "his heart and his head!"

THE FOSTERS AND THEIR LEGACY

"I think my father will be remembered as a man who believed God. Not as 'believed in God,' as the Devil does too, but rather in the matter-of-fact way he simply took God at face value…that God would keep His promises, protect in times of danger, whether from leopards and mambas to the bullets of guerrilla warriors." – Steve Foster

As has been noted, the concept of 'legacy' is a difficult one within the Fosters. "Why are there all these Fosters out there?" Pastor Calenga asks rhetorically. "They didn't create a 'mission empire.' They're not here to advance the name of Foster, but the name of Christ."

Pastor Calenga knows the legacy Steve hopes to leave is one of Angolan medical professionals; to some extent, he feels Steve is being too hard on himself: "Stephen's dream of Angolan physicians has been realized. If you look at the nurses from Kalukembe you see he has already raised up and trained many Angolans and that will continue."

The hardships of lives devoted to missions have been documented here; Rebecca Ho-Foster notes in particular, "The Foster women have been through a lot," referring to her father's three sisters. But, as this account has demonstrated again and again, the Fosters have upheld one another through very trying circumstances. Rebecca is also encouraged to note that the mantle of medical missionary was picked up in her generation by three of her female cousins: Tonya Arscott-Mills, Sara Foster Fabiano and Meghan Foster.

"The common thread through all these stories is this theme of giving and of self-sacrifice and the impact that it has," states Pastor Calenga, recalling the many trips he and Steve made in the 1990s to remote villages. "Steve would be up into the night still doing consultas, doing eye exams by lantern or flashlight. That is Steve's legacy—how much he is wanted and has given to Angola."

The final word in this historical account of the Foster family in mission and ministry belongs to Sharon Arscott-Mills: "As a family we have been blessed and gifted and we have a responsibility to use that for God's glory. Grandfather Charles and June my grandmother were very humble people, I don't think they ever thought about legacy, they just did what they felt God called them to do. I think Dad had a bit more sense of legacy because he had a higher profile and more responsibilities being international director [of AEF]. I don't even know if 'legacy' is the right word to use. I think for each of us it ought to be just daily following the Lord. Order my steps today Lord, whatever that is. I know some of us have wandered a bit off it and some of us haven't— that's life, that's how you learn. We'll see what God does with the next generation. I think maybe that sense or idea of legacy makes it hard for people to marry into the family. You are a bit more in the public eye if you marry a Foster."

"We're just ordinary people, all of us."

EPILOGUE

It's January 2013, and I'm in the home of Sheila Foster Fabiano, having a post-lunch conversation. I'm in Lubango to check up on the library at ISTEL. It's only my second visit to Angola, but it's beginning to look like the last one—the library is in fine shape and I've realized the staff there can maintain it, perhaps with the occasional emailed request directed to me. Sheila has taken responsibility for my lunches during my work at ISTEL and on this day, she's told me the story of Antonio Salomão's time spent in the custody of UNITA. "There are so many stories like this one," Sheila muses. "Someone needs to set these stories down." I feel a compulsion to respond, but quickly stifle it.

It's April 2015, and my friend Barry steps up to me wearing a grin the size of an SUV grill. "Brother," he beams radiantly, "I have a prophetic word for you!" Staunch Anglican that I am, I remind myself Barry is a Pentecostal; they do things like this. I ask him what this prophetic word is. "Habakkuk 2:2!" he answers, as though that explained it all. I pick up my New King James Bible and read:

Then the Lord answered me and said: "Write the vision and make it plain on tablets, that he may run who reads it."

Still perplexed, I ask Barry what it means. "You're a storyteller," he declares. "You're going to tell people's stories of faith; you're going to carry their words." I don't have the heart to contradict Barry. He had heard something about my career at Marvel Comics, where I had been a freelance writer for eight years. However, the type of storytelling Barry thought of simply isn't what I write. I thank Barry for his words, but I know there is nothing prophetic in them.

It's February 2018, and I'm trying to sort out papers from my previous visits to Africa. In a stack of papers I find a sheet of foolscap with 'Habakkuk 2:2' scrawled on it. Barry's words come back to me and in that moment, I realize he wasn't speaking from his own understanding after all. I'm hip-deep into the process of composing a biography of my Uncle Steve with the hope of producing an inspirational sequel to Lorry Lutz's *Sword and Scalpel*. I have become precisely the kind of storyteller Barry referred to those few years earlier.

People get the wrong idea about me when I'm introduced to them as "Steve Foster's nephew." Assumptions are made that I'm one of the Fosters, that I come from a great family tradition in missionary service. When I explain I'm related by blood only through his wife Peggy, people are thrown off; they don't know quite what to make of me. It is my hope that as a member of Steve Foster's extended family, I am near enough to the Fosters' work to tell their stories compassionately. However, at the same time I'm not a Foster, so I hope my perspective is also a little sober and open-minded.

It has been an extreme delight to have spent hours speaking to the Fosters and their friends and to have walked through Cavango, Kalukembe and Lubango, where so many of the events recorded in this book occurred. It is my hope that this book presents mission work as something approachable and achievable. After all, this story begins with Charles Foster serving in linguistics despite his lack of training. Likewise, my Aunt Peg entered into mission work without the benefit of being raised as a mission kid, but she went with a willingness to serve. Their stories—and all the stories in this book—are not intended to impress you, but to provide witnessing. God does not call the equipped but equips the called.

If you are not involved in the mission field, I hope you will provide support to those who are. And do not discard the idea that your own hands and feet can offer a special service on the mission field. I first came to Angola on a three-week trip, very sceptical of my own abilities. As of this writing, I am preparing to live in Angola as an associate missionary with SIM Canada. The experiences of my Uncle Steve and his family continues to instruct me to rely on God's provisions and remain faithful to His calling.

All glory to God,
Michael Hoskin
March 2019

AFTERWORD

Rebecca Ho-Foster

I think what I really appreciate now, about my dad, was his uncanny ability all those years ago to choose a life partner who had had a different childhood on a different continent in a different culture and yet committed herself to the greatest leap of faith imaginable. She learned a second language as an adult, gave birth and home-schooled her children in a small rural African community, during a civil war. Managing all the while to create roots, and wings, as the saying goes. Ours is a home of welcome, retreat and cheer. Our years in Kalukembe, throughout the war, had a cocooning effect for me. I felt secure, as my parents modelled an unwavering belief in the rightness of being where we were. Spending time with my dad at the hospital gave me a sense of the bigger picture, perhaps, which anchored their reasons for being there. The gift of our childhood has far-reaching impact, illustrating my parents' genuine commitment and generosity towards others. It is a privilege to have this set of parents, for whom integrity and a life of service resonate to the core.

Heather Messner

When I think of my parents, the deepest impression on my heart is that of fortitude. If I had to try to describe them to those who don't know them, this is the word I would choose. Perhaps that and "grace." They have had the courage to stick through hardship, fear, illness, uncertainty, failure, and not being understood by others. They've had the grace to hold tightly to Jesus, to grow and learn constantly, to ask for forgiveness and to offer it, and to parent four very different children through thick and thin. The crazy thing is, though, that perhaps because of these very things—fortitude and grace—there has been so much joy! I recall so many times of laughter, stories, adventures, guests from around the world, hugs upon hugs, and listening. Oh, how my parents have developed the gift of listening! Thank you, Mom and Dad, for all that you have taught us, and for making Africa our home. Thank you for living your convictions as best you've known how, and for modelling continued patience and love in so many areas of life. We love you!

Rachel Mota de Lemos

It seems impossible to authentically convey just how much I love these incredible people that made me without sounding terribly cliché or trite, but when I dig down to the real essence of it all I am overwhelmed with pride.

Far more than just his tireless dedication to treating the sick, Dad is the guy with the best hugs and most contagious laugh. Never a judgemental moment and always enthusiastic about teaching in an effort to inspire and recruit.

Though often the unsung hero, Mom's super-woman support has always been the pivotal ingredient that made it even possible for Dad to do what he does. The sacrifices that were made over all these years, coupled with her unceasing positivity, have my deepest admiration. I could not be more grateful or honoured to call them my parents.

I hope this book continues to inspire generations to come to get involved and make a difference in their own communities and abroad.

Rob Foster

In his 1854 parlour song "Hard Times Come Again No More," the great Stephen Foster (the other one), wrote:

> *Let us pause in life's pleasures and count its many tears,*
> *While we all sup sorrow with the poor*

A century and a quarter later, another Stephen Foster would put these words into action by forsaking the lucrative career of a Toronto general surgeon for the beleaguered hospital wards of an increasingly deprived and war-wrecked Angola. I couldn't be prouder to call this very man my father. His accomplishments are many; I spent much of my 20s and 30s vexed over how on earth I was going to live up to his legacy! But with time, I learned that the fountain and foundation of achievement is character, and that my father is nothing if not a man of deep moral purpose and spiritual fortitude—a man, indeed, of character. That I can follow and try to live up to.

Much to my perplexion growing up, my dad always seemed to find something redeemable in the most deplorable of people or situations: the drunken soldiers waving guns at us at checkpoints; the obstructive red tape of a sclerotic bureaucracy; the voracious inequality perpetuated by greedy men and their cadres. I wanted him to join me in my righteous indignation and anger, but he never did. He would listen to my tirades sympathetically, but then proceed to contextualize the situation and try to build empathy and understanding in his son. He did not offer judgement, but instead modelled compassion, grace, and a view of the world that was nuanced, rather than black-and-white. (During breakfast devotions, even the Pharisees and other biblical examples-of-what-not-to-do received their due diligence! Sanctimony had no place at the table.)

Above all, what I respect most about my father is his integrity. There is a congruity between his words and actions and between his public and private self that is truly rare and inspiring. Now, lest one accuse me of hagiographic excess here, I am not arguing that Stephen Foster is a perfect man! But where he stands apart from many is that he is keenly aware of this fact, and has become more so over the years. His fleshly heart is teachable, and his spirit malleable in the hands of Jesus. I count it a tremendous privilege to call him 'Dad' and I love him more deeply than ever before.

ACKNOWLEDGEMENTS

Thank you to the following people for contributing interviews and/or documents used in the preparation of this book: José Abias, Gedeão Aleque, Ann Allen, Paul Allen, Nelson André, Rodé André, Sharon Arscott-Mills, Phil Bauman, Etienne Bréchet, Jean-Pierre Bréchet, Marie-Claude Bréchet, Eduardo Calenga, Alfredo Cambonde, Mateus Capenda, Antonio Cassinda, Mateus Chave, Joaquim Chiaze, Antonio Chinjenque, Martinho Chissanga, José Chitanga, Steve Collins, Joshua Comninellis, Nicholas Comninellis, João Costa, Shelley Foster Duplantis, Daniel Estêvão, Sheila Foster Fabiano, Mark Faus, Donna Foster, Ken Foster, Luke Foster, Meghan Foster, Peggy Foster, Rob Foster, Sindia Foster, Stephen Foster, Stirling Foster, Stuart Foster, Elisabeth Gaffner, Andrew Giles, Ari Ho-Foster, Rebecca Ho-Foster, Barbara Hockersmith, Darrell Hockersmith, Daniel Holden, Elizabeth Holden, Janet Holden, Paul Holden, Collin Hong, Paul Hooper, Andrew Hoskin, Jonathan Hoskin, Mary Lou Hoskin, Paulo Ismael, Rachel Mota de Lemos, Lourendo Longenda, Carla Magna, Paulo Mateus, Heather Messner, Florence Munga, Annelise Olson, Bob Parkins, Richard Parkins, Ted Parkins, Joanna Prins, Robert Riviello, Antonio Salomão, Peggy Smith, Trevor Smith, Don Stinton, Gordon van Slingeland, Gordon Wong, Melissa Wong, Florença Zeferino, and Malaquias Zeferino.

Thank you as well to the following for their advice and encouragement: Marlene Bréchet, Liz Foster, Marijn Goud, Kelly Johnson, Megan Kauffman, Betsy Kubacki, Tim Kubacki, Brent Mudde, Helena Mudde, Karen Petkau (my proofreader), Rob Petkau, Olav Rokne, Guy Scholz, Brent Taylor, Janna Willard, and Sandy Yeh.

ABOUT THE AUTHOR

CEML, 2017: Steve (l) tells a story to his nephew Michael (r). Photo taken by Rob Foster

I am the son of Archdeacon Andrew Hoskin and Mary Lou Hoskin. I grew up in many towns throughout the province of Alberta, Canada and became a library technician, employed at the University of Calgary. I am also the archivist for the Anglican Diocese of Calgary.

From 2004-2012 I was a freelance writer at Marvel Comics where I wrote (or co-wrote) publications such as *The Official Handbook of the Marvel Universe*, *Annihilation Saga*, *War of Kings Saga* and the *All-New Iron Manual*. Am I the first Marvel Comics writer to venture into the field of non-fiction Christian biography? Likely!

I first visited Angola in 2011 and, at the time of writing, am preparing to serve on the mission field in Lubango for a one year term. Otherwise, I live and work in Calgary, where I am involved in many ministries through my home church. Although I am no longer employed in the comics industry, I volunteer my time to the Inkwell Awards nomination committee and the Grand Comics Database website. I love listening to old-time radio programs (such as Jack Benny), watching classic cinema (such as Alfred Hitchcock) and reading classic literature (such as John Buchan).

ABOUT SIM CANADA

SIM began in 1893 as the Soudan Interior Mission when three men (Walter Gowans, Roland Bingham & Thomas Kent) ventured into sub-Saharan Africa to bring the Gospel into unreached locales. Today, more than 4,000 people serve SIM worldwide and the organization is dubbed 'Serving in Mission'. Over the years, organizations such as AEF were absorbed into SIM.

"The vision of SIM is to see a witness to Christ's love where He is least known, disciples of Jesus expressing God's love in their communities, and Christ-centred churches among all peoples. A community growing in faith, in obedience to Jesus, and in ministry competence. Workers crossing barriers with the gospel, being and making disciples of Jesus, expressing His love and compassion." -SIM vision.

SIM Canada is partnered with Steve and Peggy Foster to help further God's work in Angola. You can support them by visiting https://www.sim.ca/steve-and-peggy-foster/

The author, Michael Hoskin, is also an associate missionary with SIM Canada, serving in Angola. You can support him by visiting https://www.sim.ca/michael-hoskin/

LIST OF ACRONYMS

AEA	Alliance of Evangelicals in Africa
AEF	Africa Evangelical Fellowship
AIDS	Acquired immunodeficiency syndrome
ALERT	All African Leprosy Training and Rehabilitation Centre
BMP-1	Type of Russian tank
CB	Citizen's band radio (short-distance radio communications)
CEML	Centro Evangélico Medicina do Lubango (Evangelical medical centre opened in Lubango, Angola, in 2006)
CFL	Canadian Football League
CIDA	Canadian International Development Agency
CIET	Centro de Investigación de Enfermedades Tropicales (formerly the Tropical Disease Research Centre)
CIM	China Inland Mission
CMDS	Christian Medical and Dental Society
CNIS	Canadian Network for International Surgery
D&C	Dilatation and Curettage
ER	Emergency Room
ESL	English as a Second Language
FAPLA	Forças Armadas Populares de Libertação de Angola (the MPLA's army during the Angolan civil war)
FELM	Finnish Evangelical Lutheran Mission
FIFA	Fédération Internationale de Football Association (international football association)
FLEC	Frente para a Libertação do Enclave de Cabinda (an independence movement based in Cabinda)
FNLA	Frente Nacional de Libertação de Angola (ostensibly pro-democracy party in Angola during the civil war, led by Holden Roberto, 1965)
HALO	Hazardous Area Life-support Organization (HALO Trust)
HF	High-frequency radio

IBS	Irritable bowel syndrome
ICMDA	International Christian Medical and Dental Association
ICU	Intensive Care Unit
IESA	Igreja Evangélica do Sudoeste de Angola (church denomination in Angola, founded by Swiss missionaries)
ISTEL	Instituto Superior de Teologia Evangélica do Lubango (seminary in Lubango, Angola, opened in 1981)
IT	Information Technology
IVCF	Inter-Varsity Christian Fellowship
MAF	Missionary Aviation Fellowship
MiG	Russian aircrafts
MK	Mission Kids (also called Third-Culture Kids)
MPLA	Movimento Popular de Libertação de Angola (pro-communist party in Angola, led by Agostinho Neto, 1965; later led by José dos Santos, 1979)
NFL	National Football League (American Football League)
NGO	Non-Governmental Organizations
OB/GYN	Obstetrician/Gynecologist
OISE	Ontario Institute for Studies in Education (University of Toronto)
OM	Operation Mobilization
OPEC	Organisation of the Petroleum Exporting Countries
PAACS	Pan-African Academy of Christian Surgeons
PAC	Partnership Africa-Canada
PAIGC	Partido Africano da Independência da Guiné e Cabo Verde (Guinea-Bissau's independence army)
PIDE	Polícia Internacional e de Defesa do Estado (Portuguese secret police force)
PSP	Progressive Supranuclear Palsy
RPG	Rocket-propelled grenade
RV	Recreational vehicle
SADF	South African Defence Force
SAGM	South African General Mission (founded in 1889 in Cape Town as Cape General Mission); in 1964 becomes AEF
SAM	Schweitz Alianz Mission
SIM	Formerly "Soudan Interior Mission" founded 1893; Now "Serving in Mission"
SWAPO	South-West Africa People's Organization party (Namibia)
T-55	Type of Russian tank
TAAG	Transportes Aéreos de Angola (Angolan airline)
TB	Tuberculosis

TWA	Trans World Airlines
UIEA	União De Igrejas Evangelicas De Angola (an Evangelical denomination which AEF helped found)
UNAVEM	United Nations Verification Mission
UNICEF	United Nations Children's Fund, originally known as United Nations International Children's Emergency Fund; established by the UN General Assembly 1946 post WWII
UNITA	União Nacional para a Independência Total de Angola (ostensibly pro-democracy party in Angola during the civil war; led by Jonas Savimbi until 2002)
USAID	United States Agency for International Development
YMAAP	Youth Mine Action Ambassador Programme

BIBLIOGRAPHY

Aconteceu no mundo Evangelico, No. 43 Ano IV (Fevereiro 1986).

Advancing the Gospel in Angola, Inc. *Hope for Angola: Through Healthcare, Agriculture, Education, and the Gospel of Jesus Christ.* Accessed May 29, 2019. https://www.hopeforangola.org/home.html.

Anstee, Margaret J. *Orphan of the Cold War: The Inside Story of the Collapse of the Angolan Peace Process, 1992-93.* Basingstoke: Macmillan, 1996.

Arnold, Steve. "Surgeon Haunted by Terrible Landmine Injuries." *The Spectator*, October 4 1997.

Bender, Gerald J. *Angola Under the Portuguese: The Myth and the Reality.* Berkeley, CA: University of California Press, 1978.

Brittain, Victoria. "Victims of Rebels Buried in Angola." *The Guardian*, June 7, 1993.

Calhoun, Margaret. "A False Solution to Angola's Messy War." *Wall Street Journal Europe*, June 16, 1993.

Canada News-Wire. "Canadian Aviation Charity Receives $1.2 Million Grant to Save Hospital in War-Torn Angola." April 3, 1989.

Canada News-Wire. "Canadian Wins International Award." November 23, 1988.

Canellos, Peter S. and Kevin Baron. "A US Boost to Graham's Quest for Converts." *The Boston Globe*, October 8, 2006.

CEML Angola. "About CEML Angola." Accessed May 29, 2019. http://www.ceml.org/.

Cowell, Alan. "Pope Visits Angola, Urging Amity After Long War." *New York Times*, June 5, 1992.

Crosby, Louise. "Aid Worker Struck by Horror of War; 'Brutal' Conflict Rends Angola." *Ottawa Citizen*, September 17, 1993.

Duplantis, Shelley. Duplantis Dialog. Accessed May 29, 2019. http://duplantisdialog.blogspot.com/

Fabiano, Sheila J. Foster. *Perceptions of Instituto Superior de Teologia Evangélica no Lubango Graduates in Angola: Implications for Theological Education in Learning and Ministry Practice.* PhD diss., Trinity Evangelical Divinity School, 2015.

Fennell, Tom. "The Diamond War." *Maclean's* 112, no. 12 (March 22, 1999).

Foster, Robert et. al. *Dr. Bob Foster Blog.* Accessed May 29, 2019. http://drbobfoster.blogspot.com/.

Foster, Sheila. "Refugee Relief in Angola." *African Evangel* (Summer 1984).

Foster, Stephen. "Inside the 'Sierra da Neve.'" *African Evangel* (Spring 1984).

Foster, Stuart and Sindia Foster. *Fosters in Mozambique.* Accessed May 29, 2019. http://fostersinmozambique.blogspot.com/.

Fredrikson, John C. *Biographical Dictionary of Modern World Leaders.* New York: Facts on File, 2004.

Frketich, Joanna. "Top Honour for Local Doctor: Foster Wins Humanitarian Award for Work in Angola." *The Spectator*, May 13, 2010.

Gamble, Susan. "Famed Missionary Foster Dead at 87." *Brantford Expositor*, January 12, 2012.

Gleijeses, Piero. *Conflicting Missions: Havana, Washington, and Africa; 1959-1976.*" Chapel Hill: University of North Carolina Press, 2009.

Goossen, Walfried E. "Earning the Right to Preach: A Medical Missionary to Angola Looks to Hamilton for Helping Hands." *The Spectator*, February 13, 1998.

Graham, Franklin. *Living Beyond the Limits: A Life in Sync with God.* Nashville, Tenn.: T. Nelson, 1998.

Greenaway, Norman with Sharon Oosthoek and Carolynne Wheeler. "Anti-Landmine Group Wins Nobel Prize." *The Spectator*, October 11, 1997.

Hallihan, Paul. "Ontario MD Aids Victims of Land Mines in Angola." *Toronto Star*, July 4, 1994.

Harding, Jeremy. "Apartheid's Last Stand." *London Review of Books* 38, no. 6 (March 17, 2016).

Henderson, Lawrence W. *The Church in Angola: A River of Many Currents.* Cleveland, Ohio: Pilgrim Press, 1992.

Holden, James B. *Developing A Self-Supporting Church: Implications of Foreign Funding of Mission-Church Ministry in Urban Angola.* PhD.: Trinity Evangelical Divinity School, 1995.

Holmes, Steven A. "Washington Recognizes Angola Government." *New York Times*, May 20, 1993.

Human Rights Watch. *Angola: Arms Trade and Violations of the Laws of War Since the 1992 Elections.* New York: Human Rights Watch, 1994.

Jornal do Brasil. "Missionárias Brasileiras Livres." 26 de Fevereiro de 1986.

Kissinger, Henry. *Years of Renewal.* London: Simon & Schuster, 2012.

Kristof, Nicholas. "A Little Respect for Dr. Foster." *New York Times*, March 28, 2015.

Kristof, Nicholas. "Two Women, Opposite Fortunes." *New York Times*, March 21, 2015.

Lautenbach, Dale. "Shot in Cold Blood: The Last Moments of a Tragic Safari." *Sunday Times*, January 12, 1992.

Legge, Gordon. "Missionary Carries on Family Tradition." *Calgary Herald*, May 21, 1988.

LeMaster, E. Edwin. "I Saw the Horror in Angola." *Saturday Evening Post*, May 12, 1962.

Lowes, Carol. "Laying a New Foundation; Canadians Help Angolan Churches Provide Medical Services Corruption Endemic in the African Country." *Toronto Star*, September 25, 2004.

Lutz, Lorry. *Sword and Scalpel: A Surgeon's Story of Faith and Courage.* Orange, CA: Promise Publishing, 1990.

MacQueen, Norrie. "Peacekeeping by Attrition: The United Nations in Angola." *The Journal of Modern African Studies* 36, no. 3 (1998).

Malaquias, Assis. *Rebels and Robbers: Violence in Post-Colonial Angola.* Uppsala: Nordiska Afrikainstitutet, 2007.

Manthorpe, Jonathan. "...And Angola is at War Again." *Southam News*, March 7, 1993.

McClelland, Colin. "Angola Embraces 'Wild Capitalism' Offering Swiss Cheese." *Bloomberg News*, June 27, 2014.

McClelland, Colin. "It's Sub-Sahara Africa's 3rd Richest Nation, Drives Porsches, Wears Armani—But Tops World in Under-5 Child Deaths." *Bloomberg News*, May 6, 2015.

McGreal, Chris. "Britons' Killers Elude Helpless UN." *The Independent*, January 26, 1992.

McGreal, Chris. "UN Condemns Angolan Clashes." *The Guardian*, January 5, 1993.

Montreal Gazette. "Angolan Forces Kill 100 UNITA Fighters." January 4, 1993.

Morna, Colleen Lowe. "Angola's Food Shortfall Endangers Thousands of Internal Refugees." *The Christian Science Monitor*, September 5, 1990.

Nagle, Patrick. "Angola; Rebel Land Mines Taking Toll on Civilians." *The Ottawa Citizen*, June 25, 1987.

Nida, Eugene A. *The Book of a Thousand Tongues: Catalog of All the Languages of the World in Which at Least One Complete Book of the Bible Had Been Published.* New York: United Bible Societies, 1972.

Péclard, Didier. "Religion and Politics in Angola: The Church, the Colonial State and the Emergence of Angolan Nationalism, 1940-1961." *Journal of Religion in Africa* 28, no. 2 (Jan 1988).

Phillips, Michael. "Angolans Say 300-500 Massacred by Former Soldiers." *Montreal Gazette*, February 6, 1993.

Phillips, Michael. "Government-Armed Civilians Killed UNITA Supporters." Associated Press, February 5, 1993.

PR Newswire. "Angola's Post-Election Violence Kills, Wounds Thousands." November 17, 1992.

Procter, Jack. *Fools for Christ's Sake.* Willowdale, ON: Africa Evangelical Fellowship, 1965.

Red Deer Advocate. "Missionary Surgeon Dedicates his Life to Improving Health Care in Angola." April 5, 2014.

Ross, Marvin. "Terror from the Ground: Canadian Surgeon Confronts Angola's Land Mine Horror." *Medical Post*, December 16, 1997.

Ross, Oakland. "Angola's Orphans: The Land Mine, the Amputation, the Shelter." *The Globe and Mail*, November 23, 1987.

Ross, Oakland. "Canadian MD in Angola Committed to War Work." *The Globe and Mail*, November 30, 1987.

Ross, Oakland. "Marxist Angola Staggers Westward." *The Globe and Mail*, December 5, 1987.

Sallot, Jeff. "Deadly Stakes in Land-Mine Issue; Axworthy Land-Mine Initiative Applauded." *The Globe and Mail*, September 13, 1997.

Sciolino, Elaine. "Angolan Rebel Chief Meets Reagan." *New York Times*, July 1, 1988.

Shubin, Vladimir Gennadevich. *The Hot 'Cold War': The USSR in Southern Africa.* Scottsville: University of KwaZulu-Natal Press, 2009.

Simpson, Chris. "Angola: Peace or War?" *Africa Report*, March 1, 1994.

The Christian Science Monitor. "Angola Returns to Full-Scale War in Post-Ballot Period." January 21, 1993.

The Economist. "Angola: War, Again." January 16, 1993.

The Globe and Mail. "UNITA Base Captured." January 4, 1993.

The Hutchinson Unabridged Encyclopedia with Atlas and Weather Guide. Abingdon, England: Credo Reference, 2018.

The Independent. "Angola Says 200 Dead in Fighting with UNITA." January 4, 1993.

The Independent. "MPLA 'Wiping Out Rebel Supporters.'" January 5, 1993.

The Namibian. "Reports of Nightmare Fighting." January 22, 1993.

Traber, Chris. "Guided by Positive Attitude, Smile." *Era-Banner*, August 29, 2006.

Van Niekerk, Phillip. "Human Settlements Rising from the Earth." *The Globe and Mail*, January 26, 1992.

Windsor Star. "Angolan Troops Force Rebels out of Lubango." January 4, 1993.

Winslow, Philip C. *Sowing the Dragon's Teeth: Land Mines and the Global Legacy of War.* Boston, MA: Beacon, 1999.

FOSTER FAMILY TREE

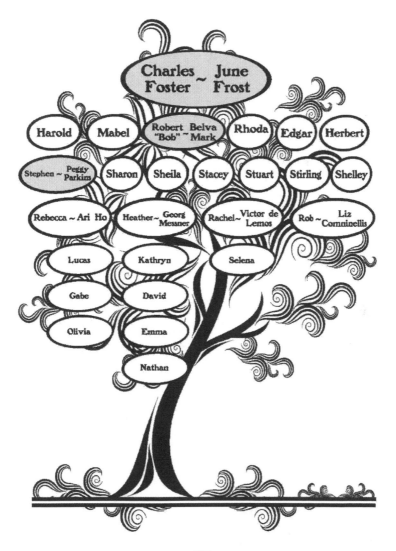

MAPS

Southern Africa. Image from Wikicommons

Map of Angola. Image from Wikicommons

PHOTOGRAPHS

Charles and June Foster. Photo courtesy of Steve Foster

(l to r) Sheila, Steve and Sharon, about to visit Angola, 1971. Photo courtesy of Rob Foster

Tundavala, the landscape which won Steve over to Angola. Photo by Michael Hoskin

Peggy and Steve prior to their honeymoon in Angola, 1973. Photo courtesy of Rob Foster

Peggy and parents (l to r): Sid Parkins, Peggy, Fran Parkins. Photo courtesy of Rob Foster

(l to r): Barb Hockersmith, Peggy Foster, Darrell Hockersmith. Photo courtesy of Rob Foster

Kalukembe Hospital. Photo taken by Marijn Goud

Steve and Jean-Pierre Bréchet at Kalukembe. Photo courtesy of Jean-Pierre Bréchet

The Fosters' home at Kalukembe, 1980s. Photo courtesy of Rob Foster

Fosters in Kalukembe: back: Steve, Peggy (holding Rob); front: Heather, Rachel, Rebecca. Photo courtesy of Rob Foster

The kids with the RV, 1988 (l to r): Heather, Rachel, Rob, Rebecca. Photo courtesy of Rob Foster

Sheila and Ezekiel Fabiano with Sara (held) and Helena (stroller). Photo courtesy of Jean-Pierre Bréchet

Cristo Rei, above Lubango. Photo courtesy of Rob Foster

Central Hospital, Lubango, 1980s. Photo courtesy of Rob Foster

Fosters in 1993; back: Stuart, Sindia, Sheila, Shelley, Heather, Steve, Rachel, Peggy, Rebecca, Rob, Donna, Stirling, Belva and Bob; front: little Belva, Cara, Sara, Helena, Daniel. Photo courtesy of Rob Foster

Fosters in 2017: Rachel, Victor, Heather, Georg (with David, Kathryn, Nathan & Emma), Peggy, Steve, Jenna, Sara, Daniel, Sheila (holding Siena), Brent, Helena (holding Emalyn), Rob, Ari, Olivia, Rebecca, Lucas, Tonya (holding her daughter Sharon), Jay (holding Paul), Sharon, Dawn (family friend), Charis, Eran, Winfer, Ken, Donna, Stirling, Meghan. Photo courtesy of Rob Foster

Steve holding Teasdale-Corti Award, 2010. Photo courtesy of Rob Foster

Ruins of the Foster's home in Cavango, 2018. Photo by Michael Hoskin

The rebuilt clinic in Cavango. Photo courtesy of Betsy Kubacki

CEML Hospital. Photo by Marijn Goud

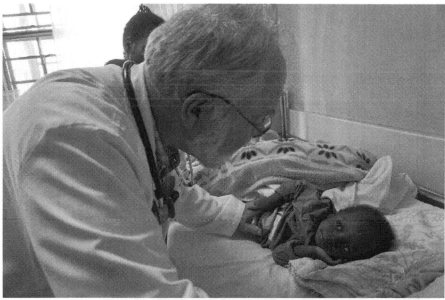

Steve visits a patient at CEML, 2016. Photo by Rob Foster

Ho-Fosters in 2014 (l to r): Olivia, Ari, Gabe, Rebecca, Lucas. Photo by Michael Hoskin

Messners, 2017: Heather, Nathan, David, Kathryn, Emma, Georg. Photo courtesy of Heather Messner

Rachel's family, 2019 (l to r): Rachel, Victor, Selena. Photo courtesy of Rachel Mota de Lemos

(l to r): Peggy, Rob, Liz and Steve at Rob's wedding. Photo courtesy of Rob Foster

Steve and Peggy, 2017. Photo courtesy of Rob Foster

Manufactured by Amazon.ca
Bolton, ON

11256087R00185